READING AND WRITING ABOUT LANGUAGE

Stephen K. Tollefson
University of California, Berkeley

Kimberly S. Davis
University of California, Berkeley

Wadsworth Publishing Company
Belmont, California
A Division of Wadsworth, Inc.

English Editor: Sheryl Fullerton

Production Editor: Jeanne Heise

Designer: Detta Penna

Copy Editor: Vicki Nelson

© 1980 by Wadsworth, Inc. All rights reserved. No part of this book may be reproduced, stored in a retrieval system, or transcribed, in any form or by any means, electronic, mechanical, photocopying, recording, or otherwise, without the prior written permission of the publisher, Wadsworth Publishing Company, Belmont, California 94002, a division of Wadsworth, Inc.

Printed in the United States of America
   2 3 4 5 6 7 8 9 10—84 83 82 81

Library of Congress Cataloging in Publication Data

Tollefson, Stephen.
  Reading and writing about language.

  Includes bibliographies.
  1. Language and languages—Addresses, essays, lectures. 2. English language—Composition and exercises. I. Davis, Kimberly Scott, joint author. II. Title.
P106.T66   400   79-10827
ISBN 0-534-00617-5

Contents

To the Student   vii

Introduction   1
    What Is Language? / Archibald A. Hill   1
    Some Dictionary Definitions of Language   6

1   The Magic of Language   9
    The Miracle of the Desert / Charlton Laird   10
    Language among Primitive People / Stuart Chase   15
    from *The Way to Rainy Mountain* / N. Scott Momaday   18
    Joey: A "Mechanical Boy" / Bruno Bettelheim   20
    Since Feeling Is First / E. E. Cummings   28
    For Further Reading   Word Magic: The Primitive Power of
                              Language / Ernst Cassirer   30

2   Backgrounds   37
    The Basic Functions of Language / Thomas Pyles and John Algeo   38
    Humpty Dumpty and Jabberwocky / Lewis Carroll   43
    Something about English / Paul Roberts   51
    For Further Reading   The View from the Babel Tower /
                              Gary Jennings   62

3   Semantics and World View   77
    Symbols / S. I. Hayakawa   78
    A Girl from Red Lion, P.A. / H. L. Mencken   87
    Classification / S. I. Hayakawa   93
    Language, Thought, and Culture / Peter Woolfson   102

For Further Reading Science and Linguistics /
Benjamin Lee Whorf 109
Chant to the Fire fly / Chippewa Song 120

4 *Usage: Dialect, Slang, and Jargon* 123
Usage Is Something Else Again / Harold B. Allen 124
Taboo: The Sacred and the Obscene / Geoffrey Wagner and
Sanford R. Radner 134
Preface to the *Dictionary of American Slang* /
Stuart Berg Flexner 142
Dialect / Dwight Bolinger 157
American Names / Stephen Vincent Benét 167
For Further Reading The Logic of Nonstandard English /
William Labov 169

5 *Children and Chimpanzees* 184
from *The Story of My Life* / Helen Keller 185
Feral and Isolated Man / Roger Brown 192
10/7 The Chimp Colony: Lucy / Eugene Linden 198
How Children Acquire Language / Carol L. Smith 210
✓The Cool Web / Robert Graves 220
✓*For Further Reading* Language and Thought / Edward Sapir 222

6 *Persuasion: Logic and Emotion* 226
Propaganda: How Not to Be Bamboozled /
Donna Woolfolk Cross 227
The Persuasive Techniques in General George Patton's Farewell
Address / Stephen K. Tollefson 238
The Persuasive Techniques in Chief Joseph's Surrender Speech /
Stephen K. Tollefson 243
The Invasion from Mars / Hadley Cantril 245
To His Coy Mistress / Andrew Marvell 258
Dulce et Decorum Est / Wilfred Owen 258
For Further Reading I Have a Dream / Martin Luther King, Jr. 262

7 *Politicians and Their Language* 267
Words and Behavior / Aldous Huxley 268
The War Prayer / Mark Twain 278
Watergate Lingo: A Language of Non-Responsibility /
Richard Gambino 282
The Destruction of Words / George Orwell 294
For Further Reading Statement: April 30, 1973 /
Richard M. Nixon 300

8   *Advertisers and Their Language*   308
      The Reality Behind Words / Jerzy Kosinski   309
      Weasel Words: God's Little Helpers / Paul Stevens   312
      How to Write Potent Copy / David Ogilvy   322
      For Further Reading   The Higher Meaning of Marlboro Cigarettes / Bruce A. Lohof   328

Postscript   336
      Artificial Intelligence: When Will Computers Understand People? / Terry Winograd   337
      Computer Poetry or, Sob Suddenly, the Bongos Are Moving / F. P. Tullius   349
      The Man Made of Words / N. Scott Momaday   353

Glossary   357

> Language is the armory of the human mind.
>
> *S. T. Coleridge*

> If language is intimately related to being human, then when we study language we are, to a remarkable degree, studying human nature.
>
> *Charlton Laird*

To the Student

Reading and Writing about Language is an anthology for college composition courses. We can think of no subject better suited to the development of good writing skills than the study of the nature and functions of language, and no activity more useful to this development than the act of writing. Because we become users of the spoken language almost effortlessly at an early age, and because language is central to all human activity, we too often take it for granted. But we seldom take writing—that most demanding of language activities—for granted. Thus, the purpose of this book is to bring together the study of language and the craft of writing in the belief that knowledge gained in the first will contribute to increasing mastery of the second. Or so has been our experience over several years in the classroom and with a great many students.

To discover in Chapter Two, for example, how a nonsense poem works is to discover also that you know more than you may think you do about how English grammar and sentence structure work. And after reading the selections on slang and jargon in Chapter Four, you are likely to gain informed control over your own uses and abuses of this kind of language. Of course, not all the selections may stir your interest or result in a measurable improvement in your writing, but they will most likely result in lively classroom discussions and thoughtful essays.

A note on the selections for further reading: Several of them make for considerably more difficult reading than their companion pieces, but we believe they represent the last word (and sometimes the first word) on the subject. We urge you to accept their challenge.

Some instructors will wish to follow the arrangement of chapters laid out in the table of contents. Others may choose to ignore it. Each chapter, however, will serve as either a sequential or self-contained unit of language study. The suggestions for review and discussion that follow each selection concern content and rhetoric. Since it is difficult in writing—some will say impossible—to separate the two, our distinction is arbitrary, intended merely to facilitate your understanding of the selection as well as its author's method of presentation. In addition, at the end of each selection we have provided exercises—sometimes short individual assignments and sometimes activities for the class as a whole—that you may use to explore further the ideas and questions each selection presents.

We hope also that, through reading this book and writing about its contents, your increasing awareness and knowledge of language will affect you beyond the immediate aims of successfully completing a composition course. We hope that you will understand better the intentions, difficulties, and successes of people using language—that you will understand why some people can express themselves clearly and persuasively while others struggle in unintelligibility and impotence, that you will understand why deceit is often couched in logic and truth is sometimes found in emotional appeals. We hope, in short, that you will become masters of language.

We would like, at this time, to thank the reviewers, Leatha Terwilliger, Mott Community College, and Vincent Gillespie, Kansas State University, for their helpful ideas and suggestions.

Berkeley, Calif.

K. S. D.
S. K. T.

INTRODUCTION

Archibald A. Hill

WHAT IS LANGUAGE?

We all use language in one form or another every day, but few of us have stopped to consider what language actually is. It seems so simple—"language is what we use when we talk or write." But this is not truly a definition of language; it is merely a description of one aspect of language. Since much of the material in this book is based on the assumption that we share a common definition of language, Archibald Hill's essay provides an appropriate introduction to our subject. He helps us to define a term that is more complex than most of us probably realize. As you read Hill, ask yourself if you can see the role that each characteristic of language plays in achieving language's principal goal—communication. Following this selection are several definitions of language from various dictionaries. Their brief explanations provide a useful contrast to Hill's detailed analysis.

[1]   Linguists can offer a set of five defining characteristics which serve to set off language from other forms of symbolic behavior and to establish language as a purely human activity. Often animal communication will have one or more of these five characteristics, but never all of them.

[2]   First, language, as has been said, is a set of sounds. This is perhaps the least important characteristic, since the communication of mammals and birds is also a set of sounds. On the other hand, the system of communication which is in some ways most strikingly like language, that of bees, is a set of body movements, not sounds. It would be easy, further, to imagine a language based on something else than sound, but no human language is so constructed. Even the manual language of the deaf is derived from the preexistent spoken language of the community.

From *Introduction to Linguistic Structures: From Sound to Sentence in English* by Archibald A. Hill, copyright, © 1958 by Harcourt Brace Jovanovich, Inc. and reprinted with their permission.

[3]   Second, the connection between the sounds, or sequences of sounds, and objects of the outside world is arbitrary and unpredictable. That is to say, a visitor from Mars would be unable to predict that in London a given animal is connected with the sound sequence *dog*, in Paris with the sequence *chien*, in Madrid with *perro*. The arbitrary quality of language symbols is not infrequently denied, for a number of reasons. Sometimes the denial is based on nothing more than the notion that the forms of one's native language are so inevitably right that they must be instinctive for all proper men. Sometimes the denial is more subtle. It is often maintained that all language, even though now largely arbitrary, must once have been a systematic imitation of objects by means of sound. It is true that there are some imitative words in all languages, but they are at best a limited part of the vocabulary. It is easy to imitate the noise of a barking dog, for instance, but difficult if not impossible to imitate a noiseless object, such as a rainbow. Though imitative words show similarity in many languages, absolute identity is rare. A dog goes "bow-wow" in English, but in related languages he often goes "wow-wow" or "bow-bow." The imitative words do not, after all, entirely escape from the general arbitrariness of language. The imitative origin of language appears, therefore, at worst unlikely and at best unprovable. The same injunction holds for theories of language origin which speculate that it is an imitation of facial or other gestures.

[4]   If it is assumed that language is arbitrary, what is meant by the statement? Just that the sounds of speech and their connection with entities of experience are passed on to all members of any community by older members of that community. Therefore, a human being cut off from contact with a speech community can never learn to talk as that community does, and cut off from all speech communities never learns to talk at all. In essence, to say that language is arbitrary is merely to say that it is social. This is perhaps the most important statement that can be made about language.

Why log. 2 sped. Type   Due Monday

[5]   In contrast, much of animal communication is instinctive rather than social. That is to say, all cats mew and purr, and would do so even if they were cut off from all communication with other cats. On the other hand, some animal communication seems to share the social nature of human speech and is therefore learned activity. A striking example is the barking of dogs, which is characteristic only of the domesticated animal, not of dogs in the wild state. Similarly, the honey dances of bees may not be altogether without an arbitrary element. It is also likely that when more is known of the cries and chatterings of the great apes in the wild state, a considerable social element in their communication may be found. Nor should it be thought that all human communication is social. A part of our communication consists of instinctive reactions which accompany language, like the trembling of fear or the suffusion of blood which accompanies anger. Yet even in the nonlinguistic accompaniments of speech, the tones of voice and the gestures, it is now clear that there is more of arbitrary and socially learned behavior than had at one time been supposed.

[6]   Third, language is systematic. I cannot hope to make this statement completely clear at this point, since the whole of this book is devoted to an exposition of the system of language. However, some observations may now be made about the system of language. As in any system, language entities are arranged in recurrent designs, so that if a part of the design is seen, predictions can be made about the whole of it, as a triangle can be drawn if one side and two angles are given. Suppose there is an incomplete sentence like "John ———s Mary an ———." A good deal about what must fill the two blanks is obvious. The first must be a verb, the second a noun. Furthermore, not all verbs will go in the first blank, since it requires a verb whose third person singular is spelled with -s and which can take two objects (that is, not such a verb as *look* or *see*). Nor will all nouns fit in the second place, since an initial vowel is required, and the noun must be one which takes an article. There is no difficulty in deciding that the sentence could be either "John gives Mary an apple" or "John hands Mary an aspirin," but not "John *gaves Mary an *book."[1]

[7]   Another observation that can be made about language systems is that every occurrence of language is a substitution frame. Any sentence is a series of entities, for each of which a whole group of other entities can be substituted without changing the frame. Thus the sentence "John gives Mary an apple" is such a substitution frame. For *John* there can be replacements like *he, Jack, William, the man, her husband,* or many others. For the verb, entities like *buys, takes, offers,* as well as the alternatives *hands* or *gives,* may be used. This characteristic of extensive substitutability for all parts of any language utterance is of some importance in that it enables us to say that parrots, no matter how startlingly human their utterances may be, are not carrying on language activity. A parakeet may produce the sentence "Birds can't talk!" with human pitch, voice tones, and nearly perfect sounds. But the bird never says "Dogs can't talk!" or "Birds can't write!" His utterance is a unit, not a multiple substitution frame.

[8]   Still another characteristic of language systems is that the entities of language are grouped into classes, always simpler, more predictable, and more sharply separated than the infinite variety of objects in the world. For instance, a whole series of objects is grouped under the single word *chair,* and *chair* is put into the large class of nouns. In dealing with objects in the outside world it may be difficult to decide whether something is a chair, a stool, or merely a rock. In language, we think of nouns and verbs as quite separate and are apt to say that the one class represents things, the other events. But in the outside world, as the physicists tell us, it is often hard to decide whether an object is best described as thing or as event.

[9]   To return once more to the defining characteristics of language, the fourth characteristic is that it is a set of symbols. That is to say, language has meaning. In

---

[1] In this essay, an asterisk placed before a form means that it is believed to be impossible. In historical treatments of language, on the other hand, an asterisk before a form indicates that it has been reconstructed by comparison but is not actually recorded. These two uses of the asterisk should not be confused.

this form the statement is a platitude and does not distinguish language from other activities which are also symbolic. The nature of language symbols turns out to be rather different from the symbols of other types of communication. The simplest nonlinguistic symbol can be defined as a substitute stimulus. Pavlov's famous dogs, fed at the sound of a bell, eventually began to drool at the sound of the bell even when no food was present. The dogs were responding to a substitute stimulus. Nonlinguistic symbols can also be substitute responses, and these can also be taught to animals. A dog who learns to "speak" at the sight of food has learned such a substitute response. In human speech, however, one of the most striking facts is that we can talk about things which are not present, and we can talk about things which ordinarily produce a strong physical reaction without experiencing that reaction. For instance, I can talk about apples even though there are none in the room, and I can talk about them without always making my mouth water, even when I am hungry. This type of language, which occurs without an immediately present stimulus or response, is called "displaced speech," and it is obviously of great importance. It is what enables man to know something of the past and of the world beyond the limited range of his vision and hearing at a given moment.

[10] The crucial fact in producing this almost miraculous and purely human effect seems to be that a given language entity can be both substitute stimulus and substitute response, and can also be a stimulus for further language responses or a response to other language stimuli. I can talk about apples when they are absent because "something reminds me of them." That is, I can make language responses to what is before me, and these language responses can stimulate the further response *apple* without any direct physical stimulus to my vision, touch, or smell. *Apple* can call forth still further language entities, like *pear* or *banana,* in an endless chain; these entities are also both stimuli and responses. When human speakers do this, they are setting up what philosophers call a "universe of discourse." The ability to make connected discourse within the symbol system is what enables men to talk at length, and profitably, about things they have never seen. By means of language men make elaborate models of distant experience and eventually test their accuracy by acting upon them. All that is known of animal communication leads to the supposition that precisely what is absent from it is the kind of symbolic activity here described, symbolic activity connected not merely with experience but with all parts of the symbol system itself. We believe, in short, that animals are incapable of displaced speech.

[11] The paragraphs above are rather general, so that a concrete example may be helpful. Let us suppose that two speakers of English are together in a room. One of them is cold. A direct response for him would be to close the window.

[12] Instead of this he can use the substitute response, which is also substitute stimulus: "John, please close the window for me." John can either close the window or reply with a further substitute: "Just a minute. Wait until I finish this page." Such a reply may produce acceptance or may lead to a discussion of John's procrastinating

character, of the fact that his parents did not discipline him properly in youth and that modern young people are generally rebellious and unmannerly. To all of this John may reply that modern times are marked by progress and the disappearance of old taboos. In the meantime the window may have been quietly closed, or completely forgotten in the warmth of discussion. What is important is that each speaker has begun reacting, not to the immediate situation, but to the other speaker's language and to his own. And in so doing, each has been building a model of general social conditions, of wide scope and ultimately of some value, even in a random and unchecked conversation of the sort described.

[13] We are now ready to turn to the last defining characteristic of language, the fact that it is complete. By this is meant that whenever a human language has been accurately observed, it has been found to be so elaborated that its speakers can make a linguistic response to any experience they may undergo. This complex elaboration is such a regular characteristic of all languages, even those of the simplest societies, that linguists have long ago accepted it as a universal characteristic. Nevertheless, in early books about language, and in the descriptions by linguistically untrained travelers today, there are statements that tribe X has a language with only two or three hundred words in it, forcing the tribe to eke out its vocabulary by gesture.[2] Linguists maintain that all such statements are the product of lack of knowledge, and are false. Skepticism about such statements is borne out by the fact that in all instances where it was possible to check on tribe X, its language proved to be complete as usual, whereupon the statement was transferred to tribe Y, whose language was as yet unknown. The statement that human language is complete once again serves to distinguish it from animal activity. In the communication of bees, for instance, the subjects of systematic discourse are severely limited. Bees cannot, apparently, make an utterance equivalent to "The beekeeper is coming."

[14] The statement that human language is always complete should not be interpreted to mean that every language has a word for everything. Obviously the ancient Greeks had no words for automobiles or atom bombs, and probably the modern Yahgan of Tierra del Fuego lack them as well. The completeness of language lies rather in the fact that a speaker of ancient Greek would have been perfectly capable of describing an automobile had he seen one, and further that had automobiles become important in ancient Greece, the speakers of Greek would have been

---

[2] A typical recent statement of this sort was reported by Leonard Bloomfield in "Secondary and Tertiary Responses to Language," *Language*, XX, 1944, p. 49 n.

"A physician, of good general background and education, who had been hunting in the north woods, told me that the Chippewa language contains only a few hundred words. Upon question, he said that he got this information from his guide, a Chippewa Indian. When I tried to state the diagnostic setting, the physician, our host, briefly and with signs of displeasure, repeated his statement and then turned his back to me. A third person, observing this discourtesy, explained that I had some experience of the language in question. This information had no effect."

For a good general account of the completeness of primitive languages and the use of gesture as a substitute among mutually unintelligible language groups, consult Ralph L. Beals and Harry Hoijer, *An Introduction to Anthropology*, Macmillan, New York, 1956, pp. 508–11.

perfectly capable of coining a word for them. It is a characteristic of vocabulary that, except in languages which have gone out of use, it is always expansible, in spite of the fact that resistance to new forms may frequently appear. Since language enables the user to make appropriate responses to all things and since vocabulary is thus characteristically "open," differences in vocabulary between two languages are not an accurate measure of the difference in efficiency or excellence of the two tongues. The fact that Eskimo does not have as highly developed a vocabulary of philosophy as does German merely indicates that the Eskimos are less interested in philosophy; on the other hand, Eskimo has a highly developed vocabulary for various kinds of snow, indicating that snow is important in Eskimo society. The completeness of human language and the openness of vocabulary make a groundless chimera of the occasionally expressed fear that a language might so degenerate as to become useless.

[15] We can now attempt a definition of language, though the definition will be cumbersome. Language is the primary and most highly elaborated form of human symbolic activity. Its symbols are made up of sounds produced by the vocal apparatus, and they are arranged in classes and patterns which make up a complex and symmetrical structure. The entities of language are symbols, that is, they have meaning, but the connection between symbol and thing is arbitrary and socially controlled. The symbols of language are simultaneously substitute stimuli and substitute responses and can call forth further stimuli and responses, so that discourse becomes independent of an immediate physical stimulus. The entities and structure of language are always so elaborated as to give the speaker the possibility of making a linguistic response to any experience. Most of the above can be paraphrased by saying that every language is a model of a culture and its adjustment to the world.

SOME DICTIONARY DEFINITIONS OF LANGUAGE

From *Webster's Third New International Dictionary*

1. The words, their pronunciation, and the methods of combining them used and understood by a considerable community and established by long usage.
2. (a) Audible, articulate, meaningful sound as produced by the action of the vocal organs; (b) a systematic means of communicating ideas or feelings by the use of conventionalized signs, sounds, gestures, or marks having understood meanings ("language of flowers," "language of painting"); (c) an artificially constructed primarily formal system of signs and symbols (as

symbolic logic) including rules for the formation of admissible expressions and for their transformation . . . ; (d) the means by which animals are thought to communicate with each other.
3. The faculty of verbal expressions and the use of words in human intercourse. . . .

From *The Shorter Oxford English Dictionary*

1. (a) The whole body of words and of methods of combining them used by a nation, people, or race; a "tongue.". . .
2. (a) Words and the methods of combining them for the expression of thought; (b) Faculty of speech; ability to speak a foreign tongue.
3. . . . (b) The phraseology or terms of a science, art, or profession. . . .
4. (a) The act of speaking; the use of speech. (b) That which is said, words, talk, report. . . .

From *The American Heritage Dictionary of the English Language*

1. The aspect of human behavior that involves the use of vocal sounds in meaningful patterns and, when they exist, corresponding written symbols to form, express, and communicate thoughts and feelings.
2. A historically established pattern of such behavior that offers substantial communication only within the culture it defines; "the English language."
3. Any method of communicating ideas, as by a system of signs, symbols, gestures, or the like: "the language of algebra."
4. The transmission of meaning, feeling, or intent by significance of act or manner: "There's language in her eye" (Shakespeare). . . .

FOR REVIEW AND DISCUSSION

Content

1. Hill writes that "a language based on something other than sound" is easy to imagine. Describe what one such language might be like.

2. What implications can you draw from Hill's observation that native speakers sometimes believe the forms of their language to be "so inevitably right that they must be instinctive for all proper men"? In what ways is this belief similar to other beliefs that people hold? What instances can you recall in which the belief Hill mentions has affected one person's (or one group's) treatment of another person (or group)?

3. What does Hill think may be "the most important statement that can be made about language"? Hill doesn't say why this may be so, but what possible reasons come to mind?

4. What areas of communication does Hill omit? For instance, does his description of language apply to "body language"?

5. Are some languages more "primitive" than others? Explain.

Rhetoric

1. What reasons can you see for the particular order in which Hill chooses to present the characteristics of language? Are the characteristics arranged in order of importance, difficulty, uniqueness, evolution?

2. Is the essay difficult or easy to understand? Why?

3. Successful writers balance the relationship among their audience, their subject, and their own writing style. For instance, if writers recognize that their audience is academic and that their subject is an esoteric one about which the audience will be knowledgeable, writers will be wise to treat the subject in depth and to write in an academic style, appropriately using precise, specialized diction. But if writers know that their audience is a general one that is unlikely to know much about the esoteric subject, it would be wise to avoid specialized diction and to treat the subject in a general way, not relying on readers' prior knowledge of the subject.

What features of Hill's writing style and his treatment of his subject help to identify his intended audience?

Classroom Exercises

1. "In human speech . . . one of the most striking facts is that we can talk about things which are not present. . . ." Hill cites this characteristic of language (called "displaced speech") as that which helps us to create a "universe of discourse." What are some *specific effects*—either desirable or undesirable—of our ability to create a "universe"? How does the characteristic of "displaced speech" affect our conception of what is real?

2. What, if any, important traits of language are missing from the dictionary definitions? List those two or three traits of language you consider to be most important in your **own** use of language. Justify your list.

1 THE MAGIC OF LANGUAGE

In the beginning was the Word. . . .
JOHN 1:1

A word has power in and of itself.
N. SCOTT MOMADAY

Sticks and stones may break my bones, but names can never hurt me.
CHILDREN'S RHYME

Because we are "modern," "enlightened" people and on such familiar terms with language, we often fail to acknowledge that it holds powerful magical properties, not only in ritual phrases and curses but in routine daily use. This chapter explores several ancient and traditional notions about the power and magic of language. In "Joey," it explores a similar theme in the context of a modern psychological case study. We hope through these readings you will discover some of the mystery and excitement that is language.

Charlton Laird

THE MIRACLE OF THE DESART

That language is a "miracle" we take for granted is Laird's theme. He wants us to sense his own wonder at the ease with which we handle a psychological and physiological process that is remarkably complex. To make us believers, he asks us to imagine ourselves in a world without language, and then takes us step by step through the act of uttering a single word. As you read, consider the appropriateness of Laird's term miracle *to describe language.*

THE LONESOME LAND

[1]   To most of us a desert is a place with too little water and too much sand, but to our ancestors a "desart" was any wild place where no one lived, presumably because no one would want to.

[2]   Imagine that you live in such a place. No other human being is near, and you have never seen anything human except the reflection of yourself in a pool. You suppose you are as unique as the sun and the moon.

[3]   You live in a world of sight and sound, but sounds of a limited sort. You know the rushing wind, the pattering sleet. You know the lonesome and terrifying howls of the wolves, the insane laughter of the loons, the chattering of chipmunks and squirrels. You can extract meaning from these sounds. You know that after the wind may come rain or snow or hail to beat upon you. You know that with the wolves abroad you want a good fire at night, and that with the loons crying a certain season of the year has come. You can guess that if the chipmunk chatters and jerks his tail with uncommon violence he is probably either hungry or angry. But to none of these sound makers, wind or wolf or chipmunk, can you say anything. Nor do they mean to say anything to you; not even the loon, in whose voice there is a human note, means to discuss the weather. You are living in a world almost devoid of communication.

[4]   And so one evening you are lonely and empty because the moon is shining and there is a strange beauty over the land. Being sad, you imagine the nicest thing that could happen to you—that there might be another creature such as you, such as you are though a little different, for there seem to be two chipmunks and numerous loons. Except that this creature, since it would be like you, would not scurry off to hide in a hole, nor disappear with a whirring of wings. It would come

From *The Miracle of Language* by Charlton Laird. Copyright 1953 by Charlton Laird. Reprinted by permission of Harper & Row, Publishers, Inc.

THE MIRACLE OF THE DESERT

and want to live with you, and the two of you could do everything together. And if you happened to like each other very much—well, you could look at each other in the moonlight and feel good inside. You might even touch each other, very intimately. Beyond that you could not go, for how can any creature, you would assume, let another know how he is feeling or what he is thinking?

[5]   Oh, you could rub your belly if you were hungry, smile and nod your head if you wanted to agree, and bellow if you were angry or got burned. But if you looked at another creature and felt very loving, how could you let the other creature know it? Or how could you find out if the other creature felt the same way? Or maybe a little bit different?

[6]   Since you have already imagined the impossible, and in the moonlight with the strange shapes and shadows everywhere it is very pleasant and strangely comforting to imagine nice and impossible things, you imagine something more. You imagine that by some sort of magic, whenever you want the other creature to know what you are thinking, your thoughts will appear in the other person. This creature, too, can give you his thoughts just by wanting you to have them. Then, if you love each other, you can tell each other all about it, only by wanting the other one to know.

[7]   But that could not happen. That would be a miracle and, being a practical fellow who takes little stock in miracles, you go off and try to drown your lonely feeling in fermented goat's milk.

[8]   Far from being fantastic, this miracle is occurring at the moment. Anyone reading this page knows essentially what I was thinking when I wrote it. Wherever this page goes, to Denver or Dublin, people will know what I was thinking, and if by some waywardness in fashion this book should have more than momentary life, people as yet unheard of will know. Similarly if any of these people were here in this room, and instead of writing I were to start creating, with my tongue and my teeth and the holes in my head, the intermittent sounds which we call speech, they would know immediately what I am thinking. Furthermore, for all or any of this to occur, neither you nor I need to be conscious of the way it occurs. I need only want you to know, and you need only refrain from leaving the room or throwing down the book.

[9]   In short "the miracle of the desart" can and does occur; it occurs so commonly that most of us never give it a thought. The very babes learn to take advantage of it, just as they learn to walk or to hold a spoon. The miracle is the subject of this book. We call it language.

THE MECHANICS OF A MIRACLE

[10]   The miracle of speech does not grow less if we examine it. Let us consider what happens. At first let us take the simplest sort of instance, in which one person

speaks a word and another hears it. Any word would do, but let us use the word *wrist*.

[11] What has the speaker done when he utters this word? By gentle pressure of the diaphragm and contraction of the intercostal muscles he has emitted a little air, scrupulously controlled, although the muscles which expelled the air are so strong they could shake his whole body if they were used vigorously. He has slightly tightened some membranes in his throat so that the column of air has forced the membranes to vibrate. Meanwhile a number of minute movements, especially of the tongue, have caused the center of vibration to spread sideways across the tongue, move suddenly forward, concentrate just back of the upper teeth, and then cease. With the cessation of this voiced sound, the column of air hisses against the upper teeth and gums, and is suddenly and momentarily stopped by a flip of the tongue. The tongue strikes the roof of the mouth with the portion just back from the tip, and spreads so that the whole column of air is suddenly dammed up and then released. All this must be done with the muscles of the throat relatively relaxed, and when the little explosion has taken place, everything must stop at once.

[12] Now the word *wrist* has been spoken, only a word, but the whole operation is so complex and delicately timed that nobody could do this by thinking about it. It can be done successfully, in the main, only when it is done unconsciously. In part it can be learned, and people having speech defects sometimes learn part of the practice by laborious study, but good speech is always mainly unconscious speech. Any tennis player, even if he could not explain this enigma, could provide an analogy for it. When he sees a rapidly flying tennis ball coming toward him, he knows what he must do. He must maneuver himself into the proper position, be poised with his weight properly distributed, meet the ball with the proper sweep of his arm and with his racket held at just the right pitch, and all this must be timed to stop the flying ball at a precise point. But if the tennis player pauses to think of all these things which must be done and how he will do them, he is lost. The ball will not skim back over the net, building air pressure as it goes until it buzzes down into the opponent's corner. If the tennis player thinks about anything except where he wants the ball to go and what he plans for the next stroke, he will probably become so awkward that he will be lucky to hit the ball at all. Rapid, precise muscular actions can be successfully carried out only by the unconscious part of the brain. And so with the speaker. He cannot speak well unless he speaks unconsciously, for his movements are as precise, as complicated, and as exactly timed as those of the tennis player. Anyone who doubts it need only observe the distress of a speaker who has not learned English as a child trying to say the word *clothes*.

[13] So much for the speaker. Now for the hearer. Sound waves which are set in motion by humming, purring, and hissing in the speaker's throat and head penetrate to the listener's inner ear, and there set up kindred vibrations. At once that marvelous agglomeration of nerves, nuclei, and whatnot which we call the brain makes the hearer aware that a familiar sound has been produced, and presents him

with various concepts associated with the sound. And here we are in the presence of meaning.

THE END AND MEANS OF MEANING

[14]   How is it possible that two people who may never have seen each other before, or who may not even live on the same continent, or be alive in the same century have immediate, similar, and complicated ideas in the presence of a sound? Especially is this event amazing when we consider that there are hundreds of thousands of these sounds with millions of meanings and still more millions of implications so delicate that they cannot be defined. Somehow hundreds of millions of people have agreed, at least roughly, as to the meaning of the word *wrist* and the other countless words in the language, and this in spite of the fact that the human animal is so varied and contentious a creature that seldom will two human beings agree about anything, whether the subject be religion, politics, or what will "go" with that hat.

[15]   Of course when the word *wrist* is spoken by one person and heard by another, communication has not as yet taken place in any very elaborate or precise way. The single word raises almost as many questions as it answers. Is the speaker thinking that his wrist is arthritic, or that certain brush strokes can best be made with the wrist? These questions can be partially answered by adding a few more words, but in spite of anything he can do the speaker is likely to remain to a degree ambiguous. He cannot be precise because the syllable he is uttering has no precise meaning.

[16]   Thus "the miracle of the desart" is far enough from the divine to exhibit a human flaw. Exact communication is impossible among men. Gertrude Stein may have felt that "a rose is a rose is a rose," but our speaker, if he considers the matter carefully, must know that a wrist is not necessarily a wrist. It may be some bones hung together by ligaments. It may be the skin outside these bones. It may be the point which marks the end of the sleeve. If the speaker is a tailor, *wrist* may be a command to hem a glove. But even granted that both speaker and hearer agree that *wrist* is here associated with the bones, flesh, and skin at the juncture of the human hand and arm, they may still associate highly varied feelings with this part of the body. The speaker may have big, bony wrists, and have hated them all her life. The hearer may have been forced out of an Olympic skiing contest when he fell and broke a wrist. There is no one thing which *wrist* calls up in exactly the same form to everyone; there are not even areas of meaning which are the same for everybody. Meanings exist only in minds, and minds result from beings and experiences; no two of them are alike, nor are the meanings they contain. Still, granted that meaning is not and never can be exact, there remains a body of agreement as to the association to be connected with certain sounds which is staggering to anyone who will contemplate it.

[17] But we have only begun, for we started with the simplest sort of example of spoken language. A word like *no* can mean *no, damn it,* or *yes,* or dozens of things between and among these meanings, depending upon the way in which the word is pronounced and the sounds modulated. The emission and comprehension of words, furthermore, become immeasurably complicated as soon as a speaker starts running them together into sentences. But let us ignore those possible ramifications and complicate the situation only slightly by making the speaker also a writer, and let him make a few marks on any sort of impressionable object. These marks can now take the place of sound and can call up the concepts associated with *wrist* wherever they go. They can continue calling up these concepts long after the man who made them is dead; they can do so for hundreds, even thousands, of years. Clay cones and slabs of stone, scratched with marks which were long undecipherable, were still able to produce something like their original meaning when their language was rediscovered, although no living man had known how to speak or write or think the language for thousands of years.

[18] Man, then, can be defined, if one wishes, as a languagized mammal. A cow may be able to communicate in a cowlike way by bawling and dogs may be able to express themselves to a degree by looking soulfully from one end while wagging the other, but man is probably more significantly distinguished from his fellow creatures by his complicated means of communication than by any other difference. In short, man as we know him could not exist without language and until there was language. Civilization could not exist until there was written language, because without written language no generation could bequeath to succeeding generations anything but its simpler findings. Culture could not be widespread until there was printed language.

[19] In the beginning was the word. Or, if in the beginning was the arboreal ape, with the word and an opposable thumb he scrambled down from the trees and found his way out of the woods.

FOR REVIEW AND DISCUSSION

Content

1. What are Laird's reasons for referring to language as a "miracle"? In what sense does he seem to mean *miracle*?

2. Why is the mere utterance of a word only the beginning of actual communication?

3. How might you test the truth of Laird's assertion that "meanings exist only in minds"?

4. What might Laird mean by saying that "good speech is always mainly unconscious speech"? Do you agree with him? What does he mean by "good speech"?

Rhetoric

1. What is the effect of Laird's introducing his ideas through an elaborate fantasy? Are his ideas as clearly presented as they might have been were he merely to have expressed—rather than to have dramatized—them?

2. What is the tone of Laird's writing? What are some of the specific ways in which that tone is created? Does the tone seem well suited to the subject?

3. What seems to be Laird's intention in describing so extensively the mechanics of saying and hearing *wrist*? Do you think that you respond to the description as he intends you to? What is your response?

4. Does Laird's use of analogy and extended example help to convince you that his argument is sound? Why?

Classroom Exercises

1. In your own words, describe what it might be like to live in a world without language. Is it possible for anyone who does speak to imagine what life really would be like without language?

2. "Exact communication is impossible among men." How does Laird support this statement? Can you think of an argument in opposition to his? Which is more convincing?

Stuart Chase

LANGUAGE AMONG PRIMITIVE PEOPLE

"Sticks and stones may break my bones, but names will never hurt me." That so many of us have resorted to this familiar, ritualistic retort in childhood should suggest that it is only half true—that indeed names can *hurt us. Chase limits his discussion to "primitive" or "ancient" peoples, but as you read consider how his observations and examples about the power of language might also apply to modern American culture.*

[1] Word magic is common to all primitive peoples. In a certain West African tribe, before setting up housekeeping it is highly desirable to obtain a Sampa. A Sampa is a prayer written in old magic letters which evil spirits are most likely to understand. It can be purchased at any wizard's for a few cowrie shells. He makes it while you wait. Into a calabash he puts a bit of clay, a feather, some twigs of straw, or whatever strikes his fancy, and over it chants a spell. Hindu parents who lose a first child by sickness may name the second by some such term as "Dunghill," on

From *The Tyranny of Words*, copyright, 1938, 1966 by Stuart Chase. Reprinted by permission of Harcourt Brace Jovanovich, Inc.

the theory that the gods, who recognize people only by their names, will not bother to waste a curse on such a lowly creature. What is a curse itself but a word winged for carrying physical harm? Frazer gives many examples of word taboos to show the universality of the practice. When a New Zealand chief was called "Wai," the word for "water," a new name for water had to be found. To cast a spell on a man's name was frequently considered as effective as casting it on his person. Names were therefore closely guarded.

[2] According to Dr. J. P. Harrington of the Smithsonian Institution, terror of the dead was so intense among American Indians that their names were not spoken aloud. Since the dead commonly bore names like "Blue Reindeer" or "Strong Bow," relatives and friends after the funeral were forced to invent new words for common objects like reindeer and bow, or at least to change the word a little. This brand of magic inevitably resulted in a welter of different names for the same object, and helped to create the babel of more than one hundred languages spoken by American Indians. How many tribal wars resulted from the babel, Dr. Harrington does not attempt to compute. The more wars, the more dead, the more new names, the more dialects, the more "foreigners," the more wars, the more dead. . . .

[3] Word magic is not confined to nature peoples. Herodotus did not dare mention the name "Osiris." The true and great name of Allah is secret, as are the names of the Brahman gods and the "real" name of Confucius. Orthodox Jews avoid the name "Jahweh." Among Christian peoples it is against the moral code to use the name of God or that of his Son except on ceremonial occasions, and in such conventions as "God bless you." Caesar gave a command in Spain to an obscure general called "Scipio" for the sake of the lucky omen his name carried. The Emperor Severus consoled himself for the immoralities of his Empress Julia because she bore the same name as the profligate daughter of Augustus. "Julias," it appeared, were a bad lot.

[4] Blasphemy, ancient and modern, is a sin based primarily on word magic. If you go out in an American street and shout "Bogom Proklyatii," citizens will not be shocked and no policeman will touch you. Yet you are shouting "God damn" in Russian. Real-estate operators frequently embellish their swampy and stony subdivisions with such names as "Floral Heights," "Cedar Gardens," and "Laurel Meadows," hoping that the customer will identify the thing with the word. He often does.

[5] A Basuto chief in 1861 delivered himself as follows:

> Sorcery only exists in the mouths of those who speak it. It is no more in the power of a man to kill his fellows by mere effort of will than it would be to raise them from the dead. That is my opinion. Nevertheless, you sorcerers who hear me speak, use moderation!

A stout speech, but taking no chances. Henshaw Ward says:

The savage has just as good a brain as we have. If we make allowances for his small amount of information, we have to admit that his power to reason is just as great as ours. He relies on his reason. As soon as he has made a vivid mental picture of an explanation, the picture seems real. He does not distinguish between what he manufactures in his own skull and what comes to his skull from the outside world. He does not understand verifying his explanations.

[6] A savage has little knowledge of natural causes. Tribes exist to whom the part played by the father in the conception of a child is unknown. It is held that a demon enters into the mother's womb. It is not quite fair to call savages superstitious in such cases, for no better explanations are available.

FOR REVIEW AND DISCUSSION

Content

1. What is *word magic*?

2. "Word magic is common to all primitive peoples." Does Chase seem to be implying that word magic is a trait limited to primitive word users, that it is not practiced by sophisticated ones? Is Chase just describing word magic, or is he evaluating it, casting judgment on it and on its users? Support your answers by referring to specific passages.

3. Chase writes that part of the power of language comes from our too literally identifying the word with the thing it names—a common semantic confusion. Refer to Chase's examples of this confusion and think of similar examples based upon your own experience.

4. What is Chase's attitude toward "primitive peoples" who are believers in word magic? What are some specific passages that make his attitude evident?

Rhetoric

1. Chase does not actually define *word magic*. How do we understand what he means by the term? Is it likely that we will all share the same definition of the term? Why?

2. Estimate what percentage of Chase's essay is general observation or opinion and what percentage is specific examples intended to support the general statements. Does he support each general statement sufficiently so that you find it convincing?

Classroom Exercises

1. If you could choose any name for yourself, what would it be? What makes you choose that name rather than another?

2. Describe your feelings about the name your parents gave you. Is there word magic working in your name?

3. Compile a list of words you find particularly attractive. Do the same for words you find distasteful. Upon what have you based your response to these words: upon their sounds, upon the personal associations that the words have, or upon their denotative meanings?

N. Scott Momaday

from THE WAY TO RAINY MOUNTAIN

The Way to Rainy Mountain, a brief history of the Kiowa Indians, is divided into sections containing a Kiowa myth or story, an anthropological or historical comment, and a personal recollection of the author, himself a Kiowa. In this section, the author continues with the story of twin brothers from the early (mythological?) days of the tribe and reveals to us some significant qualities of word magic, both ancient and modern.

[1]   Now each of the twins had a ring, and the grandmother spider told them never to throw the rings into the sky. But one day they threw them up into the high wind. The rings rolled over a hill, and the twins ran after them. They ran beyond the top of the hill and fell down into the mouth of a cave. There lived a giant and his wife. The giant had killed a lot of people in the past by building a fire and filling the cave with smoke, so that the people could not breathe. Then the twins remembered something that the grandmother spider told them: "If you ever get caught in the cave, say to yourselves the word 'thain-mom,' 'above my eyes.' " When the giant began to set fires around, the twins repeated the word "thain-mom" over and over to themselves, and the smoke remained above their eyes. When the giant had made three great clouds of smoke, his wife saw that the twins had sat without coughing or crying, and she became frightened. "Let them go," she said, "or something bad will happen to us." The twins took up their rings and returned to the grandmother spider. She was glad to see them.

[2]   A word has power in and of itself. It comes from nothing into sound and meaning; it gives origin to all things. By means of words can a man deal with the world on equal terms. And the word is sacred. A man's name is his own; he can keep it or give it away as he likes. Until recent times, the Kiowas would not speak the name of a dead man. To do so would have been disrespectful and dishonest. The dead take their names with them out of the world.

[3]   When Aho [the author's grandmother] said or heard or thought of something bad, she said the word "zei-dl-bei," "frightful." It was the one word with which she confronted evil and the incomprehensible. I liked her to say it, for she screwed up her face in a wonderful look of displeasure and clicked her tongue. It was not an exclamation so much, I think, as it was a warding off, an exertion of language upon ignorance and disorder.

N. Scott Momaday, *The Way to Rainy Mountain* (Albuquerque: University of New Mexico Press, 1969), pp. 32–33. Reprinted by permission of the publisher.

FOR REVIEW AND DISCUSSION

Content

1. What is meant by the statement that a word "gives origin to all things"?

2. Do we show reverence for the names of the dead? If so, how does our way of showing reverence differ from or resemble that of the Kiowas? If not, suggest some reasons why our culture fails to show such reverence.

3. There doesn't seem to be much logic in the Kiowa belief in the power of language. After all, as most people who have been frustrated know, "saying something doesn't make it so." Yet the twins, by saying "thain-mom," *are* able to "make it so" (and to make their escape). Does our inability to find sense in the Kiowa belief mean that their belief is false, or is there some way—perhaps not a rational way—to understand the power that the Kiowas find in words?

Rhetoric

1. The first part of the Momaday excerpt is written in the style of a myth or folk tale: Events are simply related, without explanation or interpretation, and the diction is also simple. What effect does this mode of presentation have on our response to the tale?

2. What seems to be Momaday's attitude toward his subject, the Kiowa belief in word power? Is he merely recording cultural information, along with his own memories, or is he presenting his material in a way that suggests some other purpose? Cite specific details to support your answer.

Classroom Exercises

1. Describe the circumstances in which you or someone you know might use a word similar to the one that Aho used.

2. Cite examples of and distinguish between commonplace exclamations and the kind of word that Aho used.

Bruno Bettelheim

JOEY: A "MECHANICAL BOY"

The powers we attribute to language are evident not only in our attempts to order and understand the external world but also in our attempts to order and understand ourselves. Sometimes, however, the obstacles encountered in these attempts seem insurmountable. There are numerous disorders of the brain that dramatically affect our ability to use language—dyslexia, aphasia, and autism are but three. This selection recounts the case history of a boy who suffers from autism and schizophrenia. Pay particular attention to the ways Joey both uses and misuses language, to how his attitude toward language differs from that of most people, and to what Joey's story reveals about the remarkable and at times frightening powers language can exert over us.

[1] Joey, when we began our work with him, was a mechanical boy. He functioned as if by remote control, run by machines of his own powerfully creative fantasy. Not only did he himself believe that he was a machine but, more remarkably, he created this impression in others. Even while he performed actions that are intrinsically human, they never appeared to be other than machine-started and executed. On the other hand, when the machine was not working we had to concentrate on recollecting his presence, for he seemed not to exist. A human body that functions as if it were a machine and a machine that duplicates human functions are equally fascinating and frightening. Perhaps they are so uncanny because they remind us that the human body can operate without a human spirit, that body can exist without soul. And Joey was a child who had been robbed of his humanity.

[2] Not every child who possesses a fantasy world is possessed by it. Normal children may retreat into realms of imaginary glory or magic powers, but they are easily recalled from these excursions. Disturbed children are not always able to make the return trip; they remain withdrawn, prisoners of the inner world of delusion and fantasy. In many ways Joey presented a classic example of this state of infantile autism.

[3] At the Sonia Shankman Orthogenic School of the University of Chicago it is our function to provide a therapeutic environment in which such children may start life over again. I have previously described the rehabilitation of another of our patients ["Schizophrenic Art: A Case Study"; *Scientific American*, April, 1952]. This time I shall concentrate upon the illness, rather than the treatment. In any

Reprinted with permission. Copyright © 1959 by Scientific American, Inc. All rights reserved.

age, when the individual has escaped into a delusional world, he has usually fashioned it from bits and pieces of the world at hand. Joey, in his time and world, chose the machine and froze himself in its image. His story has a general relevance to the understanding of emotional development in a machine age.

[4]   Joey's delusion is not uncommon among schizophrenic children today. He wanted to be rid of his unbearable humanity, to become completely automatic. He so nearly succeeded in attaining this goal that he could almost convince others, as well as himself, of his mechanical character. The descriptions of autistic children in the literature take for their point of departure and comparison the normal or abnormal human being. To do justice to Joey I would have to compare him simultaneously to a most inept infant and a highly complex piece of machinery. Often we had to force ourselves by a conscious act of will to realize that Joey was a child. Again and again his acting-out of his delusions froze our own ability to respond as human beings.

[5]   During Joey's first weeks with us we would watch absorbedly as this at once fragile-looking and imperious nine-year-old went about his mechanical existence. Entering the dining room, for example, he would string an imaginary wire from his "energy source"—an imaginary electric outlet—to the table. There he "insulated" himself with paper napkins and finally plugged himself in. Only then could Joey eat, for he firmly believed that the "current" ran his ingestive apparatus. So skillful was the pantomime that one had to look twice to be sure there was neither wire nor outlet nor plug. Children and members of our staff spontaneously avoided stepping on the "wires" for fear of interrupting what seemed the source of his very life.

[6]   For long periods of time, when his "machinery" was idle, he would sit so quietly that he would disappear from the focus of the most conscientious observation. Yet in the next moment he might be "working" and the center of our captivated attention. Many times a day he would turn himself on and shift noisily through a sequence of higher and higher gears until he "exploded," screaming "Crash, crash!" and hurling items from his ever present apparatus—radio tubes, light bulbs, even motors or, lacking these, any handy breakable object. (Joey had an astonishing knack for snatching bulbs and tubes unobserved.) As soon as the object thrown had shattered, he would cease his screaming and wild jumping and retire to mute, motionless nonexistence.

[7]   Our maids, inured to difficult children, were exceptionally attentive to Joey; they were apparently moved by his extreme infantile fragility, so strangely coupled with megalomaniacal superiority. Occasionally some of the apparatus he fixed to his bed to "live him" during his sleep would fall down in disarray. This machinery he contrived from masking tape, cardboard, wire and other paraphernalia. Usually the maids would pick up such things and leave them on a table for the children to find, or disregard them entirely. But Joey's machine they carefully restored: "Joey must have the carburetor so he can breathe." Similarly they were on the alert to pick up

and preserve the motors that ran him during the day and the exhaust pipes through which he exhaled.

[8] How had Joey become a human machine? From intensive interviews with his parents we learned that the process had begun even before birth. Schizophrenia often results from parental rejection, sometimes combined ambivalently with love. Joey, on the other hand, had been completely ignored.

[9] "I never knew I was pregnant," his mother said, meaning that she had already excluded Joey from her consciousness. His birth, she said, "did not make any difference." Joey's father, a rootless draftee in the wartime civilian army, was equally unready for parenthood. So, of course, are many young couples. Fortunately most such parents lose their indifference upon the baby's birth. But not Joey's parents. "I did not want to see or nurse him," his mother declared. "I had no feeling of actual dislike—I simply didn't want to take care of him." For the first three months of his life Joey "cried most of the time." A colicky baby, he was kept on a rigid four-hour feeding schedule, was not touched unless necessary and was never cuddled or played with. The mother, preoccupied with herself, usually left Joey alone in the crib or playpen during the day. The father discharged his frustrations by punishing Joey when the child cried at night.

[10] Soon the father left for overseas duty, and the mother took Joey, now a year and a half old, to live with her at her parents' home. On his arrival the grandparents noticed that ominous changes had occurred in the child. Strong and healthy at birth, he had become frail and irritable; a responsive baby, he had become remote and inaccessible. When he began to master speech, he talked only to himself. At an early date he became preoccupied with machinery, including an old electric fan which he could take apart and put together again with surprising deftness.

[11] Joey's mother impressed us with a fey quality that expressed her insecurity, her detachment from the world and her low physical vitality. We were struck especially by her total indifference as she talked about Joey. This seemed much more remarkable than the actual mistakes she made in handling him. Certainly he was left to cry for hours when hungry, because she fed him on a rigid schedule; he was toilet-trained with great rigidity so that he would give no trouble. These things happen to many children. But Joey's existence never registered with his mother. In her recollections he was fused at one moment with one event or person; at another, with something or somebody else. When she told us about his birth and infancy, it was as if she were talking about some vague acquaintance, and soon her thoughts would wander off to another person or to herself.

[12] When Joey was not yet four, his nursery school suggested that he enter a special school for disturbed children. At the new school his autism was immediately recognized. During his three years there he experienced a slow improvement. Unfortunately a subsequent two years in a parochial school destroyed this progress. He began to develop compulsive defenses, which he called his "preventions." He

could not drink, for example, except through elaborate piping systems built of straws. Liquids had to be "pumped" into him, in his fantasy, or he could not suck. Eventually his behavior became so upsetting that he could not be kept in the parochial school. At home things did not improve. Three months before entering the Orthogenic School he made a serious attempt at suicide.

[13] To us Joey's pathological behavior seemed the external expression of an overwhelming effort to remain almost nonexistent as a person. For weeks Joey's only reply when addressed was "Bam." Unless he thus neutralized whatever we said, there would be an explosion, for Joey plainly wished to close off every form of contact not mediated by machinery. Even when he was bathed he rocked back and forth with mute, engine-like regularity, flooding the bathroom. If he stopped rocking, he did this like a machine too; suddenly he went completely rigid. Only once, after months of being lifted from his bath and carried to bed, did a small expression of puzzled pleasure appear on his face as he said very softly: "They even carry you to your bed here."

[14] For a long time after he began to talk he would never refer to anyone by name, but only as "that person" or "the little person" or "the big person." He was unable to designate by its true name anything to which he attached feelings. Nor could he name his anxieties except through neologisms or word contaminations. For a long time he spoke about "master paintings" and "a master painting room" (i.e., masturbating and masturbating room). One of his machines, the "criticizer," prevented him from "saying words which have unpleasant feelings." Yet he gave personal names to the tubes and motors in his collection of machinery. Moreover, these dead things had feelings; the tubes bled when hurt and sometimes got sick. He consistently maintained this reversal between animate and inanimate objects.

[15] In Joey's machine world everything, on pain of instant destruction, obeyed inhibitory laws much more stringent than those of physics. When we came to know him better, it was plain that in his moments of silent withdrawal, with his machine switched off, Joey was absorbed in pondering the compulsive laws of his private universe. His preoccupation with machinery made it difficult to establish even practical contacts with him. If he wanted to do something with a counselor, such as play with a toy that had caught his vague attention, he could not do so: "I'd like this very much, but first I have to turn off the machine." But by the time he had fulfilled all the requirements of his preventions, he had lost interest. When a toy was offered to him, he could not touch it because his motors and his tubes did not leave him a hand free. Even certain colors were dangerous and had to be strictly avoided in toys and clothing, because "some colors turn off the current, and I can't touch them because I can't live without the current."

[16] Joey was convinced that machines were better than people. Once when he bumped into one of the pipes on our jungle gym he kicked it so violently that his teacher had to restrain him to keep him from injuring himself. When she explained

that the pipe was much harder than his foot, Joey replied: "That proves it. Machines are better than the body. They don't break; they're much harder and stronger." If he lost or forgot something, it merely proved that his brain ought to be thrown away and replaced by machinery. If he spilled something, his arm should be broken and twisted off because it did not work properly. When his head or arm failed to work as it should, he tried to punish it by hitting it. Even Joey's feelings were mechanical. Much later in his therapy, when he had formed a timid attachment to another child and had been rebuffed, Joey cried: "He broke my feelings."

[17] Gradually we began to understand what had seemed to be contradictory in Joey's behavior—why he held on to the motors and tubes, then suddenly destroyed them in a fury, then set out immediately and urgently to equip himself with new and larger tubes. Joey had created these machines to run his body and mind because it was too painful to be human. But again and again he became dissatisfied with their failure to meet his need and rebellious at the way they frustrated his will. In a recurrent frenzy he "exploded" his light bulbs and tubes, and for a moment became a human being—for one crowning instant he came alive. But as soon as he had asserted his dominance through the self-created explosion, he felt his life ebbing away. To keep on existing he had immediately to restore his machines and replenish the electricity that supplied his life energy.

[18] What deep-seated fears and needs underlay Joey's delusional system? We were long in finding out, for Joey's preventions effectively concealed the secret of his autistic behavior. In the meantime we dealt with his peripheral problems one by one.

[19] During his first year with us Joey's most trying problem was toilet behavior. This surprised us, for Joey's personality was not "anal" in the Freudian sense; his original personality damage had antedated the period of his toilet-training. Rigid and early toilet-training, however, had certainly contributed to his anxieties. It was our effort to help Joey with this problem that led to his first recognition of us as human beings.

[20] Going to the toilet, like everything else in Joey's life, was surrounded by elaborate preventions. We had to accompany him; he had to take off all his clothes; he could only squat, not sit, on the toilet seat; he had to touch the wall with one hand, in which he also clutched frantically the vacuum tubes that powered his elimination. He was terrified lest his whole body be sucked down.

[21] To counteract this fear we gave him a metal wastebasket in lieu of a toilet. Eventually, when eliminating into the wastebasket, he no longer needed to take off all his clothes, nor to hold on to the wall. He still needed the tubes and motors which, he believed, moved his bowels for him. But here again the all-important machinery was itself a source of new terrors. In Joey's world the gadgets had to move their bowels, too. He was terribly concerned that they should, but since they were so much more powerful than men, he was also terrified that if his tubes moved their

bowels, their feces would fill all of space and leave him no room to live. He was thus always caught in some fearful contradiction.

[22] Our readiness to accept his toilet habits, which obviously entailed some hardship for his counselors, gave Joey the confidence to express his obsessions in drawings. Drawing these fantasies was a first step toward letting us in, however distantly, to what concerned him most deeply. It was the first step in a year-long process of externalizing his anal preoccupations. As a result he began seeing feces everywhere; the whole world became to him a mire of excrement. At the same time he began to eliminate freely wherever he happened to be. But with this release from his infantile imprisonment in compulsive rules, the toilet and the whole process of elimination became less dangerous. Thus far it had been beyond Joey's comprehension that anybody could possibly move his bowels without mechanical aid. Now Joey took a further step forward; defecation became the first physiological process he could perform without the help of vacuum tubes. It must not be thought that he was proud of this ability. Taking pride in an achievement presupposes that one accomplishes it of one's own free will. He still did not feel himself an autonomous person who could do things on his own. To Joey defecation still seemed enslaved to some incomprehensible but utterly binding cosmic law, perhaps the law his parents had imposed on him when he was being toilet-trained.

[23] It was not simply that his parents had subjected him to rigid, early training. Many children are so trained. But in most cases the parents have a deep emotional investment in the child's performance. The child's response in turn makes training an occasion for interaction between them and for the building of genuine relationships. Joey's parents had no emotional investment in him. His obedience gave them no satisfaction and won him no affection or approval. As a toilet-trained child he saved his mother labor, just as household machines saved her labor. As a machine he was not loved for his performance, nor could he love himself.

[24] So it had been with all other aspects of Joey's existence with his parents. Their reactions to his eating or noneating, sleeping or wakening, urinating or defecating, being dressed or undressed, washed or bathed did not flow from any unitary interest in him, deeply embedded in their personalities. By treating him mechanically his parents made him a machine. The various functions of life—even the parts of his body—bore no integrating relationship to one another or to any sense of self that was acknowledged and confirmed by others. Though he had acquired mastery over some functions, such as toilet-training and speech, he had acquired them separately and kept them isolated from each other. Toilet-training had thus not gained him a pleasant feeling of body mastery; speech had not led to communication of thought or feeling. On the contrary, each achievement only steered him away from self-mastery and integration. Toilet-training had enslaved him. Speech left him talking in neologisms that obstructed his and our ability to relate to each other. In Joey's development the normal process of growth had been made to run backward. Whatever he had learned put him not at the end of his infantile development toward

integration but, on the contrary, farther behind than he was at its very beginning. Had we understood this sooner, his first years with us would have been less baffling.

[25] It is unlikely that Joey's calamity could befall a child in any time and culture but our own. He suffered no physical deprivation; he starved for human contact. Just to be taken care of is not enough for relating. It is a necessary but not a sufficient condition. At the extreme where utter scarcity reigns, the forming of relationships is certainly hampered. But our society of mechanized plenty often makes for equal difficulties in a child's learning to relate. Where parents can provide the simple creature-comforts for their children only at the cost of significant effort, it is likely that they will feel pleasure in being able to provide for them; it is this, the parents' pleasure, that gives children a sense of personal worth and sets the process of relating in motion. But if comfort is so readily available that the parents feel no particular pleasure in winning it for their children, then the children cannot develop the feeling of being worthwhile around the satisfaction of their basic needs. Of course parents and children can and do develop relationships around other situations. But matters are then no longer so simple and direct. The child must be on the receiving end of care and concern given with pleasure and without the exaction of return if he is to feel loved and worthy of respect and consideration. This feeling gives him the ability to trust; he can entrust his well-being to persons to whom he is so important. Out of such trust the child learns to form close and stable relationships.

[26] For Joey relationship with his parents was empty of pleasure in comfort-giving as in all other situations. His was an extreme instance of a plight that sends many schizophrenic children to our clinics and hospitals. Many months passed before he could relate to us; his despair that anybody could like him made contact impossible.

[27] When Joey could finally trust us enough to let himself become more infantile, he began to play at being a papoose. There was a corresponding change in his fantasies. He drew endless pictures of himself as an electrical papoose. Totally enclosed, suspended in empty space, he is run by unknown, unseen powers through wireless electricity.

[28] As we eventually came to understand, the heart of Joey's delusional system was the artificial, mechanical womb he had created and into which he had locked himself. In his papoose fantasies lay the wish to be entirely reborn in a womb. His new experiences in the school suggested that life, after all, might be worth living. Now he was searching for a way to be reborn in a better way. Since machines were better than men, what was more natural than to try rebirth through them? This was the deeper meaning of his electrical papoose.

[29] As Joey made progress, his pictures of himself became more dominant in his drawings. Through still machine-operated, he has grown in self-importance. Now he has acquired hands that do something, and he has had the courage to make a picture of the machine that runs him. Later still the papoose became a person, rather than a robot encased in glass.

JOEY: A "MECHANICAL BOY"

[30] Eventually Joey began to create an imaginary family at the school: the "Carr" family. Why the Carr family? In the car he was enclosed as he had been in his papoose, but at least the car was not stationary; it could move. More important, in a car one was not only driven but also could drive. The Carr family was Joey's way of exploring the possibility of leaving the school, of living with a good family in a safe, protecting car.

[31] Joey at last broke through his prison. In this brief account it has not been possible to trace the painfully slow process of his first true relations with other human beings. Suffice it to say that he ceased to be a mechanical boy and became a human child. This newborn child was, however, nearly twelve years old. To recover the lost time is a tremendous task. That work has occupied Joey and us ever since. Sometimes he sets to it with a will; at other times the difficulty of real life makes him regret that he ever came out of his shell. But he has never wanted to return to his mechanical life.

[32] One last detail and this fragment of Joey's story has been told. When Joey was twelve, he made a float for our Memorial Day parade. It carried the slogan: "Feelings are more important than anything under the sun." Feelings, Joey had learned, are what make for humanity; their absence, for a mechanical existence. With this knowledge Joey entered the human condition.

FOR REVIEW AND DISCUSSION

Content

1. Joey could not "name his anxieties except through neologisms or word contaminations." What is wrong with Joey's inventing neologisms (as Bettelheim uses the term)? In what ways are neologisms a sign of Joey's particular illness?

2. Consider Joey's reluctance to name unpleasantness properly or to name unpleasantness at all. What does this tell us about Joey's attitude toward language? What does Joey's reluctance tell us about the role language use is likely to play in his recovery?

3. Bettelheim says that "speech had not led to communication of thought or feeling." Why does the author consider communication important in Joey's case?

Rhetoric

1. How has Bettelheim ordered the material in his essay? Does he present different kinds of information in different sections of the essay, or is the presentation generally uniform? What effect might Bettelheim have been after by presenting material in the order he did?

2. What does Bettelheim's purpose for writing the essay seem to be? (To present a case history? To publicize his clinic? To criticize modern society?) What is there in the essay that makes his purpose evident?

3. Notice that toward the end the paragraphs become shorter and the author seems to be telescoping time. Notice too that the conclusion seems rather abrupt. Can you think of any reasons for these structural changes?

4. The diction an author uses indicates something about his intended audience: educated colleagues, the general public, students, some combination of different groups, and so forth. Look through Bettelheim's essay and select words that provide clues to whom Bettelheim sees as his audience. Then describe this audience.

Classroom Exercises

1. Look up *autism* in an unabridged dictionary (or in a psychology textbook). In what respects does Bettelheim's description of Joey match up with the dictionary or textbook definition of *autism*? Write a brief but detailed diagnosis of Joey's condition.

2. Joey's linguistic behavior is of course pathological. Yet most of us occasionally (and sometimes habitually) use language to shut us off from unpleasant realities. Identify and discuss some of these everyday aberrant uses of language. When, if ever, are they justifiable?

E. E. Cummings

SINCE FEELING IS FIRST

E. E. Cummings is well known for his linguistic and typographical unconventionality, and in this poem about love and language and poetry we find, perhaps, an explanation of why he writes the way he does.

since feeling is first
who pays any attention
to the syntax of things
will never wholly kiss you;

wholly to be a fool
while Spring is in the world

my blood approves,
and kisses are a better fate
than wisdom
lady i swear by all flowers.   Don't cry
—the best gesture of my brain is less than
your eyelids' flutter which says

Copyright 1926 by Horace Liveright; renewed 1954 by E. E. Cummings. Reprinted from *Complete Poems 1913–1962* by E. E. Cummings by permission of Harcourt Brace Jovanovich, Inc.

SINCE FEELING IS FIRST

we are for each other: then
laugh, leaning back in my arms
for life's not a paragraph

And death i think is no parenthesis

FOR REVIEW AND DISCUSSION

Content

1. Cummings is contrasting two approaches to experience. Feeling is the first of the two. What is the second? Does Cummings say that the two are incompatible or just different?

2. What is meant by "the syntax of things"?

3. *Wholly* is used both in line 4 and in line 5. Assuming that Cummings repeated the word because he wished to emphasize it, comment on the significance of wholeness in the poem.

4. Cummings has something specific in mind when he says "the best gesture of my brain." What is it?

5. What does the last line of the poem mean? Must one know the uses of the parenthesis in order to understand the line?

Rhetoric

1. What relation does *since*, the first word in the poem, have with the rest of the poem? Is *since* only a "filler word," one that adds no meaning? What effect does Cummings create by beginning his poem with this word?

2. Does it appear that throughout the poem Cummings speaks literally, or is he speaking figuratively at times? Identify any figurative expressions and think of literal replacements. Which form—the literal or the figurative—is easier to understand? Which seems more engaging?

3. Is Cummings's argument only rational, only emotional, or both? Which of his points seems more convincing? Do you find yourself responding more to rational or to emotional points in the poem? Why might this be?

4. By examining their content and syntax, explain why Cummings divides the stanzas where he does.

Classroom Exercises

1. Is a kiss just a kiss, or is Cummings correct in distinguishing between "whole" kisses and partial ones? What does Cummings mean when he says that someone who "pays any attention / to the syntax of things / will never wholly kiss you"?

2. If Cummings is to convince us that his point of view is valid, he would be wise to present an image of himself that appears reliable, competent, and sincere. Does he successfully make us trust him? What causes us to trust or to distrust him? How does the tone affect our response to the poet and to what he says?

3. Reread the poem, supplying punctuation where you think it is needed. Then write out the poem as a paragraph. Do both versions mean the same thing?

FOR FURTHER READING

Ernst Cassirer
(translated by Susanne K. Langer)

WORD MAGIC:
THE PRIMITIVE POWER OF LANGUAGE

At the beginning of this chapter Stuart Chase provided a short introduction to word magic. Here the philosopher Ernst Cassirer discusses the subject in greater and more complex detail, and explores the philosophical implications of our seemingly inherent notion that language and creation are intertwined.

[1] The original bond between the linguistic consciousness and the mythical-religious consciousness is primarily expressed in the fact that all verbal structures appear *also* as mythical entities endowed with certain mythical powers. The Word, in fact, becomes a sort of primary force, in which all being and doing originate. In all mythical cosmogonies, as far back as they can be traced, this supreme position of the Word is found. Among the texts which Preuss has collected among the Uitoto Indians there is one which he has adduced as a direct parallel to the opening passage of St. John, and which, in his translation, certainly seems to fall in with it perfectly: "In the beginning," it says, "the Word gave the Father his origin." Of course, striking though it may be, no one would try to argue from this coincidence to any direct relationship or even an analogy of material content between that primitive creation story and the speculations of St. John. And yet it presents us with a certain problem, it points to the fact that some indirect relationship must obtain, which covers everything from the most primitive gropings of mythico-religious thought to those highest products in which such thought seems to have already gone over into a realm of pure speculation.

From *Language and Myth* by Ernst Cassirer, translated by Susanne K. Langer. Copyright 1946 by Harper & Row, Publishers. Reprinted by permission of Susanne K. Langer.

[2]   A more precise insight into the foundations of this relationship can be attained only in so far as we are able to carry back the study of those examples of Word veneration, which the history of religions is always uncovering, from the mere analogy of their respective *contents* to the recognition of their common *form*. There must be some particular, essentially unchanging *function* that endows the Word with this extraordinary, religious character, and exalts it *ab initio* to the religious sphere, the sphere of the "holy." In the creation accounts of almost all great cultural religions, the Word appears in league with the highest Lord of creation; either as the tool which he employs or actually as the primary source from which he, like all other Being and order of Being, is derived. Thought and its verbal utterance are usually taken directly as one; for the mind that thinks and the tongue that speaks belong essentially together. Thus, in one of the earliest records of Egyptian theology, this primary force of "the heart and the tongue" is attributed to the creation-god Ptah, whereby he produces and governs all gods and men, all animals, and all that lives. Whatever is has come into being through the thought of his heart and the command of his tongue; to these two, all physical and spiritual being, the existence of the Ka as well as all properties of things, owe their origin. Here, as indeed certain scholars have pointed out, thousands of years before the Christian era, God is conceived as a spiritual Being who *thought* the world before he created it, and who used the Word as a means of expression and an instrument of creation. And as all physical and psychical Being rests in him, so do all ethical bonds and the whole moral order.

[3]   Those religions which base their world picture and their cosmogony essentially on a fundamental ethical contrast, the dualism of good and evil, venerate the spoken Word as the primary force by whose sole agency Chaos was transformed into an ethico-religious Cosmos. According to the Bundahish, the cosmogony and cosmography of the Parsis, the war between the power of Good and the power of Evil, i.e., between Ahura Mazda and Angra Mainyu, begins with Ahura Mazda's reciting the words of the Holy Prayer (Ahuna Vairya):

> He spake that which has twenty-one words. The end, which is his victory, the impotence of Angra Mainyu, the decline of the Daevas, the resurrection and the future life, the ending of opposition to the (good) creation for all eternity—all these he showed to Angra Mainyu . . . When a third of this prayer had been spoken, Angra Mainyu doubled up his body with terror, when two-thirds had been spoken he fell upon his knees, and when the whole had been uttered he was confounded, and powerless to abuse the creatures of Ahura Mazda, and remained confounded for three thousand years.

[4]   Here, again the words of the prayer precede the material creation, and preserve it ever against the destructive powers of the Evil One. Similarly, in India, we find the power of the Spoken Word (Vāc) exalted even above the might of the gods themselves: "On the Spoken Word all the gods depend, all beasts and men; in the Word live all creatures . . . the Word is the Imperishable, the first-born of the eternal Law, the mother of the Veddas, the navel of the divine world."

[5]   As the Word is first in origin, it is also supreme in power. Often it is the *name* of the deity, rather than the god himself, that seems to be the real source of efficacy. Knowledge of the name gives him who knows it mastery even over the being and will of the god. Thus a familiar Egyptian legend tells how Isis, the great sorceress, craftily persuaded the sun-god Ra to disclose his name to her, and how through possession of the name she gained power over him and over all the other gods. In many other ways, too, Egyptian religious life in all its phases evinces over and over again this belief in the supremacy of the name and the magic power that dwells in it. The ceremonies attending the anointment of kings are governed by minute prescriptions for the transference of the god's several names to the Pharaoh; each name conveys a special attribute, a new divine power.

[6]   Moreover, this motive plays a decisive role in the Egyptian doctrines of the soul and its immortality. The souls of the departed, starting on their journey to the land of the dead, must be given not only their physical possessions, such as food and clothing, but also a certain outfit of a magical nature: this consists chiefly of the names of the gatekeepers in the nether world, for only the knowledge of these names can unlock the doors of Death's kingdom. Even the boat in which the dead man is conveyed, and its several parts, the rudder, the mast, etc., demand that he call them by their right names; only by virtue of this appellation can he render them willing and subservient and cause them to take him to his destination.

[7]   The essential identity between the word and what it denotes becomes even more patently evident if we look at it not from the objective standpoint, but from a subjective angle. For even a person's ego, his very self and personality, is indissolubly linked, in mythic thinking, with his name. Here the name is never a mere symbol, but is part of the personal property of its bearer; property which must be carefully protected, and the use of which is exclusively and jealously reserved to him. Sometimes it is not only his name, but also some other verbal denotation, that is thus treated as a physical possession, and as such may be acquired and usurped by someone else. Georg von der Gabelentz, in his book on the science of language, mentions the edict of a Chinese emperor of the third century B.C., whereby a pronoun in the first person, that had been legitimately in popular use, was henceforth reserved to him alone. And the name may even acquire a status above the more or less accessory one of a personal possession, when it is taken as a truly substantial Being, an integral *part* of its bearer. As such it is in the same category as his body or his soul. It is said of the Eskimos that for them man consists of three elements—body, soul, and name. And in Egypt, too, we find a similar conception, for there the physical body of man was thought to be accompanied, on the one hand, by his Ka, or double, and, on the other, by his name, as a sort of spiritual double. And of all these three elements it is just the last-mentioned which becomes more and more the expression of a man's "self," of his "personality." Even in far more advanced cultures this connection between name and personality continues to be felt. When, in Roman law, the concept of the "legal person" was formally

articulated, and this status was denied to certain physical subjects, those subjects were also denied official possession of a proper name. Under Roman law a slave had no legal name, because he could not function as a legal person.

[8] In other ways, too, the unity and uniqueness of the name is not only a mark of the unity and uniqueness of the person, but actually constitutes it; the name is what first makes man an individual. Where this verbal distinctiveness is not found, there the outlines of his personality tend also to be effaced. Among the Algonquins, a man who bears the same name as some given person is regarded as the latter's other self, his alter ego. If, in accordance with a prevalent custom, a child is given the name of his grandfather, this expresses the belief that the grandfather is resurrected, reincarnated in the boy. As soon as a child is born, the problem arises which one of his departed ancestors is reborn in him; only after this has been determined by the priest can the ceremony be performed whereby the infant receives that progenitor's name.

[9] Furthermore, the mythic consciousness does not see human personality as something fixed and unchanging, but conceives every *phase* of a man's life as a new personality, a new self; and this metamorphosis is first of all made manifest in the changes which his name undergoes. At puberty a boy receives a new name, because, by virtue of the magical rites accompanying his initiation, he has ceased to exist as a boy, and has been reborn as a man, the reincarnation of one of his ancestors. In other cases the change of name sometimes serves to protect a man against impending danger; he escapes by taking on a different self, whose form makes him unrecognizable. Among the Evé it is customary to give children, and especially those whose elder brothers or sisters have died young, a name that has a frightful connotation, or attributes some non-human nature to them; the idea is that Death may be either frightened away, or deceived, and will pass them by as though they were not human at all. Similarly, the name of a man laboring under disease or bloodguilt is sometimes changed, on the same principle, that Death may not find him. Even in Greek culture this custom of altering names, with its mythic motivation, still maintained itself. Quite generally, in fact, the being and life of a person is so intimately connected with his name that, as long as the name is preserved and spoken, its bearer is still felt to be present and directly active. The dead may, at any moment, be literally "invoked," the moment those who survive him speak his name. As everyone knows, the fear of such visitation has led many savages to avoid not only every mention of the departed, whose name is tabooed, but even the enunciation of all assonances to his name. Often, for instance, an animal species whose name a defunct person had borne has to be given a different appellation, lest the dead man be inadvertently called upon by speaking of the beast. In many cases procedures of this sort, entirely mythic in their motivation, have had a radical influence on language, and modified vocabularies considerably. And the further a Being's power extends, the more mythic potency and "significance" he embodies, the greater is the sphere of influence of his name. The rule of secrecy, therefore, applies first and foremost to the Holy Name; for the mention of it would immediately release all the powers inherent in the god himself.

[10] But here let us stop; for it is not our intention to collect theological or ethnological material, but to clarify and define the problem presented by such material. Such interweaving and interlocking as we have found between the elements of language, and the various forms of religious and mythical conception cannot be due to mere chance; it must be rooted in a common characteristic of language and myth as such. Some scholars have sought to base this intimate connection on the suggestive power of words, and especially of a spoken command, to which primitive man is supposed to be particularly subject; the magical and daemonic power which all verbal utterance has for the mythic state of consciousness seems to them to be nothing more than an objectification of that experience. But such a narrow empirical and pragmatic foundation, such a detail of personal or social experience, cannot support the prime and fundamental facts of linguistic and mythic conception. More and more clearly we see ourselves faced with the question whether the close relationship of contents which certainly obtains between language and myth may not be most readily explained by the common form of their evolution, by the conditions which govern both verbal expression and mythic imagination from their earliest, unconscious beginnings.

[11] Preuss reports that, according to the Cora Indians and the Uitoto, the "Patriarch" created men and nature, but that since this creation he no longer interferes directly with the course of events. In lieu of such personal intervention, he gave to men his "Words," i.e., his cult and the religious ceremonies by means of which they now control nature and attain whatever is necessary for the welfare and perpetuation of the race. Without these holy spells which were originally given into their keeping, men would be entirely helpless, for nature yields nothing merely in return for human labor. Among the Cherokees, too, it is an accepted belief that success in hunting or fishing is due chiefly to the use of certain words of the proper magic formulas.

[12] It was a long evolutionary course which the human mind had to traverse, to pass from the belief in a physico-magical power comprised in the Word to a realization of its spiritual power. Indeed, it is the Word, it is language, that really reveals to man that world which is closer to him than any world of natural objects and touches his weal and woe more directly than physical nature. For it is language that makes his existence in a *community* possible; and only in society, in relation to a "Thee," can his subjectivity assert itself as a "Me." . . .

FOR REVIEW AND DISCUSSION

Content

1. In his introduction, Cassirer alludes to "some indirect relationship . . . which covers everything from the most primitive gropings of mythico-religious thought to those highest products . . . of pure speculation." What specifically is that relationship? Does Cassirer explain what this relationship is?

2. What is *word veneration*? What modern instances of word veneration can you think of?

3. Does there seem to be a great "sphere of influence" surrounding any holy names in modern society? If so, describe the sphere of influence of one such name. If not, discuss why we no longer seem to invest such influence in the names of holy forces.

4. In *Through the Looking Glass* (see chapter 2), Alice asks Humpty Dumpty, "Must a name mean something?" How might Cassirer answer Alice's question?

5. What does Cassirer mean by the spiritual power of the Word?

Rhetoric

1. Where does Cassirer state his main point? Did you expect to find it there? If you did, what built up your expectations? What effect upon the reader is achieved by putting the main point where it is?

2. Examine the words Cassirer uses. Assuming that he chooses words according to who he thinks his audience will be, what does his word choice reveal about his assumed audience?

Classroom Exercises

1. Do you feel about your name any of "the unity and uniqueness" that Cassirer describes as constituting "the unity and uniqueness of the person"? If you do, what occasions make these feelings evident? If you do not, what feelings *do* you have for your name?

2. Cassirer describes name changes that people go through as they enter new phases of life. Does our culture include a similar practice? Is the psychological basis for these name changes consistent with any modern attitudes toward personality or self?

FOR DISCUSSION AND WRITING

1. Momaday and Chase both discuss the Indian taboo against speaking the name of a dead person, but their attitudes toward this superstition are different. Are their attitudes compatible?

2. Cassirer says that language "reveals to man that world that is closer to him than any world of natural objects and touches his weal and woe more directly than physical nature." Would E. E. Cummings agree?

3. Language, according to Cassirer, makes our "existence in a community possible." What are the implications of his statement? Does his statement seem valid? (You may wish to refer to passages from Bettelheim's essay or to cite specific experiences you have had.)

4. Which came first, the Word or *feelings*? In what ways do the two, the Word (language) and feelings (experience), relate to each other? Is either dependent upon the other?

5. Pick one of the following questions and write an essay in response to it: Do words actually have some power, or do spells and charms only work in fairy tales and myths? Can you think of contemporary instances of word magic? Are there certain words that have power for you? What, in fact, constitutes word magic? Must it cause physical reactions in us, or can words still have power if they only affect us emotionally?

2 BACKGROUNDS

> *We view the spectacle of the world more with our words than with our eyes. . . . In speaking, the human being by his words accomplishes a purpose that quite surpasses him.*
>
> M. DUFRENNE

This chapter conveys some further ideas about the qualities and uses of language. Following a systematic discussion of the basic functions of language, Lewis Carroll's "Humpty Dumpty" exemplifies how some people view their relationship with language and how the distinctions among the functions of language sometimes become muddled. Then our ability to find meaning in Carroll's "Jabberwocky" should reassure us that despite our frequent uneasiness and blundering we nevertheless have a highly developed sense of "correct" grammar. The chapter concludes with a descriptive history of one particular language—English.

Thomas Pyles and John Algeo

THE BASIC FUNCTIONS OF LANGUAGE

If asked to explain the purpose of language, we are apt to reply that it is used to communicate. This is true, of course, but only in the broadest sense. In this selection, the authors classify the general term communication *into seven basic functions to show us the variety of ways we actually use language every day. As you read, try to match each of the authors' specific illustrations with a similar one of your own.*

[1]   Any effort to simplify our complex use of language by reducing its infinite variety to a few basic functions must be somewhat arbitrary. Neat little lists are always to be distrusted. Yet they are convenient and do no great harm as long as everyone remembers that the limits they impose are artificial. For convenience, then, we will say that language has seven basic functions: informative, interrogative, expressive, evocative, performatory, directive, and phatic.[1]

[2]   The **informative** function of language is the one we often think of as its main purpose. It is language used to tell what the speaker believes, to give information about things, and to reason about facts. It is language concerned with what we know—that is, with cognition—and thus it is the use to which language is most often put in all branches of learning. An informative statement is one that purports to be about matters of fact by asserting that something is or is not the case. Consequently it must be the kind of statement that can be either true or false—for instance, **Water boils at 212 degrees Fahrenheit, Forty-eight percent of all Americans live in igloos,** and **Cleopatra was bitten by an asp.** Of course, informative language need not be true—the information can be wrong—but it must be the sort of statement about which you can ask, "Is that true?" It makes no sense to ask of a question like **Who is he?** or of a direction like **Pass the salt** or of an exclamation like **Damn!** whether it is true or not. Such sentences are neither true nor false, but just are. Indeed, the only sort of statement to which truth and falsity are relevant is the informative utterance.

[3]   If the purpose of informative language is to give information, the aim of **interrogative** language is to get it. Because it includes all questions that need

[1] Other discussions of the functions of language are to be found in Monroe Beardsley, *Aesthetics* (New York, 1958); Roman Jakobson, "Linguistics and Poetics," in *Style in Language,* ed. Thomas A. Seboek (Cambridge, Mass., 1960); Charles W. Morris, *Signs, Language, and Behavior* (New York, 1955); I. A. Richards, *Speculative Instruments* (Chicago, 1955); and Phillip E. Wheelwright, *The Burning Fountain* (Bloomington, Ind., 1968).

From *English: An Introduction to Language* by Thomas Pyles and John Algeo © 1970 by Harcourt Brace Jovanovich, Inc. Reprinted by permission of the publishers.

answers, such as **What time is class over? Who's that?** and **How do you find the square root of 3.14?** it is language used to find out what the hearer knows or believes. Both informative and interrogative language are about cognition; but the first focuses on what the speaker knows and the second on what the hearer knows. Thus they are complementary functions, the first of several such pairs.

[4]   However important giving information may be, there are other respectable uses of language, for example, its **expressive** function, which is the use of words to reveal something about the feelings and attitudes of the speaker. At its simplest, expressive language consists of ejaculations like **ouch, good heavens, damn,** and **wow.** Such forms tell how the speaker feels, but not what he is feeling that way about. Of course, expressive words are very often added to other kinds of language to make the same sentence serve two functions at once. The difference between **The car won't start** and **The stupid car won't start** is that the first sentence tells only about the car, whereas the second tells in addition how the speaker feels about the situation. Swearing is expressive, but so are words like **glorious, beautiful, excellent,** and **good.** We can, after all, express ourselves either favorably or unfavorably.

[5]   . . . words often combine literal sense and emotional values and thus may differ from one another not in what they name but in what feelings they suggest—a distinction that is all-important in expressive language. For example, the difference between **Here come the police** and **Here come the fuzz** is not in the things the sentences are about but in the judgments expressed about those things. While informative language makes statements about what is or is not true, expressive language passes judgment on whether it is good or bad. It evaluates, appraises, and asserts the speaker's feelings.

[6]   **Evocative** language, on the other hand, tries to create feelings in the hearer. Its aim is to amuse, startle, anger, soothe, worry, or please. It is an important part of jokes, of tragedies, of advertising, and of propaganda. It is the language of a mother comforting her child, of a demagogue haranguing the crowd, and of a young man wooing a girl. Obviously, expressive and evocative language often go hand in hand—if you express your feelings about a political candidate by calling him either a slack-jawed idiot or a stalwart patriot, you probably hope to evoke the same feelings in someone else—but the difference between the two kinds of language is clear. Sometimes it may suit a man's purposes for others to have feelings he does not share. So he may want his neighbors to feel that the gubernatorial candidate of his political party is a stalwart patriot, even though he is privately convinced the fellow is a slack-jawed idiot. Language that tries to evoke a feeling the speaker does not share is often propaganda. But the evocative function . . . is also dominant in literature.

[7]   Similar in purpose to evocative use is **directive** language. It gives orders. Evocative language tries to make the hearer feel something; directive language tries to make him do something. Since it is often easier to lead a horse to water if you can first get him to feel thirsty, these two functions may go together. Clearly the chief reason for wanting people to feel that some candidate is a patriot rather than an idiot

is that they will vote for him. Directive language, however, need not be mixed with feelings. The simplest directions are requests like **Pass the salt** or **Have a seat,** which are typically quite neutral in feeling. Though directions can be given in a variety of ways, the imperative sentence is the structure most characteristic of them. However, any verbal effort, such as statements with **ought** and **must,** to control what others do, falls into the category of directive language.

[8]   A semantically odd kind of language is that known as **performatory.** Whereas directive language aims at causing an action, the function of a performatory statement is simply to be the action that it states. This seeming paradox can be illustrated more easily than it can be explained. When the defendant at a trial says, "I plead not guilty," that very statement is the act of so pleading. The defendant is not talking about any past or future pleading or about any other action that he is doing at the same time. The statement itself is the performance of the action mentioned in it. It is this characteristic of self-reference that makes performatory utterances odd. Yet they are common enough, for example *I swear to tell the truth, I name this ship H.M.S. Pinafore, I promise to love, honor, and obey, I bet you ten dollars, I declare the meeting adjourned,* and many other formulas of the same sort.

[9]   Whereas the typical sentence pattern for directive utterances is the imperative, with an actual or implied subject *you,* the typical pattern for performatory statements has *I* as its subject. Like informative and expressive language, performatory focuses on the speaker, while interrogative, evocative, and directive all focus on the hearer. Thus the foregoing six uses of language form a balanced set, differing from one another in their focus and in their reference, whether to what is known, what is felt, or what is done:

	FOCUS ON	
REFERENCE TO	Speaker	Hearer
Cognition, knowing	Informative	Interrogative
Evaluation, feeling	Expressive	Evocative
Action, doing	Performatory	Directive

[10]   The last use of language we will be concerned with is one that is easy to overlook, yet it is exceedingly common. **Phatic** language includes the everyday small talk that we use to establish rapport, make contact with our fellows, and assure mutual good will. Greetings, farewells, much chitchat, and most ritual language

serve this function, for example ***hello, goodby, nice day, How are you,*** and ***We had a lovely time—thank you for asking us.*** When someone casually says "How are you?" you know he is not really asking about your state of health. One of the most deadly bores in the world is the man who responds to that question with a detailed account of his neuralgia or his coming appendectomy when the only appropriate answer is one like "Fine" or "Not bad, how about you?" Similarly, when we say on leaving a party that we have had a nice time, we are not in fact saying anything about the party, which may well have been insufferably dull. Our words mean simply that we are leaving. Much social language is insincere if taken literally, but to chide it for its insincerity is to miss the point. It is not literal language, and its function is not to give information. It rather serves to establish an atmosphere in which people can deal easily with one another. So utterly devoid of content is it, that some have wondered whether phatic expressions should be considered true language at all. They are more like verbal handshakes.

[11] The term ***phatic*** comes from a Greek word that means 'talking,' but though phatic language is "just talk," it need not be informal or inconsequential. When a group sings the national anthem or recites a church creed, rapport is established among its members in a sober and ceremonious way. Those who flout such solemn exercises have in the past been burnt at the stake and may still be investigated by a militant society of patriots. It is by such phatic language that we decide who is safe because he is "one of us," whether in the neighborhood or the nation, and when we have phatic rapport with one another we can truthfully say, "We speak the same language."

[12] Although there may be more, seven basic functions of language have been suggested above. These functions will, however, often overlap in a single utterance, as when a drowning man calls "Help!" He gives the information that he is in trouble, expresses a feeling of distress, evokes a feeling of urgency in anyone who hears him, and finally directs anyone in earshot to pull him out of the water. To be sure, the drowning man can hardly be said to formulate all or any of those purposes; if he did, he would likely sink to a watery grave before he could get the word ***help*** out of his mouth. But that all those functions are served by the one word seems obvious, the drowning man, having been rescued and given opportunity for calmer reflection, would probably agree. Because many sentences fill more than one function simultaneously, no simple pigeonholing is possible for them.

[13] Although some functions and sentence forms seem to go naturally together, such as the directive function and the imperative, the form of a sentence is often not a reliable guide to its use. For example, the following all look like questions: ***Will alcohol freeze? Will you pass the salt? Will winter never end? Won't you be nice to a poor old helpless woman? Would you help me if you were in my shoes?*** Yet, although all have the question form, they are not all used to get information. In fact, only the first sentence is likely to have a genuine interrogative function. It is

the only one that looks for an informative answer. The second is really a direction; anyone who pretends that it is a question and answers "Yes" instead of passing the salt has a boorish sense of humor. Similarly, the third is an expression of emotion, the fourth an effort to evoke pity, and the last a roundabout way of giving some information—namely, "I am not going to help you." Thus, in deciding what use a sentence is put to, we must look not only at its form but at the whole situation of the speaker and hearer. And we must be prepared to distinguish in a single utterance overlapping uses.

FOR REVIEW AND DISCUSSION

Content

1. Do the seven functions described by Pyles and Algeo cover all possible functions of language, or can you think of others? In what ways, if any, do some of the functions overlap?

2. What value is there in knowing that language functions in these ways?

Rhetoric

1. In what specific ways do the authors attempt to make their essay entertaining as well as informative? To what extent do they succeed?

2. Do the authors make a strong case for their definition of *phatic* language as that which means nothing but provides a social atmosphere? How do they support that definition? Do they do so convincingly?

3. The conclusion makes an important point about the seven functions that is only hinted at earlier. What is this point? Why does it belong in the conclusion rather than in some other part of the essay?

4. The authors' use of transitions at the beginning of paragraphs helps readers move from one idea to the next. Besides giving the essay coherence, what else do these deliberate transitions do? Do they make reading of the essay enjoyable, easy, boring?

Classroom Exercises

1. Why might different people be likely to use one function more than they would another? Describe someone's speech that is characterized by one of the seven functions. For instance, you might describe a person who is highly expressive (in the sense meant by Pyles and Algeo), always asserting feelings by calling people creeps or great guys, referring to terrific heads of lettuce on sale at a cheap price, or speaking of his being depressed by the bad news from home.

2. What argument can you make to assert that, in fact, "Here come the police" and "Here come the fuzz" differ in what they name, and not merely in their expressive function?

3. Categorize the following sentence and explain your reasoning: "I wish you would tell me who he is."

interrogative

Lewis Carroll

HUMPTY DUMPTY and JABBERWOCKY

In these selections from Through the Looking Glass, *we see several different attitudes about the nature and function of language. Alice and Humpty Dumpty have difficulty communicating because each understands language to work in a different way. In "Jabberwocky," we see that even nonsense can conform to grammatical rules. As you read these selections, try to decide which character's view of language comes closest to your own.*

HUMPTY DUMPTY

[1]   However, the egg only got larger and larger, and more and more human: when she had come within a few yards of it, she saw that it had eyes and a nose and mouth; and, when she had come close to it, she saw clearly that it was HUMPTY DUMPTY himself. "It ca'n't be anybody else!" she said to herself. "I'm as certain of it, as if his name were written all over his face!"

[2]   It might have been written a hundred times, easily, on that enormous face. Humpty Dumpty was sitting, with his legs crossed like a Turk, on the top of a high wall—such a narrow one that Alice quite wondered how he could keep his balance—and, as his eyes were steadily fixed in the opposite direction, and he didn't take the least notice of her, she thought he must be a stuffed figure, after all.

[3]   "And how exactly like an egg he is!" she said aloud, standing with her hands ready to catch him, for she was every moment expecting him to fall.

[4]   "It's *very* provoking," Humpty Dumpty said after a long silence, looking away from Alice as he spoke, "to be called an egg—*very!*"

[5]   "I said you *looked* like an egg, Sir," Alice gently explained. "And some eggs are very pretty, you know," she added, hoping to turn her remark into a sort of compliment.

[6]   "Some people," said Humpty Dumpty, looking away from her as usual, "have no more sense than a baby!"

[7]   Alice didn't know what to say to this: it wasn't at all like conversation, she thought, as he never said anything to *her:* in fact, his last remark was evidently addressed to a tree—so she stood and softly repeated to herself:—

From Lewis Carroll, *Through the Looking Glass.*

> "Humpty Dumpty sat on a wall:
> Humpty Dumpty had a great fall.
> All the King's horses and all the King's men
> Couldn't put Humpty Dumpty in his place again."

[8] "That last line is much too long for the poetry," she added, almost out loud, forgetting that Humpty Dumpty would hear her.

[9] "Don't stand chattering to yourself like that," Humpty Dumpty said, looking at her for the first time, "but tell me your name and your business."

[10] "My *name* is Alice, but—"

[11] "It's a stupid name enough!" Humpty Dumpty interrupted impatiently. "What does it mean?"

[12] "*Must* a name mean something?" Alice asked doubtfully.

[13] "Of course it must," Humpty Dumpty said with a short laugh: "*my* name means the shape I am—and a good handsome shape it is, too. With a name like yours, you might be any shape, almost."

[14] "Why do you sit out here all alone?" asked Alice, not wishing to begin an argument.

[15] "Why, because there's nobody with me!" cried Humpty Dumpty. "Did you think I didn't know the answer to *that?* Ask another."

[16] "Don't you think you'd be safer down on the ground?" Alice went on, not with any idea of making another riddle, but simply in her good-natured anxiety for the queer creature. "That wall is so *very* narrow!"

[17] "What tremendously easy riddles you ask!" Humpty Dumpty growled out. "Of course I don't think so! Why, if ever I *did* fall off—which there's no chance of—but *if* I did—" Here he pursed up his lips, and looked so solemn and grand that Alice could hardly help laughing. "*If* I *did* fall," he went on, "*the King has promised me*—ah, you may turn pale, if you like! You didn't think I was going to say that, did you? *The King has promised me—with his very own mouth*—to—to—"

[18] "To send all his horses and all his men," Alice interrupted, rather unwisely.

[19] "Now I declare that's too bad!" Humpty Dumpty cried, breaking into a sudden passion. "You've been listening at doors—and behind trees—and down chimneys—or you couldn't have known it!"

[20] "I haven't indeed!" Alice said very gently. "It's in a book."

[21] "Ah, well! They may write such things in a *book*," Humpty Dumpty said in a calmer tone. "That's what you call a History of England, that is. Now, take a good look at me! I'm one that has spoken to a King, *I* am: mayhap you'll never see such another: and, to show you I'm not proud, you may shake hands with me!" And he

grinned almost from ear to ear, as he leant forwards (and as nearly as possible fell off the wall in doing so) and offered Alice his hand. She watched him a little anxiously as she took it. "If he smiled much more the ends of his mouth might meet behind," she thought: "And then I don't know *what* would happen to his head! I'm afraid it would come off!"

[22] "Yes, all his horses and all his men," Humpty Dumpty went on. "They'd pick me up again in a minute, *they* would! However, this conversation is going on a little too fast: let's go back to the last remark but one."

[23] "I'm afraid I ca'n't quite remember it," Alice said, very politely.

[24] "In that case we start afresh," said Humpty Dumpty, "and it's my turn to choose a subject—" ("He talks about it just as if it was a game!" thought Alice.) "So here's a question for you. How old did you say you were?"

[25] Alice made a short calculation, and said, "Seven years and six months."

[26] "Wrong!" Humpty Dumpty exclaimed triumphantly. "You never said a word like it!"

[27] "I thought you meant 'How old *are* you?' " Alice explained.

[28] "If I'd meant that, I'd have said it," said Humpty Dumpty.

[29] Alice didn't want to begin another argument, so she said nothing.

[30] "Seven years and six months!" Humpty Dumpty repeated thoughtfully. "An uncomfortable sort of age. Now if you'd asked *my* advice, I'd have said 'Leave off at seven'—but it's too late now."

[31] "I never ask advice about growing," Alice said indignantly.

[32] "Too proud?" the other enquired.

[33] Alice felt even more indignant at this suggestion. "I mean," she said, "that one ca'n't help growing older."

[34] "*One* ca'n't, perhaps," said Humpty Dumpty; "but *two* can. With proper assistance, you might have left off at seven."

[35] "What a beautiful belt you've got on!" Alice suddenly remarked. (They had had quite enough of the subject of age, she thought: and, if they really were to take turns in choosing subjects, it was *her* turn now.) "At least," she corrected herself on second thoughts, "a beautiful cravat, I should have said—no, a belt, I mean—I beg your pardon!" she added in dismay, for Humpty Dumpty looked thoroughly offended, and she began to wish she hadn't chosen that subject. "If only I knew," she thought to herself, "which was neck and which was waist!"

[36] Evidently Humpty Dumpty was very angry, though he said nothing for a minute or two. When he *did* speak again, it was in a deep growl.

[37] "It is a—*most*—*provoking*—thing," he said at last, "when a person doesn't know a cravat from a belt!"

[38] "I know it's very ignorant of me," Alice said, in so humble a tone that Humpty Dumpty relented.

[39] "It's a cravat, child, and a beautiful one, as you say. It's a present from the White King and Queen. There now!"

[40] "Is it really?" said Alice, quite pleased to find that she *had* chosen a good subject after all.

[41] "They gave it me," Humpty Dumpty continued thoughtfully as he crossed one knee over the other and clasped his hands round it, "they gave it me—for an un-birthday present."

[42] "I beg your pardon?" Alice said with a puzzled air.

[43] "I'm not offended," said Humpty Dumpty.

[44] "I mean, what *is* an un-birthday present?"

[45] "A present given when it isn't your birthday, of course."

[46] Alice considered a little. "I like birthday presents best," she said at last.

[47] "You don't know what you're talking about!" cried Humpty Dumpty. "How many days are there in a year?"

[48] "Three hundred and sixty-five," said Alice.

[49] "And how many birthdays have you?"

[50] "One."

[51] "And if you take one from three hundred and sixty-five what remains?"

[52] "Three hundred and sixty-four, of course."

[53] Humpty Dumpty looked doubtful. "I'd rather see that done on paper," he said.

[54] Alice couldn't help smiling as she took out her memorandum-book, and worked the sum for him:

$$\begin{array}{r} 365 \\ \underline{1} \\ 364 \end{array}$$

[55] Humpty Dumpty took the book and looked at it carefully. "That seems to be done right—" he began.

[56] "You're holding it upside down!" Alice interrupted.

[57] "To be sure I was!" Humpty Dumpty said gaily as she turned it round for him. "I thought it looked a little queer. As I was saying, that *seems* to be done right—though I haven't time to look it over thoroughly just now—and that shows that there are three hundred and sixty-four days when you might get un-birthday presents—"

[58] "Certainly," said Alice.

[59] "And only *one* for birthday presents, you know. There's glory for you!"

[60] "I don't know what you mean by 'glory,' " Alice said.

[61] Humpty Dumpty smiled contemptuously. "Of course you don't—till I tell you. I meant 'there's a nice knock-down argument for you!' "

[62] "But 'glory' doesn't mean 'a nice knock-down argument,' " Alice objected.

[63] "When *I* use a word," Humpty Dumpty said, in rather a scornful tone, "it means just what I choose it to mean—neither more nor less."

[64] "The question is," said Alice, "whether you *can* make words mean so many different things."

[65] "The question is," said Humpty Dumpty, "which is to be master—that's all."

[66] Alice was too much puzzled to say anything; so after a minute Humpty Dumpty began again. "They've a temper, some of them—particularly verbs: they're the proudest—adjectives you can do anything with, but not verbs—however, *I* can manage the whole lot of them! Impenetrability! That's what *I* say!"

[67] "Would you tell me please," said Alice, "what that means?"

[68] "Now you talk like a reasonable child," said Humpty Dumpty, looking very much pleased. "I meant by 'impenetrability' that we've had enough of that subject, and it would be just as well if you'd mention what you mean to do next, as I suppose you don't mean to stop here all the rest of your life."

[69] "That's a great deal to make one word mean," Alice said in a thoughtful tone.

[70] "When I make a word do a lot of work like that," said Humpty Dumpty, "I always pay it extra."

[71] "Oh!" said Alice. She was too much puzzled to make any other remark.

[72] "Ah, you should see 'em come round me of a Saturday night," Humpty Dumpty went on, wagging his head gravely from side to side, "for to get their wages, you know."

[73] (Alice didn't venture to ask what he paid them with; and so you see I ca'n't tell *you*.)

[74] "You seem very clever at explaining words, Sir," said Alice. "Would you kindly tell me the meaning of the poem called 'Jabberwocky'?"

[75] "Let's hear it," said Humpty Dumpty. "I can explain all the poems that ever were invented—and a good many that haven't been invented just yet."

[76] This sounded very hopeful, so Alice repeated the first verse:—

> " 'Twas brillig, and the slithy toves
> Did gyre and gimble in the wabe:
> All mimsy were the borogoves,
> And the mome raths outgrabe."

[77] "That's enough to begin with," Humpty Dumpty interrupted: "there are plenty of hard words there. '*Brillig*' means four o'clock in the afternoon—the time when you begin *broiling* things for dinner."

[78] "That'll do very well," said Alice: "and '*slithy*'?"

[79] "Well, '*slithy*' means 'lithe and slimy.' 'Lithe' is the same as 'active.' You see it's like a portmanteau—there are two meanings packed up into one word."

[80] "I see it now," Alice remarked thoughtfully: "and what are '*toves*'?"

[81] "Well, '*toves*' are something like badgers—they're something like lizards—and they're something like corkscrews."

[82] "They must be very curious-looking creatures."

[83] "They are that," said Humpty Dumpty: "also they make their nests under sun-dials—also they live on cheese."

[84] "And what's to '*gyre*' and to '*gimble*'?"

[85] "To '*gyre*' is to go round and round like a gyroscope. To '*gimble*' is to make holes like a gimlet."

[86] "And '*the wabe*' is the grass-plot round a sundial, I suppose?" said Alice, surprised at her own ingenuity.

[87] "Of course it is. It's called '*wabe*' you know, because it goes a long way before it, and a long way behind it—"

[88] "And a long way beyond it on each side," Alice added.

[89] "Exactly so. Well then, '*mimsy*' is 'flimsy and miserable' (there's another portmanteau for you). And a '*borogove*' is a thin shabby-looking bird with its feathers sticking out all round—something like a live mop."

[90] "And then '*mome raths*'?" said Alice. "I'm afraid I'm giving you a great deal of trouble."

[91] "Well, a '*rath*' is a sort of green pig: but '*mome*' I'm not certain about. I think it's short for 'from home'—meaning that they'd lost their way, you know."

[92] "And what does '*outgrabe*' mean?"

[93] "Well, '*outgribing*' is something between bellowing and whistling, with a kind of sneeze in the middle: however, you'll hear it done, maybe—down in the wood yonder—and, when you've once heard it, you'll be *quite* content. Who's been repeating all that hard stuff to you?"

[94] "I read it in a book," said Alice. "But I *had* some poetry repeated to me much easier than that, by—Tweedledee, I think it was."

[95] "As to poetry, you know," said Humpty Dumpty, stretching out one of his great hands, "*I* can repeat poetry as well as other folk, if it comes to that—"

[96] "Oh, it needn't come to that!" Alice hastily said, hoping to keep him from beginning.

JABBERWOCKY

[1]   'Twas brillig, and the slithy toves
      Did gyre and gimble in the wabe:
   All mimsy were the borogoves,
      And the mome raths outgrabe.

[2]   "Beware the Jabberwock, my son!
      The jaws that bite, the claws that catch!
   Beware the Jubjub bird, and shun
      The frumious Bandersnatch!"

[3]   He took his vorpal sword in hand:
      Long time the manxome foe he sought—
   So rested he by the Tumtum tree,
      And stood awhile in thought.

[4]   And, as in uffish thought he stood,
      The Jabberwock, with eyes of flame,
   Came whiffling through the tulgey wood,
      And burbled as it came!

[5]   One, two! One, two! And through and through
      The vorpal blade went snicker-snack!
   He left it dead, and with its head
      He went galumphing back.

[6]   "And hast thou slain the Jabberwock?
          Come to my arms, my beamish boy!
      O frabjous day! Callooh! Callay!"
          He chortled in his joy.

[7]   'Twas brillig, and the slithy toves
          Did gyre and gimble in the wabe:
      All mimsy were the borogoves,
          And the mome raths outgrabe.

FOR REVIEW AND DISCUSSION

Content

1. In her first linguistic confrontation with Humpty Dumpty, Alice uses a *simile*. Explain what a simile is and why Alice's gets her into trouble.

2. What does Humpty Dumpty mean when he says that a name must mean something? Do you agree or disagree with him? Why?

3. At one point Alice says, "I beg your pardon," and Humpty Dumpty replies, "I'm not offended." What does Alice mean and why does the Egg reply as he does? Who is the more literal-minded of the two?

4. "The question is," said Humpty Dumpty, "which is to be master—that's all." But is that really all that's involved in the relation between words and word users?

5. Humpty Dumpty, of course, considers himself the master of words, able to make them mean whatever he chooses. What is appealing in his "mastery" of language?

6. Do words ever mean other than what the speaker intends? Explain.

Rhetoric

1. Carroll does not *say* which, language or the language user, should be master of the other. Does he *imply* which should be master, or is the issue left unresolved? What purpose is achieved by Carroll's treatment of the proper relationship (if there is one) between language and language users?

2. "Humpty Dumpty" is intended to amuse both children and adults. Assuming that Carroll's awareness of his audience affected how he wrote the story, identify specific characteristics of style (diction, sentence length, the manner in which material is presented, and so forth) that indicate Carroll's attempt to amuse his mixed audience.

Classroom Exercises

1. Where does the meaning of a word exist? (Does it exist with the word, or is meaning in the minds of people who use the words?) If you think that meaning exists with the word, how would you explain that two people who read the same words may find different meanings? And if meaning exists only in the minds of word users, how can you explain that so many people who read the same words will find the same meaning?

2. What is happening in "Jabberwocky"? Do you think that most people who read the poem will find the same meaning in it? How close is your reading of the poem to Humpty Dumpty's reading of it?

3. Explain how you can identify the parts of speech of the nonsense words in "Jabberwocky." How do you know, for example, that *gyre* is a verb?

Paul Roberts

SOMETHING ABOUT ENGLISH

To lend some authority to our discussions about language, we should learn something about the history of our own language, which provides both focus and perspective and allows us to see our own words as part of a continuum, not isolated sounds that somehow have existed only in our lifetime. People often feel that words they hear for the first time—obscenities, for instance—are newly minted, that people in previous ages didn't say such things. We need to remember that most words have long histories extending back to other centuries and even to other languages. When you've finished this selection, you may want to examine the Oxford English Dictionary *in your campus library. It details the origins and histories of most English words.*

[1] No understanding of the English language can be very satisfactory without a notion of the history of the language. But we shall have to make do with just a notion. The history of English is long and complicated, and we can only hit the high spots.

[2] The history of our language begins a little after A.D. 600. Everything before that is pre-history, which means that we can guess at it but can't prove much. For a thousand years or so before the birth of Christ our linguistic ancestors were savages wandering through the forests of northern Europe. Their language was a part of the Germanic branch of the Indo-European family.

[3] At the time of the Roman Empire—say, from the beginning of the Christian Era to around A.D. 400—the speakers of what was to become English were scattered along the northern coast of Europe. They spoke a dialect of Low German. More exactly, they spoke several different dialects, since they were several different tribes. The names given to the tribes who got to England are *Angles, Saxons,* and *Jutes.* For convenience, we can refer to them all as Anglo-Saxons.

From *Understanding English* by Paul Roberts. Copyright © 1958 by Paul Roberts. Reprinted by permission of Harper & Row, Publishers, Inc.

[4]   Their first contact with civilization was a rather thin acquaintance with the Roman Empire on whose borders they lived. Probably some of the Anglo-Saxons wandered into the Empire occasionally, and certainly Roman merchants and traders traveled among the tribes. At any rate, this period saw the first of our many borrowings from Latin. Such words as *kettle, wine, cheese, butter, cheap, plum, gem, bishop, church* were borrowed at this time. They show something of the relationship of the Anglo-Saxons with the Romans. The Anglo-Saxons were learning, getting their first taste of civilization.

[5]   They still had a long way to go, however, and their first step was to help smash the civilization they were learning from. In the fourth century the Roman power weakened badly. While the Goths were pounding away at the Romans in the Mediterranean countries, their relatives, the Anglo-Saxons, began to attack Britain.

[6]   The Romans had been the ruling power in Britain since A.D. 43. They had subjugated the Celts whom they found living there and had succeeded in setting up a Roman administration. The Roman influence did not extend to the outlying parts of the British Isles. In Scotland, Wales, and Ireland the Celts remained free and wild, and they made periodic forays against the Romans in England. Among other defense measures, the Romans built the famous Roman Wall to ward off the tribes in the north.

[7]   Even in England the Roman power was thin. Latin did not become the language of the country as it did in Gaul and Spain. The mass of people continued to speak Celtic, with Latin and the Roman civilization it contained in use as a top dressing.

[8]   In the fourth century, troubles multiplied for the Romans in Britain. Not only did the untamed tribes of Scotland and Wales grow more and more restive, but the Anglo-Saxons began to make pirate raids on the eastern coast. Furthermore, there was growing difficulty everywhere in the Empire, and the legions in Britain were siphoned off to fight elsewhere. Finally, in A.D. 410, the last Roman ruler in England, bent on becoming emperor, left the islands and took the last of the legions with him. The Celts were left in possession of Britain but almost defenseless against the impending Anglo-Saxon attack.

[9]   Not much is surely known about the arrival of the Anglo-Saxons in England. According to the best early source, the eighth-century historian Bede, the Jutes came in 449 in response to a plea from the Celtic king, Vortigern, who wanted their help against the Picts attacking from the north. The Jutes subdued the Picts but then quarreled and fought with Vortigern, and, with reinforcements from the Continent, settled permanently in Kent. Somewhat later the Angles established themselves in eastern England and the Saxons in the south and west. Bede's account is plausible enough, and these were probably the main lines of the invasion.

[10]   We do know, however, that the Angles, Saxons, and Jutes were a long time securing themselves in England. Fighting went on for as long as a hundred years

before the Celts in England were all killed, driven into Wales, or reduced to slavery. This is the period of King Arthur, who was not entirely mythological. He was a Romanized Celt, a general, though probably not a king. He had some success against the Anglo-Saxons, but it was only temporary. By 550 or so the Anglo-Saxons were firmly established. English was in England.

[11] All this is pre-history, so far as the language is concerned. We have no record of the English language until after 600, when the Anglo-Saxons were converted to Christianity and learned the Latin alphabet. The conversion began, to be precise, in the year 597 and was accomplished within thirty or forty years. The conversion was a great advance for the Anglo-Saxons, not only because of the spiritual benefits but because it reestablished contact with what remained of Roman civilization. This civilization didn't amount to much in the year 600, but it was certainly superior to anything in England up to that time.

[12] It is customary to divide the history of the English language into three periods: Old English, Middle English, and Modern English. Old English runs from the earliest records—i.e., seventh century—to about 1100; Middle English from 1100 to 1450 or 1500; Modern English from 1500 to the present day. Sometimes Modern English is further divided into Early Modern, 1500–1700, and Late Modern, 1700 to the present.

[13] When England came into history, it was divided into several more or less autonomous kingdoms, some of which at times exercised a certain amount of control over the others. In the century after the conversion the most advanced kingdom was Northumbria, the area between the Humber River and the Scottish border. By A.D. 700 the Northumbrians had developed a respectable civilization, the finest in Europe. It is sometimes called the Northumbrian Renaissance, and it was the first of the several renaissances through which Europe struggled upward out of the ruins of the Roman Empire. It was in this period that the best of the Old English literature was written, including the epic poem *Beowulf*.

[14] In the eighth century, Northumbrian power declined, and the center of influence moved southward to Mercia, the kingdom of the Midlands. A century later the center shifted again, and Wessex, the country of the West Saxons, became the leading power. The most famous king of the West Saxons was Alfred the Great, who reigned in the second half of the ninth century, dying in 901. He was famous not only as a military man and administrator but also as a champion of learning. He founded and supported schools and translated or caused to be translated many books from Latin into English. At this time also much of the Northumbrian literature of two centuries earlier was copied in West Saxon. Indeed, the great bulk of Old English writing which has come down to us is in the West Saxon dialect of 900 or later.

[15] In the military sphere, Alfred's great accomplishment was his successful opposition to the Viking invasions. In the ninth and tenth centuries, the Norsemen

emerged in their ships from their homelands in Denmark and the Scandinavian peninsula. They traveled far and attacked and plundered at will and almost with impunity. They ravaged Italy and Greece, settled in France, Russia, and Ireland, colonized Iceland and Greenland, and discovered America several centuries before Columbus. Nor did they overlook England.

[16] After many years of hit-and-run raids, the Norsemen landed an army on the east coast of England in the year 866. There was nothing much to oppose them except the Wessex power led by Alfred. The long struggle ended in 877 with a treaty by which a line was drawn roughly from the northwest of England to the southeast. On the eastern side of the line Norse rule was to prevail. This was called the Danelaw. The western side was to be governed by Wessex.

[17] The linguistic result of all this was a considerable injection of Norse into the English language. Norse was at this time not so different from English as Norwegian or Danish is now. Probably speakers of English could understand, more or less, the language of the newcomers who had moved into eastern England. At any rate, there was considerable interchange and word borrowing. Examples of Norse words in the English language are *sky, give, law, egg, outlaw, leg, ugly, scant, sly, crawl, scowl, take, thrust*. There are hundreds more. We have even borrowed some pronouns from Norse—*they, their*, and *them*. These words were borrowed first by the eastern and northern dialects and then in the course of hundreds of years made their way into English generally.

[18] It is supposed also—indeed, it must be true—that the Norsemen influenced the sound structure and the grammar of English. But this is hard to demonstrate in detail.

[19] We may now have an example of Old English. The favorite illustration is the Lord's Prayer, since it needs no translation. This has come to us in several different versions. Here is one:

> Fæder ure þuðe eart on heofonum si þin nama gehalgod. Tobecume þin rice. Gewurðe þin willa on eorðan swa swa on heofonum. Urne gedæghwamlican hlaf syle us to dæg. And forgyf us ure gyltas swa swa we forgyfaþ urum gyltendum. And ne gelæd þu us on costnunge ac alys us of yfele. Soðlice.

[20] Some of the differences between this and Modern English are merely differences in orthography. For instance, the sign *æ* is what Old English writers used for a vowel sound like that in modern *hat* or *and*. The *th* sounds or modern *thin* or *then* are represented in Old English by þ or ð. But of course there are many differences in sound too. *Ure* is the ancestor of modern *our*, but the first vowel was like that in *too* or *ooze*. *Hlaf* is modern *loaf*; we have dropped the *h* sound and changed the vowel, which in *hlaf* was pronounced something like the vowel in *father*. Old

English had some sounds which we do not have. The sound represented by *y* does not occur in Modern English. If you pronounce the vowel in *bit* with your lips rounded, you may approach it.

[21] In grammar, Old English was much more highly inflected than Modern English is. That is, there were more case endings for nouns, more person and number endings for verbs, a more complicated pronoun system, various endings for adjectives, and so on. Old English nouns had four cases—nominative, genitive, dative, accusative. Adjectives had five—all these and an instrumental case besides. Present-day English has only two cases for nouns—common case and possessive case. Adjectives now have no case system at all. On the other hand, we now use a more rigid word order and more structure words (prepositions, auxiliaries, and the like) to express relationships than Old English did.

[22] Some of this grammar we can see in the Lord's Prayer. *Heofonum*, for instance, is a dative plural; the nominative singular was *heofon*. *Urne* is an accusative singular; the nominative is *ure*. In *urum gyltendum* both words are dative plural. *Forgyfaþ* is the third person plural form of the verb. Word order is different: "urne gedæghwamlican hlaf syle us" in place of "Give us our daily bread." And so on.

[23] In vocabulary Old English is quite different from Modern English. Most of the Old English words are what we may call native English: that is, words which have not been borrowed from other languages but which have been a part of English ever since English was a part of Indo-European. Old English did certainly contain borrowed words. We have seen that many borrowings were coming in from Norse. Rather large numbers had been borrowed from Latin, too. Some of these were taken while the Anglo-Saxons were still on the Continent (*cheese, butter, bishop, kettle*, etc.); a large number came into English after Conversion (*angel, candle, priest, martyr, radish, oyster, purple, school, spend*, etc.). But the great majority of Old English words were native English.

[24] Now, on the contrary, the majority of words in English are borrowed, taken mostly from Latin and French. Of the words in *The American College Dictionary* only about 14 percent are native. Most of these, to be sure, are common, high-frequency words—*the, of, I, and, because, man, mother, road*, etc.; of the thousand most common words in English, some 62 percent are native English. Even so, the modern vocabulary is very much Latinized and Frenchified. The Old English vocabulary was not.

[25] Sometime between the year 1000 and 1200 various important changes took place in the structure of English, and Old English became Middle English. The political event which facilitated these changes was the Norman Conquest. The Normans, as the name shows, came originally from Scandinavia. In the early tenth century they established themselves in northern France, adopted the French language, and developed a vigorous kingdom and a very passable civilization. In the year 1066, led by Duke William, they crossed the Channel and made themselves

masters of England. For the next several hundred years, England was ruled by kings whose first language was French.

[26] One might wonder why, after the Norman Conquest, French did not become the national language, replacing English entirely. The reason is that the Conquest was not a national migration, as the earlier Anglo-Saxon invasion had been. Great numbers of Normans came to England, but they came as rulers and landlords. French became the language of the court, the language of the nobility, the language of polite society, the language of literature. But it did not replace English as the language of the people. There must always have been hundreds of towns and villages in which French was never heard except when visitors of high station passed through.

[27] But English, though it survived as the national language, was profoundly changed after the Norman Conquest. Some of the changes—in sound structure and grammar—would no doubt have taken place whether there had been a Conquest or not. Even before 1066 the case system of English nouns and adjectives was becoming simplified; people came to rely more on word order and prepositions than on inflectional endings to communicate their meanings. The process was speeded up by sound changes which caused many of the endings to sound alike. But no doubt the Conquest facilitated the change. German, which didn't experience a Norman Conquest, is today rather highly inflected compared to its cousin English.

[28] But it is in vocabulary that the effects of the Conquest are most obvious. French ceased, after a hundred years or so, to be the native language of very many people in England, but it continued—and continues still—to be a zealously cultivated second language, the mirror of elegance and civilization. When one spoke English, one introduced not only French ideas and French things but also their French names. This was not only easy but socially useful. To pepper one's conversation with French expressions was to show that one was well-bred, elegant, *au courant*. The last sentence shows that the process is not yet dead. By using *au courant* instead of, say, *abreast of things*, the writer indicates that he is no dull clod who knows only English but an elegant person aware of how things are done in *le haut monde*.

[29] Thus French words came into English, all sorts of them. There were words to do with government: *parliament, majesty, treaty, alliance, tax, government*; church words: *parson, sermon, baptism, incense, crucifix, religion*; words for foods: *veal, beef, mutton, bacon, jelly, peach, lemon, cream, biscuit*; colors: *blue, scarlet, vermilion*; household words: *curtain, chair, lamp, towel, blanket, parlor*; play words: *dance, chess, music, leisure, conversation*; literary words: *story, romance, poet, literary*; learned words: *study, logic, grammar, noun, surgeon, anatomy, stomach*; just ordinary words of all sorts: *nice, second, very, age, bucket, gentle, final, fault, flower, cry, count, sure, move, surprise, plain*.

SOMETHING ABOUT ENGLISH

[30] All these and thousands more poured into the English vocabulary between 1100 and 1500, until at the end of that time many people must have had more French words than English at their command. This is not to say that English became French. English remained English in sound structure and in grammar, though these also felt the ripples of French influence. The very heart of the vocabulary, too, remained English. Most of the high-frequency words—the pronouns, the prepositions, the conjunctions, the auxiliaries, as well as a great many ordinary nouns and verbs and adjectives—were not replaced by borrowings.

[31] Middle English, then, was still a Germanic language, but it differed from Old English in many ways. The sound system and the grammar changed a good deal. Speakers made less use of case systems and other inflectional devices and relied more on word order and structure words to express their meanings. This is often said to be a simplification, but it isn't really. Languages don't become simpler; they merely exchange one kind of complexity for another. Modern English is not a simple language, as any foreign speaker who tries to learn it will hasten to tell you.

[32] For us Middle English is simpler than Old English just because it is closer to Modern English. It takes three or four months at least to learn to read Old English prose and more than that for poetry. But a week of good study should put one in touch with the Middle English poet Chaucer. Indeed, you may be able to make some sense of Chaucer straight off, though you would need instruction in pronunciation to make it sound like poetry. Here is a famous passage from the *General Prologue to the Canterbury Tales*, fourteenth century:

> Ther was also a nonne, a Prioresse,
> That of hir smyling was ful symple and coy,
> Hir gretteste oath was but by Seinte Loy,
> And she was cleped Madame Eglentyne.
> Ful wel she song the service dyvyne,
> Entuned in hir nose ful semely.
> And Frenshe she spak ful faire and fetisly,
> After the scole of Stratford-atte-Bowe,
> For Frenshe of Parys was to hir unknowe.

[33] Sometime between 1400 and 1600 English underwent a couple of sound changes which made the language of Shakespeare quite different from that of Chaucer. Incidentally, these changes contributed much to the chaos in which English spelling now finds itself.

[34] One change was the elimination of a vowel sound in certain unstressed positions at the end of words. For instance, the words *name, stone, wine, dance* were pronounced as two syllables by Chaucer but as just one by Shakespeare. The *e* in these words became, as we say, "silent." But it wasn't silent for Chaucer; it represented a vowel sound. So also the words *laughed, seemed, stored* would have been pronounced by Chaucer as two-syllable words. The change was an important one because it affected thousands of words and gave a different aspect to the whole language.

[35] The other change is what is called the Great Vowel Shift. This was a systematic shifting of half a dozen vowels and diphthongs in stressed syllables. For instance, the word *name* had in Middle English a vowel something like that in the modern word *father*; *wine* had the vowel of modern *mean*; *he* was pronounced something like modern *hey*; *mouse* sounded like *moose*; *moon* had the vowel of *moan*. Again the shift was thoroughgoing and affected all the words in which these vowel sounds occurred. Since we still keep the Middle English system of spelling these words, the differences between Modern English and Middle English are often more real than apparent.

[36] The vowel shift has meant also that we have come to use an entirely different set of symbols for representing vowel sounds than is used by writers of such languages as French, Italian, or Spanish, in which no such vowel shift occurred. If you come across a strange word—say, *bine*—in an English book, you will pronounce it according to the English system, with the vowel of *wine* or *dine*. But if you read *bine* in a French, Italian, or Spanish book, you will pronounce it with the vowel of *mean* or *seen*.

[37] These two changes, then, produced the basic differences between Middle English and Modern English. But there were several other developments that had an effect upon the language. One was the invention of printing, an invention introduced into England by William Caxton in the year 1475. Where before books had been rare and costly, they suddenly became cheap and common. More and more people learned to read and write. This was the first of many advances in communication which have worked to unify languages and to arrest the development of dialect differences, though of course printing affects writing principally rather than speech. Among other things it hastened the standardization of spelling.

[38] The period of Early Modern English—that is, the sixteenth and seventeenth centuries—was also the period of the English Renaissance, when people developed, on the one hand, a keen interest in the past and, on the other, a more daring and imaginative view of the future. New ideas multiplied, and new ideas meant new language. Englishmen had grown accustomed to borrowing words from French as a result of the Norman Conquest; now they borrowed from Latin and Greek. As we have seen, English had been raiding Latin from Old English times and before, but now the floodgates really opened, and thousands of words from the classical languages poured in. *Pedestrian, bonus, anatomy, contradict, climax, dictionary, benefit, multiply, exist, paragraph, initiate, scene, inspire* are random examples. Probably the average educated American today has more words from French in his vocabulary than from native English sources, and more from Latin than from French.

[39] The greatest writer of the Early Modern English period is of course Shakespeare, and the best-known book is the King James Version of the Bible, published in 1611. The Bible (if not Shakespeare) has made many features of Early Modern

English perfectly familiar to many people down to present times, even though we do not use these features in present-day speech and writing. For instance, the old pronouns *thou* and *thee* have dropped out of use now, together with their verb forms, but they are still familiar to us in prayer and in Biblical quotation: "Whither thou goest, I will go." Such forms as *hath* and *doth* have been replaced by *has* and *does*; "Goes he hence tonight?" would now be "Is he going away tonight?"; Shakespeare's "Fie on't, sirrah" would be "Nuts to that, Mac." Still, all these expressions linger with us because of the power of the works in which they occur.

[40] It is not always realized, however, that considerable sound changes have taken place between Early Modern English and the English of the present day. Shakespearian actors putting on a play speak the words, properly enough, in their modern pronunciation. But it is very doubtful that this pronunciation would be understood at all by Shakespeare. In Shakespeare's time, the word *reason* was pronounced like modern *raisin*; *face* had the sound of modern *glass*; the *l* in *would, should, palm* was pronounced. In these points and a great many others the English language has moved a long way from what it was in 1600.

[41] The history of English since 1700 is filled with many movements and countermovements, of which we can notice only a couple. One of these is the vigorous attempt made in the eighteenth century, and the rather half-hearted attempts made since, to regulate and control the English language. Many people of the eighteenth century, not understanding very well the forces which govern language, proposed to polish and prune and restrict English, which they felt was proliferating too wildly. There was much talk of an academy which would rule on what people could and could not say and write. The academy never came into being, but the eighteenth century did succeed in establishing certain attitudes which, though they haven't had much effect on the development of the language itself, have certainly changed the native speaker's feeling about the language.

[42] In part a product of the wish to fix and establish the language was the development of the dictionary. The first English dictionary was published in 1603; it was a list of 2500 words briefly defined. Many others were published with gradual improvements until Samuel Johnson published his *English Dictionary* in 1755. This, steadily revised, dominated the field in England for nearly a hundred years. Meanwhile in America, Noah Webster published his dictionary in 1828, and before long dictionary publishing was a big business in this country. The last century has seen the publication of one great dictionary: the twelve-volume *Oxford English Dictionary*, compiled in the course of seventy-five years through the labors of many scholars. We have also, of course, numerous commercial dictionaries which are as good as the public wants them to be if not, indeed, rather better.

[43] Another product of the eighteenth century was the invention of "English grammar." As English came to replace Latin as the language of scholarship it was felt that one should also be able to control and dissect it, parse and analyze it, as one

could Latin. What happened in practice was that the grammatical description that applied to Latin was removed and superimposed on English. This was silly, because English is an entirely different kind of language, with its own forms and signals and ways of producing meaning. Nevertheless, English grammars on the Latin model were worked out and taught in the schools. In many schools they are still being taught. This activity is not often popular with school children, but it is sometimes an interesting and instructive exercise in logic. The principal harm in it is that it has tended to keep people from being interested in English and has obscured the real features of English structure.

[44] But probably the most important force in the development of English in the modern period has been the tremendous expansion of English-speaking peoples. In 1500 English was a minor language, spoken by a few people on a small island. Now it is perhaps the greatest language of the world, spoken natively by over a quarter of a billion people and as a second language by many millions more. When we speak of English now, we must specify whether we mean American English, British English, Australian English, Indian English, or what, since the differences are considerable. The American cannot go to England or the Englishman to America confident that he will always understand and be understood. The Alabaman in Iowa or the Iowan in Alabama shows himself a foreigner every time he speaks. It is only because communication has become fast and easy that English in this period of its expansion has not broken into a dozen mutually unintelligible languages.

FOR REVIEW AND DISCUSSION

Content

1. "No understanding of the English language can be very satisfactory without a notion of the history of the language." Now that you have read Roberts's essay, do you agree with him? What does he mean by "very satisfactory"?

2. How do words become *borrowed*? When does a borrowed word become part of the language that borrowed it?

3. Most grammars arise naturally in a language. Why does Roberts refer to "the invention of English grammar" in the eighteenth century? Does the fact that a grammar was "invented" make English easier or harder to learn than other languages?

4. Do you think that we would have been better off if the eighteenth century had not begun to organize and standardize English by inventing a grammar, fixing spellings of words, and so forth? Explain your answer by describing how we might now be using language had these events not occurred.

Rhetoric

1. This essay describes a *process*, one in which a language developed. What method does the author use to organize his material (according to relative importance, according to linguistic or grammatical characteristics)? Why is the method he chooses effective or ineffective? Would another work just as well?

2. Skim the essay and identify the key transitional words that indicate major shifts in subject. Do these transitions help you to recognize the method that the author has used to organize his material?

3. Roberts mentions that many words were borrowed from Latin during the "Conversion," but he does not say what the Conversion is. What does he mean by the term? What reason might he have had for not defining it?

4. Is Roberts's intended audience linguists, or is it a general readership who will know little about the history of the English language? What clues are there? Cite specific sections to support your answer.

Classroom Exercises

1. What specific relations can you find between new words (borrowed or otherwise introduced) and conditions existing at the time the new words are introduced? What are some words that have recently become part of English? What are their backgrounds?

2. In the eighteenth century there was proposed an "academy which would rule on what people could and could not say and write." What would likely have been some of the effects of such an academy? Do you know of some similar institution in contemporary times? What roles, for example, do dictionaries and English teachers perform in this regard?

3. Using the *Oxford English Dictionary* and a current desk dictionary (which should include up-to-date meanings), study the origins and changing meanings of one pair of the following words:
bedlam—lunatic
bold—saucy
boycott—maverick
charity—welfare
dearth—starve
pagan—peasant
Try to reason out the causes of their shifts in meaning over the years.

Gary Jennings

THE VIEW FROM THE BABEL TOWER

> *The problem with any attempt to examine the general history of language is that much of it, as Gary Jennings points out, can only be guessed at, since language existed long before there were written historical records. One of the most important things we can learn from such a discussion is a sense of just how varied languages are and how complicated their histories have been. As Jennings discusses the various theories of the origin of language, try to decide which one(s) you think are most convincing.*

> Let clerks indite in Latin, and let Frenchmen in their
> French also indite their quaint terms, for it is kindly to
> their mouths; and let us show our fantasies in such
> wordes as we learned of our mother's tongue.
> THOMAS USK

[1]   When Christopher Columbus set sail into the sunset on his first voyage in 1492, one of his ships carried an under-officer specially assigned to the expedition because he spoke fluent Hebrew. Columbus expected to fetch up in Cipangu, Cathay or Ind, and there was no interpreter available to him who knew Japanese, Chinese or any of the Indian tongues. But it was a common belief in Europe at the time that Hebrew, the language of the Scriptures, was the original tongue of all mankind, so Columbus was confident that even among the Far Easterners he would be able to communicate with their scholars.

[2]   He must have been dismayed, when he finally landed in what appeared to be a backwater boondocks of the Indies, to find that the natives were as ignorant of Hebrew as they were of the Scriptures, of biblical history and of everything else in Old World experience. At any rate, there is no record of classical interpreters having been supplied for the subsequent voyages to these new Indies.

[3]   But the belief persisted until the middle of the nineteenth century that some single original language had been God's gift to man at the time of Creation, and that in happier days "the whole earth was of one language, and of one speech." The theologians took it on faith and the philologists, such as they were, tried piously to

From *Personalities of Language* by Gary Jennings. Copyright © 1965 by Gary Jennings. Reprinted by permission of T. Y. Crowell.

confirm it by tortuous rationalizing. In the 1680s Cotton Mather wrote his M.A. thesis at Harvard in a detailed defense of this supposed linguistic revelation. In 1808 the philosopher Friedrich von Schlegel persuaded himself that the ancestor of all modern tongues was the Sanskrit of ancient India. In the 1830s lexicographer Noah Webster gave it as his opinion that the prototype language must have been "Chaldee," that is, Aramaic, the language of the Holy Land in Christ's day. At various times Hungarian, German, Danish, Basque, Dutch, Swedish—all of these and many others—have been proved, at least to their speakers' satisfaction, to have been the language of Eden.

[4]   The sorry diversity of human languages in the latter-day world was neatly explained by the eleventh chapter of Genesis, and that explanation still suffices for the religious fundamentalists. When the overweening descendants of Shem, Ham and Japheth dared to begin building a tower that should rival the heights of heaven, the Lord chastised them with a thunderclap confusion of tongues. Unable even to call for the waterboy, the tower builders had to abandon their project. Each man of them wandered off, burdened with his individual and lonely language, to some far country where he could beget a whole new people of his own and have somebody to talk to.

[5]   The Bible called the city of the ill-fated ziggurat Babel (probably from the Hebrew *bilbel*, "confusion"). Hence the fundamentalists could demonstrate through a plausible folk-etymology that the Babel story was confirmed by echoes in many modern languages—the English word "babble," the Italian *balbettio*, the Spanish *balbuceo*, the French *babil*, etc.

[6]   But as the nineteenth century moved into its second half, a new generation of linguists, perhaps no less devout than their predecessors but more disposed to scientific discipline, began to question the concept of a divine Ur-language. At the same time, along came Charles Darwin to dispute the whole concept of Creation. Some scholars were so excited by his theory of evolution that they strained as hard to apply it to the origins of language as they had previously strained to validate Babel. Friedrich Max Müller earnestly suggested that the grunts and squeals of man's animal ancestors all over the earth had gradually evolved toward speech in the same way their brains had evolved toward intelligence, and that thus the world's languages would already have been infinitely various even before the genus *Homo* had attained full sapience.

[7]   That exegesis was a little too pat, and was never seriously credited. But Darwin's new timetable did at least give the scholars about a million years of human evolution to maneuver in, as against the paltry few thousand the Bible had allowed them. (According to the sober calculations of Archbishop James Ussher in the seventeenth century, Creation had taken place on an October morning in the year 4004 B.C. And Gustav Seyffarth, in the 1820s, asserted that "the alphabet of the races of the world" had been invented the day the Deluge ended: September 7, 3446 B.C.)

[8]   After Darwin, a host of anthropologists, archaeologists and paleontologists began to turn up evidence that a fair measure of human civilization had been achieved as long ago as 6000 B.C., and that man-creatures must have been living in passably peaceable intercourse—implying some degree of effective mutual communication—a good three quarters of a million years before that.

[9]   And yet to this day we are no nearer knowing how language began than are the fundamentalist endorsers of an archetype tongue divine. For all the proof we have to the contrary, we might as well join them in believing that human speech was a direct and recent gift from the Almighty. Linguists now are fairly sure they know the provenances of the major tongues of today, but the primary sources of those languages are shrouded by time past. Too, there are some current languages which refuse to fit comfortably into the linguists' scheme of things, and there must have been untold numbers of other such tongues which flourished and then fell silent over the ages.

[10]   There are probably as many different theories about the origin of languages as there are professional linguists, but four of these should suffice to show their general tenor. The linguists, though not normally inclined to persiflage, have described these four hypotheses by rather chucklesome names: the Bow-Wow theory, the Pooh-Pooh theory, the Ding-Dong theory and the Yo-He-Ho theory.

[11]   The Bow-Wow theory supposes that man learned to talk by parroting the cries of animals. Considering that man was first a hunter, the notion has a certain plausibility. Once a group of men had agreed, say, that a boar was an "oink" and an aurochs was a "moo," they would eventually have aspired to naming other things.

[12]   The Pooh-Poohists believe that man's first meaningful noises were involuntarily jolted out of him by sudden events or situations, somewhat in the manner of a duchess finding a worm in her salad. It's a little hard to believe that a caveman ever uttered anything quite as finical as "pooh-pooh" but, considering his thorny environment, it's not unlikely that he began to talk by saying a frequent "ow!"

[13]   The Ding-Dong theory is based on onomatopoeia, like the Bow-Wow, only predicating that man's first words were echoes of natural sounds other than those of animals. For instance, he may have cried "whack!" in merry mimicry of his club bouncing off a rival's skull, or muttered a fearful "bumble-boom" in imitation of the thunder.

[14]   The Yo-He-Ho theory maintains that the earliest effective speech was the result of man's beginning to cooperate and coordinate with his fellows. That is, a group of men may have learned to lighten their labors by shouting some sort of cadence count, like sailors' chanteys or soldiers' marching songs, when they were hauling home a sabertooth's carcass or levering boulders down onto an invading war party.

[15] It seems indisputable that sign language by gestures must have long preceded and then accompanied the development of any meaningful grunts and mumbles. We still find gestures handy for beckoning, shooing, threatening, and even as an aid to exposition (ask anybody, "What is a spiral staircase?" and watch). Sir Richard Paget dwelt on this to suggest, in 1930, an offbeat theory of his own as to the beginnings of speech. It was his hypothesis that the first talking man's tongue movements merely imitated his hand gestures, and that his simultaneous expiration of a breath resulted in the articulation of a specific noise to reinforce each gesture.

[16] For example, to indicate "up" a man would point a finger skyward. At the same time he would unconsciously raise the tip of his tongue to touch the roof of his mouth. If at this moment he grunted, the resulting sound would be approximately "ull" or "oll"—or, as it would be written in Latin, *al*.

[17] Sir Richard pointed out that this word element is still widespread in words signifying "up." Latin has *altus* for "high," whence the English "altitude." The Semitic *al* means "to ascend," whence the Israeli airline El Al. The Melanesian *al* means "to climb." The Kwakiutl Indian *allela* means "up." Other grunts with the tongue variously tilted against the palate give the variant sounds of *at*, *an*, *ar* and *atl*. Sir Richard thought it significant that many of the world's upthrusting mountains contain these uptongued noises in their names: the Alps, Atlas, Andes, Himalaya, Allegheny, Ararat, etc.

[18] It's easy enough to find holes in Paget's theory. For one thing, not all speech sounds involve the manipulation of the tongue, and the rest of our vocal machinery is not adapted for imitating gestures. But, because we can never know the real story of language's beginning, his theory is no more flimsy than the four previously mentioned. There have been stranger ones; Edgar Sturtevant once suggested that man developed language when he first found it profitable to deceive.

[19] The reason for the impossibility of ever tracing back to the beginnings of speech is that there is no "primitive" language surviving on earth for the scholars to study. Early explorers thought they had found something of the sort among the American Indians, the Australian aborigines and such backward peoples. But, crude though their languages sounded to the white man's ear, they proved on investigation to be of a development and complexity easily equal to any "civilized" language. And so the oldest and most basic languages available for scholarly inspection are those whose fragments of writing have been exhumed by archaeologists. But plainly, any ancient language that had attained to writing had already progressed eons beyond the primordial kindergarten.

[20] Most linguistic scholars have ceased to fret over the insoluble. They have contented themselves with visualizing modern-day languages as twigs, so to speak, and with inching backward along them to find the common branches from which the twigs sprouted, thence farther backward to the common limbs from which the

branches grew. Thus they have been able to group the world's languages into a system of fairly well-defined families. But if there ever was an archetypal, ancestral language which begat them all — a single trunk to this family tree—it is beyond discovery.

[21] Before we look into the personalities which the various languages developed as they grew, let us briefly see how they *became* separate and disparate.

[22] Our English language is a twig of the so-called Teutonic branch of a limb designated Indo-European. The heftiest and most prolific limb of the language tree, Indo-European has sprouted languages which would seem to be as dissimilar as they are far apart—from Irish in the West to the Bengali of India in the East. The belief is that all the Indo-European languages stem from a single prehistoric tongue, and that its speakers must have lived originally in the area which now comprises Austria, Czechoslovakia and Hungary.

[23] How these people came to be there, whether they had evolved there autochthonously from time beyond reckoning, can only be conjectured. But it is possible that they were a Stone Age mixture of even earlier types from both northern and Mediterranean lands, in which case their "original" language must have been an amalgam of still others. To call these people "Indo-Europeans," as most linguists do, is an obvious *ex post facto* misnomer based on the eventual geographic dispersal of their language. But if they had a name for themselves no one knows it, so we will continue to use the term for convenience's sake.

[24] The Indo-Europeans, then, were nomadic. Over the ages various groups of them went a-roving far, far from home, never to return. As they scattered to all the points of the compass, each group's language began to grow apart from the parent stock and from each of the others'. For example, the Indo-Europeans who first trekked westward gradually developed a proto-Celtic variety of their language during the long march. At one time this must have been the language of almost all western Europe, but it survives today only in its later, splinter languages of Scots Gaelic, Irish, Welsh, Breton on the farthest western coast of France, and the almost extinct Manx.

[25] Following the Celtic groups, a subsequent westward migration spread a Teutonic form of Indo-European all across the northern part of the Continent. This gradually resolved itself into a number of intermediate tongues: Gothic, Old Norse, Englisc, Old Saxon, Franconian—and thence eventually into High and Low German, Dutch, Flemish, the Scandinavian tongues and the various early forms of what finally became English.

[26] Another wave of Indo-Europeans headed straight north to become Lithuanians and Letts. Others moved east and southeast, developing the Slavic body of languages which today includes Polish, Czech, Bulgarian, Serbo-Croatian, the several Russian dialects, etc.

THE VIEW FROM THE BABEL TOWER 67

[27] Some of the Stone Age wanderers plodded southeastward all the way across Asia Minor. During this time, they developed a tongue which in a later form became Sanskrit, the oldest Indo-European language with which we are familiar. Various groups dropped out of the line of march here and there, to settle in and bequeath new languages to Armenia, Persia, Afghanistan and Baluchistan. But the most persistently footloose pushed on clear to the Indian subcontinent, where they fanned out into a multitude of settlements and dialects which became the numerous Indic tongues of today.

[28] Still other Indo-Europeans moved southward across the Balkans, developing along the way a proto-Hellenic tongue which was eventually to become classical, then modern, Greek. Another group loitered in Albania, to plant the Thraco-Illyrian still in use there.

[29] Other parties crossed the Alps, developing the Italic languages which eventuated in Latin. Much later, via Roman imperialism, Latin displaced the Celtic tongues of southern Europe to give us the whole body of Romance languages: French, Spanish, Italian, Portuguese, Catalan and Romanian.

[30] My mapping of the spread of the Indo-European tongues is admittedly oversimplified and presumptive; neither mass migrations nor changes in language ever proceed so smoothly. We don't know how long these processes did take, except that they must have occupied glacial ages. We don't know in precisely what order the various migrations took place, or how they might have been affected by rebuffs, checks, retreats and roundabout detours. We don't know how many elementary and intermediate changes the languages may have gone through. We can only trace backward from the numerous language twigs that still are green and from a few dead ones we can recognize as having withered from the same familial branches.

[31] For a small illustration of family resemblance, take the English word "three." In almost every Indo-European language the word for "three" begins with a dental consonant (*t, d* or *th*) followed by an *r*. Among the other languages of the Teutonic branch, for example, it is *thrjá* in Icelandic, *tre* in all the continental Scandinavian tongues, *drei* in German, *drie* in Dutch and Flemish. Among the Romance languages, it is *trois* in French, *tres* in Spanish and Portuguese, *tre* in Italian and *trei* in Romanian. Among the Slavic languages, it is *tri* in Russian, *tri* in Czech, and *trzy* in Polish. It is *tri* in the Celtic languages: Irish, Scots, Gaelic, Welsh and Breton; and *tris* in the Baltic languages: Lettish and Lithuanian. It is *tre* in Albanian. It was *tri* in Sanskrit, *treis* in classical Greek, *tres* in Latin and *thri* in Anglo-Saxon.

[32] The prehistoric Indo-European tide submerged what must have been innumerable earlier languages in both Europe and Asia—as in Italy, where we know that it washed away the Etruscan and Messapian. Only one European tongue dating from before the migrations managed to endure to modern times: the Basque of the French-Spanish Pyrenees. But the Indo-European tongues themselves did not everywhere survive. The Macedonian of northern Greece was extinct before history

began. The Tocharian evolved by the Indo-Europeans who penetrated farthest eastward, into the Gobi desert of remotest Turkestan, is known only from scraps of written records.

[33] And even though the Indo-European tongues are spoken today by half of the world's people, there are stubborn islands of unrelated languages flourishing right in the middle of Europe. Basque, for instance, is an entity all to itself, unallied to any other language on earth. Turkish is the European representative of a language group which includes Tataric, Kirghizic and numerous other tongues in use across wide belts of central and northern Asia. What really seems odd is that Hungary, part of the long-ago homeland of the aboriginal Indo-European, should now speak the alien Magyar, a member of a totally unrelated language family (the Finno-Ugric branch of the Ural-Altaic limb) which also includes the Finnish and Lappish of the far north.

[34] Most other languages of the world can similarly be lumped into families whose members all have a common origin. For example, while the two major tongues of India, Hindi and Bengali, are chips off the Indo-European block, the nation also has to cope with some two hundred others, most of them of the Dravidian group: Tamil, Telugu, Canarese, etc. (A ten-rupee note has to proclaim itself in nine different languages.)

[35] The Semitic group once supplied the world with its widest-used languages of commerce and diplomacy: Babylonian-Assyrian, Phœnician, Aramaic. Today its chief representatives are the Arabic of the Near East and Mediterranean Africa, the Amharic of Ethiopia, Maltese and Hebrew, the latter a "dead" language for twenty centuries but successfully resuscitated since 1948 as the national tongue of Israel.

[36] A near limb to the Semitic group is the Hamitic, whose greenest and most fruitful twig was the Egyptian of the pharaohs. A direct descendant, Coptic, is the liturgical language of African Christians, while such relations as Berber, Tamashek and Somali are still spoken by various tribes in the region of the Sahara.

[37] The peoples of the rest of Africa speak some five hundred different tongues, classified by linguists in three main groups—the Sudanese-Guinean group of the Gulf of Guinea coast and the central interior of the continent, the Bantu group farther south, and the Hottentot-Bushman languages of the southwest. It seems probable that the fierce nationalism of Africa's new autonomies will result in a gradual interweaving or lopping off of the lesser language twigs in order to surmount the current communications handicaps. But at this writing Africa is still being hampered by its multiplicity of tongues, from the level of continental progress to that of connubial peace, as witness this letter received by an African newspaper's advice-to-the-lovelorn columnist:

[38] "Being of a different tribe from my wife I do not know what to do every afternoon at four when the radio broadcasts in vernacular. She calls for one tongue, I for another. . . ."

[39] The Sinitic languages of Asia, like the Indo-European, seem to have developed during primeval times when an aboriginal race of people gradually overflowed in all directions from an oriental Eden, situated perhaps in the fertile western valleys of the Yangtze River. The family now includes the myriad spoken dialects of China, plus Tibetan, Burmese, Thai and various other languages of Indo-China. The Japanese and Korean languages may or may not be related to one another—linguists differ on this—but neither of them is related to Chinese or any other of the Sinitic tongues.

[40] The map of the pre-Columbian Americas is a jigsaw puzzle of vaguely defined linguistic families, some forty each in North and South America. This is a conservative estimate, and the families have been determined more or less by guesswork, but any more rigid classification is probably impossible. There were more than a thousand different tongues spoken in the Western hemisphere at the time the white man arrived, but most of these were dead or dying by the time comparative philologists began to study them.

[41] It may be that the first migrants to cross from Asia via the Aleutian stepping stones brought with them a proto-language like the original Indo-European master tongue. Or perhaps they made the crossing long before any of mankind had any well-developed language at all, and the numerous later tongues evolved independently. Or the crossing may have been accomplished in any number of successive waves, each new migration contributing a new tongue. Some linguists claim to have found affinities between the Eskimo family of languages and the Finno-Ugric which includes Hungarian and Finnish. Other scholars, even more imaginative, believe that the Algonquian Indian languages of northern and eastern North America contain elements borrowed from the speech of Viking explorers who visited the New World five centuries before Columbus.

[42] Like the Amerindian, the more than two hundred native languages of Australia and New Guinea had begun to dwindle before they could be seriously studied, and their familial groupings likewise must remain conjectural. The Malayo-Polynesian tongues are rather better known. This limb of language is second only to the Indo-European in its geographical spread. Its related tongues are spoken from Madagascar, off the coast of Africa, all the way to Easter Island in the eastern Pacific, more than halfway around the world. Its branches and twigs include the Tagalog of the Philippines, the Maori of New Zealand, the fast-disappearing Hawaiian, and numerous other languages of Oceania: Fijian, Tahitian, etc.

[43] Not even professional linguists know how many different languages are in use in the world today. The French Academy, a stickler for precision, used to maintain that there were exactly 2,796, exclusive of local dialects. Other estimates have ranged as high as five thousand, because few scholars can agree on just what *is* a "dialect" or when it qualifies as a "language." And, although most of the however-many thousands of tongues have been tucked cozily into families, there are a number of orphans which deny any kinfolk at all. As already mentioned,

Basque is one of them. There's an old legend to the effect that the Devil has never been able to tempt a Basque because the language is so uniquely difficult that he's never learned to speak it.

[44] Korean and Japanese may be orphans, too, unless further linguistic research somehow links them together. Others include a number of hermit languages in Kamchatka and far northeast Siberia, the tongue of the Andaman Islands in the Bay of Bengal, and that of the hairy Ainus of northern Japan.

[45] Even the nonlinguist reader has probably recognized most of the names, at least, of the languages mentioned so far in this chapter, and there are professional linguists who speak, read and write a formidable number of them (Charles Berlitz of the Berlitz Schools of Languages reputedly speaks thirty languages with varying degrees of fluency). But there are other tongues, currently or formerly in use, whose very names are little known.

[46] Just for a sampling, consider Pis, a language of the Caroline Islands; Kookie, an Indian dialect akin to Bengali; Flup, spoken along Africa's Gambia River; Saliva, an Orinoco Indian dialect; Gah, the tongue of the Malayan Alfurus; Bzub, a dialect of the Caucasus; Zaza, a Kurdish tongue of northwest Persia; Cullilan-Cunny, an Amerindian language; Kuzzilbash, a Turkish dialect; Jalloof, language of a Senegal tribe; Miao, the dialect of China's Hunan province; Yairy-Yairy and Watty-Watty, two Australian dialects of New South Wales.

[47] It is a little bit droll, a little bit pathetic, that certain peoples all speaking the same language have seen fit to invent a name for themselves which implies that they are the only people on earth, or at least the most important. This hub-of-the-universe ethnocentrism is oftenest to be found among peoples who inhabit an isolated area, or who are wary or contemptuous of their neighbors. The Eskimos, for example, call themselves the Innuit, which means "the people." The name of China comes eponymously from the dynasty of Ch'in, in turn derived from the word *chin* meaning "man," thus the Chinese are "the men." So are the Gilyads of Siberia (*nibach* in their tongue). So are the Illeni Indians (*illeni*, "the men," gave us the name of Illinois). The African name Bantu means "the men." What we call the Hottentots call themselves Khoi-Khoin, the "men among men."

[48] But no nationality and no language has been able to remain completely aloof and uncontaminated. The men of the Innuit are now well versed in GI slang, courtesy of American military outposts in the Arctic. The Hottentot men among men can probably discourse in Hollywood jargon, learned from the location crews of many a jungle movie epic.

[49] Though separate tongues were developed by the various groups of Indo-European migrants (and by the similar offshoots of all the other linguistic limbs), these languages did not just achieve variety and then petrify at that stage. They continued to change, and are still continuing to change, with every passing year.

[50] Some of a language's development is internal in nature. Its speakers invent new words to fit new things and concepts, as civilization inevitably grows more complex. They hatch colloquialisms and slang expressions, and a certain percentage of these become fixtures of the language. The natural elisions of everyday speech, vernacular differences or outright mistakes in pronunciation, passing fads in spoken language, all can become accepted and permanent usages. For example, the Middle English word *napron* became, through the slurring of "a napron," the modern English "an apron." In sixteenth-century France it became fashionable, for some queer reason, to pronounce *r* as *z* (Paris: *Pazi*). Though the cuteness eventually became tiresome and petered out, at least one leftover remains in *chaise* for the original *chaire*.

[51] Even arbitrary legislation has occasionally changed the course of a people's language. As recently as 1938 Norway decreed an end to the modified Danish that had been its "literary language" since the Middle Ages, and substituted a standardized version of the everyday vernacular called Landsmaal as its official national tongue. Kemal Ataturk, upon becoming dictator-president of Turkey in 1923, at once set about abolishing the Arabic script that had previously been used for writing Turkish and ordered the use of the Roman alphabet. The result is that Turkish children can begin to read and write now after about six months of schooling, instead of the two or three years it used to take.

[52] And there are external pressures that mold every language: wartime conquests and defeats, intergroup commerce, cultural and technological exchanges, immigration, tourism. Rome's conquest of all western Europe replaced its numerous Celtic tongues with adaptations of Latin. But the long occupation of those territories also affected the speech of the conquerors; the rankers of the legions returned home with their own language considerably mutated, so that eventually the common folk of Rome spoke a plebeian Latin quite different from the patrician language our schools still teach. For instance, *equus* was the highbrow word for "horse," but it survives only in such equally bookish words as "equine" and "equestrian." The legionnaire and the Roman-in-the-street said *caballus*, which is much more widely represented in the Romance languages of today—the French *cheval*, the Italian *cavallo*, the Spanish *caballo*—and in the English "cavalry," "cavalcade," etc.

[53] Switzerland shows one remarkable effect of commerce on language. Traditionally the world's bank, referee and middleman, Switzerland has never aspired to developing a distinctive language of its own, unless one counts the provincial tongue called Romansch spoken by less than 2 per cent of the population. The Swiss have found it more expedient, prudent and profitable to make do with the French, German and Italian of their three abutting neighbors.

[54] The linguistic largesse of immigration is too well known, especially in the United States, to require elaboration here. The linguistic souvenirs brought home by tourists are perhaps best exemplified in the cocktail-party conversation of any

debutante just returned from her "finishing" in Europe. As for cultural exchanges of language, the Western world's musical terminology is predominantly Italian (*piano, fortissimo*, etc.), while art critics rely on both French and Italian expressions (*trompe l'oeil, chiaroscuro*, etc.). Because France gave aviation its earliest impetus, the flyer's technology is still full of French terms (*fuselage, aileron*, etc.).

[55] There is no language in the world whose structure or vocabulary does not exhibit the results of one or several internal ferments and external jostlings. And of them all, English is the one which best illustrates the many ways in which language can change, develop and grow.

[56] Whatever tongue the neolithic Britons may have chanted in their dawn-worship ceremonies at Stonehenge, no one knows. We do know that their language gave way to the Celtic brought from the Continent by the so-called Indo-Europeans. And *that* was largely supplanted by the Teutonic dialects of the later invading Angles, Saxons and Jutes. Their Englisc, which became Anglo-Saxon, gave English its basic structure, its grammar and its stock of common words for common things, acts, concepts and emotions. But Anglo-Saxon words, though the oftenest used, are a minority in modern English, because the vocabulary has so often been enriched by other conquerors, skirmishers and settlers—and it is their words we use most in science, art, religion, technology, politics, literature and other supracommon fields.

[57] Latin came with the Roman legions, the later Christian missionaries and the still later cultural cosmopolitanism of the Renaissance. Norse words were contributed by the Viking invaders. The Norman conquerors brought a sort of bastard French, while Parisian French attended the later succession of the Angevin kings.

[58] By the fourteenth century, the blend of court French (with its admixture of Latin) and the London dialect of Anglo-Saxon (with its traces of Norse and Celtic) had been established as *the* English language. But its speakers continued to borrow words from all the Continental tongues and, during Britannia's heyday of ruling the waves, her explorers and colonizers collected still more words from a multitude of exotic sources.

[59] Meantime, English was constantly enjoying or enduring every possible change from within: simplification of its grammar, shifts in pronunciation and spelling, the invention of neologisms, changes in the meaning of many words, the formalization of slang, colloquialisms and idioms. It gradually sloughed off most of the word-endings—indications of gender, number, case, tense and mood—which still complicate the Continental languages. The inflections which do remain in English are few (*-s* for plural, *'s* for possessive, *-ed* for past tense, etc.) and are seldom irregular (as "men" instead of mans, "his" instead of he's, "went" instead of goed, etc.). In the main, English relies on word order and the addition of modifying words to make its sentences clear. In this it is structurally more like Chinese than like any of its Indo-European cousins.

[60] Its insatiable appetite for other people's words and its uninhibited talent for invention have given English, of all languages, probably the widest scope of expression and the richest potential for euphony. It has a store of synonyms to convey just about every conceivable nuance of meaning; it would be possible to write a lengthy monograph on the subject of Love, for instance, without once repeating the word. And in the rare event that a writer cannot find just the precise locution for his purpose, he can ransack the language's vast stockpile of word elements to compound a brand-new coinage of his own.

[61] The one pressure to which English has never bent is that of legislation, although self-appointed improvers have had a go at it from time to time. The Norman kings decreed the use of their brand of French at court, in the courts of law, in trade and in literature. In 1450 Reginald Pecock sought to jettison the Gallicisms and Latinisms that had crept into English, offering pure Anglian alternatives like "ungothroughable" for impenetrable and "nottobethoughtuponable" for imponderable. When the Puritans came into the ascendancy in England they tried to abolish Roman Catholicism from the language by such sleazy stratagems as substituting "Sir" for Saint in church names—Sir Peter's, Sir Mary's *(sic)*, etc.—and promoting "Christ-tide" to delete the despised "mass" from Christmas.

[62] Shortly after the American Revolution, several of the United States founding fathers favored setting up an academy like that of France or Sweden, to standardize and sanctify an "official" American language. And there have been meaningless gestures like the 1923 attempt to have Congress establish that "the national and official language of the Government and people of the United States of America . . . is hereby defined as and declared to be the American language, [i.e.] words and phrases generally accepted as being in good use by the people of the United States of America. . . ." But no do-good decree, proposal or ban has ever stopped the English-speaking people from conducting their lives in whatever vernacular they chose.

[63] I should mention here that any praise of the virtues and advantages of English is an automatic appreciation of the many other tongues which have so heavily contributed to it. And also that the foregoing capsule history of English is intended as microcosm; every other language has manifested similar changes, developments and growth. Thus, every language equally testifies to man's adaptability to shifting circumstances and conditions.

[64] But things do not change everywhere in the same direction or degree. One society becomes urbanized, another remains agrarian; a land-cramped people become migrants or marauders, a comfortable people turn to contemplation and aesthetics. This is not to say that every individual person conforms to a societal way of life—but his native language may. Doubtless the Araucanian Indians of the South American pampas have their sages, rascals, idlers, wits and half-wits, but they all speak the same basic tongue. And that language reflects the pitiful rigors of their

existence in that it includes a wide vocabulary of words just to express varying intensities of hunger.

[65] The reasonable man is aware that not all Scots are miserly, not all Frenchmen are excitable, not all Russians are gloomy—and ditto for all the other facile labels fabricated by superstition, false tradition and standing jokes. But, while it is impossible to assign a stereotyped temperament to every individual of a specific race, color or nationality, it *is* often possible to detect differing and distinctive "personalities" among their languages.

[66] To a non-Scot, the word "burr" perfectly describes both the Gaelic pronunciation and the national flower of Scotland: the language and the thistle are equally rough-edged. The liquid vowels of the Polynesian tongues conjure up visions of loveliness and languor, full moon and blue lagoon.

[67] Contrariwise, the gutturals of the German language sound, to a non-German, as harsh and forbidding as winter in the Black Forest. The swoops and swirls of Persian script seem, to a Westerner, as voluptuous and sensual as the quatrains of Omar Khayyám. But Goethe wrote tender and lyrical word-music in German, and Persian is prosaically utilitarian for keeping the accounts of Iranian oil companies. The personality of a language, like that of a man, is the sum of many things not always apparent to the casual eye or ear.

[68] One factor in the makeup of a language is what the Germans call *Sprachgefühl*, or speech-feeling. In *Words and Their Ways in English Speech* philologists J. B. Greenough and G. L. Kittredge define it as "a regular and persistent mode of thought, and consequently of expression, which more or less dominates the form of the language in the mouths of all its speakers. . . . It affects every word that we utter, though we may think that we are speaking as the whim of the moment dictates; and thus it is the strongest and most pervasive of all conservative forces, and has kept [each] language true to itself." They cite as examples Latin's majestic simplicity of style and the epigrammatic scintillation of French, then add, "Men of genius may take great liberties with their mother tongue without offense; but let them once run counter to its characteristic tendencies, let them violate [its] *Sprachgefühl*, and their mannerism becomes, as it were, a foreign language."

[69] While the national language of a people has its own personality, a *Sprachgefühl* distinct from even closely related tongues, it is at the same time a complex of sublanguages—regional dialects, trade jargons and the like—each of which has its own idiosyncrasies. Take a New York stockbroker and an Alabama sharecropper, a Moscow ballerina and a Pskov muzhik—or, for that matter, any teen-ager and his grandfather. Each pair speaks one national language, but with what worlds-apart difference.

[70] It may be hard to imagine a world in which every town or every social group or even every family spoke a separate language—but it could conceivably have happened. Oral language, like gossip, can undergo remarkable changes even across

the space of two backyards, let alone across a country or a century. There is every reason to believe that the world's peace and progress have been retarded by its multifarious tongues. But, horrible to contemplate, these thousands of mutually incomprehensible languages might well have wisped and splintered into thousands of thousands—and mankind into even more fragmented, insular and dissident subcultures—except for one thing. Along came writing.

FOR REVIEW AND DISCUSSION

Content

1. Jennings cites the absence of *primitive* languages as the reason for its being impossible to discover the beginnings of speech. What does he mean, though, by a primitive language? How might one distinguish a primitive language from a *civilized* one?

2. Jennings mentions a number of theories about the origin of language. Think of another theory, one that is not mentioned in the essay.

3. Based on how Jennings has described the study of language origin and families, define his attitude toward linguists. Does he seem to respect their work, for instance, or is he disdainful? Make your definition as precise as possible and support it with references to passages in the essay.

4. What are the implications in Edgar Sturtevant's suggestion that language was developed so that people could profit from deceit? Should Sturtevant's theory be taken seriously? What is Jennings's attitude toward it?

Rhetoric

1. What is Jennings's purpose in writing this essay? Is there a thesis sentence or paragraph that makes his purpose clear?

2. What is the general tone of the essay? Why might Jennings have chosen such a tone for this essay?

3. Jennings uses *chucklesome* [paragraph 10] rather than, say, *humorous* or *funny* or *amusing*. What effect has the strange word when you read it? How does it affect your attitude toward Jennings or toward the hypotheses whose names he is describing?

4. Reread the conclusion of the essay. How much can you tell about the content of the essay from reading only its conclusion?

5. Does the conclusion seem effectively dramatic and provocative, or does it seem hackneyed—overdone? Describe your response to the last sentence. What image comes to mind?

Classroom Exercises

1. "There is every reason to believe that the world's peace and progress have been retarded by its multifarious tongues. But, horrible to contemplate, these thousands of mutually incomprehensible languages might well have wisped and splintered into thousands of thousands—and mankind into even more fragmented, insular and dissident subcultures—except for one thing. Along came writing." What does this concluding thought suggest about the relationship of writing to language and, more importantly, to human history? Discuss why you think that writing is or is not so important as Jennings suggests.

2. Many people propose that the worldwide adoption of a single language would lead to greater peace and prosperity among nations. Some advocate the adoption of an artificial language (Esperanto, for example), while others advocate the adoption of an existing language (English, French, Russian, Spanish, etc.). Discuss the merits, weaknesses, and complexities of this proposal.

FOR DISCUSSION AND WRITING

1. Humpty Dumpty says that words mean what he wants them to mean, and his use of words such as *glory* and *impenetrability* illustrates that what he wants them to mean is often not what they normally mean. Which of the language functions described by Pyles and Algeo does Humpty Dumpty make most use of when he treats language in this way?

2. Discuss how the seven functions of language figure in the conversation between Alice and Humpty Dumpty.

3. How would Humpty Dumpty have gotten along with those people in the eighteenth century who, according to Roberts, favored an academy to purify English? Describe a scene in which Humpty Dumpty and a few of these language purists try to converse.

4. Jennings notes the belief, held until midway through the nineteenth century, "that some single original language had been God's gift to man at the time of the Creation" and that at one time all people spoke that one language. Imagine that all people now speak that original language; then describe specific ways in which our daily lives would be changed from how they are now.

Then imagine what our lives would be like if we all "mastered" language as Humpty Dumpty does. Describe this imagined way of life.

What are the benefits and shortcomings of each imagined existence?

5. In the argument about our relationship to language, whose side are you on, Alice's or Humpty Dumpty's? Explain your answer.

3 SEMANTICS AND WORLD VIEW

There are as many different worlds upon the earth as there are languages.
CLYDE KLUCKHOHN
The limits of my language are the limits of my world.
L. WITTGENSTEIN

Semantics is "the study of meaning in language, particularly with regard to its historical change." In this chapter, S. I. Hayakawa and others discuss *how* words mean and how their meanings often differ from the things they stand for. Once we understand this basic principle of semantics and how, for example, English speakers classify the things of the world, we can better understand the idea that people who speak languages quite different from our own may not see the world in the same way we do.

S. I. Hayakawa

SYMBOLS

That words are merely symbols for ideas and things—and not the things themselves—is something we often forget, and, as Hayakawa points out, is an oversight that frequently causes us problems. In this selection, the well-known semanticist explains how misconstruing the symbolic nature of words can affect our daily behavior and use of language. Ask yourself how often you have committed the semantic errors he discusses.

THE SYMBOLIC PROCESS

[1] Animals struggle with each other for food or for leadership but they do not, like human beings, struggle with each other for things that *stand for* food or leadership: such things as our paper symbols of wealth (money, bonds, titles), badges of rank to wear on our clothes, or low-number license plates, supposed by some people to stand for social precedence. For animals, the relationship in which one thing *stands for* something else does not appear to exist except in very rudimentary form.[1]

[2] The process by means of which human beings can arbitrarily make certain things *stand for* other things may be called the *symbolic process*. Whenever two or more human beings can communicate with each other, they can, by agreement, make anything stand for anything. For example, here are two symbols:

X   Y

---

[1] One investigator, J. B. Wolfe, trained chimpanzees to put poker chips into an especially constructed vending machine ("chimpomat") which supplied grapes, bananas, and other food. The chimpanzees proved to be able to distinguish chips of different "values" (one grape, two grapes, zero, and so on) and also proved to be willing to work for them if the rewards were fairly immediate. They tended, however, to stop work as they accumulated more chips. Their "money system" was definitely limited to rudimentary and immediate transactions. See Robert M. Yerkes' *Chimpanzees: A Laboratory Colony* (1943).

Other examples of animals successfully learning to react meaningfully to things-that-stand-for-other-things can readily be offered, but as a general rule these animal reactions are extremely simple and limited when contrasted with human possibilities in this direction. For example, it appears likely that a chimpanzee might be taught to drive a simplified car, but there would be one thing wrong with its driving: its reactions are such that if a red light showed when it was halfway across a street, it would stop in the middle of the crossing, while, if a green light showed when another car was stalled in its path, it would go ahead regardless of consequences. In other words, so far as such a chimpanzee would be concerned, the red light could hardly be said to stand for "stop"; it *is* stop.

From *Language in Thought and Action*, Second Edition, by S. I. Hayakawa, copyright © 1964 by Harcourt Brace Jovanovich, Inc. Reprinted by permission of the publishers.

SYMBOLS

We can agree to let X stand for buttons and Y stand for bows; then we can freely change our agreement and let X stand for the Chicago White Sox and Y for the Cincinnati Reds; or let X stand for Chaucer and Y for Shakespeare, X for North Korea, and Y for South Korea. *We are, as human beings, uniquely free to manufacture and manipulate and assign values to our symbols as we please.* Indeed, we can go further by making symbols that stand for symbols. If necessary we can, for instance, let the symbol M stand for all the X's in the previous example (buttons, White Sox, Chaucer, North Korea) and let N stand for all the Y's (bows, Cincinnati Reds, Shakespeare, South Korea). Then we can make another symbol, T, stand for M and N, which would be an instance of a symbol of symbols of symbols. This freedom to create symbols of *any* assigned value and to create *symbols that stand for symbols* is essential to what we call the symbolic process.

[3]   Everywhere we turn, we see the symbolic process at work. Feathers worn on the head or stripes on the sleeve can be made to stand for military rank; cowrie shells or rings of brass or pieces of paper can stand for wealth; crossed sticks can stand for a set of religious beliefs; buttons, elks' teeth, ribbons, special styles of ornamental haircutting or tattooing, can stand for social affiliations. The symbolic process permeates human life at the most primitive and the most civilized levels alike. Warriors, medicine men, policemen, doormen, nurses, cardinals, and kings wear costumes that symbolize their occupations. American Indians collected scalps, college students collect membership keys in honorary societies, to symbolize victories in their respective fields. There are few things that men do or want to do, possess or want to possess, that have not, in addition to their mechanical or biological value, a symbolic value.

[4]   All fashionable clothes, as Thorstein Veblen has pointed out in his *Theory of the Leisure Class* (1899), are highly symbolic: materials, cut, and ornament are dictated only to a slight degree by considerations of warmth, comfort, or practicability. The more we dress up in fine clothes, the more we restrict our freedom of action. But by means of delicate embroideries, easily soiled fabrics, starched shirts, high heels, long and pointed fingernails, and other such sacrifices of comfort, the wealthy classes manage to symbolize, among other things, the fact that they don't have to work for a living. On the other hand, the not-so-wealthy, by imitating these symbols of wealth, symbolize their conviction that, even if they do work for a living, they are just as good as anybody else.

[5]   With the changes in American life since Veblen's time, many changes have taken place in our ways of symbolizing social status. Except for evening and party wear, fashionable clothes nowadays are often designed for outdoor life and therefore stress comfort, informality, and above all, freedom from the conventions of business life—hence the gaily colored sports shirts for men and capri pants for women.

[6]   In Veblen's time a deeply tanned skin was indicative of a life spent in farming and other outdoor labor, and women in those days went to a great deal of trouble shielding themselves from the sun with parasols, wide hats, and long sleeves.

Today, however, a pale skin is indicative of confinement in offices and factories, while a deeply tanned skin suggests a life of leisure—of trips to Florida, Sun Valley, and Hawaii. Hence, a sun-blackened skin, once considered ugly because it symbolized work, is now considered beautiful because it symbolizes leisure. "The idea is," as Stanton Delaplane said in the San Francisco *Chronicle,* "to turn a color which, if you were born with it, would make it extremely difficult to get into major hotels." And pallid people in New York, Chicago, and Toronto who cannot afford midwinter trips to the West Indies find comfort in browning themselves with drugstore tanning solutions.

[7] Food, too, is highly symbolic. Religious dietary regulations, such as those of the Catholics, Jews, and Mohammedans, are observed in order to symbolize adherence to one's religion. Specific foods are used to symbolize specific festivals and observances in almost every country—for example, cherry pie on George Washington's birthday; haggis on Burns' Nicht. And eating together has been a highly symbolic act throughout all of man's known history: "companion" means one with whom you share your bread.

[8] The white Southerner's apparently illogical attitude toward Negroes can also be accounted for on symbolic grounds. People from outside the South often find it difficult to understand how many white Southerners accept close physical contact with Negro servants and yet become extremely upset at the idea of sitting beside Negroes in restaurants or buses. The attitude of the Southerner rests on the fact that the ministrations of a Negro servant—even personal care, such as nursing—have the symbolic implication of social inequality; while admission of Negroes to buses, restaurants, and nonsegregated schools has the symbolic implication of social equality.

[9] We select our furniture to serve as visible symbols of our taste, wealth, and social position. We often choose our residences on the basis of a feeling that it "looks well" to have a "good address." We trade in perfectly good cars for later models, not always to get better transportation, but to give evidence to the community that we can afford it.[2]

[10] Such complicated and apparently unnecessary behavior leads philosophers, both amateur and professional, to ask over and over again, "Why can't human beings live simply and naturally?" Often the complexity of human life makes us look enviously at the relative simplicity of such lives as dogs and cats lead. But the

---

[2] The writer once had an eight-year-old car in good running condition. A friend of his, a repairman who knew the condition of the car, kept urging him to trade it for a new model. "But why?" the writer asked. "The old car's in fine shape still." The repairman answered scornfully, "Yeah, but what the hell. All you've got is transportation."

Recently, the term "transportation car" has begun to appear in advertisements: for example, "'48 Dodge—Runs perfectly good; transportation car. Leaving, must sell. $100." (Classified section of the *Pali Press,* Kailua, Hawaii.) Apparently it means a car that has no symbolic or prestige value and is good only for getting you there and bringing you back—a miserable kind of vehicle indeed!

symbolic process, which makes possible the absurdities of human conduct, also makes possible language and therefore all the human achievements dependent upon language. The fact that more things can go wrong with motorcars than with wheelbarrows is no reason for going back to wheelbarrows. Similarly, the fact that the symbolic process makes complicated follies possible is no reason for wanting to return to a cat-and-dog existence. A better solution is to understand the symbolic process so that instead of being its victims we become, to some degree at least, its masters.

LANGUAGE AS SYMBOLISM

[11] Of all forms of symbolism, language is the most highly developed, most subtle, and most complicated. It has been pointed out that human beings, by agreement, can make anything stand for anything. Now, human beings have agreed, in the course of centuries of mutual dependency, to let the various noises that they can produce with their lungs, throats, tongues, teeth, and lips systematically stand for specified happenings in their nervous systems. We call that system of agreements *language*. For example, we who speak English have been so trained that, when our nervous systems register the presence of a certain kind of animal, we may make the following noise: "There's a cat." Anyone hearing us expects to find that, by looking in the same direction, he will experience a similar event in his nervous system—one that will lead him to make an almost identical noise. Again, we have been so trained that when we are conscious of wanting food, we make the noise "I'm hungry."

[12] There is, as has been said, *no necessary connection between the symbol and that which is symbolized*. Just as men can wear yachting costumes without ever having been near a yacht, so they can make the noise "I'm hungry" without being hungry. Furthermore, just as social rank can be symbolized by feathers in the hair, by tattooing on the breast, by gold ornaments on the watch chain, or by a thousand different devices according to the culture we live in, so the fact of being hungry can be symbolized by a thousand different noises according to the culture we live in: "*J'ai faim*," or "*Es hungert mich*," or "*Ho appetito*," or "*Hara ga hetta*," and so on.

[13] However obvious these facts may appear at first glance, they are actually not so obvious as they seem except when we take special pains to think about the subject. Symbols and things symbolized are independent of each other; nevertheless, we all have a way of feeling as if, and sometimes acting as if, there were necessary connections. For example, there is the vague sense we all have that foreign languages are inherently absurd: foreigners have such funny names for things, and why can't they call things by their right names? This feeling exhibits itself most strongly in those tourists who seem to believe that they can make the natives of any country understand English if they shout loud enough. Like the little

boy who was reported to have said, "Pigs are called pigs because they are such dirty animals," they feel that the symbol is inherently connected in some way with the thing symbolized. Then there are the people who feel that since snakes are "nasty, slimy creatures" (incidentally, snakes are *not* slimy), the word "snake" is a *nasty, slimy word*.

THE PITFALLS OF DRAMA

[14] Naïveté regarding the symbolic process extends to symbols other than words, of course. In the case of drama (stage, movies, television), there appear to be people in almost every audience who never quite fully realize that a play is a set of fictional, symbolic representations. An actor is one who symbolizes other people, real or imagined. In a movie some years ago, Fredric March enacted with great skill the role of a drunkard. Florence Eldridge (Mrs. March) reports that for a long time thereafter she got letters of advice and sympathy from women who said that they too were married to alcoholics. Also some years ago it was reported that when Edward G. Robinson, who used to play gangster roles with extraordinary vividness, visited Chicago, local hoodlums would telephone him at his hotel to pay their professional respects.

[15] One is reminded of the actor, playing the role of a villain in a traveling theatrical troupe, who, at a particularly tense moment in the play, was shot by an excited cowpuncher in the audience. But this kind of confusion does not seem to be confined to unsophisticated theatergoers. In recent times, Paul Muni, after playing the part of Clarence Darrow in *Inherit the Wind*, was invited to address the American Bar Association; Ralph Bellamy, after playing the role of Franklin D. Roosevelt in *Sunrise at Campobello*, was invited by several colleges to speak on Roosevelt. Also, there are those astonishing patriots who rushed to the recruiting offices to help defend the nation when, on October 30, 1938, the United States was "invaded" by an "army from Mars" in a radio dramatization.[3]

THE WORD IS NOT THE THING

[16] The above, however, are only the more striking examples of confused attitudes toward words and symbols. There would be little point in mentioning them if we were *uniformly and permanently aware* of the independence of symbols from things symbolized, as all human beings, in the writer's opinion, *can be* and *should be*. But we are not. Most of us have, in some area or other of our thinking, improper

---

[3] See Hadley Cantril's *The Invasion from Mars* (1940) [Ed. note: see Chapter Six]; also John Houseman's "The Men from Mars," *Harper's* (December 1948).

habits of evaluation. For this, society itself is often to blame: most societies systematically encourage, concerning certain topics, the habitual confusion of symbols with things symbolized. For example, if a Japanese schoolhouse caught on fire, it used to be obligatory in the days of emperor-worship to try to rescue the emperor's *picture* (there was one in every schoolhouse), even at the risk of one's life. (If you got burned to death, you were posthumously ennobled.) In our society, we are encouraged to go into debt in order that we may display, as symbols of prosperity, shiny new automobiles. Strangely enough, the possession of shiny automobiles even under these conditions makes their "owners" *feel* prosperous. In all civilized societies (and probably in many primitive ones as well), the symbols of piety, of civic virtue, or of patriotism are often prized above actual piety, civic virtue, or patriotism. In one way or another, we are all like the brilliant student who cheats on his exams in order to make Phi Beta Kappa: it is so much more important to have the symbol than the things it stands for.

[17] The habitual confusion of symbols with things symbolized, whether on the part of individuals or societies, is serious enough at all levels of culture to provide a perennial human problem.[4] But with the rise of modern communications systems, the problem of confusing verbal symbols with realities assumes peculiar urgency. We are constantly being talked at, by teachers, preachers, salesmen, public-relations counsels, governmental agencies, and moving-picture sound tracks. The cries of the hawkers of soft drinks, detergents, and laxatives pursue us into our homes, thanks to radio and television—and in some houses the sets are never turned off from morning to night. The mailman brings direct-mail advertising. Billboards confront us on the highway, and we even take portable radios with us to the seashore.

[18] We live in an environment shaped and largely created by hitherto unparalleled semantic influences: mass-circulation newspapers and magazines which are given to reflecting, in a shocking number of cases, the weird prejudices and obsessions of their publishers and owners; radio programs, both local and network, almost completely dominated by commercial motives; public-relations counsels who are simply highly paid craftsmen in the art of manipulating and reshaping our semantic environment in ways favorable to their clients. It is an exciting environment, but fraught with danger: it is only a slight exaggeration to say that Hitler conquered Austria by radio. Today, the full resources of advertising agencies, public-relations counsels, radio, television, and slanted news stories are brought to bear in order to influence our decisions in election campaigns, especially in years of presidential elections.

[19] Citizens of a modern society need, therefore, more than that ordinary "common sense" which was defined by Stuart Chase as that which tells you that the

---

[4]The charge against the Pharisees, it will be remembered, was that they were obsessively concerned with the symbols of piety at the expense of an adequate concern with its spirit.

world is flat. They need to be systematically aware of the powers and limitations of symbols, especially words, if they are to guard against being driven into complete bewilderment by the complexity of their semantic environment. The first of the principles governing symbols is this: The symbol is NOT the thing symbolized; the word is NOT the thing; the map is NOT the territory it stands for.

MAPS AND TERRITORIES

[20] There is a sense in which we all live in two worlds. First, we live in the world of happenings which we know at first hand. This is an extremely small world, consisting only of that continuum of the things that we have actually seen, felt, or heard—the flow of events constantly passing before our senses. So far as this world of personal experience is concerned, Africa, South America, Asia, Washington, New York, or Los Angeles do not exist if we have never been to these places. Jomo Kenyetta is only a name if we have never seen him. When we ask ourselves how much we know at first hand, we discover that we know very little indeed.

[21] Most of our knowledge, acquired from parents, friends, schools, newspapers, books, conversation, speeches, and television, is received *verbally*. All our knowledge of history, for example, comes to us only in words. The only proof we have that the Battle of Waterloo ever took place is that we have had reports to that effect. These reports are not given us by people who saw it happen, but are based on other reports: reports of reports of reports, which go back ultimately to the first-hand reports given by people who did see it happening. It is through reports, then, and through reports of reports, that we receive most knowledge: about government, about what is happening in Korea, about what picture is showing at the downtown theater—in fact, about anything that we do not know through direct experience.

[22] Let us call this world that comes to us through words the *verbal world*, as opposed to the world we know or are capable of knowing through our own experience, which we shall call the *extensional world*. (The reason for the choice of the word "extensional" will become clear later.) The human being, like any other creature, begins to make his acquaintance with the extensional world from infancy. Unlike other creatures, however, he begins to receive, as soon as he can learn to understand, reports, reports of reports, reports of reports of reports. In addition he receives inferences made from reports, inferences made from other inferences, and so on. By the time a child is a few years old, has gone to school and to Sunday school, and has made a few friends, he has accumulated a considerable amount of second- and third-hand information about morals, geography, history, nature, people, games—all of which information together constitutes his verbal world.

[23] Now, to use the famous metaphor introduced by Alfred Korzybski in his *Science and Sanity* (1933), this verbal world ought to stand in relation to the

SYMBOLS

extensional world as a *map* does to the *territory* it is supposed to represent. If a child grows to adulthood with a verbal world in his head which corresponds fairly closely to the extensional world that he finds around him in his widening experience, he is in relatively small danger of being shocked or hurt by what he finds, because his verbal world has told him what, more or less, to expect. He is prepared for life. If, however, he grows up with a false map in his head—that is, with a head crammed with error and superstition—he will constantly be running into trouble, wasting his efforts, and acting like a fool. He will not be adjusted to the world as it is; he may, if the lack of adjustment is serious, end up in a mental hospital.

[24] Some of the follies we commit because of false maps in our heads are so commonplace that we do not even think of them as remarkable. There are those who protect themselves from accidents by carrying a rabbit's foot. Some refuse to sleep on the thirteenth floor of hotels—a situation so common that most big hotels, even in the capitals of our scientific culture, skip "13" in numbering their floors. Some plan their lives on the basis of astrological predictions. Some play fifty-to-one shots on the basis of dream books. Some hope to make their teeth whiter by changing their brand of tooth paste. All such people are living in verbal worlds that bear little, if any, resemblance to the extensional world.

[25] Now, no matter how beautiful a map may be, it is useless to a traveler unless it accurately shows the relationship of places to each other, the structure of the territory. If we draw, for example, a big dent in the outline of a lake for, let us say, artistic reasons, the map is worthless. But if we are just drawing maps for fun without paying any attention to the structure of the region, there is nothing in the world to prevent us from putting in all the extra curlicues and twists we want in the lakes, rivers, and roads. No harm will be done *unless someone tries to plan a trip by such a map.*

[26] Similarly, by means of imaginary or false reports, or by false inferences from good reports, or by mere rhetorical exercises, we can manufacture at will, with language, "maps" which have no reference to the extensional world. Here again no harm will be done unless someone makes the mistake of regarding such "maps" as representing real territories.

[27] We all inherit a great deal of useless knowledge, and a great deal of misinformation and error (maps that were formerly thought to be accurate), so that there is always a portion of what we have been told that must be discarded. But the cultural heritage of our civilization that is transmitted to us—our socially pooled knowledge, both scientific and humane—has been valued principally because we have believed that it gives us accurate maps of experience. The analogy of verbal worlds to maps is an important one and will be referred to frequently throughout this book. It should be noticed at this point, however, that there are two ways of getting false maps of the world into our heads: first, by having them given to us; second, by creating them ourselves when we misread the true maps given to us.

FOR REVIEW AND DISCUSSION

Content

1. Listen to people speak—friends, other students, your family, even strangers—and note errors in their use of words. What are some examples of their semantic confusion?

2. In paragraph 11, Hayakawa describes a "system of agreements" that he says is *language*. Explain how this description of language is either complete or incomplete.

3. To illustrate that confusion in the symbolic process is not limited to word use, Hayakawa mentions actors who have been associated with the roles they played. Do these actors' cases really illustrate confusion in the symbolic process, or might other factors be involved? Discuss each actor's case.

4. What does Hayakawa mean by *semantic influences?*

Rhetoric

1. Hayakawa spends several pages describing symbols in general, but his specific concern is the symbolism of language. What is the purpose of his more general discussion?

2. When discussing the prevalence of the symbolic process, Hayakawa offers two examples in one sentence: "American Indians collected scalps, college students collect membership keys in honorary societies, to symbolize victories in their respective fields." By placing scalps and honorary societies together, Hayakawa has made an implicit comparison. What is that comparison? How can we be satisfied that we get from the sentence what Hayakawa put into it?

3. While writing about semantic confusion caused by misapprehension of symbols, Hayakawa invokes Korzybski's metaphor of map and territory. Does this metaphor (which is intended as a map of the territory Hayakawa is discussing) cause its own semantic confusion, or is it an accurate map detailing the terrains of the two worlds we live in? Explain.

Classroom Exercises

1. Hayakawa mentions a number of misuses of symbols, a number of ways in which the extensional world and the verbal world become misaligned. But does he suggest how we might improve our use of symbols, how we might become "aware of the independence of symbol from things symbolized"? Do you have any suggestions?

2. Describe some symbols in our present styles of dress. What particular "symbols" do you try to wear? Why do you choose these symbolic styles of dress rather than others? Why don't you favor the other styles?

3. What specific words do you usually respond to as though their meaning were inherent? Hayakawa mentions *pig* and *snake*. Another might be *cancer*. Compile a list of words that you have trouble separating from what they symbolize. Select one such word and give it a new meaning, one that is pleasant if the original is unpleasant, or unpleasant if the original is pleasant. For instance, you might decide to make *cancer* mean *spring* (the season) or *rolling stream*. After you have had a chance to use your word in its new symbolic role, evaluate your response to the word (to the *symbol*, not to what is symbolized). How much of the old meaning is retained? Are you able to separate words from the things they symbolize?

H. L. Mencken

A GIRL FROM RED LION, P.A.

We are frequently told not to believe everything we read; this story concerns a young woman who evidently hasn't been warned. She fails to distinguish between fact and fiction, and thus the novels of her day, and her boyfriend, get her into a lamentable and amusing situation.

[1]   Somewhere in his lush, magenta prose Oscar Wilde speaks of the tendency of nature to imitate art—a phenomenon often observed by persons who keep their eyes open. I first became aware of it, not through the pages of Wilde, but at the hands of an old-time hack-driver named Peebles, who flourished in Baltimore in the days of this history. Peebles was a Scotsman of a generally unfriendly and retiring character, but nevertheless he was something of a public figure in the town. Perhaps that was partly due to the fact that he had served twelve years in the Maryland Penitentiary for killing his wife, but I think he owed much more of his eminence to his adamantine rectitude in money matters, so rare in his profession. The very cops, indeed, regarded him as an honest man, and said so freely. They knew about his blanket refusal to take more than three or four times the legal fare from drunks, they knew how many lost watches, wallets, stick-pins and walking-sticks he turned in every year, and they admired as Christians, though deploring as cops, his absolute refusal to work for them in the capacity of stool-pigeon.

[2]   Moreover, he was industrious as well as honest, and it was the common belief that he had money in five banks. He appeared on the hack-stand in front of the old Eutaw House every evening at nine o'clock, and put in the next five or six hours shuttling merrymakers and sociologists to and from the red-light districts. When this trade began to languish he drove to Union Station, and there kept watch until his two old horses fell asleep. Most of the strangers who got off the early morning trains wanted to go to the nearest hotel, which was only two blocks away, so there was not a great deal of money in their patronage, but unlike the other hackers Peebles never resorted to the device of driving them swiftly in the wrong direction and then working back by a circuitous route.

[3]   A little after dawn one morning in the early Autumn of 1903, just as his off horse began to snore gently, a milk-train got in from lower Pennsylvania, and out of it issued a rosy-cheeked young woman carrying a pasteboard suitcase and a pink

From *Newspaper Days*, by H. L. Mencken. Copyright 1941 and renewed 1969 by August Mencken and Mercantile-Safe Deposit and Trust Co. Reprinted by permission of Alfred A. Knopf, Inc.

parasol. Squired up from the train-level by a car-greaser with an eye for country beauty, she emerged into the sunlight shyly and ran her eye down the line of hacks. The other drivers seemed to scare her, and no wonder, for they were all grasping men whose evil propensities glowed from them like heat from a stove. But when she saw Peebles her feminine intuition must have told her that he could be trusted, for she shook off the car-greaser without further ado, and came up to the Peebles hack with a pretty show of confidence.

[4] "Say, mister," she said, "how much will you charge to take me to a house of ill fame?"

[5] In telling of it afterward Peebles probably exaggerated his astonishment a bit, but certainly he must have suffered something rationally describable as a shock. He laid great stress upon her air of blooming innocence, almost like that of a cavorting lamb. He said her two cheeks glowed like apples, and that she smelled like a load of hay. By his own account he stared at her for a full minute without answering her question, with a wild stream of confused surmises racing through his mind. What imaginable business could a creature so obviously guileless have in the sort of establishment she had mentioned? Could it be that her tongue had slipped—that she actually meant an employment office, the Y.W.C.A., or what not? Peebles, as he later elaborated the story, insisted that he had cross-examined her at length, and that she had not only reiterated her question in precise terms, but explained that she was fully determined to abandon herself to sin and looked forward confidently to dying in the gutter. But in his first version he reported simply that he had stared at her dumbly until his amazement began to wear off, and then motioned to her to climb into his hack. After all, he was a common carrier, and obliged by law to haul all comers, regardless of their private projects and intentions. If he yielded anything to his Caledonian moral sense it took the form of choosing her destination with some prudence. He might have dumped her into one of the third-rate bagnios that crowded a street not three blocks from Union Station, and then gone on about his business. Instead, he drove half way across town to the high-toned studio of Miss Nellie d'Alembert, at that time one of the leaders of her profession in Baltimore, and a woman who, though she lacked the polish of Vassar, had sound sense, a pawky humor, and progressive ideas.

[6] I had become, only a little while before, city editor of the *Herald*, and in that capacity received frequently confidential communications from her. She was, in fact, the source of a great many useful news tips. She knew everything about everyone that no one was supposed to know, and had accurate advance information, in particular, about Page 1 divorces, for nearly all the big law firms of the town used her facilities for the manufacture of evidence. There were no Walter Winchells in that era, and the city editors of the land had to depend on volunteers for inside stuff. Such volunteers were moved (*a*) by a sense of public duty gracefully performed, and (*b*) by an enlightened desire to keep on the good side of newspapers. Not infrequently they cashed in on this last. I well remember the night when two visiting

A GIRL FROM RED LION, P.A.

Congressmen from Washington got into a debate in Miss Nellie's music-room, and one of them dented the skull of the other with a spittoon. At my suggestion the other city editors of Baltimore joined me in straining journalistic ethics far enough to remove the accident to Mt. Vernon place, the most respectable neighborhood in town, and to lay the fracture to a fall on the ice.

[7]   My chance leadership in this public work made Miss Nellie my partisan, and now and then she gave me a nice tip and forgot to include the other city editors. Thus I was alert when she called up during the early afternoon of Peebles' strange adventure, and told me that something swell was on ice. She explained that it was not really what you could call important news, but simply a sort of human-interest story, so I asked Percy Heath to go to see her, for though he was now my successor as Sunday editor, he still did an occasional news story, and I knew what kind he enjoyed especially. He called up in half an hour, and asked me to join him. "If you don't hear it yourself," he said, "you will say I am pulling a fake."

[8]   When I got to Miss Nellie's house I found her sitting with Percy in a basement room that she used as a sort of office, and at once she plunged into the story.

[9]   "I'll tell you first," she began, "before you see the poor thing herself. When Peebles yanked the bell this morning I was sound asleep, and so was all the girls, and Sadie the coon had gone home. I stuck my head out of the window, and there was Peebles on the front steps. I said: 'Get the hell away from here! What do you mean by bringing in a drunk at this time of the morning? Don't you know us poor working people gotta get some rest?' But he hollered back that he didn't have no drunk in his hack, but something he didn't know what to make of, and needed my help on, so I slipped on my kimono and went down to the door, and by that time he had the girl out of the hack, and before I could say 'scat' he had shoved her in the parlor, and she was unloading what she had to say.

[10]   "Well, to make a long story short, she said she came from somewheres near a burg they call Red Lion, P.A., and lived on a farm. She said her father was one of them old rubes with whiskers they call Dunkards, and very strict. She said she had a beau in York, P.A., of the name of Elmer, and whenever he could get away he would come out to the farm and set in the parlor with her, and they would do a little hugging and kissing. She said Elmer was educated and a great reader, and he would bring her books that he got from his brother, who was a train butcher on the Northern Central, and him and her would read them. She said the books was all about love, and that most of them was sad. Her and Elmer would talk about them while they set in the parlor, and the more they talked about them the sadder they would get, and sometimes she would have to cry.

[11]   "Well, to make a long story short, this went on once a week or so, and night before last Elmer come down from York with some more books, and they set in the parlor, and talked about love. Her old man usually stuck his nose in the door now and then, to see that there wasn't no foolishness, but night before last he had a

bilious attack and went to bed early, so her and Elmer had it all to theirself in the parlor. So they quit talking about the books, and Elmer began to love her up, and in a little while they was hugging and kissing to beat the band. Well, to make a long story short, Elmer went too far, and when she came to herself and kicked him out she realized she had lost her honest name.

[12] "She laid awake all night thinking about it, and the more she thought about it the more scared she got. In every one of the books her and Elmer read there was something on the subject, and all of the books said the same thing. When a girl lost her honest name there was nothing for her to do except to run away from home and lead a life of shame. No girl that she ever read about ever done anything else. They all rushed off to the nearest city, started this life of shame, and then took to booze and dope and died in the gutter. Their family never knew what had became of them. Maybe they landed finally in a medical college, or maybe the Salvation Army buried them, but their people never heard no more of them, and their name was rubbed out of the family Bible. Sometimes their beau tried to find them, but he never could do it, and in the end he usually married the judge's homely daughter, and moved into the big house when the judge died.

[13] "Well, to make a long story short, this poor girl lay awake all night thinking of such sad things, and when she got up at four thirty a.m. and went out to milk the cows her eyes was so full of tears that she could hardly find their spigots. Her father, who was still bilious, give her hell, and told her she was getting her just punishment for setting up until ten and eleven o'clock at night, when all decent people ought to be in bed. So she began to suspect that he may have snuck down during the evening, and caught her, and was getting ready to turn her out of the house and wash his hands of her, and maybe even curse her. So she decided to have it over and done with as soon as possible, and last night, the minute he hit the hay again, she hoofed in to York, P.A., and caught the milk-train for Baltimore, and that is how Peebles found her at Union Station and brought her here. When I asked her what in hell she wanted all she had to say was 'Ain't this a house of ill fame?', and it took me an hour or two to pump her story out of her. So now I have got her upstairs under lock and key, and as soon as I can get word to Peebles I'll tell him to take her back to Union Station, and start her back for Red Lion, P.A. Can you beat it?"

[14] Percy and I, of course, demanded to see the girl, and presently Miss Nellie fetched her in. She was by no means the bucolic Lillian Russell that Peebles' tall tales afterward made her out, but she was certainly far from unappetizing. Despite her loss of sleep, the dreadful gnawings of her conscience and the menace of an appalling retribution, her cheeks were still rosy, and there remained a considerable sparkle in her troubled blue eyes. I never heard her name, but it was plain that she was of four-square Pennsylvania Dutch stock, and as sturdy as the cows she serviced. She had on her Sunday clothes, and appeared to be somewhat uncomfortable in them, but Miss Nellie set her at ease, and soon she was retelling her story to two strange and, in her sight, probably highly dubious men. We listened without interrupting her, and when she finished Percy was the first to speak.

[15] "My dear young lady," he said, "you have been grossly misinformed. I don't know what these works of fiction are that you and Elmer read, but they are as far out of date as Joe Miller's Jest-Book. The stuff that seems to be in them would make even a newspaper editorial writer cough and scratch himself. It may be true that, in the remote era when they appear to have been written, the penalty of a slight and venial slip was as drastic as you say, but I assure you that it is no longer the case. The world is much more humane than it used to be, and much more rational. Just as it no longer burns men for heresy or women for witchcraft, so it has ceased to condemn girls to lives of shame and death in the gutter for the trivial dereliction you acknowledge. If there were time I'd get you some of the more recent books, and point out passages showing how moral principles have changed. The only thing that is frowned on now seems to be getting caught. Otherwise, justice is virtually silent on the subject.

[16] "Inasmuch as your story indicates that no one knows of your crime save your beau, who, if he has learned of your disappearance, is probably scared half to death, I advise you to go home, make some plausible excuse to your pa for lighting out, and resume your care of his cows. At the proper opportunity take your beau to the pastor, and join him in indissoluble love. It is the safe, respectable and hygienic course. Everyone agrees that it is moral, even moralists. Meanwhile, don't forget to thank Miss Nellie. She might have helped you down the primrose way; instead, she has restored you to virtue and happiness, no worse for an interesting experience."

[17] The girl, of course, took in only a small part of this, for Percy's voluptuous style and vocabulary were beyond the grasp of a simple milkmaid. But Miss Nellie, who understood English much better than she spoke it, translated freely, and in a little while the troubled look departed from those blue eyes, and large tears of joy welled from them. Miss Nellie shed a couple herself, and so did all the ladies of the resident faculty, for they had drifted downstairs during the interview, sleepy but curious. The practical Miss Nellie inevitably thought of money, and it turned out that the trip down by milk-train and Peebles' lawful freight of $1 had about exhausted the poor girl's savings, and she had only some odd change left. Percy threw in a dollar and I threw in a dollar, and Miss Nellie not only threw in a third, but ordered one of the ladies to go to the kitchen and prepare a box-lunch for the return to Red Lion.

[18] Sadie the coon had not yet come to work, but Peebles presently bobbed up without being sent for, and toward the end of the afternoon he started off for Union Station with his most amazing passenger, now as full of innocent jubilation as a martyr saved at the stake. As I have said, he embellished the story considerably during the days following, especially in the direction of touching up the girl's pulchritude. The cops, because of their general confidence in him, swallowed his exaggerations, and I heard more than one of them lament that they had missed the chance to handle the case professionally. Percy, in his later years, made two or three attempts to put it into a movie scenario, but the Hays office always vetoed it.

[19] How the girl managed to account to her father for her mysterious flight and quick return I don't know, for she was never heard from afterward. She promised to send Miss Nellie a picture postcard of Red Lion, showing the new hall of the Knights of Pythias, but if it was ever actually mailed it must have been misaddressed, for it never arrived.

FOR REVIEW AND DISCUSSION

Content

1. What makes the girl's decision to enter a "house of ill fame" humorous? Cite specific details from the story.

2. What is the narrator's attitude toward the girl's flight from home, Peebles's history and nature, and Percy's speech to the girl? What makes us aware of the narrator's attitude?

3. Percy's speech is directed toward the girl, whom Percy is trying to help. But does his speech throw light on any other elements in the story?

4. Does the story have a "moral"? What might it be?

Rhetoric

1. The characters speak in ways that distinguish them from each other. Identify the tone, the kinds of expressions (colloquial, euphemistic, learned, and so forth), and other stylistic features that set each character apart.

2. Miss Nellie repeatedly says, "Well, to make a long story short—" but her story just gets longer. How does this "refrain" affect your understanding of and response to Miss Nellie?

3. Are we ever made to feel sorry for the girl, or is her plight merely humorous? What details affect our attitude toward her?

4. What is the relation between how Mencken makes us feel toward the girl and what the themes of the story are?

Classroom Exercises

1. In fiction we often ignore the structure we have been taught to look for in essays. Usually we describe structure by identifying the unity in what we read, by noting how the various elements in the writing share a common purpose. In Mencken's story there are actually several minor lines, or *substories*. Try to sort them out and explain why Mencken would create such a complex structure.

2. We have all known people who talk like Miss Nellie or Percy, people whose speech displays readily identifiable quirks or characteristics. Describe the speech habits of such a person you have known and speculate about the reasons for that person's way of speaking.

CLASSIFICATION

S. I. Hayakawa

CLASSIFICATION

We turn again to S. I. Hayakawa, this time for a discussion of how we use language to name and classify the people and things around us, and how the process of classification influences our attitudes about the world in general. Consider, as you read this selection, how easily and frequently we fall into misclassifying and stereotyping things—how easily we distort reality.

GIVING THINGS NAMES

[1] The figure below shows eight objects, let us say animals, four large and four small, a different four with round heads and another four with square heads, and still another four with curly tails and another four with straight tails. These animals, let us say, are scampering about your village, but since at first they are of no importance to you, you ignore them. You do not even give them a name.

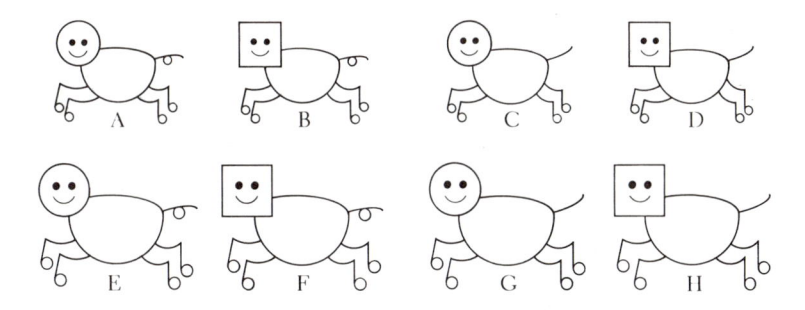

[2] One day, however, you discover that the little ones eat up your grain, while the big ones do not. A differentiation sets itself up, and abstracting the common characteristics of A, B, C, and D, you decide to call these *gogo*; E, F, G, and H you decide to call *gigi*. You chase away the *gogo*, but leave the *gigi* alone. Your neighbor, however, has had a different experience; he finds that those with square heads bite, while those with round heads do not. Abstracting the common characteristics of B, D, F, and H, he calls them *daba*, and A, C, E, and G he calls *dobo*. Still another neighbor discovers, on the other hand, that those with curly tails kill

From *Language in Thought and Action*, Second Edition, by S. I. Hayakawa, copyright © 1964 by Harcourt Brace Jovanovich, Inc. Reprinted by permission of the publishers.

snakes, while those with straight tails do not. He differentiates them, abstracting still another set of common characteristics: A, B, E, and F are *busa*, while C, D, G, and H are *busana*.

[3]   Now imagine that the three of you are together when E runs by. You say, "There goes the *gigi*"; your first neighbor says, "There goes the *dobo*"; your other neighbor says, "There goes the *busa*." Here immediately a great controversy arises. What is it really, a *gigi*, a *dobo*, or a *busa*? What is its *right name*? You are quarreling violently when along comes a fourth person from another village who calls it a *muglock*, an edible animal, as opposed to *uglock*, an inedible animal—which doesn't help matters a bit.

[4]   Of course, the question, "What is it *really*? What is its *right name*?" is a nonsense question. By a nonsense question is meant one that is not capable of being answered. Things can have "right names" only if there is a necessary connection between symbols and things symbolized, and we have seen that there is not. That is to say, in the light of your interest in protecting your grain, it may be necessary for you to distinguish the animal E as a *gigi*; your neighbor, who doesn't like to be bitten, finds it practical to distinguish it as a *dobo*; your other neighbor, who likes to see snakes killed, distinguishes it as a *busa*. What we call things and where we draw the line between one class of things and another depend upon the interests we have and the purposes of the classification. For example, animals are classified in one way by the meat industry, in a different way by the leather industry, in another different way by the fur industry, and in a still different way by the biologist. None of these classifications is any more final than any of the others; each of them is useful for its purpose.

[5]   This holds, of course, for everything we perceive. A table "is" a table to us, because we can understand its relationship to our conduct and interests; we eat at it, work on it, lay things on it. But to a person living in a culture where no tables are used, it may be a very big stool, a small platform, or a meaningless structure. If our culture and upbringing were different, that is to say, our world would not even look the same to us.

[6]   Many of us, for example, cannot distinguish between pickerel, pike, salmon, smelts, perch, crappies, halibut, and mackerel; we say that they are "just fish, and I don't like fish." To a seafood connoisseur, however, these distinctions are real, since they mean the difference to him between one kind of good meal, a very different kind of good meal, or a poor meal. To a zoologist, even finer distinctions become of great importance, since he has other and more general ends in view. When we hear the statement, then, "This fish is a specimen of the pompano, *Trachinotus carolinus*," we accept this as being "true," even if we don't care, not because that is its "right name," but because that is how it is *classified* in the most complete and most general system of classification which people most deeply interested in fish have evolved.

CLASSIFICATION 95

[7] When we name something, then, we are classifying. *The individual object or event we are naming, of course, has no name and belongs to no class until we put it in one.* To illustrate again, suppose that we were to give the *extensional* meaning of the word "Korean." We would have to point to all "Koreans" living at a particular moment and say, "The word 'Korean' denotes at the present moment these persons: $A_1, A_2, A_3 \ldots A_n$." Now, let us say, a child, whom we shall designate as Z, is born among these "Koreans." *The extensional meaning of the word "Korean," determined prior to the existence of Z, does not include Z.* Z is a new individual belonging to no classification, since all classifications were made without taking Z into account. Why, then, is Z also a "Korean?" *Because we say so.* And, saying so—fixing the classification—we have determined to a considerable extent future attitudes toward Z. For example, Z will always have certain rights in Korea; he will always be regarded in other nations as an "alien" and will be subject to laws applicable to "aliens."

[8] In matters of "race" and "nationality," the way in which classifications work is especially apparent. For example, the present writer is by birth a "Canadian," by "race" a "Japanese," and is now an "American." Although he was legally admitted to the United States on a Canadian passport as a "nonquota immigrant," he was unable to apply for American citizenship until after 1952. According to American immigration law (since 1952 as well as before), a Canadian entering the United States as a permanent resident has no trouble getting in, unless he happens to be of Oriental extraction, in which case his "nationality" becomes irrelevant and he is classified by "race." If the quota for his "race"—for example, Japanese—is filled (and it usually is), and if he cannot get himself classified as a non-quota immigrant, he is not able to get in at all. Are all these classifications "real"? Of course they are, and *the effect that each of them has upon what he may and may not do constitutes their "reality."*

[9] The writer has spent his entire life, except for short visits abroad, in Canada and the United States. He speaks Japanese haltingly, with a child's vocabulary and an American accent; he does not read or write it. Nevertheless, because classifications seem to have a kind of hypnotic power over some people, he is occasionally credited with (or accused of) having an "Oriental mind." Since Buddha, Confucius, General Tojo, Mao Tse-tung, Pandit Nehru, Syngman Rhee, and the proprietor of the Golden Pheasant Chop Suey House all have "Oriental minds," it is difficult to know whether to feel complimented or insulted.

[10] When is a person a "Negro"? By the definition accepted in the United States, any person with even a small amount of "Negro blood"—that is, whose parents or ancestors were classified as "Negroes"—is a "Negro." *It would be exactly as justifiable to say that any person with even a small amount of "white blood" is "white."* Why do they say one rather than the other? Because the former system of classification *suits the purposes of those making the classification.* Classification is not a matter of identifying "essences," as is widely believed. It is simply a reflection of

social convenience and necessity—and different necessities are always producing different classifications.

[11] There are few complexities about classifications at the level of dogs and cats, knives and forks, cigarettes and candy, but when it comes to classifications at high levels of abstraction—for example, those describing conduct, social institutions, philosophical and moral problems—serious difficulties occur. When one person kills another, is it an act of murder, an act of temporary insanity, an act of homicide, an accident, or an act of heroism? As soon as the process of classification is completed, our attitudes and our conduct are to a considerable degree determined. We hang the murderer, we lock up the insane man, we free the victim of circumstances, we pin a medal on the hero.

THE BLOCKED MIND

[12] Unfortunately, people are not always aware of the way in which they arrive at their classifications. Unaware of those characteristics of the extensional Mr. Miller not covered by classifying him as "a Jew," and attributing to Mr. Miller all the characteristics *suggested* by the affective connotations of the term with which he has been classified, they pass final judgment on Mr. Miller by saying, "Well, a Jew's a Jew. There's no getting around that!"

[13] We need not concern ourselves here with the injustices done to "Jews," "Roman Catholics," "Republicans," "redheads," "chorus girls," "sailors," "Brass-hats," "Southerners," "Yankees," "school teachers," "government regulations," "socialistic proposals," and so on, by such hasty judgments or, as it is better to call them, fixed reactions. "Hasty judgments" suggests that such errors can be avoided by thinking more slowly; this, of course, is not the case, for some people think very slowly with no better results. What we are concerned with is the way in which we block the development of our own minds by such automatic reactions.

[14] To continue with our example of the people who say, "A Jew's a Jew. There's no getting around that!"—they are, as we have seen, confusing the denoted, extensional Jew with the fictitious "Jew" inside their heads. Such persons, the reader will have observed, can usually be made to admit, on being reminded of certain "Jews" whom they admire—perhaps Albert Einstein, perhaps Associate Justice Arthur Goldberg, perhaps Jascha Heifetz, perhaps Mort Sahl—that "there are exceptions, of course." They have been compelled by experience, that is to say, to take cognizance of at least a few of the multitude of "Jews" who do not fit their preconceptions. At this point, however, they continue triumphantly, "But exceptions only prove the rule!"[1]—which is another way of saying, "Facts don't count."

---

[1] This extraordinarily fatuous saying originally meant, "The exception *tests* the rule"—*Enceptio probat regulam*. This older meaning of the word "prove" survives in such an expression as "automobile proving ground."

[15] The writer, who lives in Marin County, California, once attended hearings at the county court house concerning a proposed ordinance to forbid racial discrimination in the rental and sale of housing. (Such discrimination in Marin is chiefly directed against Negroes.) He was impressed by the fact that a large majority of those who rose to speak were in favor of the ordinance; but he was also impressed by the number who, though maintaining that they counted Negroes among their best and most admired friends, still spoke heatedly against a law that would, by forbidding racial discrimination in the sale and rental of housing, enable Negroes to live anywhere in the county. Presumably, all the Negroes whom they loved and admired were "exceptions," and the stereotyped "Negro" remained in their heads in spite of their experience.

[16] People like this may be said to be impervious to new information. They continue to vote for their party *label*, no matter what mistakes their party makes. They continue to object to "socialists," no matter what the socialists propose. They continue to regard "mothers" as sacred, no matter which mother. A woman who had been given up both by physicians and psychiatrists as hopelessly insane was being considered by a committee whose task it was to decide whether or not she should be committed to an asylum. One member of the committee doggedly refused to vote for commitment. "Gentlemen," he said in tones of deepest reverence, "you must remember that this woman is, after all, a mother."[2] Similarly such people continue to hate "Protestants," no matter which Protestant. Unaware of characteristics left out in the process of classification, they overlook, when the term "Republican" is applied to the party of Abraham Lincoln, the party of Warren Harding, the party of Herbert Hoover, and the party of Dwight Eisenhower, the rather important differences between them.

COW$_1$ IS NOT COW$_2$

[17] How do we prevent ourselves from getting into such intellectual blind alleys, or, finding we are in one, how do we get out again? One way is to remember that practically all statements in ordinary conversation, debate, and public controversy taking the form, "Republicans are Republicans," "Business is business," "Boys will be boys," "Women drivers are women drivers," and so on, are *not true*. Let us put one of these back into a context in life.

> "I don't think we should go through with this deal, Bill. Is it altogether fair to the railroad company?"
> "Aw, forget it! *Business is business*, after all."

Such an assertion, although it looks like a "simple statement of fact," is not simple and is not a statement of fact. The first "business" *denotes* transaction under discus-

---

[2] One wonders how this committee member would have felt about Elizabeth Duncan, executed for murder in San Quentin in 1962, whose possessive love of her son led her to hire assassins to kill her pregnant daughter-in-law.

sion; the second "business" invokes the *connotations* of the word. The sentence is a *directive*, saying, "Let us treat this transaction with complete disregard for considerations other than profit, as the word 'business' suggests." Similarly, when a father tries to excuse the mischief done by his sons, he says, "Boys will be boys"; in other words, "Let us regard the actions of my sons with that indulgent amusement customarily extended toward those whom we call 'boys,' " though the angry neighbor will say, of course, "Boys, my eye! They're little hoodlums; that's what they are!" These too are not informative statements but directives, directing us to classify the object or event under discussion in given ways, in order that we may feel or act in the ways suggested by the terms of the classification.

[18] There is a simple technique for preventing such directives from having their harmful effect on our thinking. It is the suggestion made by Korzybski that we add "index numbers" to our terms, thus; $Englishman_1$, $Englishman_2$, $Englishman_3$, . . .; cow_1, cow_2, cow_3, . . .; $Frenchman_1$, $Frenchman_2$, $Frenchman_3$, . . . ; $communist_1$, $communist_2$, $communist_3$, . . . The terms of the classification tell us what the individuals in that class have in common; *the index numbers remind us of the characteristics left out*. A rule can then be formulated as a general guide in all our thinking and reading: *Cow_1 is not cow_2, Jew_1 is not Jew_2, $politician_1$ is not $politician_2$, and so on*. This rule, if remembered, prevents us from confusing levels of abstraction and forces us to consider the facts on those occasions when we might otherwise find ourselves leaping to conclusions which we might later have cause to regret.

"TRUTH"

[19] Most intellectual problems are, ultimately, problems of classification and nomenclature. Some years ago there was a dispute between the American Medical Association and the Antitrust Division of the Department of Justice as to whether the practice of medicine was a "profession" or "trade." The American Medical Association *wanted* immunity from laws prohibiting "restraint of trade"; therefore, it insisted that medicine *is* a "profession." The Antitrust Division *wanted* to stop certain economic practices connected with medicine, and therefore it insisted that medicine *is* a "trade." Partisans of either side accused the other of perverting the meanings of words and of not being able to understand plain English.

[20] Can farmers operate oil wells and still be "farmers"? In 1947 the attorney general of the state of Kansas sued to dissolve a large agricultural cooperative, Consumers Cooperative Association, charging that the corporation, in owning oil wells, refineries, and pipe-lines, was exceeding the statutory privileges of purchasing cooperatives under the Cooperative Marketing Act, which permits such organizations to "engage in any activity in connection with manufacturing, selling, or supplying to its members machinery, equipment or supplies." The attorney general

held that the cooperative, under the Act, could not handle, let alone process and manufacture, general farm supplies, but only those supplies used in the marketing operation. The Kansas Supreme Court decided unanimously in favor of the defendant (CCA). In so deciding, the court held that gasoline and oil *are* "farm supplies," and producing crude oil *is* "part of the business of farming." The decision which thus enlarged the definition of "farming" read,

> This court will take judicial notice of the fact that in the present state of the art of farming, gasoline . . . is one of the costliest items in the production of agricultural commodities. . . . Anyway, gasoline and tractors are here, and this court is not going to say that motor fuel is not a supply necessary to carrying on of farm operations. . . . Indeed it is about as well put as can be on Page 18 of the state's Exhibit C where the defendant (CCA) says: "*Producing crude oil, operating pipe-lines and refineries, are also part of the business of farming. It is merely producing synthetic hay for iron horses. It is 'off-the-farm farming' which the farmer, in concert with his neighbors, is carrying on.* . . . Production of power farming equipment, then, is logically an extension of the farmers' own farming operations." (Italics supplied.)

[21] Is a harmonica player a "musician"? Until 1948, the American Federation of Musicians had ruled that the harmonica was a "toy." Professional harmonica players usually belonged, therefore, to the American Guild of Variety Artists. Even as distinguished a musician as Larry Adler, who has often played the harmonica as a solo instrument with symphony orchestras, was by the union's definition "not a musician." In 1948, however, the AFM, finding that harmonica players were getting popular and competing with members of the union, decided that they were "musicians" after all—a decision that did not sit well with the president of AGVA, who promptly declared jurisdictional war on the AFM.[3]

[22] Thurman Arnold tells of another instance of a problem in classification:

> A plaster company was scraping gypsum from the surface of the ground. If it was a mine, it paid one tax; if a manufacturing company, it paid another. Expert witnesses were called who almost came to blows, such was their disgust at the stupidity of those who could not see that the process was essentially mining, or manufacturing. A great record was built up to be reviewed by the State Supreme Court on this important question of "fact."[4]

[23] Is aspirin a "drug" or not? In some states, it is legally classified as a "drug," and therefore it can be sold only by licensed pharmacists. If people want to be able to buy aspirin in groceries, lunchrooms, and pool halls (as they can in other states), they must have it reclassified as "not a drug."

[24] Is medicine a "profession" or a "trade"? Is the production of crude oil "a part of farming"? Is a harmonica player a "musician"? Is aspirin a "drug"? Such ques-

---

[3] "The S.F. Police Dept. Bagpipe Band . . . will soon be decked out in the traditional finery of bagpipers. Pan-Am is flying over from Scotland twenty-one uniforms. . . . The pipers, by the way, don't have to belong to the Musicians Union since the bagpipe is classified as 'an instrument of war.' Has there ever been any doubt?" Herb Caen in the San Francisco *Chronicle.*
[4] *The Folklore of Capitalism* (1938), p. 182.

tions are commonly settled by appeals to dictionaries to discover the "real meanings" of the words involved. It is also common practice to consult past legal decisions and all kinds of learned treatises bearing on the subject. The decision finally rests, however, not upon appeals to past authority, but upon *what people want*. If they want the AMA to be immune from antitrust action, they will go to the Supreme Court if necessary to get medicine "defined" as a "profession." If they want the AMA prosecuted, they will get a decision that it is a "trade." (They got, in this case, a decision from the Court that it did not matter whether the practice of medicine was a "trade" or not; what mattered was that the AMA had, as charged, *restrained* the trade of Group Health Association, Inc., a cooperative which procured medical services for its members. The antitrust action was upheld.)

[25] If people want agricultural cooperatives to operate oil wells, they will get the courts to define the activity in such a way as to make it possible. If the public doesn't care, the decision whether a harmonica player is or is not a "musician" will be made by the stronger trade union. The question whether aspirin is or is not a "drug" will be decided neither by finding the dictionary definition of "drug" nor by staring long and hard at an aspirin tablet. It will be decided on the basis of where and under what conditions people want to buy their aspirin.

[26] In any case, society as a whole ultimately gets, on all issues of wide public importance, the classifications it wants, even if it has to wait until all the members of the Supreme Court are dead and an entirely new court is appointed. When the desired decision is handed down, people say, "Truth has triumphed." *In short, society regards as "true" those systems of classification that produce the desired results.*

[27] The scientific test of "truth," like the social test, is strictly practical, except for the fact that the "desired results" are more severely limited. The results desired by society may be irrational, superstitious, selfish, or humane, but the results desired by scientists are only that our systems of classification produce predictable results. Classifications, as amply indicated already, determine our attitudes and behavior toward the object or event classified. When lightning was classified as "evidence of divine wrath," no courses of action other than prayer were suggested to prevent one's being struck by lightning. As soon, however, as it was classified as "electricity," Benjamin Franklin achieved a measure of control over it by his invention of the lightning rod. Certain physical disorders were formerly classified as "demonic possession," and this suggested that we "drive the demons out" by whatever spells or incantations we could think of. The results were uncertain. But when those disorders were classified as "bacillus infections," courses of action were suggested that led to more predictable results.

[28] Science seeks only the *most general useful systems* of classification; these it regards for the time being, until more useful classifications are invented, as "true."

FOR REVIEW AND DISCUSSION

Content

1. What does Hayakawa mean when he says that "What is it *really*?" and "What is its *right name*?" are nonsense questions?

2. We sometimes think that scientific systems of classification are true because we know that scientists are said to be objective, to conduct their studies without injecting personal bias. According to Hayakawa, is there any truth in scientific systems? Do you think that there can ever be true systems of classification?

3. In what ways are classification systems beneficial? Illustrate your answer by discussing a specific system.

4. Explain Hayakawa's contention that "most intellectual problems are, ultimately, problems of classification and nomenclature."

Rhetoric

1. Numerous examples accompany the points Hayakawa makes in this essay. Are all examples useful? Are there more examples presented than are needed? Support your answer with references to specific passages in the essay.

2. Hayakawa refers to himself in several sections of the essay. Why might he have done this? How is your attitude toward him affected by his use of personal anecdotes?

Classroom Exercises

1. Hayakawa asserts that questions of classification rest "upon what people want." What purposes—good or bad—do you detect in some systems presently used to classify people? To classify types of work? To classify types of food?

2. What experiences can you recall in which someone else's classification system was forced upon you, but you could not make use of it? For instance, you may have been asked whether you like *cold* sandwiches more than you like *hot* sandwiches, only to find that you could not answer the question because you do not value sandwiches according to their temperature.

When confronted with a classification system you could not use, did you try to replace it with a useful one of your own? If you did, what response did the first system's user have to yours?

3. One way to classify people is, of course, by race. Another is by sex. What other ways are there? Develop your own classification system for people. What are the rationale and purpose of your system?

Peter Woolfson

LANGUAGE, THOUGHT, AND CULTURE

It is one thing for us to understand that others see the world differently than we do (such differences are apparent enough even among the closest of family and friends). It is quite another thing to understand that our language actually shapes our perception of reality, and that people of other cultures and languages may perceive reality in profoundly different ways. Peter Woolfson's essay examines these second kinds of differences within the framework of the controversial "Sapir-Whorf hypothesis." As you read Woolfson, try to imagine yourself belonging to some of the other cultures he discusses—it won't be easy.

[1]   Psycholinguists and linguistic anthropologists share a common concern with the relationship between language and thought. Several questions have been raised about this relationship, but the dominant one can be stated very simply: does the language we speak determine the way we think? One well-known attempt to answer the question is the *linguistic relativity hypothesis* (also called the Sapir-Whorf hypothesis or the Whorfian hypothesis).[1] In essence, the hypothesis suggests that a given language, especially in its grammar, provides its speakers with habitual grooves of expression which predispose these speakers to see the world in ready-made patterns. Since grammars vary from language to language, it is likely that the habitual patterns of thought vary from language to language. If so, the world view of a speaker of a particular language will be different from the world view of a speaker of a different language. Although the hypothesis seems to affirm the view that language determines thought, one should remember that it concentrates on habitual patterns; and habitual patterns may be ignored or circumvented. What is necessary is that we become aware of these patterns by conscious introspection, scientific study, or cross-cultural comparison.

[2]   Why are habitual patterns of expression so important? We all have approximately the same set of physical organs for perceiving reality—eyes to see, ears to hear, noses to smell, tongues to taste, and skins to feel. Reality should be the same for us all. Our nervous systems, however, are being bombarded by a continual flow of sensations of different kinds, intensities, and durations. It is obvious that all of these sensations do not reach our consciousness; some kind of filtering system

---

[1] Benjamin L. Whorf, *Language, Thought, and Reality,* ed. J. B. Carroll (New York: John Wiley & Sons, 1964).

Copyright 1972 by Peter Woolfson. Reprinted by permission of the author.

LANGUAGE, THOUGHT, AND CULTURE

reduces them to manageable proportions. The Whorfian hypothesis suggests that the filtering system is one's language. Our language, in effect, provides us with a special pair of glasses that heightens certain perceptions and dims others. Thus, while all sensations are received by the nervous system, only some are brought to the level of consciousness. One of Whorf's classic examples, *snow*, illustrates the role of language in this process:

> We have the same word for falling snow, snow on the ground, snow packed hard like ice, slushy snow, wind-driven flying snow—whatever the situation may be. To an Eskimo, this all-inclusive word would be almost unthinkable; he would say that falling snow, slushy snow, and so on, are sensually and operationally different, different things to contend with; he uses different words for them and for other kinds of snow. The Aztecs go even farther than we in the opposite direction with "cold," "ice," and "snow" all represented by the same basic word. . . .[2]

[3] Although Whorf demonstrated that different languages use words differently to classify reality, he also indicated by his techniques of illustration that these concepts can be expressed, in a language that lacks them, by other means. Thus, the different types of snow may be described by adjectival words and phrases. Using these alternatives in English grammar, he makes it possible for us to visualize the different types of snow and to perceive the differences among them. Because the differences are specifically labeled, we become conscious of them. The important point to remember is that we are not *habitually conscious* of these distinctions. But if it becomes necessary for us to perceive these distinctions, as a skier might with snow, then they would become conscious, and the vocabulary or descriptive items would follow. In the case of the skier, he borrows his terms for snow from the more specialized vocabulary of the Austrians.

[4] *Snow*, however, is an example of a word with obvious cultural and environmental emphases. In many instances the relationship between cultural emphasis and vocabulary is much less apparent. For example, Americans are a mobile people and transportation plays an extremely important role culturally in our society. And yet we use the word *go* whether we are going by foot, car, train, or plane. Germans, on the other hand, use *gehen* when they go by foot, and *fahren* when they go by vehicle. The Navaho, according to Kluckholn and Leighton, make an even more complex set of distinctions:

> When a Navaho says that he went somewhere he never fails to specify whether it was afoot, astride, by wagon, auto, train, or airplane. This is done partly by using different verb stems which indicate whether the traveler moved under his own steam or was transported, partly by naming the actual means. . . .
> Moreover the Navaho language insists upon another type of splitting of the generic idea of "going" to which German is as indifferent as English. The Navaho always differentiates between starting to go, going along, arriving at, returning from a point. . . .[3]

---

[2] Whorf, p. 216.
[3] Clyde Kluckhohn and Dorothea Leighton, *The Navaho* (New York: Doubleday & Company, 1962), pp. 274–75.

And so, although transportation is a major cultural emphasis in American society, our word *go* is certainly considerably less precise than the terms used by the Navaho for this activity. It becomes apparent, then, that even when an activity has considerable cultural emphasis, certain perceptions may be heightened by the language while others may remain dim.

[5]   Does having separate words for different aspects of a thing or an event really make a difference in our consciousness, our awareness? For example, we commonly make distinctions between the colors *purple, blue, green, yellow, orange,* and *red*. If we have special interests like painting or dress designing, we may have a much wider vocabulary which includes distinctions between shades such as "cerise," "burgundy," or "magenta." These distinctions, however, are not part of the ordinary vocabulary of the American male, for instance. Investigations show that other languages are more restricted in their color vocabulary than English. The Shona of Rhodesia have only three major terms: *cips^{w}uka* (orange, red, purple and some blue); *citema* (blue and some green); and *cicena* (green and yellow). The Bassa of Liberia have only two major color terms: *hui* which represents purple, blue, and green; and *zīza* which represents yellow, orange, and red.[4] In one sense, these more restricted vocabularies do not affect consciousness. If the speaker of one of these languages finds it necessary to make color distinctions not indicated by his color terms, he can still express the distinction by using the objects in the environment— "that's leaf *citema*" or "that's sky *citema*," for example. On the other hand, psycholinguists like Lantz, Brown, and Lenneberg have shown that having a number of terms for color distinctions is particularly useful for remembering colors that have been seen at an earlier time.[5] The more color terms the subjects in these experiments had, the better their memories were for sorting out the colors they had seen. These examples show that there is a relationship between vocabulary, cultural emphasis, and habitual consciousness.

[6]   But does the language of a speaker provide him with a structure for seeing the world in ready-made patterns? In other words, is the Whorfian hypothesis valid? It should be obvious that the Whorfian hypothesis is just that, a hypothesis: an idea to be tested, an informed guess. In spite of numerous attempts at verification, it has never been satisfactorily proved or disproved. But it remains plausible. For example, the grammatical categories of singular and plural are important ones in English grammar, so important that they are expressed redundantly:

> One boy goes outside.
> Two boys go outside.

Plurality, in these examples, is reiterated by the use of a number word, a noun suffix, and a specific verbal form. Singular and plural are categories that can hardly

---

[4] H. A. Gleason, Jr., *An Introduction to Descriptive Linguistics*, rev. ed. (New York: Holt, Rinehart and Winston, 1961), pp. 4–5.
[5] Joseph DeVito, *The Psychology of Speech and Language* (New York: Random House, 1970), p. 200.

LANGUAGE, THOUGHT, AND CULTURE

be ignored. A speaker of English finds it natural to divide his universe into things that are either singular or plural. To a speaker of Taos, an American Indian language, however, this view would represent a gross oversimplification. According to Trager:

> ... In the Taos linguistic universe there is no such simple distinction: some things are indeed unitary, and others are multiple, but some unitary things can be multiple only in sets, while others are multiple as aggregates: moreover, a set can be unitary, if it is inanimate, or it can be multiple—but then only if it is animate. . . .[6]

Thus, the Taos Indian classifies the objects in his universe differently from a native speaker of English. The Whorfian hypothesis suggests that because of this difference in classification, the Taos Indian actually sees the world differently from a native speaker of English.

[7] The apparent relationship between grammar and world view can be seen in the basic types of sentence structures. Probably the most typical kind of sentence in English is the declarative sentence made up of a subject, verb, and direct object and associated with our conceptual focus of an actor, an action, and the object of an action. For example, the answer to the question "What happened?" could be either

John	*dropped*	*the ball*
Subject	Verb	Direct Object
Actor	Action	Object of Action

or

The car	*hit*	*the bridge*
Subject	Verb	Direct Object
Actor	Action	Object of Action

This sentence form is so common in English that we use the form metaphorically without being the least bit conscious of imposing the form "actor, action, object of action" where it does not literally apply. As a result, English commonly produces sentences such as:

Communism	*threatens*	*Southeast Asia*
Subject	Verb	Direct Object
Actor	Action	Object of Action

Northern Chinese, however, does not ordinarily use this kind of sentence structure. If one asked a speaker of Chinese the equivalent of the question "What happened?" he would probably get the answer in the form of *topic* and *comment*. In other words, where the American would say, "John dropped the ball," the Chinese would say, "Ball-particle (type of object)-dropping." It is not necessary for the Chinese to indicate the actor or the time of the action. Speakers of English, in contrast, specify whether the action was in the past or not. However, they do have a sentence form

---

[6] George L. Trager, *Languages of the World* (Buffalo, New York: unpublished manuscript), IV, 17.

where the actor is not specified: subject and passive verb: "The ball was dropped." Nevertheless, many speakers of English feel uneasy about this construction; it does not appear complete. Since only two of the three habitual components are present, they feel compelled to ask, "Dropped by whom?" In short, Americans and Chinese have different basic sentence structures which focus on different aspects of a situation.[7]

[8]   In order to deal systematically with the question of the validity of the Whorfian hypothesis, it is necessary to ask several other questions. First, is thought possible without speech? If it is, then at least some perceptions are possible without the mediation of language. Studies of animal behavior suggest some answers. W. H. Thorpe, an ethologist, maintains that all animals perceive—that is, anticipate and recognize. He writes, "Some essential ability to deal with events in time as in space is, by definition, to be expected throughout the world of living things."[8] For example, when a cat runs up a tree after seeing a dog, he exhibits this ability. The cat sees the dog (perception); it identifies the dog as dangerous (cognition); it foresees trouble (anticipation); it quickly checks its environment (evaluation); and it runs up the nearest tree (resolution). The cat does all this without the aid of language, and therefore it seems reasonable to assume that we are capable of some processes of thought without the mediation of language.

[9]   Second, are the grammars of various languages really different? Do not all languages possess features in common? Is there not a universal grammar, a general grammar of human languages? Are not the differences between languages, in reality, superficial, of little consequence in determining man's perceptions of reality? Let us look at the kinds of language universals that have been identified by Charles Hockett and Joseph Greenberg. Hockett[9] outlines thirteen design features of language, such as *semanticity* (shared associations), *arbitrariness* (noniconicity), and *productivity* (open-endedness). Greenberg[10] discusses such universals as *multimodality: indicative mode* (statement) and *imperative mode* (command), for example. There are, to be sure, very broad and general, universal statements about language that can be made to which no exceptions can be found. However, it is equally true that the grammars of the languages of the world show considerable variety in the devices they employ to classify reality. It is this level of classification, dissection, and organization, the level of diversity rather than universality, with which Whorf's linguistic relativity hypothesis is concerned.

[10]   Third, what effect does culture—learned and shared behavior patterns—have on the way we perceive the world? Although language is our principal means of

---

[7] Charles F. Hockett, *A Course in Modern Linguistics* (New York: The Macmillan Company, 1958), pp. 201–03.
[8] W. H. Thorpe, *Learning and Instinct in Animals* (Cambridge, Mass.: Harvard Univ. Press, 1958), p. 4.
[9] Charles Hockett, "The Origin of Speech," *American Scientist*, 203 (1960), 89–96.
[10] Joseph Greenberg, *Anthropological Linguistics* (New York: Random House, 1968).

transmitting culture from generation to generation, much of our learning, especially while we are young, takes place without explicit verbalizations: that is, much of our behavior is learned informally through observation and imitation. All kinds of sensory data may be used to recognize, classify, anticipate, and evaluate experiences. For example, a child whose first experiences of life take place within a single-roomed structure such as an igloo, tipi, or tent develops a sense of reality which is quite different from the child whose early experiences take place in a multi-partitioned structure in which his own place, the nursery, is safely insulated from the adult experiences around him. The different settings, themselves, affect the child's image of self, his relationship to others, to events, and to things. Thus culture provides many avenues for developing our perception of reality.

[11] In spite of these questions, social scientists have attempted to devise tests for verifying the Whorfian hypothesis. One major consideration in such testing has been the nature of Whorf's evidence. Frequently, he named a grammatical device in one language and a different device for handling a similar situation in another language, and assumed that the difference demonstrated a difference in perception. This assumption is not necessarily valid. For example, French classifies all nouns as either masculine or feminine—*le soleil,* "the sun," is masculine, but *la lune,* "the moon," is feminine. Despite this classification, the Frenchman does not actually perceive these gender distinctions as real; they are simply grammatical devices. Whatever relationships these classifications once had with reality are now very remote.

[12] In an attempt to provide a more defensible way of verifying the hypothesis, social scientists began to look for non-verbal behavioral concomitants for linguistic categories. One test, given by John Carroll, involved showing English and Hopi subjects three pictures from which they were to select the two that they felt were most alike. The pictures were based on differences in the way objects are handled. For example, one series of pictures showed three men, one unloading a carton of fruit, one spilling milk, and one dropping a coin. English subjects most often grouped the accidental actions, whereas the Hopi grouped the first two because words in their language for these actions are similar.[11]

[13] Another experiment, conducted by Joseph Casagrande, involved Navaho and English-speaking children:

> Navaho and English-speaking children were presented with two objects which differed from each other in both form and color, for example, a blue stick and a yellow rope. They were then shown a third object which matched one of the original objects in color and the other in form, for example, a blue rope. They were asked to select one of the two original objects which best matched this third object. A number of such sets were used and the results confirmed the hypothesis. Navaho children, in the example cited above, selected the yellow rope, whereas English-speaking children selected the blue stick.[12]

[11] DeVito, p. 205.
[12] DeVito, p. 206.

[14] When middle-class English-speaking children in metropolitan Boston were given the same test, however, there were unexpected results.[13] They made choices similar to those of the Navaho children. Apparently, the Boston children were accustomed to having "creative" toys to play with, toys that involve the child in manipulating objects. Certainly the results achieved in Boston weaken the conclusiveness of the original experiment. An additional problem with the validity of these tests is that they are designed to show relationships between language and behavior on a relatively concrete level, and the selection of a yellow rope or a blue stick hardly qualifies as an example of philosophical orientation. In reality, the Whorfian hypothesis has most relevance in the areas that are most difficult to pin down: philosophy, religion, ethics, and values. Behavioral concomitants on this level are difficult to find and test.

[15] Another difficulty in testing the Whorfian hypothesis is that of controlling variables. Ideally, tests should be conducted on subjects whose backgrounds include a unilingual-unicultural environment. Unfortunately, the kind of geographic and cultural isolation necessary for this kind of environment is very rare. The modern world is one that fosters cultures which are multilingual and languages which are multicultural.

[16] In the final analysis, Whorf's linguistic relativity hypothesis will probably remain only a hypothesis. But this does not mean that we should abandon it as a useful tool. On the contrary, by comparing patterns of grammatical usage—becoming conscious of them, studying them, and evaluating them—we will gain insights into the categories our language forces us to pay attention to, the ideas that are easy for us to express, and the ideas that are difficult to voice. We can, as Whorf put it, turn background into foreground. Thus, both science and man are served.

FOR REVIEW AND DISCUSSION

Content

1. "Does having separate words for different aspects of a thing or an event really make a difference in our consciousness, our awareness?" The question is Woolfson's. How does he answer it?

2. Woolfson asks if thought is possible without speech. He then describes a cat's process of thinking about a dog, a process completed without, we can assume, the help of language. Is Woolfson suggesting that a cat's thought is similar to or the same as human thought? What does Woolfson mean by *thought*? Is his meaning clear?

3. Why does Woolfson stress the idea of our not being "habitually conscious" of certain linguistic distinctions?

---

[13] John B. Carroll and Joseph B. Casagrande, "The Function of Language Classifications in Behavior," *Communication and Culture*, ed. Alfred Smith (New York: Holt, Rinehart & Winston, 1966), pp. 503–04.

Rhetoric

1. Woolfson frequently begins paragraphs with direct questions—a technique that often marks a writer as amateurish and unskillful. Can you see any useful rhetorical purpose for Woolfson's questions?

2. Woolfson neither totally accepts nor rejects the Sapir-Whorf hypothesis. How would you describe his attitude toward it? What makes his attitude apparent?

Classroom Exercises

1. Review Woolfson's discussion of typical English and North Chinese sentence structures, and try to imagine yourself as part of a culture whose language tends to describe events without attributing their causes, a culture in which patterns of perception are less bound by the subject-verb-object structure than are most English sentences. Then write, in North Chinese sentence structures, a paragraph describing an event. Can you express all that you wish to express? Does the event "change" in your mind as you try to translate it from English thought to North Chinese thought?

2. Imagine yourself looking at modern American culture from the viewpoint of a nonnative speaker of English. What clusters of words in American English might reflect conditions peculiar to our culture or environment, much in the same way as the Eskimos' many words for snow reflect its special significance for them?

FOR FURTHER READING

Benjamin Lee Whorf

SCIENCE AND LINGUISTICS

This selection provides an excellent overview of Whorf's theories about language, thought, and culture. As you read Whorf, weigh his powers of description, analysis, and persuasion against those of his interpreter and critic, Peter Woolfson. Which writer do you find more convincing?

[1] Every normal person in the world, past infancy in years, can and does talk. By virtue of that fact, every person—civilized or uncivilized—carries through life certain naïve but deeply rooted ideas about talking and its relation to thinking. Because of their firm connection with speech habits that have become unconscious and automatic, these notions tend to be rather intolerant of opposition. They are by no means entirely personal and haphazard; their basis is definitely systematic, so

From *Technology Review* 42 (April 1940): 229–31, 247–48. Reprinted by permission of the publisher.

that we are justified in calling them a system of natural logic—a term that seems to me preferable to the term common sense, often used for the same thing.

[2] According to natural logic, the fact that every person has talked fluently since infancy makes every man his own authority on the process by which he formulates and communicates. He has merely to consult a common substratum of logic or reason which he and everyone else are supposed to possess. Natural logic says that talking is merely an incidental process concerned strictly with communication, not with formulation of ideas. Talking, or the use of language, is supposed only to "express" what is essentially already formulated nonlinguistically. Formulation is an independent process, called thought or thinking, and is supposed to be largely indifferent to the nature of particular languages. Languages have grammars, which are assumed to be merely norms of conventional and social correctness, but the use of language is supposed to be guided not so much by them as by correct, rational, or intelligent THINKING.

[3] Thought, in this view, does not depend on grammar but on laws of logic or reason which are supposed to be the same for all observers of the universe—to represent a rationale in the universe that can be "found" independently by all intelligent observers, whether they speak Chinese or Choctaw. In our own culture, the formulations of mathematics and of formal logic have acquired the reputation of dealing with this order of things: i.e., with the realm and laws of pure thought. Natural logic holds that different languages are essentially parallel methods for expressing this one-and-the-same rationale of thought and, hence, differ really in but minor ways which may seem important only because they are seen at close range. It holds that mathematics, symbolic logic, philosophy, and so on are systems contrasted with language which deal directly with this realm of thought, not that they are themselves specialized extensions of language. The attitude of natural logic

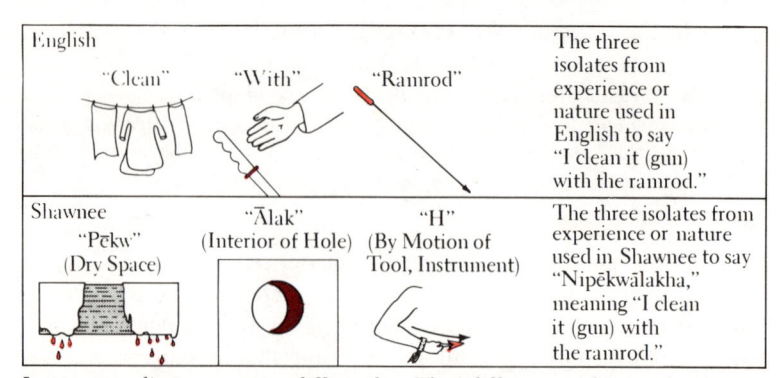

English			The three isolates from experience or nature used in English to say "I clean it (gun) with the ramrod."
"Clean"	"With"	"Ramrod"	
Shawnee	"Ālak"	"H"	The three isolates from experience or nature used in Shawnee to say "Nipēkwālakha," meaning "I clean it (gun) with the ramrod."
"Pēkw" (Dry Space)	(Interior of Hole)	(By Motion of Tool, Instrument)	

Languages dissect nature differently. The different isolates of meaning (thoughts) used by English and Shawnee in reporting the same experience, that of cleaning a gun by running the ramrod through it. The pronouns 'I' and 'it' are not shown by symbols, as they have the same meaning in each language. In Shawnee ni- equals 'I'; -a equals 'it.'

SCIENCE AND LINGUISTICS

is well shown in an old quip about a German grammarian who devoted his whole life to the study of the dative case. From the point of view of natural logic, the dative case and grammar in general are an extremely minor issue. A different attitude is said to have been held by the ancient Arabians: Two princes, so the story goes, quarreled over the honor of putting on the shoes of the most learned grammarian of the realm; whereupon their father, the caliph, is said to have remarked that it was the glory of his kingdom that great grammarians were honored even above kings.

[4] The familiar saying that the exception proves the rule contains a good deal of wisdom, though from the standpoint of formal logic it became an absurdity as soon as "prove" no longer meant "put on trial." The old saw began to be profound psychology from the time it ceased to have standing in logic. What it might well suggest to us today is that, if a rule has absolutely no exceptions, it is not recognized as a rule or as anything else; it is then part of the background of experience of which we tend to remain unconscious. Never having experienced anything in contrast to it, we cannot isolate it and formulate it as a rule until we so enlarge our experience and expand our base of reference that we encounter an interruption of its regularity. The situation is somewhat analogous to that of not missing the water till the well runs dry, or not realizing that we need air till we are choking.

[5] For instance, if a race of people had the physiological defect of being able to see only the color blue, they would hardly be able to formulate the rule that they saw only blue. The term blue would convey no meaning to them, their language would lack color terms, and their words denoting their various sensations of blue would answer to, and translate, our words "light, dark, white, black," and so on, not our word "blue." In order to formulate the rule or norm of seeing only blue, they would need exceptional moments in which they saw other colors. The phenomenon of gravitation forms a rule without exceptions; needless to say, the untutored person is utterly unaware of any law of gravitation, for it would never enter his head to conceive of a universe in which bodies behaved otherwise than they do at the earth's surface. Like the color blue with our hypothetical race, the law of gravitation is a part of the untutored individual's background, not something he isolates from that background. The law could not be formulated until bodies that always fell were seen in terms of a wider astronomical world in which bodies moved in orbits or went this way and that.

[6] Similarly, whenever we turn our heads, the image of the scene passes across our retinas exactly as it would if the scene turned around us. But this effect is background, and we do not recognize it; we do not see a room turn around us but are conscious only of having turned our heads in a stationary room. If we observe critically while turning the head or eyes quickly, we shall see, no motion it is true, yet a blurring of the scene between two clear views. Normally we are quite unconscious of this continual blurring but seem to be looking about in an unblurred world. Whenever we walk past a tree or house, its image on the retina changes just

as if the tree or house were turning on an axis; yet we do not see trees or houses turn as we travel about at ordinary speeds. Sometimes ill-fitting glasses will reveal queer movements in the scene as we look about, but normally we do not see the relative motion of the environment when we move; our psychic makeup is somehow adjusted to disregard whole realms of phenomena that are so all-pervasive as to be irrelevant to our daily lives and needs.

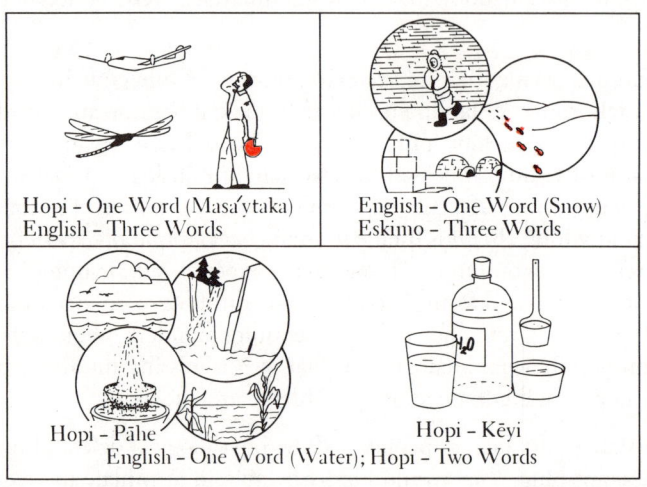

Hopi - One Word (Masa'ytaka) English - Three Words	English - One Word (Snow) Eskimo - Three Words
Hopi - Pāhe English - One Word (Water); Hopi - Two Words	Hopi - Kēyi

Languages classify items of experience differently. The class corresponding to one word and one thought in language A may be regarded by language B as two or more classes corresponding to two or more words and thoughts.

[7] Natural logic contains two fallacies: First, it does not see that the phenomena of a language are to its own speakers largely of a background character and so are outside the critical consciousness and control of the speaker who is expounding natural logic. Hence, when anyone, as a natural logician, is talking about reason, logic, and the laws of correct thinking, he is apt to be simply marching in step with purely grammatical facts that have somewhat of a background character in his own language or family of languages but are by no means universal in all languages and in no sense a common substratum of reason. Second, natural logic confuses agreement about subject matter, attained through use of language, with knowledge of the linguistic process by which agreement is attained: i.e., with the province of the despised (and to its notion superfluous) grammarian. Two fluent speakers, of English let us say, quickly reach a point of assent about the subject matter of their speech; they agree about what their language refers to. One of them, A, can give directions that will be carried out by the other, B, to A's complete satisfaction. Because they thus understand each other so perfectly, A and B, as natural logicians, suppose they must of course know how it is all done. They think, e.g., that it is simply a matter of choosing words to express thoughts. If you ask A to explain how

he got B's agreement so readily, he will simply repeat to you, with more or less elaboration or abbreviation, what he said to B. He has no notion of the process involved. The amazingly complex system of linguistic patterns and classifications, which A and B must have in common before they can adjust to each other at all, is all background to A and B.

[8] These background phenomena are the province of the grammarian—or of the linguist, to give him his more modern name as a scientist. The word linguist in common, and especially newspaper, parlance means something entirely different, namely, a person who can quickly attain agreement about subject matter with different people speaking a number of different languages. Such a person is better termed a polyglot or a multilingual. Scientific linguists have long understood that ability to speak a language fluently does not necessarily confer a linguistic knowledge of it, i.e., understanding of its background phenomena and its systematic processes and structure, any more than ability to play a good game of billiards confers or requires any knowledge of the laws of mechanics that operate upon the billiard table.

[9] The situation here is not unlike that in any other field of science. All real scientists have their eyes primarily on background phenomena that cut very little ice, as such, in our daily lives; and yet their studies have a way of bringing out a close relation between these unsuspected realms of fact and such decidedly foreground activities as transporting goods, preparing food, treating the sick, or growing potatoes, which in time may become very much modified, simply because of pure scientific investigation in no way concerned with these brute matters themselves. Linguistics presents a quite similar case; the background phenomena with which it deals are involved in all our foreground activities of talking and of reaching agreement, in all reasoning and arguing of cases, in all law, arbitration, conciliation, contracts, treaties, public opinion, weighing of scientific theories, formulation of scientific results. Whenever agreement or assent is arrived at in human affairs, and whether or not mathematics or other specialized symbolisms are made part of the procedure, THIS AGREEMENT IS REACHED BY LINGUISTIC PROCESSES, OR ELSE IT IS NOT REACHED.

[10] As we have seen, an overt knowledge of the linguistic processes by which agreement is attained is not necessary to reaching some sort of agreement, but it is certainly no bar thereto; the more complicated and difficult the matter, the more such knowledge is a distinct aid, till the point may be reached—I suspect the modern world has about arrived at it—when the knowledge becomes not only an aid but a necessity. The situation may be likened to that of navigation. Every boat that sails is in the lap of planetary forces; yet a boy can pilot his small craft around a harbor without benefit of geography, astronomy, mathematics, or international politics. To the captain of an ocean liner, however, some knowledge of all these subjects is essential.

[11] When linguists became able to examine critically and scientifically a large number of languages of widely different patterns, their base of reference was expanded; they experienced an interruption of phenomena hitherto held universal, and a whole new order of significances came into their ken. It was found that the background linguistic system (in other words, the grammar) of each language is not merely a reproducing instrument for voicing ideas but rather is itself the shaper of ideas, the program and guide for the individual's mental activity, for his analysis of impressions, for his synthesis of his mental stock in trade. Formulation of ideas is not an independent process, strictly rational in the old sense, but is part of a particular grammar, and differs, from slightly to greatly, between different grammars. We dissect nature along lines laid down by our native languages. The categories and types that we isolate from the world of phenomena we do not find there because they stare every observer in the face; on the contrary, the world is presented in a kaleidoscopic flux of impressions which has to be organized by our minds—and this means largely by the linguistic systems in our minds. We cut nature up, organize it into concepts, and ascribe significances as we do, largely because we are parties to an agreement to organize it in this way—an agreement that holds throughout our speech community and is codified in the patterns of our language. The agreement is, of course, an implicit and unstated one, BUT ITS TERMS

Objective Field	Speaker (Sender)	Hearer (Receiver)	Handling of Topic, Running of Third Person
Situation 1a.			English ... "He is running" Hopi ... "Wari" (Running, Statement of Fact)
Situation 1b. Objective Field Blank Devoid of Running			English ... "He ran" Hopi ... "Wari" (Running, Statement of Fact)
Situation 2			English ... "He is running" Hopi ... "Wari" (Running, Statement of Fact)
Situation 3 Objective Field Blank			English ... "He ran" Hopi ... "Era Wari" (Running, Statement of Fact from Memory)
Situation 4 Objective Field Blank			English ... "He will run" Hopi ... "Warikni" (Running, Statement of Expectation)
Situation 5 Objective Field Blank			English ... "He runs" (e.g. on the Track Team) Hopi ... "Warikngwe" (Running, Statement of Law)

Contrast between a "temporal" language (English) and a "timeless" language (Hopi). What are to English differences of time are to Hopi differences in the kind of validity.

ARE ABSOLUTELY OBLIGATORY; we cannot talk at all except by subscribing to the organization and classification of data which the agreement decrees.

[12] This fact is very significant for modern science, for it means that no individual is free to describe nature with absolute impartiality but is constrained to certain modes of interpretation even while he thinks himself most free. The person most nearly free in such respects would be a linguist familiar with very many widely different linguistic systems. As yet no linguist is in any such position. We are thus introduced to a new principle of relativity, which holds that all observers are not led by the same physical evidence to the same picture of the universe, unless their linguistic backgrounds are similar, or can in some way be calibrated.

[13] This rather startling conclusion is not so apparent if we compare only our modern European languages, with perhaps Latin and Greek thrown in for good measure. Among these tongues there is a unanimity of major pattern which at first seems to bear out natural logic. But this unanimity exists only because these tongues are all Indo-European dialects cut to the same basic plan, being historically transmitted from what was long ago one speech community; because the modern dialects have long shared in building up a common culture; and because much of this culture, on the more intellectual side, is derived from the linguistic backgrounds of Latin and Greek. Thus this group of languages satisfies the special case of the clause beginning "unless" in the statement of the linguistic relativity principle at the end of the preceding paragraph. From this condition follows the unanimity of description of the world in the community of modern scientists. But it must be emphasized that "all modern Indo-European-speaking observers" is not the same thing as "all observers." That modern Chinese or Turkish scientists describe the world in the same terms as Western scientists means, of course, only that they have taken over bodily the entire Western system of rationalizations, not that they have corroborated that system from their native posts of observation.

[14] When Semitic, Chinese, Tibetan, or African languages are contrasted with our own, the divergence in analysis of the world becomes more apparent; and, when we bring in the native languages of the Americas, where speech communities for many millenniums have gone their ways independently of each other and of the Old World, the fact that languages dissect nature in many different ways becomes patent. The relativity of all conceptual systems, ours included, and their dependence upon language stand revealed. That American Indians speaking only their native tongues are never called upon to act as scientific observers is in no wise to the point. To exclude the evidence which their languages offer as to what the human mind can do is like expecting botanists to study nothing but food plants and hothouse roses and then tell us what the plant world is like!

[15] Let us consider a few examples. In English we divide most of our words into two classes, which have different grammatical and logical properties. Class 1 we call nouns, e.g., 'house, man'; class 2, verbs, e.g., 'hit, run.' Many words of one class can act secondarily as of the other class, e.g., 'a hit, a run,' or 'to man (the boat),'

but, on the primary level, the division between the classes is absolute. Our language thus gives us a bipolar division of nature. But nature herself is not thus polarized. If it be said that 'strike, turn, run,' are verbs because they denote temporary or short-lasting events, i.e., actions, why then is 'fist' a noun? It also is a temporary event. Why are 'lightning, spark, wave, eddy, pulsation, flame, storm, phase, cycle, spasm, noise, emotion' nouns? They are temporary events. If 'man' and 'house' are nouns because they are long-lasting and stable events, i.e., things, what then are 'keep, adhere, extend, project, continue, persist, grow, dwell,' and so on doing among the verbs? If it be objected that 'possess, adhere' are verbs because they are stable relationships rather than stable percepts, why then should 'equilibrium, pressure, current, peace, group, nation, society, tribe, sister,' or any kinship term be among the nouns? It will be found that an "event" to US means "what our language classes as a verb" or something analogized therefrom. And it will be found that it is not possible to define 'event, thing, object, relationship,' and so on, from nature, but that to define them always involves a circuitous return to the grammatical categories of the definer's language.

[16] In the Hopi language, 'lightning, wave, flame, meteor, puff of smoke, pulsation' are verbs—events of necessarily brief duration cannot be anything but verbs. 'Cloud' and 'storm' are at about the lower limit of duration for nouns. Hopi, you see, actually has a classification of events (or linguistic isolates) by duration type, something strange to our modes of thought. On the other hand, in Nootka, a language of Vancouver Island, all words seem to us to be verbs, but really there are no classes 1 and 2; we have, as it were, a monistic view of nature that gives us only one class of word for all kinds of events. 'A house occurs' or 'it houses' is the way of saying 'house,' exactly like 'a flame occurs' or 'it burns.' These terms seem to us like verbs because they are inflected for durational and temporal nuances, so that the suffixes of the word for house event make it mean long-lasting house, temporary house, future house, house that used to be, what started out to be a house, and so on.

[17] Hopi has one noun that covers every thing or being that flies, with the exception of birds, which class is denoted by another noun. The former noun may be said to denote the class (FC–B)—flying class minus bird. The Hopi actually call insect, airplane, and aviator all by the same word, and feel no difficulty about it. The situation, of course, decides any possible confusion among very disparate members of a broad linguistic class, such as this class (FC–B). This class seems to us too large and inclusive, but so would our class 'snow' to an Eskimo. We have the same word for falling snow, snow on the ground, snow packed hard like ice, slushy snow, wind-driven flying snow—whatever the situation may be. To an Eskimo, this all-inclusive word would be almost unthinkable; he would say that falling snow, slushy snow, and so on, are sensuously and operationally different, different things to contend with; he uses different words for them and for other kinds of snow. The Aztecs go even farther than we in the opposite direction, with 'cold,' 'ice,' and

'snow' all represented by the same basic word with different terminations; 'ice' is the noun form; 'cold,' the adjectival form; and for 'snow,' "ice mist."

[18]   What surprises most is to find that various grand generalizations of the Western world, such as time, velocity, and matter, are not essential to the construction of a consistent picture of the universe. The psychic experiences that we class under these headings are, of course, not destroyed; rather, categories derived from other kinds of experiences take over the rulership of the cosmology and seem to function just as well. Hopi may be called a timeless language. It recognizes psychological time, which is much like Bergson's "duration," but this "time" is quite unlike the mathematical time, T, used by our physicists. Among the peculiar properties of Hopi time are that it varies with each observer, does not permit of simultaneity, and has zero dimensions; i.e., it cannot be given a number greater than one. The Hopi do not say, "I stayed five days," but "I left on the fifth day." A word referring to this kind of time, like the word day, can have no plural. The puzzle picture (page 114) will give mental exercise to anyone who would like to figure out how the Hopi verb gets along without tenses. Actually, the only practical use of our tenses, in one-verb sentences, is to distinguish among five typical situations, which are symbolized in the picture. The timeless Hopi verb does not distinguish between the present, past, and future of the event itself but must always indicate what type of validity the SPEAKER intends the statement to have: (a) report of an event (situations 1, 2, 3 in the picture); (b) expectation of an event (situation 4); (c) generalization or law about events (situation 5). Situation 1, where the speaker and listener are in contact with the same objective field, is divided by our language into the two conditions, 1*a* and 1*b*, which it calls present and past, respectively. This division is unnecessary for a language which assures one that the statement is a report.

[19]   Hopi grammar, by means of its forms called aspects and modes, also makes it easy to distinguish among momentary, continued, and repeated occurrences, and to indicate the actual sequence of reported events. Thus the universe can be described without recourse to a concept of dimensional time. How would a physics constructed along these lines work, with no T (time) in its equations? Perfectly, as far as I can see, though of course it would require different ideology and perhaps different mathematics. Of course V (velocity) would have to go too. The Hopi language has no word really equivalent to our 'speed' or 'rapid.' What translates these terms is usually a word meaning intense or very, accompanying any verb of motion. Here is a clue to the nature of our new physics. We may have to introduce a new term I, intensity. Every thing and event will have an I, whether we regard the thing or event as moving or as just enduring or being. Perhaps the I of an electric charge will turn out to be its voltage, or potential. We shall use clocks to measure some intensities, or, rather, some RELATIVE intensities, for the absolute intensity of anything will be meaningless. Our old friend acceleration will still be there but doubtless under a new name. We shall perhaps call it V, meaning not velocity but variation. Perhaps all growths and accumulations will be regarded as V's. We should not have the

concept of rate in the temporal sense, since, like velocity, rate introduces a mathematical and linguistic time. Of course we know that all measurements are ratios, but the measurements of intensities made by comparison with the standard intensity of a clock or a planet we do not treat as ratios, any more than we so treat a distance made by comparison with a yardstick.

[20] A scientist from another culture that used time and velocity would have great difficulty in getting us to understand these concepts. We should talk about the intensity of a chemical reaction; he would speak of its velocity or its rate, which words we should at first think were simply words for intensity in his language. Likewise, he at first would think that intensity was simply our own word for velocity. At first we should agree, later we should begin to disagree, and it might dawn upon both sides that different systems of rationalization were being used. He would find it very hard to make us understand what he really meant by velocity of a chemical reaction. We should have no words that would fit. He would try to explain it by likening it to a running horse, to the difference between a good horse and a lazy horse. We should try to show him, with a superior laugh, that his analogy also was a matter of different intensities, aside from which there was little similarity between a horse and a chemical reaction in a beaker. We should point out that a running horse is moving relative to the ground, whereas the material in the beaker is at rest.

[21] One significant contribution to science from the linguistic point of view may be the greater development of our sense of perspective. We shall no longer be able to see a few recent dialects of the Indo-European family, and the rationalizing techniques elaborated from their patterns, as the apex of the evolution of the human mind, nor their present wide spread as due to any survival from fitness or to anything but a few events of history—events that could be called fortunate only from the parochial point of view of the favored parties. They, and our own thought processes with them, can no longer be envisioned as spanning the gamut of reason and knowledge but only as one constellation in a galactic expanse. A fair realization of the incredible degree of diversity of linguistic system that ranges over the globe leaves one with an inescapable feeling that the human spirit is inconceivably old; that the few thousand years of history covered by our written records are no more than the thickness of a pencil mark on the scale that measures our past experience on this planet; that the events of these recent millenniums spell nothing in any evolutionary wise, that the race has taken no sudden spurt, achieved no commanding synthesis during recent millenniums, but has only played a little with a few of the linguistic formulations and views of nature bequeathed from an inexpressibly longer past. Yet neither this feeling nor the sense of precarious dependence of all we know upon linguistic tools which themselves are largely unknown need be discouraging to science but should, rather, foster that humility which accompanies the true scientific spirit, and thus forbid that arrogance of the mind which hinders real scientific curiosity and detachment.

FOR REVIEW AND DISCUSSION

Content

1. What is the commonly held *(natural logic)* assumption about the relation of language to thought? Briefly explain Whorf's argument against this assumption.

2. What does Whorf mean by *background of experience* (paragraph 4)?

3. We would all like to believe that we think well, or that we think *correctly*. Is Whorf saying that we do not think correctly? Is correctness an issue in Whorf's essay?

4. Explain the basic differences between the Hopi conception of time and our own.

Rhetoric

1. What purpose is served in this essay by the careful and detailed introductory material on thought and the linguistic process? For example, although disagreeing with the system of natural logic, Whorf discusses it in some detail. Why? In what way would the essay suffer if the lengthy introduction were condensed and the Whorfian hypothesis were presented earlier than it is?

2. Examine Whorf's frequent use of analogies (for instance, "the situation may be likened to that of navigation"). What do these analogies suggest about the nature of his subject? About the nature of his audience?

Classroom Exercises

1. Every individual is "constrained to certain modes of interpretation even while he thinks himself most free." But is freedom in this regard something to desire? Does Whorf find anything "wrong" with the constraints of one's language?

2. What effect does Whorf's hypothesis have on how you value your own interpretations of experiences and objects, events, and ideas?

Chippewa Song

CHANT TO THE FIRE-FLY

This short song was recorded by an anthropologist who studied the Chippewa Indians in the mid-1800s. The three versions give us an idea of the difficulties encountered in translating into English from a language so different as Chippewa. Pay particular attention to the changes that the chant goes through in each version and consider whether it "loses something in the translation."

Chippewa Original

Wau wau tay see!
Wau wau tay see!
E mow e shin
Tahe bwau ne baun-e wee!
Be eghaun—be eghaun—ewee!
Wau wau tay see!
Wau wau tay see!
Was sa koon ain je gun.
Was sa koon ain je gun.

Literal Translation

Flitting-white-fire-insect! waving-white-fire-bug! give me light before I go to bed! give me light before I go to sleep. Come, little dancing white-fire-bug! Come, little flitting white-fire-beast! Light me with your bright white-flame-instrument—your little candle.

Literary Translation

Fire-fly, fire-fly! bright little thing,
Light me to bed, and my song I will sing.
Give me your light, as you fly o'er my head,
That I may merrily go to my bed.
Give me your light o'er the grass as you creep,
That I may joyfully go to my sleep.

From *The Sky Clears*, by A. Grove Day. Copyright 1951 by A. Grove Day, 1968 by Bison Books. Reprinted by permission of the University of Nebraska Press.

CHANT TO THE FIRE-FLY

Come, little fire-fly, come, little beast—
Come! and I'll make you tomorrow a feast.
Come, little candle that flies as I sing,
Bright little fairy-bug—night's little king;
Come, and I'll dance as you guide me along,
Come, and I'll pay you, my bug, with a song.

FOR REVIEW AND DISCUSSION

Content

1. What kind of poem is this? A lullaby, a spell, a simple entertainment? What do you think is the purpose of the poem?

2. Why might a line such as the first (*wau wau tay see*) in the original be translated two ways, as it is in the literal translation? How might both translations be accurate to the sense of the original?

3. What does the poem suggest about the Chippewa's relation to nature? What songs and poems of the 1970s suggest something about our relation to nature?

Rhetoric

1. Does the literary translation convey the same attitude toward the firefly as the literal one does? In what way are the attitudes in the two versions similar? Different?

2. How is the attitude in each version conveyed (for example, through tone, rhythm, diction)?

3. Does the rhyme in the literary translation help or hinder the poem's effectiveness for you? Explain.

4. Why is the literary version so much longer than the literal one?

Classroom Exercises

1. Humpty Dumpty (see chapter 2) might say that he can just as well master two languages as one, and that the original chant means whatever he translates it to mean. Assuming, however, that neither the literal nor literary translation is the work of Humpty Dumpty, offer some possible reasons for their seeming difference in meaning. Is one necessarily less like the original than the other?

2. If you have studied a foreign language, discuss the problems you have encountered in doing a straightforward literal translation of a poem and in moving from a literal to a literary translation.

FOR DISCUSSION AND WRITING

1. How might Hayakawa explain the girl's fleeing to the city (in Mencken's story)? Are the causes Hayakawa would ascribe different from those you would ascribe? In what way?

2. What similarities are there between the Whorfian hypothesis and Hayakawa's description of how we classify things? Are the two compatible?

3. Woolfson asks if having a separate word for specific aspects of things can change our awareness. How might Hayakawa answer Woolfson's question?

4. Based on your reading of Whorf, Hayakawa, and Woolfson, draw up your own hypothesis about the relationship between language and reality. Consider the following questions: Does reality determine how language is used? Does language create reality? Is there actually a reality? If reality exists, does it seem likely that language can accurately describe it?

5. First from the point of view of Hayakawa, and then from that of Whorf, explain why literature from one language can or cannot be translated accurately into another language, especially one that is unrelated to the original. In what respect are Hayakawa and Whorf in agreement?

6. Discuss how classification can lead to stereotyping and how we can avoid unfair and negative stereotyping.

7. Discuss a particular kind of stereotyping with which you are familiar—perhaps something that has affected you personally.

4 USAGE: DIALECT, SLANG, AND JARGON

> *If you tell me something is a pleasure, I don't know whether it is more like revenge, or buttered toast, or success, or adoration, or relief from danger, or a good scratch.*
>
> C. S. LEWIS

Usage—"the actual or expressed way in which a language is used, interrelated or pronounced in expression"—is a constant problem for all of us. When should we use certain words or phrases and when should we avoid them? The selections in this chapter attempt to resolve this problem, with particular attention to the misuse of jargon and the significance of slang and dialects. Harold B. Allen, in "Usage is Something Else Again," has a message for both students and teachers about the distinctions between "correct" and "incorrect" usage.

Harold B. Allen

USAGE IS SOMETHING ELSE AGAIN

> As students and teachers of writing, we constantly hear phrases such as "That's not the way it's said." But who determines how it is said is often a mystery to us, a mystery which Allen tries to unravel in this essay. What is proper, he points out, frequently has more to do with the situation than with a set of arbitrary rules, although such rules do apply in many cases. As you read, examine the differences between speaking and writing as he discusses them, and ask yourself whether you have ever been guilty of imposing your own preferences on others under the guise of "propriety."

[1] The exploding popular concern with man's abuse of his environment is curiously relevant to a long-standing concern of our schools, the teaching of "correct English." The language of man, his means of human communication and control, is also part of his environment. This amazingly complex system exists without his doing anything about it. But some men want to do something about it; they want to make changes in it and in how men use it. For whatever reasons, some men have tried to interfere with the system without understanding the complex relationships within it. Some have insisted upon *It is I* in speech and thereby have polluted the language with the unanticipated *between you and I*. Some have insisted upon the pronunciation /ask/ and hence have unwittingly encouraged such odd forms as /hat/ for /hæt/. Some have insisted upon spelling as a guide to pronunciation and hence have helped to produce such forms as /æntarktik/. Today some would like to change the way millions of Americans talk, the so-called culturally different in Appalachia, Harlem, Washington, Chicago, and Detroit, with a possible effect upon their speech and their social attitudes that can hardly be estimated. Then we always have with us such people as those who served as the "Usage Panel" for the *American Heritage Dictionary of the English Language,* people who apparently are not unwilling to have their personal linguistic prejudices and biases considered as guides to language behavior for those whose linguistic insecurity has been fostered by the correctness concept taught in the schools.

[2] I would suggest that a sound attitude must rest upon as much solid support as can be provided rather than upon personal opinion and feeling. Here I would like to propose a pragmatic approach to the problem of developing such an attitude.

From *Focusing on Language* by Harold B. Allen, Enola Borgh and Verna L. Newsome (T. Y. Crowell). Copyright © 1975 by Harper & Row, Publishers, Inc. Reprinted by permission of the publisher.

[3]   Ultimately three kinds of persons are involved in the development of a sound attitude toward language matters. Theoretically, any one person could be all three, but at different times. Practically, it is not very often that any one person has the opportunity or the ability to act in all three capacities.

[4]   The first person studies language as language. He is a scientific scholar in the field of language, a linguist. To such a person a language is a system primarily manifested in vocal symbols used for the communication of meaning among human beings. Any given language is such a system. English is such a system. We infer the existence of the system only by perceiving its overt manifestations. Its primary overt manifestation is in human speech; its secondary overt manifestation is in human writing or printing. A possible tertiary manifestation could occur through symbols related to alphabetic letters, such as the Morse code or Braille.

[5]   In what he hears or sees this first person finds combinations of sounds or letters that seem to point to things or associations outside the language, that is, that have referential or dictionary meaning—and he so classifies and describes them. He also observes different kinds of signals that show how these lexical symbols are related to each other in a given utterance. These signals he classifies according to shape and tune and volume and position. Statements based upon observations constitute what is known as a grammar. If the statements are confined to the description of the overt manifestations, it is the relatively weak kind of grammar called structural. If it consists of a series of sequential rules, the operation of which accounts for or explains any and all possible acceptable sentences in the language, then it is the much more powerful kind of grammar called generative.

[6]   Note that the concern of this first person is simply to describe the working of the system in all its complexity. Whether this approach is that of the structuralist or that of the transformationalist with his generative grammar, he is still dealing with the system itself. He is not concerned with what is outside the system, even though he may limit his concern to the language used by one person (an idiolect) or that used by a community of people (a dialect).

[7]   In observing the language forms of some individual, for example, the linguist may record *I did it* and *It was me* and *Me and him did it*. His rules would have to state that in preverbal position and after a certain type of verb both *I* and *me* appear, but that in preverbal position *me* does not occur alone (that is, as in *Me did it*). He might also observe *He saw me* and *between you and I*, and will accordingly have a rule that *me* occurs after a certain type of verb as object and that *I* occurs in this combination after a prepositional function word.

[8]   Now there is a second kind of person involved in all this. Unlike the linguist or grammarian, he looks not into the language but away from it. He is concerned not with the internal operation of the language, but with the correlation of linguistic matters with the nonlinguistic environment in which people use language. This

person may be a linguistic geographer, or a sociolinguist, or a psycholinguist, or a dictionary editor—or a graduate student writing a dissertation! Such a person would ascertain the situation in which *me* occurs after a form of *be* and the situation in which *me* occurs in a coordination before a verb as in *Me and him did it*. His description of the situation would include details about the speaker's education and social group, the kind of rapport with the listener, the time and nature of the occurrence, and the audience. This relationship between a language feature and the complex nonlinguistic contexts is the usage of the feature. Any description of such a relationship is a statement about that usage. A set of such statements about a number of language features is a description of usage of that language. Such a set may be in expository form, with the support of tables and charts, or it may be in alphabetical or other sequential lists, as in a dictionary of usage.

[9] I do not want to seem to be laboring this point, to be unnecessarily obvious. But I do want to be very clear about this matter that has been seriously misrepresented in many textbooks and classrooms. Grammar is a set of statements about what goes on inside a language. That is one thing. Usage is the relationship between what occurs in a language and the external context of speaker, purpose, time, place, mood, and audience. Usage is something else again.

[10] Now there is a third person involved in all this. He is the teacher, the professor—usually of English, but also of speech. This person has a very special job, one derived from the very nature of our democratic society. As Charles C. Fries wrote in his *American English Grammar* in 1940, the schools and colleges in this country assume the obligation of helping students to gain control of those language matters that correlate with the speech and writing of educated people, that is, of what we call Standard English. At least until recently a high degree of such control has been held essential for the individual citizen with respect to his personal advancement through the utilization of all his personal capabilities and as essential for the individual citizen in a society where full communication is a *sine qua non* in economics and political life.

[11] This third person, then, has an obligation to center attention upon those particular language matters, those particular correlations of language and context, that are peculiar to one or more varieties of Standard English. If he has students who lack control over some of these correlations, that is, who cannot imitate them, then he has the problem of helping them to modify their speech and writing habits. If the students actually have nonstandard dialect quite different in essential features, then he has the problem of helping them to acquire control of a second dialect, almost as if it were a second language, not to replace their original dialect but rather to be added to it. In short, this third person is a teacher of usage.

[12] Clearly this third person is not the first person. But some serious misunderstanding has resulted from confusing these two jobs. The linguist observes, describes, generalizes, and theorizes about language, but he does not prescribe. The teacher, on the other hand, must assume the responsibility of prescribing, of indi-

cating the choice between Standard and Nonstandard English. He is prescriptive in the same way that a foreign-language teacher is prescriptive, for he is teaching control of a different set of language forms. But there are two kinds of prescriptiveness. One has been manifested in certain traditional textbooks often found in high schools and colleges today. This prescriptiveness is often associated with some kind of indefinable mystique called "correctness," a mystique more transcendental than objective, more unreal than real.

[13] There is another kind of prescriptiveness, based upon some awareness of the facts of language. This second kind cannot exist except as the third in a sequence of activities. First, the linguist analyzes a language and describes it in a grammar. Second, the student of usage determines the relationships between language and context and describes those in statements about usage—in general principles as in Martin Joos's little monograph *The Five Clocks* or in various compendiums ranging from Margaret Bryant's *Dictionary of Current American Usage* to *Webster's Third New International*. Third, the teacher of usage chooses those particular correlations characteristic of Standard English and endeavors to teach them. The second person cannot do his job unless the linguist has done his. The third person, the teacher, cannot do his job unless the usage scholar has done his. If he tries to, then he is in grave danger of elevating personal taste and private prejudice to the status of public dogma.

[14] Clearly it is the second person, the student of usage, who is critical in the teaching of usage. It is to him we must now turn as the one to rescue us from the unhappy and untenable position from which can be seen only a right and a wrong, only a correct and an incorrect form. Life—and the language of life—is not quite so simple.

[15] I would suggest that instead of this two-valued split, this dichotomy between two extremes, we should less naively and more realistically look at language correlations in terms of the dimensions provided by the second person.

[16] The first important step in this direction was taken by the late John S. Kenyon. Of course, for two millenniums scholars had had before them the classical Horatian statement that usage is the standard of speaking, *Usus est norma loquendi*, and in the eighteenth century the rhetorician George Campbell had elaborated that simple dictum by declaring that the standard, the *norma*, has three characteristics: contemporary, standard, and reputable. It was not until 1939 that the late Porter Perrin introduced the notion of levels in his book, *Index to Usage*, but Perrin made the mistake of assigning colloquial to one level and Standard English to another. Textbooks adopting this analysis were soon confusing students everywhere by suggesting to them that one can't talk Standard English, one can only write it. Kenyon, in his articles in *College English* and in *The English Journal* in October, 1948, for the first time recognized the important distinction of functional varieties that exist upon one level. He pointed out that colloquial standard and written standard, for example, exist on the same level.

[17] But even Kenyon's analysis retains the concept of level, one I think which is misleading in its implicit analogy to floors in a building or levels in a mine. I would offer instead the term *dimension* as a deliberate attempt to present the idea of a range, a continuum. I would offer specifically the consideration of five dimensions as a frame of reference for English usage. The limitation to five is admittedly an oversimplification, but it is pedagogically workable. Any analysis, even Joos's in *The Five Clocks*, is bound to be an oversimplification, so complex is the language-culture context. But the concept of five dimensions is pragmatically sound.

[18] This concept will also admit easy visual demonstration. Let a line represent the continuum between the primary manifestation of language, speech, and the secondary manifestation of language, writing. Some language matters fall peculiarly at the speech end of the continuum; others occur at the writing end. Some words people scarcely ever write. Such a word is *ficety* or *feisty*, a term widely heard in the South Midland area. Rarely will a speaker admit having written it, and then he is unsure of the spelling. At the other extreme is a word like *tergiversation*. Semantically it would be possible to say, "Some ficety people are subject to tergiversation," but actually it is an impossible combination, for these two terms are at opposite ends of the first dimension. All our words are locatable, then, somewhere along this dimension with respect to the relative frequency with which they occur in speech and in writing, somewhere between the exclusively spoken and exclusively literary.

[19] Grammatical forms also range along this dimension. *If it's true* is at a point different from where we would place *If it be true*. *It's me* is colloquial and *It is I* is uncommonly literary written English. Contractions like *won't, ain't, she's, I'd've* are clearly spoken forms. *There's some books on the table* is much more likely to be heard than to be read. So many forms are close to this end of the continuum that there actually can be a grammar of spoken English in contrast to that of written English.

[20] Such a grammar would have to include also the differences in syntax, for here too there is a range between speech and writing. Some written English offers the Latinate expressions *to whom, from whom,* and *than whom* at the one extreme end of the continuum. *That's the boy that his father owns a supermarket* is a kind of construction much closer to the other end. A nonrestrictive clause is common in writing; it is rare in speech. Coordination between clauses is common in the speech of most persons; it is much less common in writing. In short, we simply do not write precisely as we speak and we do not speak precisely as we write. Some language forms may be typically found in speech; other language forms may be typically found in writing. All language forms can be placed somewhere along this dimension.

[21] But as you consider these sample forms I just cited you notice, of course, that they differ in other ways. In reading aloud his sermon, a minister may say, "It is not I who thus admonish you. These are not my words, but Paul's." Yet an hour later

he may answer the telephone with, "Yes, it's me. Oh, no, I wasn't really trying to scold you, Norman." The difference here between *It's me* and *It's I*, and between *scold* and *admonish*, points to a second dimension, a second range of relative frequencies of occurrence—the range between formality and informality. This dimension extends from all points on the first dimension, so that to illustrate it you now need a two-dimensional figure, a square. Any language matter is identifiable in terms of its position somewhere in that square.

[22] Some written matters vary between formal and informal. Punctuation features do, for instance. The dash is much more informal than the colon or semicolon. Certain abbreviations are more informal than the full words they represent. Even numerals are sometimes more informal than written words. Notice the style, for example, on a formal wedding invitation with June Fourth carefully spelled out in elegant type. Likewise, some exclusively speech matters range from formality to informality. In formal public address a speaker will use much more precise articulation than in intimate conversation; he may even use spelling pronunciations such as "pumpkin" and "antarctic" for "punkin" or "antartic."

[23] At the same time, language matters that occur in both speech and writing still exhibit contrasts of formality and informality. Take, for example, the whole body of terms comprised under the headings of slang, cant, jargon, and the like. These tend to bunch up toward the informal end of this dimension. But some technical cant or jargon may bunch up at the other end. None of us will have any difficulty in placing these two quotations:

> Man, you just play it real cool and quit puttin' us on.

> This maximal, nondiscrete sphere of social relationships has no corporate organization and is not segmented into lineages, age-sets, secret societies, territorial districts, political factions, and the like.

[24] Many occupations, of course, have two sets of terms in their special jargons—one set for formal communications such as top-level reports and committee sessions and descriptive literature, and another set, colorful, slangy, even obscene, used by the working force, such as the men on the machines. Similar contrasts occur in the language of teen-agers who like to make over old automobiles and in the language of music fans and hi-fi enthusiasts.

[25] Martin Joos's analysis in *The Five Clocks* would break this dimension into these sections, these five kinds of style: (1) intimate (the language of people emotionally close to each other and not concerned at the moment with communication as much as empathy.) (2) casual (the style of a social group with common understandings.) Its speech is marked by ellipsis:

> Nice day. Been pretty warm, though. Thanks. OK.

(3) consultative (the style of ordinary communication, usually with some kind of feedback from the audience, if only an occasional "Mmh, mmh.") (4) formal (a

style not characterized by feedback. It is the style of the formal public address, of the magazine article, and essay. It is marked, says Joos, by detachment and by cohesion.) (5) frozen (the style of formal edited English, ranging from the rewritten textbook to the rewritten sermon, whether rewritten by the writer or by an editor. At its extreme the frozen style may be the language of ritual.)

[26] Now we add lines to suggest a three-dimensional figure, a cube, in order to allow for the third dimension, the one uppermost in the concerns of many teachers of English. This is the range or scale of variations between Standard English and Nonstandard English. Remember that these are designations undefinable in terms of absolutes. They can be defined only in terms of correlation with nonlinguistic features of our cultures. Professor Fries, back in 1927, defined Standard English, Good English, as that used habitually by men and women who carry on the affairs of the English-speaking world. This is surely a matter of relativity, of frequency of occurrence.

[27] A college graduate in a given community is vice-president of a bank, a director on the local hospital board, chairman of the Community Chest campaign, and past commander of the American Legion post. He goes on a hunting trip with three friends. That night they relax with a little game of poker. And a tape recording of the conversation would reveal that at one time he said, "Say, I'm doing all right, ain't I?" This single occurrence in the speech of even a community leader does not make *ain't I?* Standard English.

[28] An unskilled laborer in the same community left school when he finished the fourth grade. He has no social life except that of his home and the beer tavern. He has accepted no community responsibilities. But he has a television set. By sheer chance some dramatic program impresses him with the statement, "And if he were here now, I'd shoot him." The next night in the tavern he comes out with this: "And if he were here now, I'd slug him." This single occurrence in such a context does not make *If he were* Nonstandard English.

[29] On the contrary, determination of what is and is not Standard English must necessarily be a matter of judgment based upon the accumulation of evidence. The vast majority of linguistic matters—of pronunciation, vocabulary, grammar, and syntax—occur in the standard part of the continuum as well as in the nonstandard. They are common in the language of all users of English. Other matters, like much of the vocabulary, occur only in the writing of educated persons. In either case judgment is automatic. But a small minority of language matters can cause trouble, some because they are borderline cases and hence induce dogmatic judgments not always justified, and others because they are so indubitably nonstandard that they handicap the user socially, educationally, and occupationally.

[30] Here is where the growing body of evidence now available helps to underlie a reasonable judgment. Let's take some speech items for example. Throughout the country many teachers for years have tried to get children to pronounce the adverb

just as it is spelled. Indeed, that is their criterion—the spelling. But evidence from the *Linguistic Atlas* projects is clear; the usual pronunciation is /jɨst/* as in *Just a minute*. Actually four words contrast in this sentence: "The just judge said that he just couldn't get the gist of the jest." Spelling is also the criterion with another shibboleth—*government*. The presence of the medial *n* is used as an argument that it should be pronounced. Again, evidence collected by *Webster's* reveals that in ordinary use educated people do not pronounce the *n*. Some teachers and others have tried to promote the British forms /ask/, /dants/, etc., instead of /æsk/ and /dænts/. Again, evidence is clear that on all levels the /æ/ vowel is normal in most of the United States.

[31] Should I mention *It's me*? There are still people who object to it; yet studies show that this is the normal conversational use all over the United States. How about *like* as a joiner of clauses, in such a construction as *It looks like it'll rain*? One of my Ph.D. students several years ago found that 66 per cent of 155 school textbooks flatly said that *like* cannot be used as a conjunction; and 48 college freshman texts took the same position. But the New England Atlas shows that *like* is so used by 46 percent of the college graduates; and in the Midwest 47 percent so use it. Clearly, with the third dimension of usage as with the first and second, we have a continuum, a range, from one extreme to the other rather than a dichotomy of right and wrong, correct and incorrect. With respect to all three dimensions, then, an attempt to locate any given language item will be inadequate unless the attempt is made with awareness of the relation of the language item to other items and to the correlated nonlinguistic features.

[32] But there is a fourth dimension as well—and to illustrate it we move our imaginary cube from one place to another. It is the dimension of space, from here to there or anywhere. And as we move the cube we find that what is nonstandard or nonexistent in one area may be standard and common in another; what is formal written in one may be informal spoken in another, and standard, or perhaps nonstandard, in both places.

[33] Schools in the northern part of the country have long insisted upon /ruwf/ as the correct pronunciation of *roof*, that is, with the vowel of *loose*. This is of course the common form in the South, but in the Upper Midwest 68 percent of the informants for the *Linguistic Atlas* have my normal pronunciation, /ruf/, with the vowel of *put*. Schools also, and likewise on the basis of spelling, insist upon /kriyk/ for *creek*. This too is normal standard in the South; but in my region 79 percent of the people actually say what I say, /krik/, riming with *pick*. Take *due*. My pronunciation /duw/ is considered pretty lowbrow by some teachers of speech—and it may sound pretty bad to you—but in the Upper Midwest it is, by 83 percent, the majority form.

* The symbol /ɨ/ represents a vowel not identified in English spelling. It is a sound made with the tongue higher than for the vowel in *bun* and farther back than the position in *bit*. Northern and Southern speakers usually have it in the second syllable of *horses*.

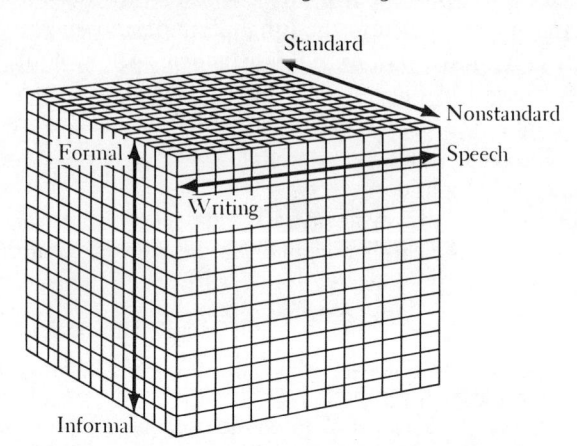

The Five Dimensions of English Usage

Any given language element may undergo a change of position within the cube, or disappear completely, as the cube is moved into the fourth and fifth dimensions, space and time.

[34] Until I began teaching in southern Illinois many years ago, I had never heard anyone say *I'd like for you to do this*. I dutifully tried to correct my students but gave up when I discovered that my colleagues said it too. Now I realize that this is standard spoken informal English in a very large section of the country, even though it simply doesn't exist in my own Northern dialect.

[35] When several centuries ago the plural *you* displaced the singular *thou*, there still was some felt need for a distinctive plural. In the United States this need was met in the North by *youse*, in the Midland area by *you ones*, usually as *you'uns*, and in the South by *you all*, usually *y'all*. But the first two have never gained social respectability, and are nonstandard. Southern *y'all*, however, is standard spoken English in the South. As a matter of fact, sometimes there is no possible term except a regional term. There is no national word, for example, for the strip of grass between sidewalk and street. In the Upper Midwest two dozen names for it have been recorded—from *boulevard*, *parking*, *parking strip*, *terrace*, *tree lawn*, *curbing*, *curb strip*, and *devil strip* to the curious word *berm*. They are all regional, and all standard!

[36] Finally, let's move our imaginary cube slowly, ever so slowly—and now we represent the passage of time. As we move it back to 1900, back to 1600, back to 1400, many language matters will shift their relative positions and perhaps disappear, while new ones will take their place. Even in our own lifetime we can experience this shift. The change is slow with syntactic forms, as when over the centuries the wandering adjective settled firmly into place before the noun; it may be more rapid, as with the swift acceptance of the progressive *-ing* verb phrase in the

eighteenth century; it may be almost overnight, as with such words as *beatnik* and *hippie*. We who teach need to keep this fact in mind as we ourselves grow older, for otherwise we'll find ourselves trying to make our students use our own sometimes old-fashioned forms. My own pronunciations, *isolate* with the vowel of *fit*, *economic* with the vowel of *bet*, *cigaret* with the stress on the final syllable, and *juvenile* with the last syllable rhyming with *pill*, are different from those used by my students—and probably by you.

[37] Usage, we see, is not a simple black-and-white contrast. To assume that it is, and to criticize others accordingly, is the easy way out. It is easy to follow the dictates of a given textbook without questioning by what right the author makes his judgments. It is easy for the teacher to correct by the book and to drill accordingly. But that is not real teaching. Real teaching is educating, not drilling. And education is the process of developing discriminative reactions. That calls for sensitivity. With respect to language it means that we seek to have not correct-incorrect distinctions but rather active awareness of what is appropriate for the speaker and the occasion and the audience.

[38] I have suggested a point of view that rests squarely upon observation of language in use and upon recognition of the fact that language is a social phenomenon integral with the complex fabric of our social structure. This point of view rejects the presentation of personal whim, preconceptions, and unsupported generalizations as guidelines for others to follow. It is, I submit, a point of view that makes sense—and for better control of our language as we use it day by day.

FOR REVIEW AND DISCUSSION

Content

1. Are distinctions among Martin Joos's five kinds of style clear? Is the style of Allen's essay primarily *formal* or *frozen*? Explain.

2. Why is *dimension* a better term than *level* when discussing usage?

3. According to Allen, "Determination of what is and is not Standard English must necessarily be a matter of judgment based upon the accumulation of evidence." What does Allen mean? Is this judgment he speaks of objective or subjective?

Rhetoric

1. Examine this sentence in the first paragraph: "Then we always have with us. . . ." What is the tone of the sentence? What words reinforce the tone? Is this tone typical of the tone throughout the essay?

2. Study the following sentence: "Now there is a second kind of person involved in all this" (paragraph 8). Many teachers tell students to avoid the false substantive *there is*

because it takes up the main part of a sentence and does not add substance or meaning to a statement. Can you account for its use here? Is its use *appropriate*?

3. What effect might Allen be trying to achieve by discussing his own usages? Does his having done so make you more or less inclined to accept his attitude toward language use?

Classroom Exercises

1. Select a form of expression now considered to be Standard English usage. Then accumulate evidence of its use around campus. What judgment can you make on the form of expression? Is it actually an appropriate usage on campus?

2. "With respect to language it [education] means that we seek to have not correct-incorrect distinctions but rather active awareness of what is appropriate for the speaker and the audience and the occasion." How might a teacher foster *awareness of what is appropriate*? What is the difference between *appropriate* and *correct*?

3. Listen to yourself speak to friends. Then listen to yourself talk to teachers. In what ways do you use language differently on these different occasions? Explain whether you were using language appropriately or inappropriately during each conversation.

*Geoffrey Wagner
and Sanford R. Radner*

TABOO: THE SACRED AND THE OBSCENE

A taboo is "*a prohibition excluding something from use, approach, or mention because of its sacred and inviolable nature.*" All cultures and languages are filled with taboos, and our own modern, mechanized American culture is no exception. We don't openly discuss many facets of our existence—death, excretory functions, and sex, for example—because we have learned that they are taboo. In this selection, Wagner and Radner discuss taboo in general as well as its significance in particular areas. Pay special attention to the euphemisms we use that allow us to discuss these taboo subjects without embarrassment.

[1]   *Taboo* is a Tongan word (sometimes spelled *tabu*) supposedly adopted from Polynesian culture by Captain Cook, an eighteenth-century English explorer. Today most Americans probably associate it with the perfume of that name showing, in the celebrated Kreisler Sonata ad, the longest kiss on record. Freud, however, assured us of the double, or "ambivalent," meaning of taboo: (1) as sacred, (2) as forbidden-unclean. The unutterable pair form a sort of self-complementary

From *Language and Reality* by Geoffrey Wagner and Sanford R. Radner. Copyright 1974 by Thomas Y. Crowell Company, Inc. Reprinted by permission of the authors.

antithesis—"so that," as he writes, "the objects of veneration become objects of aversion." If this dynamic were understood, we should not be supporting by our taxes small armies of official snoopers all trying to detect something called obscenity in our midst, and world statesmen would not be making damn fools of themselves in public by calling pornography the origin of Communism.

[2]   The way in which taboo collects this strange semantic pair-bond in our culture is curious. Until not too long ago in England, at any rate, authors who had infringed laws governing sexual purity were sometimes also prosecuted for profanity or blasphemy.[1] Relatively recently, Gerard-Kornelis Van Het Reve was prosecuted under Article 147 of the Dutch Penal Code concerning blasphemy, when it was considered likely that he would get off on the score of obscenity.

[3]   Here, in the neat phrasing of Kenneth Burke, "scatology and eschatology overlap." The objects of aversion and the objects of veneration illide (*veneration* itself is close to *venery*). We are all familiar with G-d avoidances. Totemism was the ritual preservation of taboo, and not to write God's name in full, or that of Yahweh (a protective tetragrammaton meaning *I am who shall be*), was avoiding visually identifiable blasphemy. Moses was rebuked for wanting to know God's name—"the Lord will not hold him guiltless that taketh his name in vain" (Exodus 21:7).

[4]   *Gee, Jeepers* for Jesus, *heck* for hell, the *deuce* for the devil, *shucks* for shit, and *bloody* (in England) for By Our Lady are all examples of Freud's point, as well as Kenneth Burke's extension of it. Taboo involved the "blindness" of a sense: *Holy Tchee!* thus fulfills the source of the taboo for the ear, while making no verbal infringement, but it is a "dirty" word, one for which an excremental alias could well be (and often is) substituted.

[5]   A few years ago an enterprising West German marketed a toilet paper, rather appropriately bearing the trade name *Adios*. For a while the product sold pretty well. Then it was brought to the attention of the Bishop of Munich, who protested violently (*Der Spiegel*, March 14, 1962). A less sacrilegious name had to be, and was in fact, found. Generically, what the good bishop was saying in his objection was that the sacred and the fecal are both exceptional, and exceptionally nonutterable. There was even a hint of this taboo when Rolls Royce marketed their revered Silver Mist model in Germany, and had hastily to retitle it; *Mist* is German shit, or at any rate manure.

[6]   Egyptian pyramidal tombs are supposed to have mimicked dung piles, while it is said that the Dalai Lamas believed their excrement to be notably holy (cp. U.S. *head*). That the organs of sex are also those of excretion has been called God's final joke on man. Privacy taboos resulting from the vetoes available in this area proliferated in Puritanism, of course, and repeatedly crisscrossed the tracks of capitalism. For money has been called a kind of dung, and there is still a great deal of

---

[1] From *Webster's New World Dictionary*. **obscenity**: "offensive to modesty or decency"; **profanity**: "showing disregard or contempt for sacred things"; **blasphemy**: "speaking irreverently of God."

touchiness about bank balances and the like ("May we anticipate an early remittance?"); in fact, this sometimes reaches the point of real confusion.[2]

[7] Essentially we must remember, however, that the savages studied in Freud's *Totem and Taboo* were living in small societies literally threatened by uncleanness. Dead bodies putrefied and carried disease. They were actually unclean and so cast out—"untouchable."

[8] Such could be called behavioral taboo (with its relic in our charges of "indecent behavior"). Linguistic taboo ("insulting language") involves phonemic situations, and Edmund Leach shows us the same Freudian pair-bond operating in *quim*, one of the most taboo terms (*the* most, he claims) for the feminine pudenda—euphemism! euphemism!—yet one etymologically associated with *queen*.

[9] God-dog, dog collar, God damn, son of a bitch (one doesn't say, You son of a kangaroo)—this area of taboo rests on social valuation of animals and, if Leach is correct, the classifying of animals as regards their edibility involves sex. It is well known that we cringe from consuming dog—or even horse, which the French eat—and are yet surprised by the Indians' similar fastidiousness about cow (or the pious Jews about pork).

SUBJECTS OF TABOO IN OUR CULTURE

[10] The social environment of a child is a continuum which is then broken up into discrete entities. The gaps between these naturally form the taboo part of the environment since they are full of uncertainty. The same anxiety must pertain, too, about the human body itself. The child needs to find itself finite, to identify itself as apart from its surroundings, with the result that nearly all exudations of the body come under some sort of taboo. This certainly varies in degree, excreta being more tabooed than menstrual flow, say, and the latter more than mere tears; but even hair and nails are often subject to ritual fears.

[11] The greatest outlaw of all, here, is not unnaturally death, the binary antithesis of life in most world religions. This is understandable. In small Royal Air Force squadrons during the Battle of Britain of World War II, the casualty rate was so high that fighter pilots had, for the sake of some sort of sanity, to invent a death-diminishing slang. This touching jargon, with its terms like *gone for a burton* (a special kind of beer) to replace "blown to smithereens," was later made the subject

---

[2] This kind of confusion was best highlighted by the boy who was told by his mother to avoid his schoolmates' synonyms for urination and substitute *whisper*.
"Daddy," he said that evening to his father, who was not yet in on the code, "I want to whisper."
"Sure, son," came the answer. "Do it in my ear.'"

of an illuminating article by Eric Partridge. But this was essentially a private, protective slang; it was not used for hiding reality, and it was not disseminated beyond the group using it.

[12] There is no doubt that death taboos are universal. Only a year or so ago, a village in central Italy called Camposanto, successfully petitioned to change its name because of its connotations of cemetery. Yet it is significant that it did so only recently. In our own technological society, death is a living criticism and a reiterated public defeat. Consequently, our terms for neutralizing this event can become truly absurd, as in certain California mortuaries.

[13] It is not simply that we coin *passed on, joined the majority, no longer with us*, and the like; I defy anyone who has lost a close and dear relative to not want to grope for some such expression directly thereafter. All cultures euphemize death, even those, like the Japanese, where the dead are sometimes conceived as still present.

[14] But when the reluctance grossly exceeds the human need, something is afoot, and the semanticist takes note. No one wants to die. And stink. But when the "leave-taking" in Forest Lawn of millionaire mortician Hubert Eaton resembles, verbally and physically, a minor Fascist ceremony, taboo turns into phobia. The concealment becomes so much social rococo.

[15] Similarly, when military shorthand refers to dead Marines as H.R.'s, meaning is demeaned if this term is passed on to the American public as a verbal antiseptic. It may be that it is easier for combat troops to talk about *horizontally repatriated* rather than dead, or to call wounded W.I.A.'s (wounded in action), but to tell press reporters, as has been the case, "The weeklies are on the rack" for *Dead and wounded figures have been posted* looks close to obfuscation of the type that tried to turn napalm into *incendigel*. Euphemisms are not intended to hide; they are, rather, transparent veils to soften the starkness of our human existences.

[16] Taboo is a reluctance to utter which is not necessarily an inhibition; it may be a kind of linguistic self-protection, which is to say that it is, in Anatol Rapoport's sense, "operational." It may of course be either oral or written, and the meeting of these twain can be, in our semantic society, a very bloody crossroad indeed.

[17] Excremental taboos are, in fact, so extreme in American society—the deodorant society, after all—that they form as good a place as any at which to come to grips with some of the most glaring conflicts about taboo. For instance: a ladies' REST ROOM (or LOUNGE) scarcely describes "operationally" what goes on inside it. Yet even this euphemism, REST ROOM, does not apparently anesthetize sufficiently the reality, and thousands of dollars have been spent reshooting sequences of movies so that the supposedly more innocuous POWDER ROOM will appear.

[18] Despite decades of "liberation," sex is still the area in American life where taboo operates most powerfully. According to Professor H. J. Eysenck, Freud's true importance with regard to sex lay in his formulation (and subsequent populariza-

tion) of a language which contained ideas people could use—so that what was previously unutterable could be uttered. The Kinsey Report, whatever its failings, undoubtedly showed that elementary sexual matters were not being rendered into a vocabulary in our culture. Since they were not, parents had scant terms with which to discuss such matters with their children—much to the derision of the latter.

[19] To *sleep with* or *go to bed with* has been shown up as a seriously inadequate language deputy for the sexual act. Naturally there are many other such, ranging from *having relations* to the (legal) *sexual congress*. Partridge found a virtual dictionary of such in his *Shakespeare's Bawdy*. Ozark women used to *lay down* for the same activity. There is the Biblical *know*.

[20] A few years ago a British lawyer put a prostitute on the stand in a famous case and asked her if she had *slept with* the accused. She replied that she had not. This considerably disconcerted counsel, since the lady involved had frankly admitted that she had indeed had sexual intercourse with the man identified. The question had to be rephrased in sterner terms so that she might understand that *sleeping with* meant "sleeping with," not merely sleeping with. A hoary chestnut of British colonial days has it that a district administrator of the pukka sahib type enjoyed for years the sexual services of a native concubine; but when asked by his friends, who knew of this, whether he had ever *gone to bed with* the woman, he fervently denied having done so. On being pressed, over cups, to come clean, he got out stertorously the three words, "On the mat!"

EUPHEMISM: USE AND ABUSE

[21] We have already defined euphemism as a less direct symbol for the tabooed word, and we have discussed examples in various areas of taboo in our culture. Sometimes the original euphemism does not do the job of sufficiently quieting anxiety about the taboo, and a further step of *reeuphemizing* is necessary: *manure* gets dumped as *fertilizer* which then gets too closely attached to its stink so that it has to be called *plant food*. Similarly, *face-lifting* is disguised as *cosmetic surgery* which then turns into *skin sculpture*. A *garbage man* becomes a *sanitation engineer* who is now talked about in some parts as an *environmental expert*.

[22] Euphemism certainly performs a serious function in survival—cancer is genuinely easier to bear when it is called a *tumor,* and some addicts prefer to have a fix known as *inoculation;* but it clearly loses all purpose when it so clouds reality that no one knows what is happening at all. In such extreme cases, symbol loses all contact with referent.

[23] Lincoln, Nebraska's Hospital for the Crippled and Deformed is now the Nebraska Orthopedic Hospital, and New York's Hospital for the Society for the Relief of the Ruptured and Crippled has become the Hospital for Special Surgery. In this same spirit, artificial limbs are sometimes termed *prosthetic devices*.

TABOO: THE SACRED AND THE OBSCENE 139

[24] This has been shown genuinely to help, rather than hinder. Reality can, after all, become so unpleasant as to be unbearable. Someone who is called *crippled* by one society may be assisted by being reclassified *handicapped* or *disabled* by another. Are not sports players in the best of health also "handicapped"? To be blind is, surely, to be *visually handicapped* rather than *crippled*, since the blind are capable of extraordinary tactile and auditory sensitivity. An expert typist or concert pianist may well lack the use of eyes.

[25] Where, then, comes the borderline or breaking point at which the taboo totem gets worshiped for itself, as a kind of verbal golden calf? Of course, it is hard to be semantically specific. Since the renaming of a reality cannot change that reality, calling gelled gasoline fluid which is being dropped on Asiatic peasantry *napalm* is merely so much verbalized shame.

[26] Napalm was a technological neologism drawn from naphthenic and palmitic acids; but it soon became so closely attached to the dreadful reality that *incendigel*, even more technically neutral, it was hoped, was coined, and South Vietnamese newspapers were instructed to use the term. To the rice-paddy peasant anointed with one or the other, such subtleties of semantics must have seemed the luxury of a very rich and callous society indeed.

[27] The same attempt at reality-concealment of course proceeds on a more mundane level. At a point in our unsaying, we reach a moment when we hinder, rather than help, by such terms. The *environmental expert* is still shifting trash and the *grief therapist* (for which read funeral director) is still burying bodies—or *stiffs*. Ladies who do not want to mention *nose jobs* have been known to refer to them as *deviated septum operations*; however, a plain and simple deviated septum is a serious matter and should certainly not be confused with a *nose job*.

[28] Society gets the euphemisms it wants. The White House tried to induce journalists to eschew the term *escalation* and rename it *supplementary bombing*, without notable success. You might say—the way in which our lies are told us is important. The motive of the user is well revealed in a euphemism.

[29] Take our reiterated importation of the term *engineer*. Surely here the totem-creature is in danger of becoming more sacred than the being in reality. The plumber becomes a *household engineer*, the ditchdigger a *construction engineer*, a salesman a *sales engineer*, and a moving truck has *Moving Engineers* emblazoned on its flanks. Mencken unearthed a bedding manufacturer terming himself a *sleep-engineer*, and also an *exterminator-engineer*. The list could be continued indefinitely, and has been in fact; in 1935 the National Society of Professional Engineers protested against all these pseudo-engineers in our midst, in an action to try to get American railroads to call their locomotive engineers *enginemen*.

[30] Once again science admires itself in a mirror. There is a reflection, as we write, of the same tendency in the common substitution on all sides of *technologist* for technician. The Laverne-Pisani Bill was the result of one of these very conten-

tions in the field of nursing; it was aimed at precisely defining what a *nurse* was, in the inclusion or exclusion of certain medical regimens. The American Medical Association now wants to reclassify all GPs as *specialists*.

[31] The neologisms of technology, which artificially swell our dictionaries every year, are generally emotion-poor and depriving in effect. The man in the street still has problems using simple terms like amps and ohms. Now words like *polyunsaturates, quasars, rhochromatics,* and the like spatter our breakfast-food semantic, and to tell the layman that he has *agrypnia* or *cephalalgia* or *pyrexia* in lieu of the complaints they actually stand for (insomnia, headache, fever) is simply to confuse and probably alarm him. A *cold* is a *respiratory infection*. Most people would probably rather have a cold.

[32] Once again, it should be emphasized that the use of these terms often depends on context. They may be genuinely helpful. Thus a doctor can discuss a cancer innocently enough in front of an alarmed patient by referring to it as *neoplasia;* alcoholism may be called *extensive two-carbon fragment intake,* or just *etch* (from ethanol). Yet all too often technological euphemism can merely turn into another Humpty Dumpty. The effect of continual euphemism is really to make everything rather foggily similar and in the end to work against individuality and eccentricity. "The smatterer in science," Herman Melville has a character in *White Jacket* say, "thinks that by mouthing hard words he proves that he understands hard things."

[33] To conclude the entire subject of this chapter, we should see that taboo stands for a stage in language. It is not mutism, nor is it substitute physical activity. It is essentially a semantic transaction, and to utter an unutterable in the form of euphemism is perhaps an important pace forward in communication and makes certain dialogues easier and more "normal." But the *space where no language is* remains constant—the gap between symbol and reality.

FOR REVIEW AND DISCUSSION

Content

1. What is the relation between taboo and euphemism?

2. What euphemisms are associated with death? Pick one and analyze its meaning. In what contexts would it be useful?

3. The opposite of euphemism is *dysphemism*, a word that is harsher than a word it replaces. What are some dysphemisms associated with death? *Croak* is one. When would use of dysphemism be appropriate?

4. How are euphemisms less accurate than are the names they replace? Or are they equally accurate? How can we be sure?

5. What is meant by "the space where no language is"? Where is this space?

6. Do the authors imply that speakers control the use of euphemism or that euphemism controls (or affects) the ways users think? Do they imply neither of these relations? Both?

Rhetoric

1. The tone of this essay might be described as *glib*—a quality that is not usually desirable. Explain what *glib* means and point to specific places in the text that reveal this tone.

2. Why might the authors have chosen this tone? Is the tone appropriate?

3. Is the authors' attitude toward the use of euphemism clear throughout the essay, or is it developed as the essay progresses? As you read the essay, were you at any point uncertain of their attitude?

Classroom Exercises

1. What are some of the taboos in our culture? Can they be divided into categories based on similarity in the *object* of the taboo or the *purpose* of the taboo?

2. "The motive of a user is well revealed in a euphemism." To illustrate the authors' point, listen to people talking—on the radio or television, in the market, on campus, or wherever you happen to be—and record interesting euphemisms you hear. Then take each and determine what, if anything, it says about the person who used it.

Stuart Berg Flexner

PREFACE TO THE DICTIONARY OF AMERICAN SLANG

Slang is one of the most common and popular modes of spoken English; we get into trouble only when we use it in writing. Yet telling a slang term from its counterpart in "standard" usage can be difficult at times. In this selection, the author not only defines slang and attempts to explain its origins, he provides us with a number of categories for our slang terms. After reading the selection, you may want to look at the Dictionary of American Slang *in your campus library.*

[1] American slang, as used in the title of this dictionary, is the body of words and expressions frequently used by or intelligible to a rather large portion of the general American public, but not accepted as good, formal usage by the majority. No word can be called slang simply because of its etymological history; its source, its spelling, and its meaning in a larger sense do *not* make it slang. Slang is best defined by a dictionary that points out who uses slang and what "flavor" it conveys.

[2] I have called all slang used in the United States "American," regardless of its country of origin or use in other countries.

[3] In this preface I shall discuss the human element in the formation of slang (what American slang is, and how and why slang is created and used). . . .

[4] The English language has several levels of vocabulary:

[5] *Standard usage* comprises those words and expressions used, understood, and accepted by a majority of our citizens under any circumstances or degree of formality. Such words are well defined and their most accepted spellings and pronunciations are given in our standard dictionaries. In standard speech one might say: *Sir, you speak English well.*

[6] *Colloquialisms* are familiar words and idioms used in informal speech and writing, but not considered explicit or formal enough for polite conversation or business correspondence. Unlike slang, however, colloquialisms are used and understood by nearly everyone in the United States. The use of slang conveys the suggestion that the speaker and the listener enjoy a special "fraternity," but the use of colloqualisms emphasizes only the informality and familiarity of a general social

From *Dictionary of American Slang* edited by Harold Wentworth and Stuart Berg Flexner. Copyright © 1975, 1967, 1960 by Harper & Row, Publishers, Inc. Reprinted by permission of T. Y. Crowell.

situation. Almost all idiomatic expressions, for example, could be labeled colloquial. Colloquially, one might say: *Friend, you talk plain and hit the nail right on the head.*

[7] *Dialects* are the words, idioms, pronunciations, and speech habits peculiar to specific geographical locations. A dialecticism is a regionalism or localism. In popular use "dialect" has come to mean the words, foreign accents, or speech patterns associated with any ethnic group. In Southern dialect one might say: *Cousin, y'all talk mighty fine.* In ethnic-immigrant "dialects" one might say: *Paisano, you speak good the English,* or *Landsman, your English is plenty all right already.*

[8] *Cant, jargon,* and *argot* are the words and expressions peculiar to special segments of the population. *Cant* is the conversational, familiar idiom used and generally understood only by members of a specific occupation, trade, profession, sect, class, age group, interest group, or other sub-group of our culture. *Jargon* is the technical or even secret vocabulary of such a sub-group; jargon is "shop talk." *Argot* is both the cant and the jargon of any professional criminal group. In such usages one might say, respectively: *CQ-CQ-CQ . . . the tone of your transmission is good; You are free of anxieties related to interpersonal communication;* or *Duchess, let's have a bowl of chalk.*

[9] *Slang*[1] is generally defined above. In slang one might say: *Buster, your line is the cat's pajamas,* or *Doll, you come on with the straight jazz, real cool like.*

[10] Each of these levels of language, save standard usage, is more common in speech than in writing, and slang as a whole is no exception. Thus, very few slang words and expressions (hence very few of the entries in this dictionary) appear in standard dictionaries.

[11] American slang tries for a quick, easy, personal mode of speech. It comes mostly from cant, jargon, and argot words and expressions whose popularity has increased until a large number of the general public uses or understands them. Much of this slang retains a basic characteristic of its origin: it is *fully* intelligible only to initiates.

[12] Slang may be represented pictorially as the more popular portion of the cant, jargon, and argot from many sub-groups (only a few of the sub-groups are shown in the figure). The shaded areas represent only general overlapping between groups.

[13] Eventually, some slang passes into standard speech; other slang flourishes for a time with varying popularity and then is forgotten; finally, some slang is never fully accepted nor completely forgotten. *O.K., jazz* (music), and *A-bomb* were recently considered slang, but they are now standard usages. *Bluebelly, Lucifer,* and

---

[1] For the evolution of the word "slang," see F. Klaeber, "Concerning the Etymology of Slang," *American Speech*, April, 1926.

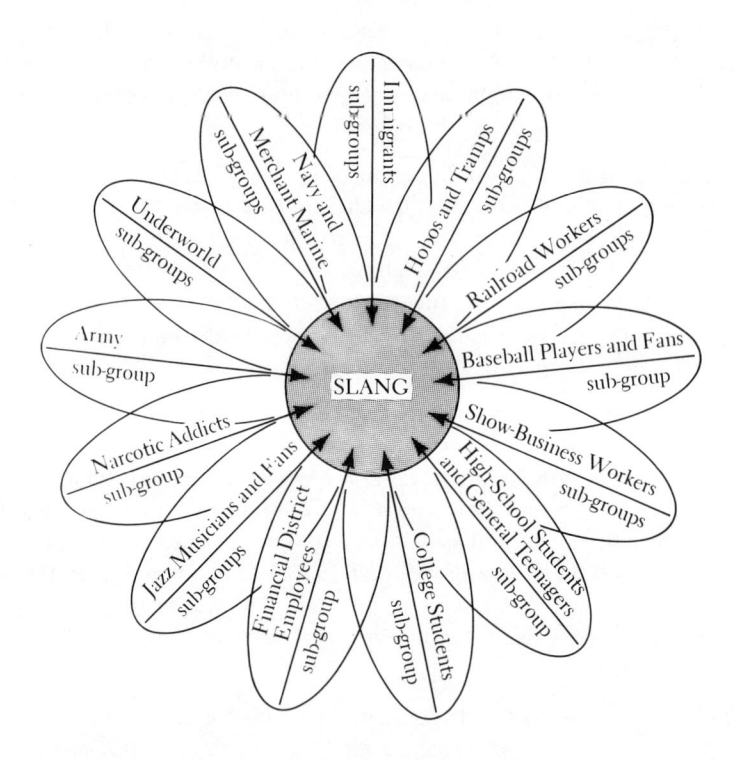

[Figure: A daisy-shaped diagram with "SLANG" at the center, surrounded by petals labeled: Immigrants sub-groups; Navy and Merchant Marine sub-groups; Underworld sub-groups; Hobos and Tramps sub-groups; Railroad Workers sub-groups; Army sub-group; Baseball Players and Fans sub-group; Narcotic Addicts sub-group; Show-Business Workers sub-groups; Jazz Musicians and Fans sub-groups; Financial District Employees sub-group; College Students sub-group; High-School Students and General Teenagers sub-group.]

the bee's knees have faded from popular use. *Bones* (dice) and *beat it* seem destined to remain slang forever: Chaucer used the first and Shakespeare used the second.

[14] It is impossible for any living vocabulary to be static. Most new slang words and usages evolve quite naturally: they result from specific situations. New objects, ideas, or happenings, for example, require new words to describe them. Each generation also seems to need some new words to describe the same old things.

[15] Railroaders (who were probably the first American sub-group to have a nationwide cant and jargon) thought *jerk water town* was ideally descriptive of a community that others called a *one-horse town*. The changes from *one-horse town* and *don't spare the horses* to a *wide place in the road* and *step on it* were natural and necessary when the automobile replaced the horse. The automobile also produced such new words and new meanings (some of them highly specialized) as *gas buggy, jalopy, bent eight, Chevvie, convertible,* and *lube*. Like most major innovations, the automobile affected our social history and introduced or encouraged *dusters, hitch hikers, road hogs, joint hopping, necking, chicken* (the game), *car coats,* and *suburbia*.

[16] The automobile is only one obvious example. Language always responds to new concepts and developments with new words.

PREFACE TO THE DICTIONARY OF AMERICAN SLANG 145

[17] Consider the following:

> wars: *redcoats, minutemen, bluebelly, over there, doughboy, gold brick, jeep.*
> mass immigrations: *Bohunk, greenhorn, shillalagh, voodoo, pizzeria.*
> science and technology: *'gin, side-wheeler, wash-and-wear, fringe area, fallout.*
> turbulent eras: *Redskin, maverick, speak, Chicago pineapple, free love, fink, breadline.*
> evolution in the styles of eating: *applesauce, clambake, luncheonette, hot dog, coffee and.*
> dress: *Mother Hubbard, bustle, shimmy, sailor, Long Johns, zoot suit, Ivy League.*
> housing: *lean-to, bundling board, chuckhouse, W.C., railroad flat, split-level, sectional.*
> music: *cakewalk, bandwagon, fish music, long hair, rock.*
> personality: *Yankee, alligator, flapper, sheik, hepcat, B.M.O.C., beetle, beat.*
> new modes of transportation: *stage, pinto, jitney, kayducer, hot shot, jet jockey.*
> new modes of entertainment: *barnstormer, two-a-day, clown alley, talkies, d.j., Spectacular.*
> changing attitudes toward sex: *painted woman, fast, broad, wolf, jailbait, sixty-nine.*
> human motivations: *boy crazy, gold-digger, money-mad, Momism, Oedipus complex, do-gooder, sick.*
> personal relationships: *bunky, kids, old lady, steady, ex, gruesome twosome, John.*
> work and workers: *clod buster, scab, pencil pusher, white collar, graveyard shift, company man.*
> politics: *Tory, do-nothing, mug-wump, third party, brain trust, fellow traveler, Veep.*
> and even hair styles: *bun, rat, peroxide blonde, Italian cut, pony tail, D.A.*

[18] Those social groups that first confront a new object, cope with a new situation, or work with a new concept devise and use new words long before the population at large does. The larger, more imaginative, and useful a group's vocabulary, the more likely it is to contribute slang. To generate slang, a group must either be very large and in constant contact with the dominant culture or be small, closely knit, and removed enough from the dominant culture to evolve an extensive, highly personal, and vivid vocabulary. Teen-agers are an example of a large sub-group contributing many words. Criminals, carnival workers, and hoboes are examples of the smaller groups. The smaller groups, because their vocabulary is personal and vivid, contribute to our general slang out of proportion to their size.

[19] Whether the United States has more slang words than any other country (in proportion to number of people, area, or the number of words in the standard vocabulary) I do not know.[2] Certainly the French and the Spanish enjoy extremely large slang vocabularies. Americans, however, do use their general slang more than any other people.

---

[2] The vocabulary of the average American, most of which he knows but never uses, is usually estimated at 10,000–20,000 words. Of this quantity I estimate conservatively that 2,000 words are slang. Slang, which thus forms about 10 per cent of the words known by the average American, belongs to the part of his vocabulary most frequently *used.*

The English language is now estimated to have at least 600,000 words; this is over four times the 140,000 recorded words of the Elizabethan period. Thus over 450,000 *new words or meanings* have been added since Shakespeare's day, without counting the replacement words or those that have been forgotten

[20] American slang reflects the kind of people who create and use it. Its diversity and popularity are in part due to the imagination, self-confidence, and optimism of our people. Its vitality is in further part due to our guarantee of free speech and to our lack of a national academy of language or of any "official" attempt to purify our speech. Americans are restless and frequently move from region to region and from job to job. This hopeful wanderlust, from the time of the pioneers through our westward expansion to modern mobility, has helped spread regional and group terms until they have become general slang. Such restlessness has created constantly new situations which provoke new words. Except for a few Eastern industrial areas and some rural regions in the South and West, America just doesn't look or sound "lived in." We often act and speak as if we were simply visiting and observing. What should be an ordinary experience seems new, unique, or colorful to us, worthy of words and forceful speech. People do not "settle down" in their jobs, towns, or vocabularies.

[21] Nor do we "settle down" intellectually, spiritually, or emotionally. We have few religious, regional, family, class, psychological, or philosophical roots. We don't believe in roots, we believe in teamwork. Our strong loyalties, then, are directed to those social groups—or sub-groups as they are often called—with which we are momentarily identified. This ever-changing "membership" helps to promote and spread slang.

between then and now. There are now approximately 10,000 slang words in American English, and about 35,000 cant, jargon, and argot words.

Despite this quantity, 25 per cent of all communication is composed of just nine words. According to McKnight's study, another 25 per cent of all speech is composed of an additional 34 words (or: 43 words comprise 50 per cent of all speech). Scholars do differ, however, on just which nine words are the most popular. Three major studies are: G. H. McKnight, *English Words and Their Background*, Appleton-Century-Crofts, Inc., 1923 (for spoken words only); Godfrey Dewey, "Relative Frequency of English Speech Sounds," *Harvard Studies in Education*, vol. IV, 1923 (for written words only); and Norman R. French, Charles W. Carter, and Walter Koenig, Jr., "Words and Sounds of Telephone Conversations," *Bell System Technical Journal*, April, 1930 (telephone speech only). Their lists of the most common nine words are:

McKnight's (speech)	Dewey's (written)	Bell Telephone (conversations)
	a	a
and	and	
be		
have		
	in	
		I
	is	is
it	it	it
		on
of	of	
	that	that
the	the	the
to	to	to
will		
you		you

[22] But even within each sub-group only a few new words are generally accepted. Most cant and jargon are local and temporary. What persist are the exceptionally apt and useful cant and jargon terms. These become part of the permanent, personal vocabulary of the group members, giving prestige to the users by proving their acceptance and status in the group. Group members then spread some of this more honored cant and jargon in the dominant culture. If the word is also useful to non-group members, it is on its way to becoming slang. Once new words are introduced into the dominant culture, via television, radio, movies, or newspapers, the rapid movement of individuals and rapid communication between individuals and groups spread the new word very quickly.

[23] For example, consider the son of an Italian immigrant living in New York City. He speaks Italian at home. Among neighborhood youths of similar background he uses many Italian expressions because he finds them always on the tip of his tongue and because they give him a sense of solidarity with his group. He may join a street gang, and after school and during vacations work in a factory. After leaving high school, he joins the navy; then he works for a year seeing the country as a carnival worker. He returns to New York, becomes a longshoreman, marries a girl with a German background, and becomes a boxing fan. He uses Italian and German borrowings, some teen-age street-gang terms, a few factory terms, slang with a navy origin, and carnival, dockworker's, and boxing words. He spreads words from each group to all other groups he belongs to. His Italian parents will learn and use a few street-gang, factory, navy, carnival, dockworker's, and boxing terms; his German in-laws will learn some Italian words from his parents; his navy friends will begin to use some of his Italian expressions; his carnival friends a few navy words; his co-workers on the docks some carnival terms, in addition to all the rest; and his social friends, with whom he may usually talk boxing and dock work, will be interested in and learn some of his Italian and carnival terms. His speech may be considered very "slangy" and picturesque because he has belonged to unusual, colorful sub-groups.

[24] On the other hand, a man born into a Midwestern, middle-class, Protestant family whose ancestors came to the United States in the eighteenth century might carry with him popular high-school terms. At high school he had an interest in hot rods and rock-and-roll. He may have served two years in the army, then gone to an Ivy League college where he became an adept bridge player and an enthusiast of cool music. He may then have become a sales executive and developed a liking for golf. This second man, no more usual or unusual than the first, will know cant and jargon terms of teen-age high-school use, hotrods, rock-and-roll, Ivy League schools, cool jazz, army life, and some golf player's and bridge player's terms. He knows further a few slang expressions from his parents (members of the Jazz Age of the 1920's), from listening to television programs, seeing both American and British movies, reading popular literature, and from frequent meetings with people having completely different backgrounds. When he uses cool terms on the golf course,

college expressions at home, business words at the bridge table, when he refers to whiskey or drunkenness by a few words he learned from his parents, curses his next-door neighbor in a few choice army terms—then he too is popularizing slang.

[25] It is, then, clear that three cultural conditions especially contribute to the creation of a large slang vocabulary: (1) hospitality to or acceptance of new objects, situations, and concepts; (2) existence of a large number of diversified sub-groups; (3) democratic mingling between these sub-groups and the dominant culture. Primitive peoples have little if any slang because their life is restricted by ritual; they develop few new concepts; and there are no sub-groups that mingle with the dominant culture. (Primitive sub-groups, such as medicine men or magic men, have their own vocabularies; but such groups do not mix with the dominant culture and their jargon can never become slang because it is secret or sacred.)

[26] But what, after all, are the advantages that slang possesses which make it useful? Though our choice of any specific word may usually be made from habit, we sometimes consciously select a slang word because we believe that it communicates more quickly and easily, and more personally, than does a standard word. Sometimes we resort to slang because there is no one standard word to use. In the 1940's *WAC, cold war,* and *cool* (music) could not be expressed quickly by any standard synonyms. Such words often become standard quickly, as have the first two. We also use slang because it often is more forceful, vivid, and expressive than are standard usages. Slang usually avoids the sentimentality and formality that older words often assume. Taking a girl to a *dance* may seem sentimental, may convey a degree of formal, emotional interest in the girl, and has overtones of fancy balls, fox trots, best suits, and corsages. At times it is more fun to go to a *hop*. To be *busted* or without a *hog* in one's *jeans* is not only more vivid and forceful than being penniless or without funds, it is also a more optimistic state. A *mouthpiece* (or *legal beagle*), *pencil pusher, sawbones, boneyard, bottle washer* or a course in *biochem* is more vivid and forceful than a lawyer, clerk, doctor, cemetery, laboratory assistant, or a course in biochemistry—and is much more real and less formidable than a legal counsel, junior executive, surgeon, necropolis (or memorial park), laboratory technician, or a course in biological chemistry.

[27] Although standard English is exceedingly hospitable to polysyllabicity and even sesquipedalianism, slang is not. Slang is sometimes used not only because it is concise but just because its brevity makes it forceful. As this dictionary demonstrates, slang seems to prefer short words, especially monosyllables, and, best of all, words beginning with an explosive or an aspirate.[3]

---

[3] Many such formations are among our most frequently used slang words. As listed in this dictionary, *bug* has 30 noun meanings, *shot* 14 noun and 4 adjective meanings, *can* 11 noun and 6 verb, *bust* 9 verb and 6 noun, *hook* 8 noun and 5 verb, *fish* 14 noun, and *sack* 8 noun, 1 adjective, and 1 verb meaning. Monosyllabic words also had by far the most citations found in our source reading of popular literature. Of the 40 words for which we found the most quotations, 29 were monosyllabic. Before condensing, *fink*

PREFACE TO THE DICTIONARY OF AMERICAN SLANG 149

[28] We often use slang *fad* words as a bad habit because they are close to the tip of our tongue. Most of us apply several favorite but vague words to any of several somewhat similar situations; this saves us the time and effort of thinking and speaking precisely. At other times we purposely choose a word because it is vague, because it does not commit us too strongly to what we are saying. For example, if a friend has been praising a woman, we can reply "she's *the bee's knees*" or "she's a real *chick*," which can mean that we consider her very modern, intelligent, pert, and understanding—or can mean that we think she is one of many nondescript, somewhat confused, followers of popular fads. We can also tell our friend that a book we both have recently read is *the cat's pajamas* or *the greatest*. These expressions imply that we liked the book for exactly the same reasons that our friend did, without having to state what these reasons were and thus taking the chance of ruining our rapport.

[29] In our language we are constantly recreating our image in our own minds and in the minds of others. Part of this image, as mentioned above, is created by using sub-group cant and jargon in the dominant society; part of it is created by our choice of both standard and slang words. A sub-group vocabulary shows that we have a group to which we "belong" and in which we are "somebody"—outsiders had better respect us. Slang is used to show others (and to remind ourselves of) our biographical, mental, and psychological background; to show our social, economic, geographical, national, racial, religious, educational, occupational, and group interests, memberships, and patriotisms. One of the easiest and quickest ways to do this is by using counter-words. These are automatic, often one-word responses of like or dislike, of acceptance or rejection. They are used to counter the remarks, or even the presence, of others. Many of our fad words and many student and quasi-intellectual slang words are counter-words. For liking: *beat, the cat's pajamas, drooly, gas, George, the greatest, keen, nice, reet, smooth, super, way out*, etc. For rejection of an outsider (implying incompetence to belong to our group): *boob, creep, dope, drip, droop, goof, jerk, kookie, sap, simp, square, weird*, etc. Such automatic counters are overused, almost meaningless, and are a substitute for thought. But they achieve one of the main purposes of speech: quickly and automatically they express our own sub-group and personal criteria. Counter-words are often fad words creating a common bond of self-defense. All the rejecting counters listed above could refer to a moron, an extreme introvert, a birdwatcher, or a genius. The counters merely say that the person is rejected—he does not belong to the group. In uttering the counter we don't care what the person is; we are pledging our own group loyalty, affirming our identity, and expressing our satisfaction at being accepted.

had citations from 70 different sources, *hot* 67, *bug* 62, *blow* and *dog* 60 each, *joint* 59, *stiff* 56, *punk* 53, *bum* and *egg* 50 each, *guy* 43, *make* 41, *bull* and *mug* 37 each, *bird* 34, *fish* and *hit* 30 each, *ham* 25, *yak* 23, *sharp* 14, and *cinch* 10. (Many of these words, of course, have several slang meanings; many of the words also appeared scores of times in the same book or article.)

[30] In like manner, at various periods in history, our slang has abounded in words reflecting the fear, distrust, and dislike of people unlike ourselves. This intolerance is shown by the many derogatory slang words for different immigrant, religious, and racial groups: *Chink, greaser, Heinie, hunkie, mick, mockie, nigger, spik.* Many counters and derogatory words try to identify our own group status, to dare others to question our group's, and therefore our own, superiority.

[31] Sometimes slang is used to escape the dull familiarity of standard words, to suggest an escape from the established routine of everyday life. When slang is used, our life seems a little fresher and a little more personal. Also, as at all levels of speech, slang is sometimes used for the pure joy of making sounds, or even for a need to attract attention by making noise. The sheer newness and informality of certain slang words produces a pleasure.

[32] But more important than this expression of a more or less hidden esthetic motive on the part of the speaker is slang's reflection of the personality, the outward, clearly visible characteristics of the speaker. By and large, the man who uses slang is a forceful, pleasing, acceptable personality. Morality and intellect (too frequently not considered virtues in the modern American man) are overlooked in slang, and this has led to a type of reverse morality: many words, once standing for morally good things, are now critical. No one, for example, though these words were once considered complimentary, wants to be called a *prude* or *Puritan.* Even in standard usage they are mildly derisive.

[33] Moreover, few of the many slang synonyms for drunk are derogatory or critical. To call a person a standard drunk may imply a superior but unsophisticated attitude toward drinking. Thus we use slang and say someone is *boozed up, gassed, high, potted, stinking, has a glow on,* etc., in a verbal attempt to convey our understanding and awareness. These slang words show that we too are human and know the effects of excessive drinking.

[34] In the same spirit we refer to people sexually as *big ass man, fast, John, sex pot, shack job, wolf,* etc., all of which accept unsanctioned sexual intercourse as a matter of fact. These words are often used in a complimentary way and in admiration or envy. They always show acceptance of the person as a "regular guy." They are never used to express a moral judgment. Slang has few complimentary or even purely descriptive words for "virgin," "good girl," or "gentleman." Slang has *bag, bat, ex, gold digger, jerk, money mad, n.g., old lady, square,* etc.; but how many words are there for a good wife and mother, an attractive and chaste woman, an honest, hard-working man who is kind to his family, or even a respected elderly person? Slang—and it is frequently true for all language levels—always tends toward degradation rather than elevation. As slang shows, we would rather share or accept vices than be excluded from a social group. For this reason, for self-defense, and to create an aura (but not the fact) of modernity and individuality, much of our slang purposely expresses amorality, cynicism, and "toughness."

[35] Reverse morality also affects slang in other ways. Many use slang just because it is not standard or polite. Many use slang to show their rebellion against *boobs*, *fuddy-duddies*, *marks*, and *squares*. Intellectuals and politicians often use slang to create the "common touch" and others use slang to express either their anti-intellectualism or avant-garde leanings. Thus, for teen-agers, entertainers, college students, beatniks, jazz fans, intellectuals, and other large groups, slang is often used in preference to standard words and expressions. Slang is the "official" modern language of certain vociferous groups in our population.

[36] In my work on this dictionary, I was constantly aware that most American slang is created and used by males. Many types of slang words—including the taboo and strongly derogatory ones, those referring to sex, women, work, money, whiskey,[4] politics, transportation, sports, and the like—refer primarily to male endeavor and interest. The majority of entries in this dictionary could be labeled "primarily masculine use." Men belong to more sub-groups than do women; men create and use occupational cant and jargon; in business, men have acquaintances who belong to many different sub-groups. Women, on the other hand, still tend to be restricted to family and neighborhood friends. Women have very little of their own slang. The new words applied to women's clothing, hair styles, homes, kitchen utensils and gadgets are usually created by men. Except when she accompanies her boy friend or husband to *his* recreation (baseball, hunting, etc.) a woman seldom mingles with other groups. When women do mingle outside of their own neighborhood and family circles, they do not often talk of the outside world of business, politics, or other fields of general interest where new feminine names for objects, concepts, and viewpoints could evolve.

[37] Men also tend to avoid words that sound feminine or weak. Thus there are sexual differences in even the standard vocabularies of men and women. A woman may ask her husband to set the table for dinner, asking him to put out the *silver*, *crystal*, and *china*—while the man will set the table with *knives*, *forks*, *spoons*, *glasses*, and *dishes*. His wife might think the *table linen attractive*, the husband might think the *tablecloth* and *napkins* pretty. A man will buy a *pocketbook* as a gift for his wife, who will receive a *bag*. The couple will live under the same roof, the wife in her *home*, the man in his *house*. Once outside of their domesticity the man will begin to use slang quicker than the woman. She'll get into the *car* while he'll get into the *jalopy* or *Chevvie*. And so they go: she will learn much of her general slang from him; for any word she associates with the home, her personal belongings, or any female concept, he will continue to use a less descriptive, less personal one.

[38] Males also use slang to shock. The rapid tempo of life, combined with the sometimes low boiling point of males, can evoke emotions—admiration, joy, contempt, anger—stronger than our old standard vocabulary can convey. In the stress

---

[4] It would appear that the word having the most slang synonyms is *drunk*.

of the moment a man is not just in a standard "untenable position," he is *up the creek*. Under strong anger a man does not feel that another is a mere "incompetent"—he is a *jerk* or a *fuck-off*.

[39] Men also seem to relish hyperbole in slang. Under many situations, men do not see or care to express fine shades of meaning: a girl is either a *knockout* or a *dog*, liquor either *good stuff* or *panther piss*, a person either has *guts* or is *chicken*, a book is either *great* or nothing but *crap*. Men also like slang and colloquial wording because they express action or even violence: we *draw pay, pull a boner, make a score, grab some sleep, feed our face, kill time*—in every instance we tend to use the transitive verb, making ourselves the active doer.

[40] The relation between a sub-group's psychology and its cant and jargon is interesting, and the relation between an individual's vocabulary and psychological personality is even more so. Slang can be one of the most revealing things about a person, because our own personal slang vocabulary contains many words used by choice, words which we use to create our own image, words which we find personally appealing and evocative—as opposed to our frequent use of standard words merely from early teaching and habit. Whether a man calls his wife *baby, doll, honey, the little woman, the Mrs.*, or *my old lady* certainly reveals much about him. What words one uses to refer to a mother *(Mom, old lady)*, friend *(buddy, bunkie, old man)*, the bathroom *(can, John, little boy's room)*, parts of the body and sex acts *(boobies, gigi, hard, laid, score)*, being tired *(all in, beat)*, being drunk *(clobbered, high, lit up like a Christmas tree, paralyzed)*, and the like, reveal much about a person and his motivations.[5]

[41] The basic metaphors, at any rate, for all levels of language depend on the five senses. Thus *rough, smooth, touch; prune, sour puss, sweet; fishy, p.u., rotten egg; blow, loud; blue, red, square*. In slang, many metaphors refer to touch (including the sense of heat and cold) and to taste.

[42] Food is probably our most popular slang image. Food from the farm, kitchen, or table, and its shape, color, and taste suggest many slang metaphors. This is because food can appeal to taste, smell, sight, and touch, four of our five senses; because food is a major, universal image to all people, all sub-groups; because men work to provide it and women devote much time to buying and preparing it; because food is before our eyes three times every day.

[43] Many standard food words mean money in nonstandard use: *cabbage, kale, lettuce*. Many apply to parts of the body: *cabbage head, cauliflower ear, meat hooks, nuts, plates of meat*. Many food words refer to people: *apple, cold fish, Frog, fruitcake, honey, sweetie pie*. Others refer to general situations and attitudes: to *brew*

---

[5] For just the last example, *clobbered* may indicate that a drinker is punishing himself, *high* that he is escaping, *lit up like a Christmas tree* that he is seeking attention and a more dominant personality, and *paralyzed* that he seeks punishment, escape or death.

PREFACE TO THE DICTIONARY OF AMERICAN SLANG   153

a plot, to receive a *chewing out*, to find oneself *in a pickle* or something *not kosher*, to be unable to *swallow* another's story, to ask *what's cooking?* Many drunk words also have food images: *boiled, fried, pickled;* and so do many words for nonsense; *applesauce, banana oil, spinach.* Many standard food words also have sexual meanings in slang. The many food words for money, parts of the body, people, and sex reveal that food means much more to us than mere nourishment. When a *good egg brings home the bacon* to his *honey*, or when a *string bean* of a *sugar daddy* takes his *piece* of *barbecue* out to get *fried* with his hard-earned *kale*, food images have gone a long way from the farm, kitchen, and table.

[44] Sex has contributed comparatively few words to modern slang,[6] but these are among our most frequently used. The use of sex words to refer to sex in polite society and as metaphors in other fields is increasing. Sex metaphors are common for the same conscious reasons that food metaphors are. Sex appeals to, and can be used to apply to, most of the five senses. It is common to all persons in all sub-groups, and so we are aware of it continually.

[45] Slang words for sexual attraction and for a variety of sexual acts, positions, and relationships are more common than standard words. Standard non-taboo words referring to sex are so scarce or remote and scientific that slang is often used in referring to the most romantic, the most obscene, and the most humorous sexual situations. Slang is so universally used in sexual communication that when "a man meets a maid" it is best for all concerned that they know slang.[7] Slang words for sex carry little emotional connotation; they express naked desire or mechanical acts, devices, and positions. They are often blunt, cynical and "tough."

[46] The subconscious relating of sex and food is also apparent from reading this dictionary. Many words with primary, standard meanings of food have sexual slang meanings. The body, parts of the body, and descriptions of each, often call food terms into use: *banana, bread, cheese cake, cherry, jelly roll, meat,* etc. Beloved, or simply sexually attractive, people are also often called by food names: *cookie, cup of tea, honey, peach, quail, tomato,* etc. This primary relation between sex and food depends on the fact that they are man's two major sensuous experiences. They are shared by all personalities and all sub-groups and they appeal to the same senses— thus there is bound to be some overlapping in words and imagery. However, there are too many standard food words having sexual meanings in slang for these conscious reasons to suffice. Sex and food seem to be related in our subconscious.

[47] Also of special interest is the number of slang expressions relating sex and cheating. Used metaphorically, many sex words have secondary meanings of being

---

[6] Many so-called bedroom words are not technically slang at all, but are sometimes associated with slang only because standard speech has rejected them as taboo. However, many of these taboo words do have further metaphorical meanings in slang: *fucked, jerk, screw you,* etc.

[7] On the other hand, Madam de Staël is reported to have complimented one of her favorite lovers with "speech is not his language."

cheated, deceived, swindled, or taken advantage of, and several words whose primary meaning is cheating or deceiving have further specific sexual meanings: *cheating, fucked, make, royal screwing, score, turn a trick,* etc. As expressed in slang, sex is a trick somehow, a deception, a way to cheat and deceive us. To curse someone we can say *fuck you* or *screw you,* which expresses a wish to deprive him of his good luck, his success, perhaps even his potency as a man.[8] Sex is also associated with confusion, exhausting tasks, and disaster: *ball buster, screwed up, snafu,* etc. It seems clear, therefore, that, in slang, success and sexual energy are related or, to put it more accurately, that thwarted sexual energy will somehow result in personal disaster.

[48] Language is a social symbol. The risk of the middle class coincided with the period of great dictionary makers, theoretical grammarians, and the "correct usage" dogma. The new middle class gave authority to the dictionaries and grammarians in return for "correct usage" rules that helped solidify their social position. Today, newspaper ads still implore us to take mail-order courses in order to "learn to speak like a college graduate," and some misguided English instructors still give a good speaking ability as the primary reason for higher education.

[49] The gap between "correct usage" and modern practice widens each day. Are there valid theoretical rules for speaking good English, or should "observed usage" be the main consideration? Standard words do not necessarily make for precise, forceful, or useful speech. On the other hand, "observed usage" can never promise logic and clarity. Today, we have come to depend on "observed usage," just as eighteenth- and nineteenth-century social climbers depended on "correct usage," for social acceptance.

[50] Because it is not standard, formal, or acceptable under all conditions, slang is usually considered vulgar, impolite, or boorish. As this dictionary shows, however, the vast majority of slang words and expressions are neither taboo, vulgar, derogatory, nor offensive in meaning, sound, or image. There is no reason to avoid any useful, explicit word merely because it is labeled "slang." Our present language has not decayed from some past and perfect "King's English," Latin, Greek, or pre-Tower of Babel tongue. All languages and all words have been, are, and can only be but conventions mutually agreed upon for the sake of communicating. Slang came to America on the Mayflower. In general, it is not vulgar, new, or even peculiarly

---

[8] See F. P. Wood, "The Vocabulary of Failure," *Better English,* Nov., 1938, p. 34. The vocabulary of failure is itself very revealing. Failure in one's personality, school, job, business, or an attempted love affair are all expressed by the same vocabulary. One gets the *brush off,* the *gate,* a *kiss off,* or *walking papers* in both business and personal relationships. As the previous discussion of counterwords demonstrates, slang allows no distinction or degree among individual failures. Incompetence does not apply to just one job or facet of life—either one belongs or is considered unworthy. This unworthiness applies to the entire personality, there are no alternate avenues for success or happiness. One is not merely of limited intelligence, not merely an introvert, not merely ugly, unknowing, or lacking in aggression—but one is a failure in all these things, a complete *drip, jerk,* or *square.* The basic failure is that of personality, the person is not a mere failure—he is an outcast, an untouchable; he is taboo.

American: an obvious illustration of this is the polite, old French word *tête*, which was originally slang from a Latin word *testa*—cooking pot.

[51] Cant and jargon in no way refer only to the peculiar words of undesirable or underworld groups. Slang does not necessarily come from the underworld, dope addicts, degenerates, hoboes, and the like. Any cultural sub-group develops its own personal cant and jargon which can later become general slang. All of us belong to several of these specific sub-groups using our own cant and jargon. Teen-agers, steel workers, soldiers, Southerners, narcotic addicts, churchgoers, truck drivers, advertising men, jazz musicians, pickpockets, retail salesmen in every field, golf players, immigrants from every country, college professors, baseball fans—all belong to typical sub-groups from which slang originates. Some of these sub-groups are colorful; most are composed of prosaic, average people.

[52] Many people erroneously believe that a fundamental of slang is that it is intentionally picturesque, strained in metaphor, or jocular. Picturesque metaphor (and metonymy, hyperbole, and irony) does or should occur frequently in all levels of speech. Picturesque metaphor is a frequent characteristic of slang, but it does not define slang or exist as an inherent part of it. The picturesque or metaphorical aspect of slang is often due to its direct honesty or to its newness. Many standard usages are just as picturesque, but we have forgotten their original metaphor through habitual use. Thus slang's *jerk* and *windbag* are no more picturesque than the standard *incompetent* and *fool*. *Incompetent* is from the Latin *competens* plus the negating prefix *in-* and = "unable or unwilling to compete"; *fool* is Old French, from the Latin *follis* which actually = "bellows or wind bag"; slang's *windbag* and the standard *fool* actually have the same metaphor.

[53] As for picturesque sounds, I find very few in slang. Onomatopoeia, reduplications, harsh sounds and pleasing sounds, even rhyming terms, exist on all levels of speech. Readers of this dictionary will find no more picturesque or unusual sounds here than in a similar length dictionary of standard words. Many slang words are homonyms for standard words.

[54] As has been frequently pointed out, many slang words have the same meaning. There seems to be an unnecessary abundance of counterwords, synonyms for "drunk," hundreds of fad words with almost the same meaning, etc. This is because slang introduces word after word year after year from many, many sub-groups. But slang is a scatter-gun process; many new words come at the general public; most are ignored; a few stick in the popular mind.

[55] Remember that "slang" actually does not exist as an entity except in the minds of those of us who study the language. People express themselves and are seldom aware that they are using the artificial divisions of "slang" or "standard." First and forever, language is language, an attempt at communication and self-expression. The fact that some words or expressions are labeled "slang" while others are labeled "jargon" or said to be "from the Anglo-Saxon" is of little value except to scholars.

Thus this dictionary is a legitimate addition to standard dictionaries, defining many words just as meaningful as and often more succinct, useful, and popular than many words in standard dictionaries.

FOR REVIEW AND DISCUSSION

Content

1. Is it always possible to distinguish between jargon and slang? When does jargon become slang?

2. What does Flexner mean by *counter-words*? How are these words used differently than are other words?

3. Discuss some modern slang that expresses "amorality, cynicism, and 'tough-mindedness.' "

4. Why can *observed usage* "never promise logic and clarity"? Does this failing invalidate *observed usage*?

Rhetoric

1. How would you describe the author's own level of vocabulary? How does an awareness of his level of vocabulary help you to understand his approach to his subject?

2. Does Flexner build a strong argument for his assertion that Americans do not "settle down," that America does not seem "lived in"? How does he support his assertion?

Classroom Exercises

1. Flexner comments in 1960 that "women have very little of their own slang." Does his comment hold true now?

2. "American slang reflects the kind of people who create and use it." Discuss one or two examples of slang that reflect its creators and users.

3. "Slang can be one of the most revealing things about a person. . . ." Observe how someone you know uses slang, and discuss what slang reveals about that person.

Dwight Bolinger

DIALECT

>All of us (with the possible exception of Walter Cronkite) speak a dialect, a particular version of our native language. In American English, however, we usually notice only those dialects that are most evident, such as Southern drawls or Brooklynese. In this selection, Dwight Bolinger examines the various kinds of dialects and then discusses several in detail. As you read, try to apply his discussion to your own experience with people from various parts of the country.

[1]   Linguistic history records sweeping changes that affect vast bodies of speakers over long periods—some abrupt, even cataclysmic, so that everyone is conscious of what is happening, others so gradual that speakers may be unaware of them during their lifetimes. Dialectology looks upon the differences that set one community apart from another, that characterize the individual speaker even when they do not necessarily interfere with communication, that give society its flavor and no small amount of its mirth. Linguistic history is dialectology writ large, and dialectology is the idiosyncrasies of particular speakers writ medium. There is no clear separation of what one speaker does that others of his community do not do; nor is there any between what communities do that makes them different from one another or what it is that distinguishes one language from another. Techniques of discovery may differ—historical linguistics has elaborate strategies to hypothesize what cannot be observed because the evidence has long since vanished, whereas dialectology may be contemporary, capturing many of its facts almost as they happen. The facts in both fields are the same; the size of the bite is what distinguishes them.

[2]   But size makes a difference in our appreciation, for dialect differences are cut to the measure of our comprehension, while differences between languages may overwhelm us. Comparatively few individuals are bilingual. Every speaker is multilingual in the sense of understanding more than one dialect. And most speakers command different styles of speech which, if they are not to be called different dialects, are denied the name only because we want to reserve it for contrasts that are more pronounced. Whenever we speak in a more "reserved" or "decorous" manner, whenever we strive to avoid "grammatical mistakes," we pass from one dialect to another.

Excerpted from *Aspects of Language* by Dwight Bolinger, copyright © 1968 by Harcourt Brace Jovanovich, Inc. and reprinted with their permission.

KINDS OF DIALECT

[3] Every speaker speaks as many dialects as there are groups among which he moves that have different modes of speech. Some groups are biologically determined. Others are formed by more or less voluntary association. Here are some important ones:

[4] **[1] Profession** The speech of the minister differs from the speech of the merchant. Each occupation has its own things to talk about. But the difference goes beyond merely having different words for different things. It often embodies a variety of names for the same thing: the soothsayer has his ***augury,*** the weather man his ***forecast,*** the doctor his ***prognosis,*** and the scientist his ***prediction.***

[5] **[2] Sex** Men's talk differs from women's talk. This line is somewhat blurred in our society, but it remains legible. Adjectives like ***dreadful, precious, darling*** are more apt to be encountered in women's speech than in men's—in fact, women are more liberal with adjectives in general. In some levels of society men are less inhibited in their choice of words than women. Women are less inhibited in their intonational range.

[6] **[3] Age** The infant differs from the child, the child from the adolescent, the adolescent from the adult. The most extreme case is baby talk, which, in the sense that its speakers are physically unable to speak otherwise, is not really a dialect, but it becomes one when its forms are imitated—and sometimes fabricated—by adults and used by them with young children. As with all dialects, forms from this one may be picked up and broadcast; a recent instance is ***bye-bye,*** which is heard more and more as an ordinary friendly farewell, not necessarily an intimate one. At the other extreme is the dialect that time imposes on us all: older speakers do not always adopt newer ways of speaking, and the older they grow the more quaint their speech becomes. Nor is the process always purely automatic—a transition between age levels may be made consciously. Among the Ainu of Japan, "there is a kind of speech that is characteristic of older people which persists in its own right and is adopted by younger people as they gradually mature"—an "old speech" which does not itself grow old and die out.[1]

[7] **[4] Occasion** Even the most careful speakers permit themselves a style of speech at home that is different from the one they use in public. Many societies set up—not by legislation but by tacit consent—a standard dialect that is used on formal occasions and that serves as a kind of inter-lingua, available to any speaker when he wants to identify himself with speakers at large rather than with speakers at home. The standard dialect takes on the local color of the speaker but is nevertheless different from the relaxed style used with friends, family, and neighbors. It is more

---

[1] Shiro Hattori, "A Special Language of the Older Generations Among the Ainu," *General Linguistics* 6.43–58 (1964).

neutral and as a rule is more generally understood, but intelligibility is not essential to its authority.[2] In some countries, any relaxation of the formal standard in occasions that call for it is resented even if, as happens sometimes, speakers have difficulty understanding it (this may be likened to the reactions of some people in our own culture to attempts to make the Bible more intelligible by modernizing the English).[3] In India, formal Hindi is stiffened by generous doses of Sanskrit.[4] In Chinese, a formal lecture and a conversation may even differ syntactically: the idea that one group of officials (A) is more numerous than another group (B) is expressed in the lecture as

A	dwō	yú	B
A	numerous	than	B

and in the conversation as

A	bĭ	B	dwō
A	compared to	B	numerous[5]

[8]   The standard in English is not clear-cut (it is never entirely so anywhere), but certain tendencies mark it off. The obvious ones are in the choice of words. Where a university press, announcing a competition, reserves to itself the *"first refusal* of manuscripts," the intent is not to be candidly pessimistic but to avoid the more accurate but too colloquial *first chance at.*[6] At a graduation one hears *All seniors will please rise* (or possibly *stand*); a relaxed occasion would call for *get up* or *stand up.* Certain contractions are avoided on formal occasions: the easygoing *show* harmonizes with *'em* in *Let's show 'em* but would hardly be used with the stiff verb *reveal: Let's reveal them.* In the supremely formal atmosphere of the church, even *let's* may be avoided: *Let's pray* would sound secular, if not sporting. And there are syntactic differences here and there. Take the use of adverbs. There is a variety of English, regarded as substandard, in which most adverbs are distinguished from adjectives not by the suffix *-ly* but by position after the verb or verb phrase: in *He wrote the letter real careful, careful* is an adverb; in *He wrote a careful letter* it is an adjective. (All dialects of English do this part of the time: *He made the trip fast, He made a fast trip.*) Standard English adds the *-ly* and uses the resulting adverbs rather freely as to position: *They left rapidly, They rapidly left.* But very informal—not necessarily substandard—English does not favor *-ly* adverbs before the verb or verb phrase. It prefers the other position or some adverb not ending in

---

[2] Experiments have shown that "speakers of high status are more comprehensible for speakers of all statuses." See L. S. Harms, "Status Cues in Speech: Extra-race and Extra-region Identification," *Lingua* 12.300–06 (1963).

[3] Charles A. Ferguson, "Diglossia," *Word* 15.330 (1959).

[4] Paul W. Friedrich, *Language* 37.168 (1961).

[5] John de Francis in *Georgetown University Monograph Series on Languages and Linguistics*, September, 1951, p. 50.

[6] MLA-Oxford Award, 1952–53: "Under the terms of the competition, Oxford will have first refusal of all manuscripts submitted," *Hispania* 36.116 (1953).

-ly: instead of ***He grew steadily worse, I promptly told him,*** and ***She's constantly complaining*** it will say ***He grew worse and worse, I told him right there,*** and ***She's all the time complaining.***

[9] There is practically no limit to the number of social affinities revealed in differences of language. To age, sex, occupation, and occasion it would be necessary to add religion, politics, lodge affiliation, preference as to sports or amusements, and any other circumstances under which people meet and speak. But overshadowing them all are two coordinates laid on every society that determine far wider differences than any thus far mentioned. One is horizontal, as on a map: Bostonese, for example, differs from the speech of the rest of New England, and the speech of New England differs from that of the Coastal South; geographical dialects are inevitable, because people do more talking to their neighbors than to those who are farther away, and where more is shared, differences are fewer. The other is vertical, as with layers: in stratified societies people are born to a social class; nothing stigmatizes a class more indelibly than its language, and differences in speech are often cultivated for this very purpose.

[10] Probably because they touch us in a tender spot, the vertical and horizontal differences are the ones that come first to mind when dialects are mentioned. Geographical differences have ties with our loyalties to home, town, and state. Social differences are nourished on feelings of superiority and inferiority, and to some extent color all other differences. In a society where women and farmers are regarded as inferior, sex differences and occupational differences become class differences. As for differences due to occasion, inability to handle the standard dialect when the occasion calls for it is especially likely to be taken as a class difference, for the dominant social class is the one whose traits of speech are most fully embodied in the standard.

[11] The linguist and the sociologist are selective in different ways in their attitudes toward dialect. The linguist focuses mainly on the horizontal coordinate. Differences from region to region are the specimens that attract him most, probably because they are the same, though on a smaller scale, as the ones already familiar to him from language to language. When he speaks of dialectology it is almost always in this sense, more specifically referred to as "linguistic geography," "areal linguistics," or "dialect geography." The sociologist focuses mainly on the vertical coordinate. He is interested in how social groups interact within a single speech community, in how language influences our opportunities and our behavior. He views language as a series of codes by which the individual acts out his roles in society.

LINGUISTIC CODES

[12] The language of a profession, say that of law, is social distinction in its crudest form. It is part of an economic order in which everyone's way of earning a living somehow influences his speech because of the need to manipulate a certain set of

DIALECT 161

objects and concepts that are the tools of the profession. But ordinarily it goes no deeper than the choice of terms to match the objects. What really counts for the sociologist is how the lawyer interacts with his banker and his grocer, and how the banker's son and the grocer's son are able, through having certain models to emulate in their parents, teachers, and others, to define themselves and by so doing to open or close the doors to growth and change of status.

[13] The sociologist Basil Bernstein distinguishes two types of code that are socially significant: restricted and elaborated.[7] A restricted code allows one to interact with one's fellows in a highly predictable way. It is associated with a certain social set or activity where only a limited number of things can be done. They are not necessarily prescribed in a particular order, as they would be in a game, but the choices are few. An example is the cocktail party, where the nature of the language used and the nature of the things talked about is known in advance and what one learns about new-made acquaintances is transmitted not so much by language as by look and gesture. The conventionality of the language enables speakers to relax in one another's company and communicate in other ways, much as the set movements of a dance remove the necessity of deciding what to do next. In a restricted code, individuality is submerged. The speaker and listener are in a well-defined relationship with each other, with verbal routines laid out in advance. There is not much choice of what to say simply because there is no need to say much, and the little that is said carries a heavy load of implicit meaning. The speaker is acting a role with speeches perhaps not fully written for him as they would be on the stage, but well supplied with stock items by the small department within the social structure where he happens to be moving at the moment. There is room for a bit of ad-libbing but little more.

[14] In an elaborated code, the speaker and listener are acting parts in which they must improvise. Their standing with each other is such that neither can take much for granted about the other. Intentions and purposes have to be brought into the open and defined. What the speaker will say is hard to predict, because it is not about commonplaces but about something more or less unique, related less to some foreseeable role and more to him as an individual. He is wearing not a comic nor a tragic mask but his own face, and that is harder to put into words. An example would be that of a man told to do something by his boss and having to explain why it is impossible for him to comply.

[15] All speakers communicate with both restricted and elaborated codes, but not all are able to switch codes with the ease that is needed to interact to their advantage with other members of their society. Some speakers have little practice except with restricted codes, and unfortunately some of the roles in the social structure that are carried by those codes—implanted in the child by his exposure to them—are looked down upon. A speaker who is forced to operate with a certain code because

---

[7] "A Socio-linguistic Approach to Social Learning," in *Survey of the Social Sciences, 1965*, ed. Julius Gould (Baltimore, Md.: Penguin Books, Inc., 1965), pp. 144–68.

he has never had any other models to imitate will find that his only communication will be with other speakers who use the same code—it becomes self-enforcing and self-perpetuating. One of the tasks of education is to lead to an awareness of the limitations of one's code and to a large amount of practice with elaborated codes, where the speaker is forced to become conscious of his language, to "orient towards the verbal channel."[8] This is the individual's road of escape from the confinement of his every act by restricted codes laid on him by the social structure without regard for his individuality, capacities, or intelligence.

LINGUISTIC GEOGRAPHY

[16] Serious investigation of geographical dialects began in the latter part of the nineteenth century. The first comprehensive study was made in North and Central Germany by Georg Wenker. A smaller study followed in Denmark, and between 1902 and 1908 Jules Gilliéron published his *Atlas Linguistique de la France,* the most influential work of its kind. Since the turn of the century materials have been collected for similar atlases all over the world. In the United States the model has been the *Linguistic Atlas of New England,* directed by Hans Kurath and published between 1939 and 1943. Other regional atlases covering most of the country have been drawn up as part of a comprehensive *Linguistic Atlas of the United States and Canada,* still in preparation.

[17] As the name implies, a linguistic atlas is a collection of maps showing the prevalence of particular speech forms in particular areas. What the dialect geographer most often selects to mark off a dialect area is simply its preference for certain words. Differences in pronunciation or syntax yield a more reliable measure, but words are easier to work with; information can even be gathered by mail through a questionnaire that asks what words a speaker uses for particular meanings: is a field enclosure made of stone called a ***stone wall,*** a ***stone fence,*** a ***rock wall,*** or a ***rock fence***? Are drains that take rainwater off a roof called ***eaves troughs, water spouting, gutters,*** or ***rain spouts***? For greater accuracy, detailed phonetic information is needed. Trained interviewers must be sent to the scene and may spend hours with a single informant. Does he pronounce ***soot*** to rime with ***boot*** or with ***put***? Is his final consonant in ***with*** like that of ***bath*** or that of ***bathe***? Does his pronunciation of ***tomato*** end with the same vowel sound as ***panda*** or is it like ***grotto***? The Swiss German atlas, published in 1962, was based on a questionnaire containing 2,600 items, which took from four to eight days to administer. Its phonetic discriminations were exquisite—as many as twenty-one different tongue heights, for example, in front unrounded vowels.[9] The items chosen for a questionnaire to test differences in

---

[8] Bernstein, *op. cit.,* p. 161.
[9] William Moulton, review in *Journal of English and German Philology* 62.831 (1963).

vocabulary, pronunciation, and syntax are the ones most likely to reveal the peculiarities of everyday speech: names of household objects, foods, parts of the body, weather phenomena, numbers, and so on.

American Dialect Geography

[18] Unless he is combining his interest as a linguist with an extracurricular one as a folklorist or sociologist, the dialect geographer is less concerned with the items in a questionnaire for their own sake than as indicators of where to draw the boundary lines and how to trace the routes of speakers as they migrated from one area to another. The latter—the fanning out of dialects from their original centers and their crisscrossing and blending as the wave moves outward—is of special significance in a country like the United States, with its extraordinarily mobile population.

Boundaries are set by mapping the farthest points to which a given form has penetrated. When a line—termed an *isogloss* if it has to do with words, an *isophone* if with sounds—is drawn connecting these points, it is usually found to lie close to the lines drawn for other forms—for instance, the same speakers who say **snake feeder** for 'dragonfly' are also apt to pronounce the word **greasy** as **greazy**. The interlocking lines form a bundle of isoglosses (or isophones) and represent the frontier of the dialect in question.

[19] American English divides rather clearly into three grand dialect areas in the eastern part of the country. They reflect the settlement of these areas by early migrants from England who brought their dialects with them. One such dialectal transplant from England is the vowel in words like **half, bath, aunt, glass,** and **laugh.** We easily recognize one way of pronouncing these words as a feature of cultivated speech in the East and of over-cultivated speech elsewhere. It is by no means uniform (in Eastern Virginia, for example, it will be heard in **master** and **aunt** but not in many other words), and represents one side of a split that took place in the eastern counties of England before the American Revolution. The /a/ was transplanted from those counties as folk speech by immigrants to New England, but it also took root in London and so became established as fashionable speech in the parts of the country that maintained the closest ties with England.[10]

[20] As the population spread westward the boundaries became more and more blurred. The earlier, more gradual movement extended them fairly evenly as far as the Mississippi. By the time the migrants had flowed up against the Rocky Mountains, the three tides had broken into a series of rivulets and eddies. Where a given area was settled mainly by speakers of a given dialect, that dialect of course pre-

---

[10] Hans Kurath, "Some Aspects of Atlantic Seaboard English Considered in Their Connections with British English," in *Communications et Rapports du Premier Congrès International de Dialectologie Générale* (Louvain, Belgium, 1965), pp. 239–40.

vailed. The area around Hayden, Colorado, was turned into a kind of Northern island by a group of women schoolteachers who came out from Ann Arbor, Michigan, and married ranchers there. Later, as younger speakers grew up and intermarried, Northern and Midland traits were blended.

[21] Dialect blending is not confined to the West but goes on wherever the streams of communication, which seem to grow swifter every day, overflow the earlier lines. In northern Illinois, for example, the lines again are growing dim. The following list—of interest also as a sample of the kind of vocabulary used—enumerates words that are receding in the predominantly Midland area of Illinois, even though half of them were Midland to begin with:

1. window blind 'shade for a window, on a spring roller' (Midland)
2. woodshed
3. pigpen
4. pulley bone 'breastbone of a chicken, wishbone' (Southern, South Midland)
5. light bread 'bread made with yeast' (Southern, South Midland)
6. hay doodle 'small pile of hay' (Midland)
7. trestle 'saw horse with an X-frame'
8. poo-wee!, a call to hogs
9. poison vine 'poison ivy'
10. cement road 'concrete road'
11. to favor 'to resemble,' as in **John favors his father**
12. baby cab 'baby carriage' (Midland)
13. belling 'shivaree' (Midland)
14. belly buster 'dive in coasting prone on a sled, belly flop' (Midland)[11]

[22] Two metaphors describe the extremes of diffusion. One is the relay race, the other the cross-country. In the first, a speaker picks up something from his neighbor to the east and runs with it as far as his neighbor to the west, always staying between them. In the second, a speaker breaks loose from the paternal neighborhood and travels to all points of the compass, picking up pieces at each stop and dropping them all along the way. The latter is the kind of diffusion that makes dialectology a hazardous business. As Robert Louis Stevenson wrote in *The Amateur Emigrant,*

> I knew I liked Mr. Jones from the moment I saw him. I thought him by his face to be Scottish; nor could his accent undeceive me. For as there is a *lingua franca* of many tongues on the moles and in the feluccas of the Mediterranean, so there is a free or common accent among English-speaking men who follow the sea. They catch a twang of a New England port, from a cockney skipper, even a Scotsman sometimes learns to drop an *h*; a word of a dialect is picked up from another hand in the forecastle; until often the result is undecipherable, and you have to ask for a man's place of birth.[12]

---

[11] Roger W. Shuy, "The Northern-Midland Dialect Boundary in Illinois," *Publications of the American Dialect Society* No. 38, November, 1962, p. 59. Professor Shuy was kind enough to provide definitions.
[12] South Seas Edition (New York: Charles Scribner's Sons, Inc., 1925), p. 9.

[23] The compilers of the new *Dictionary of American Regional English* are at present engaged in one of the largest word-gathering projects in history—a five-year (1965–70) survey of the dialects of the United States from Florida to Alaska in an effort "to collect the greater part . . . of the words and phrases, pronunciations, spellings, and meanings used . . . up to the present time."[13] Besides bringing to light the quantities of unregistered written forms in obscure places, this project will rescue uncounted expressions that would otherwise be lost as their users died away because the forms existed only in the spoken language. The estimated five million entries will be processed by computers. (The compilers of the vast *Oxford Dictionary* assembled three and a half million entries by hand.)

[24] But geography is not all. The fading of differences is accelerated by social pressures. Where a normalized, cultivated speech gains in favor—and this, we should remember, was until recently the largest single result of formal schooling—everything with a pronounced local or, especially, rustic flavor tends to be rooted out. Thus, in the area of northern Illinois already discussed, the cultivated forms *I ran home yesterday, He did it, I'm going to lie down* are replacing the uncultivated—whether Northern or Midland—*I run home yesterday, He done it, I'm going to lay down.*[14]

THE HORIZONTAL IMPOSED ON THE VERTICAL

[25] When a rubber manufacturer in Akron, Ohio, imports low-wage laborers from West Virginia, he unwittingly turns a geographical dialect into a social one. The newcomers are readily identified by their strange forms of speech, and they are poor and uneducated. No matter how carefully they dress and conduct themselves, they cannot change their dialect quickly enough to merge with the rest of the community, and the result is that the one trait that marks them most distinctly is taken as a badge of their "class."

[26] Or, to complicate things further, the imported laborers may speak a dialect that was socially non-standard even in the place of origin and is still further out of line with the standard speech of the new area. The most radically deviant form of English likely to be encountered in this country echoes the trade language that was used in the early part of the eighteenth century on the West African coast and was probably carried to the plantations of the South and used by speakers who had no other means of communication.[15]

---

[13] Frederic G. Cassidy, "American Regionalism and the Harmless Drudge," *Publications of the Modern Language Association* 82:3.14 (1967).
[14] Shuy, *op. cit.*, p. 64.
[15] William A. Stewart, "Sociolinguistic Factors in the History of American Negro Dialects," *The Florida FL Reporter*, Spring, 1976, pp. 1–4.

[27] This transplanting, as American dialectologist Raven McDavid points out, has happened and continues to happen all over the United States, and constitutes a grave social problem. For the fact is that nothing more thoroughly excludes a person from a social group than a manner of speech that has come to be identified as uncultivated. And, given the fact that the most extensive recent migrations have been from the poorest rural areas, especially those of the South, to the most tightly structured urban societies, those of our large cities, one understands how much language has contributed to the creation or deepening of class lines.

[28] The best solution seems to be an enlightened "bi-dialectalism," fostered by the schools, where the basic job of integration has to be done. The form of speech approved by the local community is taught not as something that must be acquired and used under all circumstances but as something useful for general communication, while the imported speech is respected in its place on the playground, in the home, and in relaxed conversation.[16] "The first principle of any language program is that, whatever the target, it must respect the language that the students bring with them to the classroom."[17] The schools will need to be more sophisticated in their teaching of English. This calls for helping teachers to see that when students come to them limited to restricted codes in a nonstandard dialect what they need is not to be corrected in supposed mistakes but to be introduced to a new and in many ways different but related system, no better and no worse than the old one but more useful in their new contacts.[18] It may even be useful to teach some of the nonstandard dialect to the speakers of the standard. Acceptance, not just toleration, implies both knowledge and use.

FOR REVIEW AND DISCUSSION

Content

1. How is *dialect* distinguished from *language*? Why is it sometimes difficult to make this distinction?

2. Bolinger suggests that one's profession and sex influence one's dialect. In what ways may sex and profession also influence the use of jargon?

3. What factors in modern society are causing dialect differences to fade? What benefits and drawbacks do you see to everyone's speaking the same dialect?

---

[16] Raven I. McDavid, Jr., "American Social Dialects," *College English*, January, 1965, pp. 254–60.
[17] Raven I. McDavid, Jr., "Sense and Nonsense about American Dialects," *Publications of the Modern Language Association* 81:2.7–17 (1966), p. 9.
[18] This is being attempted in Washington, D.C., by the Urban Language Study. See J. L. Dillard in *The Linguistic Reporter*, October, 1966, pp. 1–2.

Rhetoric

1. To what extent does Bolinger seem to be describing the nature of dialect, the study of dialect, a particular attitude toward dialect? What else might he be doing in this essay? What seems to be his main purpose?

2. How well has Bolinger's examination of dialect prepared us to accept his closing argument in favor of "enlightened bi-dialectalism"?

Classroom Exercises

1. How would you classify the dialect you speak—ethnically, regionally, socially, or by some other classification? Describe the characteristics of your dialect.

2. Describe the linguistic code of your class. Is the code *restricted*, *elaborated*, or a combination of both?

Stephen Vincent Benét

AMERICAN NAMES

A common error among many students of literature is to assume that all poems hold hidden meaning, that poets seldom really mean what they say. This poem is not filled with mystery or obscurity, although it may refer to an out-of-the-way place or two. It is not a complex poem, but it does make a significant point about language. For a moment we are not concerned with the theoretical or even the practical aspects of language that occupy much of this anthology. We are concerned merely with the sound of language, the sound of names.

[1]   I have fallen in love with American names,
      The sharp names that never get fat,
      The snakeskin-titles of mining-claims,
      The plumed war-bonnet of Medicine Hat,
      Tucson and Deadwood and Lost Mule Flat.

[2]   Seine and Piave are silver spoons,
      But the spoonbowl-metal is thin and worn,
      There are English counties like hunting-tunes
      Played on the keys of a postboy's horn,
      But I will remember where I was born.

[3]   I will remember Carquinez Straits,
      Little French Lick and Lundy's Lane,

From *Ballads and Poems* by Stephen Vincent Benét. Copyright 1931 by Stephen Vincent Benét. Copyright © 1959 by Rosemary Carr Benét. Reprinted by permission of Holt, Rinehart & Winston, Publishers.

> The Yankee ships and the Yankee dates
> And the bullet-towns of Calamity Jane.
> I will remember Skunktown Plain.
>
> [4] I will fall in love with a Salem tree
> And a rawhide quirt from Santa Cruz,
> I will get me a bottle of Boston tea
> And a blue-gum nigger to sing me blues.
> I am tired of loving a foreign muse.
>
> [5] Rue des Martyrs and Bleeding-Heart-Yard,
> Senlis, Pisa, and Blindman's Oast,
> It is a magic ghost you guard
> But I am sick for a newer ghost,
> Harrisburg, Spartanburg, Painted Post.
>
> [6] Henry and John were never so
> And Henry and John were always right?
> Granted, but when it was time to go
> And the tea and the laurels had stood all night,
> Did they never watch for Nantucket Light?
>
> [7] I shall not rest quiet in Montparnasse.
> I shall not lie easy at Winchelsea.
> You may bury my body in Sussex grass,
> You may bury my tongue at Champmedy.
> I shall not be there. I shall rise and pass.
> Bury my heart at Wounded knee.

FOR REVIEW AND DISCUSSION

Content

1. What does Benét mean by the line "The sharp names that never get fat"?

2. Do you think that this poem would have more meaning for those who have some acquaintance with a foreign language than it would for others?

Rhetoric

1. At first glance, little seems to happen in this poem, but if you review each stanza, you will see that the poem does move toward a particular ending. What is it? What are the stages through which the poem moves toward that ending?

2. Benét uses a first person point of view in which there are frequent references to "I." What effect has this point of view on the focus of the poem? Would a third person point of view have worked just as well?

3. What is the predominant verb tense in the poem? Why might Benét have decided to use it?

4. Benét uses a number of figurative expressions—for instance, "Seine and Piave are silver spoons." Can they easily be "translated" into their literal meanings? How do we understand what Benét means by "silver spoons"?

Classroom Exercises

1. What qualities seem to distinguish American and foreign place names? Why do you think Benét responds so strongly to American place names?

2. What are some American place names that particularly appeal to you? What causes their appeal? Their sounds and imagery? The associations you have with them? Something else?

FOR FURTHER READING

William Labov

THE LOGIC OF NONSTANDARD ENGLISH

Most of the selections in this chapter deal with American English in very broad terms, but this article is a detailed examination of one particular kind—what we often refer to as "Black English" or "Black dialect." The author analyzes particularly the logic of this dialect, perhaps because those of us who don't speak it have frequently assumed that it is illogical and somehow "incorrect"—in spite of what we know about language.

[1] In the past decade, a great deal of federally sponsored research has been devoted to the educational problems of children in ghetto schools. In order to account for the poor performance of children in these schools, educational psychologists have attempted to discover what kind of disadvantage or defect they are suffering from. The viewpoint that has been widely accepted and used as the basis for large scale intervention programs is that the children show a cultural deficit as a result of an impoverished environment in their early years. Considerable attention has been given to language. In this area the deficit theory appears as the concept of verbal deprivation. Black children from the ghetto area are said to receive little verbal stimulation, to hear very little well-formed language, and as a result are

From *Language in the Inner City* by William Labov. Copyright 1972 by the University of Pennsylvania Press. Reprinted by permission of the publisher.

impoverished in their means of verbal expression. They cannot speak complete sentences, do not know the names of common objects, cannot form concepts or convey logical thoughts.

[2]   Unfortunately, these notions are based upon the work of educational psychologists who know very little about language and even less about black children. The concept of verbal deprivation has no basis in social reality. In fact, black children in the urban ghettos receive a great deal of verbal stimulation, hear more well-formed sentences than middle-class children, and participate fully in a highly verbal culture. They have the same basic vocabulary, possess the same capacity for conceptual learning, and use the same logic as anyone else who learns to speak and understand English. . . .

VERBALITY AND VERBOSITY

[3]   The general setting in which the deficit theory arises consists of a number of facts which are known to all of us. One is that black children in the central urban ghettos do badly in all school subjects, including arithmetic and reading. . . .

[4]   The most extreme view which proceeds from this orientation—and one that is now being widely accepted—is that lower-class black children have no language at all. The notion is first drawn from Basil Bernstein's writings that "much of lower-class language consists of a kind of incidental 'emotional' accompaniment to action here and now" (Jensen 1968, p. 118). Bernstein's views are filtered through a strong bias against all forms of working-class behavior, so that middle-class language is seen as superior in every respect—as "more abstract, and necessarily somewhat more flexible, detailed and subtle" (p. 119). . . .

[5]   Here, for example, is a complete interview with a black child, one of hundreds carried out in a New York City school. The boy enters a room where there is a large, friendly, white interviewer, who puts on the table in front of him a toy and says: "Tell me everything you can about this." (The interviewer's further remarks are in parentheses.)

>   [12 seconds of silence]
> (What would you say it looks like?)
>   [8 seconds of silence]
> A space ship.
> (Hmmmm.)
>   [13 seconds of silence]
> Like a je-et.
>   [12 seconds of silence]
> Like a plane.
>   [20 seconds of silence]

(What color is it?)
Orange. (2 seconds) An' whi-ite. (2 seconds)
          An' green.
     [6 seconds of silence]
(An' what could you use it for?)
     [8 seconds of silence]
A je-et.
     [6 seconds of silence]
(If you had two of them, what would you
     do with them?)
     [6 seconds of silence]
Give one to some-body.
(Hmmm. Who do you think would like to have
     it?)
     [10 seconds of silence]
Cla-rence.
(Mm. Where do you think we could get
     one of these?)
At the store.
(Oh ka-ay!)

[6]   We have here . . . defensive, monosyllabic behavior. . . . What is the situation that produces it? The child is in an asymmetrical situation where anything he says can literally be held against him. He has learned a number of devices to avoid saying anything in this situation, and he works very hard to achieve this end. . . .

[7]   If one takes this interview as a measure of the verbal capacity of the child, it must be as his capacity to defend himself in a hostile and threatening situation. But unfortunately, thousands of such interviews are used as evidence of the child's total verbal capacity, or more simply his verbality. It is argued that this lack of verbality explains his poor performance in school. Operation Head Start and other intervention programs have largely been based upon the deficit theory—the notions that such interviews give us a measure of the child's verbal capacity and that the verbal stimulation which he has been missing can be supplied in a preschool environment. . . .

[8]   The view of the black speech community which we obtain from our work in the ghetto areas is precisely the opposite from that reported by Deutsch or by Bereiter and Engelmann. We see a child bathed in verbal stimulation from morning to night. We see many speech events which depend upon the competitive exhibition of verbal skills—sounding, singing, toasts, rifting, louding—a whole range of activities in which the individual gains status through his use of language (see Labov, et al., 1968, section 4.2). We see the younger child trying to acquire these skills from older children, hanging around on the outskirts of older peer groups, and imitating this behavior to the best of his ability. We see no connection

between verbal skill in the speech events characteristic of the street culture and success in the schoolroom. . . .

[9] Our work in the speech community makes it painfully obvious that in many ways working-class speakers are more effective narrators, reasoners, and debaters than many middle-class speakers who temporize, qualify, and lose their argument in a mass of irrelevant detail. Many academic writers try to rid themselves of that part of middle-class style that is empty pretension, and keep that part that is needed for precision. But the average middle-class speaker that we encounter makes no such effort; he is enmeshed in verbiage, the victim of sociolinguistic factors beyond his control.

[10] I would like to contrast two speakers dealing with roughly the same topic—matters of belief. The first is Larry H., a fifteen-year-old core member of the Jets, being interviewed by John Lewis. Larry is one of the loudest and roughest members of the Jets, one who gives the least recognition to the conventional rules of politeness. For most readers of this paper, first contact with Larry would produce some fairly negative reactions on both sides. It is probable that you would not like him any more than his teachers do. Larry causes trouble in and out of school. He was put back from the eleventh grade to the ninth, and has been threatened with further action by the school authorities.

> *JL:* What happens to you after you die? Do you know?
> *Larry:* Yeah, I know. (What?) After they put you in the ground, your body turns into—ah—bones, an' shit.
> *JL:* What happens to your spirit?
> *Larry:* Your spirit—soon as you die, your spirit leaves you. (And where does the spirit go?) Well, it all depends . . . (On what?) You know, like some people say if you're good an' shit, your spirit goin' t'heaven . . . 'n' if you bad, your spirit goin' to hell. Well, bullshit! Your spirit goin' to hell anyway, good or bad.
> *JL:* Why?
> *Larry:* Why? I'll tell you why. 'Cause, you see, doesn' nobody really know that it's a God, y'know, 'cause I mean I have seen black gods, pink gods, white gods, all color gods, and don't nobody know it's really a God. An' when they be sayin' if you good, you goin' t'heaven, tha's bullshit, 'cause you ain't goin' to no heaven, 'cause it ain't no heaven for you to go to.

[11] Larry is a paradigmatic speaker of the Black English Vernacular (BEV) as opposed to standard English. His grammar shows a high concentration of such characteristic BEV forms as negative inversion ("don't nobody know . . ."), negative concord ("you ain't goin' to no heaven . . ."), invariant *be* ("when they be sayin'. . ."), dummy *it* for standard *there* ("it ain't no heaven . . ."), optional copula deletion ("if you're good . . . if you bad . . .") and full forms of auxiliaries ("I have seen . . ."). The only standard English influence in this passage is the one case of "doesn't" instead of the invariant "don't" of BEV. Larry also provides a paradigmatic example of the rhetorical style of BEV: he can sum up a complex argument in a few words, and the full force of his opinions come through without qualification or reservation. He is eminently quotable, and his interviews give us

THE LOGIC OF NONSTANDARD ENGLISH

many concise statements of the BEV point of view. One can almost say that Larry speaks the BEV culture (see Labov, et al. 1968, vol. 2, pp. 38, 71–73, 291–92).

[12] It is the logical form of this passage which is of particular interest here. Larry presents a complex set of interdependent propositions which can be explicated by setting out the standard English equivalents in linear order. The basic argument is to deny the twin propositions:

(A) If you are good, (B) then your spirit will go to heaven.
(~A) If you are bad, (C) then your spirit will go to hell.

Larry denies (B) and asserts that if (A) or (~A), then (C). His argument may be outlined as follows:

1. Everyone has a different idea of what God is like.
2. Therefore nobody really knows that God exists.
3. If there is a heaven, it was made by God.
4. If God doesn't exist, he couldn't have made heaven.
5. Therefore heaven does not exist.
6. You can't go somewhere that doesn't exist.

(~B) Therefore you can't go to heaven.
(C) Therefore you are going to hell.

The argument is presented in the order: (C), because (2) because (1), therefore (2), therefore (~B) because (5) and (6). Part of the argument implicit: the connection (2) therefore (~B) leaves unstated the connecting links (3) and (4), and in this interval Larry strengthens the propositions from the form (2) "Nobody knows if there is . . ." to (5) "There is no. . . ." Otherwise, the case is presented explicitly as well as economically. The complex argument is summed up in Larry's last sentence, which shows formally the dependence of (~B) on (5) and (6):

> An' when they be sayin' if you good, you goin' t'heaven (the proposition, if A, then B),
> Tha's bullshit (is absurd),
> 'cause you ain't goin' to no heaven (because B)
> 'cause it ain't no heaven for you to go to (because (5) and (6)).

This hypothetical argument is not carried on at a high level of seriousness. It is a game played with ideas as counters, in which opponents use a wide variety of verbal devices to win. There is no personal commitment to any of these propositions, and no reluctance to strengthen one's argument by bending the rules of logic as in the (2)–(5) sequence. But if the opponent invokes the rules of logic, they hold. In John Lewis's interviews, he often makes this move, and the force of his argument is always acknowledged and countered within the rules of logic. In this case, he pointed out the fallacy that the argument (2)-(3)-(4)-(5)-(6) leads to (~C) as well as (~B), so it cannot be used to support Larry's assertion (C):

> JL: Well, if there's no heaven, how could there be a hell?
> Larry: I mean—ye-eah. Well, let me tell you, it ain't no hell, 'cause this is hell right here, y'know! (This is hell?) Yeah, this is hell right here!

[13] Larry's answer is quick, ingenious, and decisive. The application of the (3)-(4)-(5) argument to hell is denied, since hell is here, and therefore conclusion (C) stands. These are not ready-made or preconceived opinions, but new propositions devised to win the logical argument in the game being played. The reader will note the speed and precision of Larry's mental operations. He does not wander, or insert meaningless verbiage. The only repetition is (2), placed before and after (1) in his original statement. It is often said that the nonstandard vernacular is not suited for dealing with abstract or hypothetical questions, but in fact speakers from the black community take great delight in exercising their wit and logic on the most improbable and problematical matters. Despite the fact that Larry H. does not believe in God, and has just denied all knowledge of him, John Lewis advances the following hypothetical question:

> JL: . . . but, just say that there is a God, what color is he? White or black?
> Larry: Well, if it is a God . . . I wouldn' know what color, I couldn' say—couldn' nobody say what color he is or really *would* be.
> JL: But now, jus' suppose there was a God—
> Larry: Unless'n they say . . .
> JL: No, I was jus' sayin' jus' suppose there is a God, would he be white or black?
> Larry: . . . He'd be white, man.
> JL: Why?
> Larry: Why? I'll tell you why. 'Cause the average whitey out here got everything, you dig? And the nigger ain't got shit, y'know? Y'unnerstan'? So—um—for—in order for *that* to happen, you know it ain't no black God that's doin' that bullshit.

No one can hear Larry's answer to this question without being convinced that they are in the presence of a skilled speaker with great "verbal presence of mind," who can use the English language expertly for many purposes. Larry's answer to John Lewis is again a complex argument. The formulation is not standard English, but it is clear and effective even for those not familiar with the vernacular. The nearest standard English equivalent might be: "So you know that God isn't black, because if he was, he wouldn't have arranged things like that."

[14] The reader will have noted that this analysis is being carried out in standard English, and the inevitable challenge is: why not write in BEV, then, or in your own nonstandard dialect? The fundamental reason is, of course, one of firmly fixed social conventions. All communities agree that standard English is the proper medium for formal writing and public communication. Furthermore, it seems likely that standard English has an advantage over BEV in explicit analysis of surface forms, which is what we are doing here. We will return to this opposition between explicitness and logical statement in subsequent sections on grammaticality and logic. First, however, it will be helpful to examine standard English in its primary natural setting, as the medium for informal spoken communication of middle-class speakers.

[15] Let us now turn to the second speaker, an upper-middle-class, college-educated black man (Charles M.) being interviewed by Clarence Robins in our survey of adults in Central Harlem.

THE LOGIC OF NONSTANDARD ENGLISH 175

CR: Do you know of anything that someone can do, to have someone who has passed on visit him in a dream?

Charles: Well, I even heard my parents say that there is such a thing as something in dreams some things like that, and sometimes dreams do come true. I have personally never had a dream come true. I've never dreamt that somebody was dying and they actually died (Mhm) or that I was going to have ten dollars the next day and somehow I got ten dollars in my pocket (Mhm). I don't particularly believe in that, I don't think it's true. I do feel, though, that there is such a thing as—ah—witchcraft. I do feel that in certain cultures there is such a thing as witchcraft, or some sort of *science* of witchcraft; I don't think that it's just a matter of believing hard enough that there is such a thing as witchcraft. I do believe that there is such a thing that a person can put himself in a state of *mind* (Mhm), or that—er—something could be given them to intoxicate them in a certain—to a certain frame of mind—that—that could actually be considered witchcraft.

[16] Charles M. is obviously a good speaker who strikes the listener as well-educated, intelligent, and sincere. He is a likeable and attractive person, the kind of person that middle-class listeners rate very high on a scale of job suitability and equally high as a potential friend. His language is more moderate and tempered than Larry's; he makes every effort to qualify his opinions, and seems anxious to avoid any misstatements or overstatements. From these qualities emerge the primary characteristic of this passage—its verbosity. Words multiply, some modifying and qualifying, others repeating or padding the main argument. The first half of this extract is a response to the initial question on dreams, basically:

1. Some people say that dreams sometimes come true.
2. I have never had a dream come true.
3. Therefore I don't believe (1).

Some characteristic filler phrases appear here: *such a thing as, some things like that,* and *particularly*. Two examples of dreams given after (2) are afterthoughts that might have been given after (1). Proposition (3) is stated twice for no obvious reason. Nevertheless, this much of Charles M.'s response is well-directed to the point of the question. He then volunteers a statement of his beliefs about witchcraft which shows the difficulty of middle-class speakers who (a) want to express a belief in something but (b) want to show themselves as judicious, rational, and free from superstitions. The basic proposition can be stated simply in five words:

"But I believe in witchcraft."

However, the idea is enlarged to exactly 100 words, and it is difficult to see what else is being said. In the following quotations, padding which can be removed without change in meaning is shown in parentheses.

(1) "I (do) feel, though, that there is (such a thing as) witchcraft." *Feel* seems to be a euphemism for "believe."

(2) "(I do feel that) in certain cultures (there is such a thing as witchcraft)." This repetition seems designed only to introduce the word *culture*, which lets us know that the speaker knows about anthropology. Does *certain cultures* mean "not in ours" or "not in all"?

(3) "(or some sort of *science* of witchcraft.)" This addition seems to have no clear meaning at all. What is a "science" of witchcraft as opposed to just plain witchcraft? The main function is to introduce the word *science*, though it seems to have no connection to what follows.

(4) "I don't think that it's just (a matter of) believing hard enough that (there is such a thing as) witchcraft." The speaker argues that witchcraft is not merely a belief; there is more to it.

(5) "I (do) believe that (there is such a thing that) a person can put himself in a state of mind . . . that (could actually be considered) witchcraft." Is witchcraft as a state of mind different from the state of belief, denied in (4)?

(6) "or that something could be given them to intoxicate them (to a certain frame of mind). . . ." The third learned word, *intoxicate*, is introduced by this addition. The vacuity of this passage becomes more evident if we remove repetitions, fashionable words and stylistic decorations:

> But I believe in witchcraft.
> I don't think witchcraft is just a belief.

[17] A person can put himself or be put in a state of mind that is witchcraft. Without the extra verbiage and the "OK" words like *science, culture,* and *intoxicate,* Charles M. appears as something less than a first-rate thinker. The initial impression of him as a good speaker is simply our long-conditioned reaction to middle-class verbosity. We know that people who use these stylistic devices are educated people, and we are inclined to credit them with saying something intelligent. Our reactions are accurate in one sense. Charles M. is more educated than Larry. But is he more rational, more logical, more intelligent? Is he any better at thinking out a problem to its solution? Does he deal more easily with abstractions? There is no reason to think so. Charles M. succeeds in letting us know that he is educated, but in the end we do not know what he is trying to say, and neither does he.

[18] In the previous section I have attempted to explain the origin of the myth that lower-class black children are nonverbal. The examples just given may help to account for the corresponding myth that middle-class language is in itself better suited for dealing with abstract, logically complex, or hypothetical questions. These examples are intended to have certain negative force. They are not controlled experiments. On the contrary, this and the preceding section are designed to convince the reader that the controlled experiments that have been offered in evidence are misleading. The only thing that is controlled is the superficial form of the stimulus. All children are asked "What do you think of capital punishment?" or "Tell me everything you can about this." But the speaker's interpretation of these requests, and the action he believes is appropriate in response is completely uncontrolled. One can view these test stimuli as requests for information, commands for action, threats of punishment, or meaningless sequences of words. They are probably intended as something altogether different—as requests for display, but in any case the experimenter is normally unaware of the problem of interpretation. The

methods of educational psychologists such as used by Deutsch, Jensen, and Bereiter follow the pattern for animal experiments where motivation is controlled by simple methods as withholding food until a certain weight reduction is reached. With human subjects, it is absurd to believe that identical stimuli are obtained by asking everyone the same question.

[19] Since the crucial intervening variables of interpretation and motivation are uncontrolled, most of the literature on verbal deprivation tells us nothing about the capacities of children. They are only the trappings of science, approaches which substitute the formal procedures of the scientific method for the activity itself. With our present limited grasp of these problems, the best we can do to understand the verbal capacities of children is to study them within the cultural context in which they were developed.

[20] It is not only the black vernacular which should be studied in this way, but also the language of middle-class children. The explicitness and precision which we hope to gain from copying middle-class forms are often the product of the test situation, and limited to it. For example, it was stated in the first part of this paper that working-class children hear more well-formed sentences than middle-class children. This statement may seem extraordinary in the light of the current belief of many linguists that most people do not speak in well-formed sentences, and that their actual speech production, or performance, is ungrammatical. But those who have worked with any body of natural speech know that this is not the case. Our own studies (Labov 1966) of the grammaticality of everyday speech show that the great majority of utterances in all contexts are complete sentences, and most of the rest can be reduced to grammatical form by a small set of editing rules. The proportions of grammatical sentences vary with class backgrounds and styles. The highest percentage of well-formed sentences are found in casual speech, and working-class speakers use more well-formed sentences than middle-class speakers. The widespread myth that most speech is ungrammatical is no doubt based upon tapes made at learned conferences, where we obtain the maximum number of irreducibly ungrammatical sequences.

[21] It is true that technical and scientific books are written in a style which is markedly middle-class. But unfortunately, we often fail to achieve the explicitness and precision which we look for in such writing, and the speech of many middle-class people departs maximally from this target. All too often, standard English is represented by a style that is simultaneously overparticular and vague. The accumulating flow of words buries rather than strikes the target. It is this verbosity which is most easily taught and most easily learned, so that words take the place of thoughts, and nothing can be found behind them.

[22] When Bernstein (e.g., 1966) describes his elaborated code in general terms, it emerges as a subtle and sophisticated mode of planning utterances, where the speaker is achieving structural variety, taking the other person's knowledge into

account, and so on. But when it comes to describing the actual difference between middle-class and working-class speakers (Bernstein 1966), we are presented with a proliferation of "I think," of the passive, of modals and auxiliaries, of the first-person pronoun, of uncommon words, and so on. But these are the bench marks of hemming and hawing, backing and filling, that are used by Charles M., the devices which so often obscure whatever positive contribution education can make to our use of language. When we have discovered how much of middle-class style is a matter of fashion and how much actually helps us express ideas clearly, we will have done ourselves a great service. We will then be in a position to say what standard grammatical rules must be taught to nonstandard speakers in the early grades. . . .

LOGIC

[23] For many generations, American schoolteachers have devoted themselves to correcting a small number of nonstandard English rules to their standard equivalents, under the impression that they were teaching logic. This view has been reinforced and given theoretical justification by the claim that BEV lacks the means for the expression of logical thought.

[24] Let us consider for a moment the possibility that black children do not operate with the same logic that middle-class adults display. This would inevitably mean that sentences of a certain grammatical form would have different truth values for the two types of speakers. One of the most obvious places to look for such a difference is in the handling of the negative, and here we encounter one of the nonstandard items which has been stigmatized as illogical by schoolteachers—the double negative, or as we term it, *negative concord*. A child who says "He don't know nothing" is often said to be making an illogical statement without knowing it. According to the teacher, the child wants to say "He knows nothing" but puts in an extra negative without realizing it, and so conveys the opposite meaning, "He does not know nothing," which reduces to "He knows something." I need not emphasize that this is an absurd interpretation. If a nonstandard speaker wishes to say that "He does not know *nothing*," he does so by simply placing contrastive stress on both negatives as I have done here ("He *don't* know *nothing*") indicating that they are derived from two underlying negatives in the deep structure. But note that the middle-class speaker does exactly the same thing when he wants to signal the existence of two underlying negatives: "He *doesn't* know *nothing*." In the standard form with one underlying negative ("He doesn't know anything"), the indefinite *anything* contains the same superficial reference to a preceding negative in the surface structure as the nonstandard *nothing* does. In the corresponding positive sentences, the indefinite *something* is used. The dialect difference, like most of the differences between the standard and nonstandard forms, is one of surface form, and has nothing to do with the underlying logic of the sentence.

[25] We can summarize the ways in which the two dialects differ:

	Standard English, SE	Black English Vernacular, BEV
Positive:	He knows something.	He know something.
Negative:	He doesn't know anything.	He don't know nothing.
Double Negative:	He *doesn't* know *nothing*.	He *don't* know *nothing*.

This array makes it plain that the only difference between the two dialects is in superficial form. When a single negative is found in the deep structure, standard English converts *something* to the indefinite *anything*; BEV converts it to *nothing*. When speakers want to signal the presence of two negatives, they do it the same way. No one would have any difficulty constructing the same table of truth values for both dialects. English is a rare language in its insistence that the negative particle be incorporated in the first indefinite only. The Anglo-Saxon authors of the Peterborough Chronicle were surely not illogical when they wrote *For ne waeren nan martyrs swa pined alse he waeron,* literally, "For never weren't no martyrs so tortured as they were." The "logical" forms of current standard English are simply the accepted conventions of our present-day formal style. Russian, Spanish, French, and Hungarian show the same negative concord as nonstandard English, and they are surely not illogical in this. What is termed "logical" in standard English is of course the conventions which are habitual. The distribution of negative concord in English dialects can be summarized in this way (Labov, et al. 1968, section 3.6; Labov 1968):

1. In all dialects of English, the negative is attracted to a lone indefinite before the verb: "Nobody knows anything," not "Anybody doesn't know anything."
2. In some nonstandard white dialects, the negative also combines optionally with all other indefinites: "Nobody knows nothing," "He never took none of them."
3. In other white nonstandard dialects, the negative may also appear in preverbal position in the same clause: "Nobody doesn't know nothing."
4. In Black English Vernacular, negative concord is obligatory to all indefinites within the clause, and it may even be added to preverbal position in following clauses: "Nobody didn't know he didn't" (meaning, "Nobody knew he did").

[26] Thus all dialects of English share a categorical rule which attracts the negative to an indefinite subject, and they merely differ in the extent to which the negative particle is also distributed to other indefinites in preverbal position. It would have been impossible for us to arrive at this analysis if we did not know that black speakers are using the same underlying logic as everyone else.

[27] Negative concord is more firmly established in Black English Vernacular than in other nonstandard dialects. The white nonstandard speaker shows variation in this rule, saying one time, "Nobody ever goes there" and the next, "Nobody never goes there." Core speakers of the BEV vernacular consistently use the latter form. In repetition tests which we conducted with adolescent blacks (Labov, et al. 1968, section 3.9), standard forms were repeated with negative concord. Here, for example, are three trials by two thirteen-year-old members (Boot and David) of the Thunderbirds:

Model by interviewer: "Nobody ever sat at any of those desks, anyhow."
Boot:
(1) Nobody never sa—No [whitey] never sat at any o' tho' dess, anyhow.
(2) Nobody never sat any any o' tho' dess, anyhow.
(3) Nobody as ever sat at no desses, anyhow.
David:
(1) Nobody ever sat in-in-in-in- none o'—say it again?
(2) Nobody never sat in none o' tho' desses anyhow.
(3) Nobody—aww! Nobody never ex—Dawg!

It can certainly be said that Boot and David fail the test; they have not repeated the sentence correctly—that is, word for word. But have they failed because they could not grasp the meaning of the sentence? The situation is in fact just the opposite; they failed because they perceived only the meaning and not the superficial form. Boot and David are typical of many speakers who do not perceive the surface details of the utterance so much as the underlying semantic structure, which they unhesitatingly translate into the vernacular form.

Model:
I asked Alvin if he knows how to play basketball.
Boot:
I ax Alvin do he know how to play basketball.
Money:
I ax Alvin if—do he know how to play basketball.
Model:
I asked Alvin whether he knows how to play basketball.
Larry F:
(1) I axt Alvin does he know how to play basketball.
(2) I axt Alvin does he know how to play basketball.

Here the difference between the words used in the model sentence and in the repetition is striking. Again, there is a failure to pass the test. But it is also true that these boys understand the standard sentence, and translate it with extraordinary speed into the BEV form, which is here the regular Southern colloquial form.

[28] To pass the repetition test, Boot and the others have to learn to listen to surface detail. They do not need a new logic; they need practice in paying attention to the explicit form of an utterance rather than its meaning. Careful attention to surface features is a temporary skill needed for language learning—and neglected thereafter by competent speakers. . . .

[29] Linguists are in an excellent position to demonstrate the fallacies of the verbal deprivation theory. All linguists agree that nonstandard dialects are highly structured systems. They do not see these dialects as accumulations of errors caused by the failure of their speakers to master standard English. When linguists hear black children saying "He crazy" or "Her my friend," they do not hear a primitive language. Nor do they believe that the speech of working-class people is merely a form of emotional expression, incapable of expressing logical thought. . . .

[30] When linguists say that BEV is a system, we mean that it differs from other dialects in regular and rule-governed ways, so that it has equivalent ways of expressing the same logical content. When we say that it is a separate subsystem, we mean that there are compensating sets of rules which combine in different ways to preserve the distinctions found in other dialects. Thus as noted above BEV does not use the *if* or *whether* complementizer in embedded questions, but the meaning is preserved by the formal device of reversing the order of subject and auxiliary. . . .

[31] Linguists now agree that teachers must know as much as possible about the Black English Vernacular as a communicative system. . . .

[32] The exact nature and relative importance of the structural differences between BEV and standard English are not in question here. It is agreed that the teacher must approach the teaching of the standard through a knowledge of the child's own system. The methods used in teaching English as a foreign language are recommended, not to declare that BEV is a foreign language, but to underline the importance of studying the native dialect as a coherent system for communication. This is in fact the method that should be applied in any English class. . . .

[33] That educational psychology should be strongly influenced by a theory so false to the facts of language is unfortunate; but that children should be the victims of this ignorance is intolerable. It may seem that the fallacies of the verbal deprivation theory are so obvious that they are hardly worth exposing. I have tried to show that such exposure is an important job for us to undertake. If linguists can contribute some of their available knowledge and energy toward this end, we will have done a great deal to justify the support that society has given to basic research in our field.

FOR REVIEW AND DISCUSSION

Content

1. How do we determine what "logic" is in standard English? Discuss whether the logic of standard English is different from or similar to the logic of some other English dialect.

2. The author says that middle-class language is verbose. What does he mean? To what extent do you agree with him?

3. Explain the difference between what Labov calls the "surface forms" or "surface features" of language and what is sometimes called the "deep structure" of language.

Rhetoric

1. Is Labov's purpose to argue for a particular thesis or to present his and other researchers' findings? How is his purpose made apparent?

2. Does Labov adequately explain *why* "the best we can do to understand the verbal capacities of children is to study them within the cultural context in which they were developed"? Is the explanation stated or implied?

3. Labov's argument seems to rest largely on his revealing analysis of the speech habits of only two subjects—Larry H. and Charles M. How does the author avoid the possible criticism that his conclusions rest on too narrow a research base?

4. Does Labov fall into the trap of verbosity that he complains exists in middle-class writing and speaking? If you think that he does, cite specific instances.

5. The author employs a number of examples in his writing. Examine the discussion that follows each one and comment on its completeness and accuracy.

Classroom Exercises

1. Paragraph 11 contains a list of characteristic BEV forms. Using these forms as a guide, write in Black English a description of some event. Then "translate" the Black English version into standard English. Did you feel equally at ease thinking in both dialects?

2. From *Students' Right to Their Own Language*, a 1974 publication of the National Council of Teachers of English: "American schools and colleges have, in the last decade, been forced to take a stand on a basic educational question: what should the schools do about the language habits of students who come from a wide variety of social, economic, and cultural backgrounds?" Some possible answers are:
   The schools should try to uphold language variety.
   They should try to modify it.
   They should try to complement it.
   They should try to eradicate it.
Discuss where you, your classmates, and your instructor stand on this issue.

FOR DISCUSSION AND WRITING

1. When, according to Allen's meaning of *appropriate usage*, would specific euphemisms for *pregnancy, insanity,* or *cancer* be appropriately used? When would the same euphemisms be inappropriate?

2. Flexner and Bolinger distinguish between the way men and women speak. Does such a distinction seem valid? Study the way men and women speak—their word choice, tone, sentence structure, and so forth—and draw a tentative thesis of your own.

3. What—if any—relation is there between dialect and the use of slang? Do some dialects use more slang than others?

4. Select a short story and analyze how the author uses dialect, slang, cant, jargon, and euphemism in the dialogue of the characters. Consider what these elements of language tell us about each character.

5. Choose a word or phrase that people of your generation frequently use but which may not be understood by someone of your parents' generation. Write an extended definition of the word or phrase, illustrating its usage, that will make its meaning clear to your audience. You may want to speculate about why you use it.

5 CHILDREN AND CHIMPANZEES

> *Real thinking is possible only in the light of genuine language, no matter how limited, how primitive: in her [Helen Keller's] case, it became possible with the discovery that w-a-t-e-r was not necessarily a sign that water was wanted or expected, but was the name of this substance, by which it could be mentioned, conceived, remembered.*
> SUSANNE K. LANGER

> *It is reported that monkeys, when not involved in arboreal distractions, can speak our language but refrain from doing so lest they be mistaken for men.*
> NOAH JONATHAN JACOBS

> *Roger tickle Lucy.*
> LUCY THE CHIMPANZEE

The process by which we acquire language is at once simple and complex, and remains something of a mystery despite the continuing investigations of modern science. The selections in this chapter explore language acquisition from several revealing perspectives. For example, the experiences of Helen Keller and Lucy the chimpanzee and Roger Brown's account of wild children are extraordinary and fascinating, and should help us to understand better how this process has occurred in each of us and how it leads to our becoming true *homo sapiens*.

Helen Keller

from THE STORY OF MY LIFE

Helen Keller (1880–1968) contracted a disease in infancy that left her deaf and blind. This excerpt from her autobiography recounts the early part of her education and the painstaking process by which her teacher, Anne Sullivan, taught her to speak. In its time, Helen Keller's triumph over silence and darkness was unique. As you read, consider what it must be like to acquire language while deprived of sight and sound, having to rely primarily on a sense of touch.

[1] The beginning of my life was simple and much like every other little life. I came, I saw, I conquered, as the first baby in the family always does. There was the usual amount of discussion as to a name for me. The first baby in the family was not to be lightly named, every one was emphatic about that. My father suggested the name of Mildred Campbell, an ancestor whom he highly esteemed, and he declined to take any further part in the discussion. My mother solved the problem by giving it as her wish that I should be called after her mother, whose maiden name was Helen Everett. But in the excitement of carrying me to church my father lost the name on the way, very naturally, since it was one in which he had declined to have a part. When the minister asked him for it, he just remembered that it had been decided to call me after my grandmother, and he gave her name as Helen Adams.

[2] I am told that while I was still in long dresses I showed many signs of an eager, self-asserting disposition. Everything that I saw other people do I insisted upon imitating. At six months I could pipe out "How d'ye," and one day I attracted every one's attention by saying "Tea, tea, tea" quite plainly. Even after my illness I remembered one of the words I had learned in these early months. It was the word "water," and I continued to make some sound for that word after all other speech was lost. I ceased making the sound "wah-wah" only when I learned to spell the word.

[3] They tell me I walked the day I was a year old. My mother had just taken me out of the bath-tub and was holding me in her lap, when I was suddenly attracted by the flickering shadows of leaves that danced in the sunlight on the smooth floor. I slipped from my mother's lap and almost ran toward them. The impulse gone, I fell down and cried for her to take me up in her arms.

From Helen Keller, *The Story of My Life* (New York, 1903).

[4]   These happy days did not last long. One brief spring, musical with the song of robin and mocking-bird, one summer rich in fruit and roses, one autumn of gold and crimson sped by and left their gifts at the feet of an eager, delighted child. Then, in the dreary month of February, came the illness which closed my eyes and ears and plunged me into the unconsciousness of a new-born baby. They called it acute congestion of the stomach and brain. The doctor thought I could not live. Early one morning, however, the fever left me as suddenly and mysteriously as it had come. There was great rejoicing in the family that morning, but no one, not even the doctor, knew that I should never see or hear again.

[5]   I fancy I still have confused recollections of that illness. I especially remember that tenderness with which my mother tried to soothe me in my waking hours of fret and pain, and the agony and bewilderment with which I awoke after a tossing half sleep, and turned my eyes, so dry and hot, to the wall, away from the once-loved light, which came to me dim and yet more dim each day. But, except for these fleeting memories, if, indeed, they be memories, it all seems very unreal, like a nightmare. Gradually I got used to the silence and darkness that surrounded me and forgot that it had ever been different, until she came—my teacher—who was to set my spirit free. But during the first nineteen months of my life I had caught glimpses of broad, green fields, a luminous sky, trees and flowers which the darkness that followed could not wholly blot out. If we have once seen, "the day is ours, and what the day has shown."

[6]   I cannot recall what happened during the first months after my illness. I only know that I sat in my mother's lap or clung to her dress as she went about her household duties. My hands felt every object and observed every motion, and in this way I learned to know many things. Soon I felt the need of some communication with others and began to make crude signs. A shake of the head meant "No" and a nod, "Yes," a pull meant "Come" and a push, "Go." Was it bread that I wanted? Then I would imitate the acts of cutting the slices and buttering them. If I wanted my mother to make ice-cream for dinner I made the sign for working the freezer and shivered, indicating cold. My mother, moreover, succeeded in making me understand a good deal. I always knew when she wished me to bring her something, and I would run upstairs or anywhere else she indicated. Indeed, I owe to her loving wisdom all that was bright and good in my long night.

[7]   I understood a good deal of what was going on about me. At five I learned to fold and put away the clean clothes when they were brought in from the laundry, and I distinguished my own from the rest. I knew by the way my mother and aunt dressed when they were going out, and I invariably begged to go with them. I was always sent for when there was company, and when the guests took their leave, I waved my hand to them, I think with a vague remembrance of the meaning of the gesture. One day some gentlemen called on my mother, and I felt the shutting of the front door and other sounds that indicated their arrival. On a sudden thought I ran upstairs before any one could stop me, to put on my idea of a company dress.

Standing before the mirror, as I had seen others do, I anointed mine head with oil and covered my face thickly with powder. Then I pinned a veil over my head so that it covered my face and fell in folds down to my shoulders, and tied an enormous bustle around my small waist, so that it dangled behind, almost meeting the hem of my skirt. Thus attired I went down to help entertain the company.

[8] I do not remember when I first realized that I was different from other people; but I knew it before my teacher came to me. I had noticed that my mother and friends did not use signs as I did when they wanted anything done, but talked with their mouths. Sometimes I stood between two persons who were conversing and touched their lips. I could not understand, and was vexed.

[9] The most important day I remember in all my life is the one on which my teacher, Anne Mansfield Sullivan, came to me. I am filled with wonder when I consider the immeasurable contrasts between the two lives which it connects. It was the third of March, 1887, three months before I was seven years old.

[10] On the afternoon of that eventful day, I stood on the porch, dumb, expectant. I guessed vaguely from my mother's signs and from the hurrying to and fro in the house that something unusual was about to happen, so I went to the door and waited on the steps. The afternoon sun penetrated the mass of honeysuckle that covered the porch, and fell on my upturned face. My fingers lingered almost unconsciously on the familiar leaves and blossoms which had just come forth to greet the sweet southern spring. I did not know what the future held of marvel or surprise for me. Anger and bitterness had preyed upon me continually for weeks and a deep languor had succeeded this passionate struggle.

[11] Have you ever been at sea in a dense fog, when it seemed as if a tangible white darkness shut you in, and the great ship, tense and anxious, groped her way toward the shore with plummet and sounding-line, and you waited with beating heart for something to happen? I was like that ship before my education began, only I was without compass or sounding-line, and had no way of knowing how near the harbour was. "Light! give me light!" was the wordless cry of my soul, and the light of love shone on me in that very hour.

[12] I felt approaching footsteps. I stretched out my hand as I supposed to my mother. Some one took it, and I was caught up and held close in the arms of her who had come to reveal all things to me, and, more than all things else, to love me.

[13] The morning after my teacher came she led me into her room and gave me a doll. The little blind children at the Perkins Institution had sent it and Laura Bridgman had dressed it; but I did not know this until afterward. When I had played with it a little while, Miss Sullivan slowly spelled into my hand the word "d-o-l-l." I was at once interested in this finger play and tried to imitate it. When I finally succeeded in making the letters correctly I was flushed with childish pleasure and pride. Running downstairs to my mother I held up my hand and made the letters for

doll. I did not know that I was spelling a word or even that words existed; I was simply making my fingers go in monkey-like imitation. In the days that followed I learned to spell in this uncomprehending way a great many words, among them *pin, hat, cup* and a few verbs like *sit, stand* and *walk*. But my teacher had been with me several weeks before I understood that everything has a name.

[14] One day, while I was playing with my new doll, Miss Sullivan put my big rag doll into my lap also, spelled "d-o-l-l" and tried to make me understand that "d-o-l-l" applied to both. Earlier in the day we had had a tussle over the words "m-u-g" and "w-a-t-e-r." Miss Sullivan had tried to impress it upon me that "m-u-g" is *mug* and that "w-a-t-e-r" is *water*, but I persisted in confounding the two. In despair she had dropped the subject for the time, only to renew it at the first opportunity. I became impatient at her repeated attempts and, seizing the new doll, I dashed it upon the floor. I was keenly delighted when I felt the fragments of the broken doll at my feet. Neither sorrow nor regret followed my passionate outburst. I had not loved the doll. In the still, dark world in which I lived there was no strong sentiment or tenderness. I felt my teacher sweep the fragments to one side of the hearth, and I had a sense of satisfaction that the cause of my discomfort was removed. She brought me my hat, and I knew I was going out into the warm sunshine. This thought, if a wordless sensation may be called a thought, made me hop and skip with pleasure.

[15] We walked down the path to the well-house, attracted by the fragrance of the honeysuckle with which it was covered. Some one was drawing water and my teacher placed my hand under the spout. As the cool stream gushed over one hand she spelled into the other the word *water*, first slowly, then rapidly. I stood still, my whole attention fixed upon the motions of her fingers. Suddenly I felt a misty consciousness as of something forgotten—a thrill of returning thought; and somehow the mystery of language was revealed to me. I knew then that "w-a-t-e-r" meant the wonderful cool something that was flowing over my hand. That living word awakened my soul, gave it light, hope, joy, set it free! There were barriers still, it is true, but barriers that could in time be swept away.

[16] I left the well-house eager to learn. Everything had a name, and each name gave birth to a new thought. As we returned to the house every object which I touched seemed to quiver with life. That was because I saw everything with the strange, new sight that had come to me. On entering the door I remembered the doll I had broken. I felt my way to the hearth and picked up the pieces. I tried vainly to put them together. Then my eyes filled with tears; for I realized what I had done, and for the first time I felt repentance and sorrow.

[17] I learned a great many new words that day. I do not remember what they all were; but I do know that *mother, father, sister, teacher* were among them—words that were to make the world blossom for me, "like Aaron's rod, with flowers." It would have been difficult to find a happier child than I was as I lay in my crib at the

close of that eventful day and lived over the joys it had brought me, and for the first time longed for a new day to come.

[18] I had now the key to all language, and I was eager to learn to use it. Children who hear acquire language without any particular effort; the words that fall from others' lips they catch on the wing, as it were, delightedly, while the little deaf child must trap them by a slow and often painful process. But whatever the process, the result is wonderful. Gradually from naming an object we advance step by step until we have traversed the vast distance between our first stammered syllable and the sweep of thought in a line of Shakespeare.

[19] At first, when my teacher told me about a new thing I asked very few questions. My ideas were vague, and my vocabulary was inadequate; but as my knowledge of things grew, and I learned more and more words, my field of inquiry broadened, and I would return again and again to the same subject, eager for further information. Sometimes a new word revived an image that some earlier experience had engraved on my brain.

[20] I remember the morning that I first asked the meaning of the word, "love." This was before I knew many words. I had found a few early violets in the garden and brought them to my teacher. She tried to kiss me: but at that time I did not like to have any one kiss me except my mother. Miss Sullivan put her arm gently round me and spelled into my hand, "I love Helen."

[21] "What is love?" I asked.

[22] She drew me closer to her and said, "It is here," pointing to my heart, whose beats I was conscious of for the first time. Her words puzzled me very much because I did not then understand anything unless I touched it.

[23] I smelt the violets in her hand and asked, half in words, half in signs, a question which meant, "Is love the sweetness of flowers?"

[24] "No," said my teacher.

[25] Again I thought. The warm sun was shining on us.

[26] "Is this not love?" I asked, pointing in the direction from which the heat came. "Is this not love?"

[27] It seemed to me that there could be nothing more beautiful than the sun, whose warmth makes all things grow. But Miss Sullivan shook her head, and I was greatly puzzled and disappointed. I thought it strange that my teacher could not show me love.

[28] A day or two afterward I was stringing beads of different sizes in symmetrical groups—two large beads, three small ones, and so on. I had made many mistakes, and Miss Sullivan had pointed them out again and again with gentle patience. Finally I noticed a very obvious error in the sequence and for an instant I concen-

trated my attention on the lesson and tried to think how I should have arranged the beads. Miss Sullivan touched my forehead and spelled with decided emphasis, "Think."

[29] In a flash I knew that the word was the name of the process that was going on in my head. This was my first conscious perception of an abstract idea.

[30] For a long time I was still—I was not thinking of the beads in my lap, but trying to find a meaning for "love" in the light of this new idea. The sun had been under a cloud all day, and there had been brief showers; but suddenly the sun broke forth in all its southern splendour.

[31] Again I asked my teacher, "Is this not love?"

[32] "Love is something like the clouds that were in the sky before the sun came out," she replied. Then in simpler words than these, which at that time I could not have understood, she explained: "You cannot touch the clouds, you know; but you feel the rain and know how glad the flowers and the thirsty earth are to have it after a hot day. You cannot touch love either; but you feel the sweetness that it pours into everything. Without love you would not be happy or want to play."

[33] The beautiful truth burst upon my mind—I felt that there were invisible lines stretched between my spirit and the spirits of others.

[34] From the beginning of my education Miss Sullivan made it a practice to speak to me as she would speak to any hearing child; the only difference was that she spelled the sentences into my hand instead of speaking them. If I did not know the words and idioms necessary to express my thoughts she supplied them, even suggesting conversation when I was unable to keep up my end of the dialogue.

[35] This process was continued for several years; for the deaf child does not learn in a month, or even in two or three years, the numberless idioms and expressions used in the simplest daily intercourse. The little hearing child learns these from constant repetition and imitation. The conversation he hears in his home stimulates his mind and suggests topics and calls forth the spontaneous expression of his own thoughts. This natural exchange of ideas is denied to the deaf child. My teacher, realizing this, determined to supply the kinds of stimulus I lacked. This she did by repeating to me as far as possible, verbatim, what she heard, and by showing me how I could take part in the conversation. But it was a long time before I ventured to take the initiative, and still longer before I could find something appropriate to say at the right time.

[36] The deaf and the blind find it very difficult to acquire the amenities of conversation. How much more this difficulty must be augmented in the case of those who are both deaf and blind! They cannot distinguish the tone of the voice or, without assistance, go up and down the gamut of tones that give significance to words; nor can they watch the expression of the speaker's face, and a look is often the very soul of what one says.

FOR REVIEW AND DISCUSSION

Content

1. Describe Keller's method of communication before she learned language. What were its limitations?

2. Describe the process by which Keller acquired language. What does she mean when she observes, "I had now the key to all language"?

3. What seems to have been the hardest language lesson for her to learn? Would that lesson also be difficult for children who can hear and see? Explain.

4. She remarks, "I quickly learned that each printed word stood for an object, an act, or a quality." How would S. I. Hayakawa ("Symbols," chapter 3) respond to what she learned?

5. At various points in her story, Keller suggests a relationship between language and thinking. What specifically is the relationship?

Rhetoric

1. Speculate about Keller's assumed audience and her purpose in telling her story.

2. As you read through the selection, did you find yourself accepting or questioning the accuracy of her remembrances? What contributed to your response?

3. How are we to read Keller's meaning when she describes herself standing "dumb" on the porch on the afternoon of Anne Sullivan's arrival?

4. What is the effect of her addressing the reader directly in paragraph 11?

5. What significance can you attach to the first word that she learns?

Classroom Exercises

1. Imagine that you are deprived of your sight or your hearing—or both. In what ways would this handicap affect your use of language?

2. Have a blindfolded classmate dictate a description of an unfamiliar object placed in his hands. Have a second classmate (absent during the first dictation) dictate a description of the same object, which he can see but cannot touch. (For best results use four or more classmates instead of two.) Compare and contrast the descriptions. What might they reveal about the language characteristics of persons handicapped in these ways?

Roger Brown

FERAL AND ISOLATED MAN

Throughout history there have been various more or less well documented cases of "wild children"—children who have grown up either in isolation or with animals. Roger Brown is interested in these children primarily for what we can learn from them about language, its acquisition and importance in human development. Here for the first time we see some scientific evidence that language may be one of the keys to "humanness." As you read, consider the similarities and differences between these children and Helen Keller.

[1] In the tenth edition of his *Systemae Naturae*, published in 1758, Linnaeus listed *Homo Ferus* (L. wild man) as a subdivision of the genus *Homo Sapiens*. The defining characteristics of feral man, succinctly listed by Linnaeus, were *tetrapus, mutus, hursutus*. There were nine historical records of wild men available to the great taxonomist. These included the Hessian wolf-boy of 1349, the Lithuanian bear-boy of 1661, and Wild Peter of Hanover of 1724. Since Linnaeus' time about thirty additional cases have accumulated. These cases have generally conformed to two of Linnaeus' specifications: They have lacked speech and have gone on all fours. The majority have not been especially hirsute and that characteristic does not help define feral man. An attribute not mentioned by Linnaeus, but reliably found in these cases, is the depression of sexuality. It appears, like speech, to be a function that a society must develop. Within the class of feral men a distinction should be made between those known to have been nurtured by wild animals and those who lived on their own in the wilds. It must be assumed that these latter cases lived in human society until they were old enough to wander off and look after themselves. They fall between true feral man and cases of extreme isolation. It has sometimes happened that a child has been shut away from human society except for routine feeding. These cases, living with minimal human aid, are called isolated man.

[2] Feral and isolated man interest the psychologist, philosopher, and sociologist because they provide an important natural experiment on the relative importance of genetic and environmental factors in the determination of all aspects of human behavior. The importance of feral man to the science of man was perceived long ago. Lord Monboddo proclaimed the discovery of Wild Peter of Hanover to be more important than the discovery of 30,000 new stars. Wild Peter was brought from Hanover to England by King George so that he might be used to test the doctrine of

---

Reprinted with permission of Macmillan Publishing Co., Inc. from *Words and Things* by Roger Brown. Copyright © 1958, 1968 by The Free Press, a Division of Macmillan Publishing Co., Inc.

innate ideas. The king presented Peter to the enlightened princess of Wales and she placed him in charge of Dr. Arbuthnot, that good friend of Pope and Swift.

[3] While Peter began the tradition of scientific interest in feral man, he also, unfortunately, began an equally hardy tradition of scientific difficulty in interpreting the data so obtained. There was, first of all, the problem of determining the exact circumstances of Peter's earlier life. From a number of sources it seems clear that he had lived for some time in human society. He was probably the child of a certain widower whose second wife drove Peter from the house. There was, secondly, the problem of estimating Peter's native intelligence. The behavior of feral man somewhat resembles that of the ament living in human society. If one cannot decide whether or not these cases are congenitally deficient, the results obtained are all open to the following directly opposed interpretations.

[4] The extreme environmentalists, like Rousseau, have found in feral man proof of the infinite plasticity of man. The feral cases violate all parochial notions of human nature and prove that human nature is created in society and may take any form that society dictates. However, the extreme environmentalist cannot deny the importance of genetic factors since, as Zingg remarks, there is something lacking to make this case complete—a wolf or dog who has been trained to human behavior. He can acknowledge that the character of the species sets limits on behavioral development but that, within these limits, environment is the principal factor.

[5] The student who is inclined to give more importance to heredity will interpret the cases of feral man quite differently. He believes them all to be congenitally feeble-minded; their behavior simply demonstrates the strong determining power of innate intelligence. Aments, whether in human or wolf society, are much alike. To be sure some feral cases have recovered and demonstrated considerable learning ability, but these cases cannot have been true aments, in the opinion of the men backing heredity. Their recovery proves that when there is no genetic deficiency the most unfavorable environment has only a temporary handicapping effect. With this uncertainty about native intelligence the environmentalist cannot prove that genetically normal human specimens are rendered permanently inhuman by the lack of society in their early years. Those that remain *mutus* and *tetrapus* may be feeble-minded. Those that recover have not remained inhuman. The environmentalist points out, with irritation, the improbability that all feral cases would be feeble-minded. The heredity-man counters that the feeble-minded child is just the one to be driven out of his home or exposed to wild beasts and furthermore, not all feral men are assumed to be feeble-minded—only those who do not recover. In the opinion of the environmentalist, anyone who thinks that a child who has survived in the wilds on his own initiative could possibly be feeble-minded . . .—the man who thinks that must himself be suspected of feeble-mindedness. We tiptoe out and softly close the door behind us. Let us look at several of the best documented cases to see if they do not teach something more modest than the truth about human nature, perhaps something about the nature of language.

THE WILD BOY OF AVEYRON

[6] . . . Victor, the wild boy of Aveyron, . . . was about twelve years old when he was captured in the Caune Woods and Dr. Itard tried for five years to teach him to speak and read. Victor succeeded in understanding a large number of words and phrases but he could produce no speech except the two exclamations: "*Oh, Dieu!*" and "*Lait!*" These came out, in very imperfect form, quite early in training. The discrepancy between the boy's achievements in reading and in speech production requires some explanation.

[7] It is conceivable that Victor's mentality was adequate to the full use of language and that he was simply held back by inability to master the business of articulation and phonation. Perhaps the impulse to babble which is so evident in infants operates on a maturational timetable such that it must receive social support when the readiness is there or the impulse will die. The pecking response in chicks is an example of this kind of timed skill. A bright spot elicits the pecking response in newborn chicks. When chicks were raised in the dark and fed by dropper for fourteen days it was found that they would not peck though exposed to daylight. The original study includes a dramatic photograph of a starving chick standing in the midst of a pile of grain—not pecking! Itard's experience with Victor suggests that speech in man, like pecking in chicks, may require social reinforcement at the crucial age when the impulse is ripe or else it will not develop at all. To evaluate this proposal we will look at other cases of feral and isolated man.

KAMALA AND AMALA

[8] Since 1850, at least, there have been constant reports of wolf-children in India. Some of the Indian people have a superstitious reluctance to kill wolves and there has also been a practice of exposing unwanted children. Most of those carried off have certainly been killed but occasionally the child is taken to the wolf den and survives for a time as an extra cub.

[9] In 1920 the Rev. A. L. Singh was told of a *manushbhaga*, a man ghost, haunting a certain Indian village. The ghost had been seen in the company of wolves going in and out of a giant dead ant hill which the animals presumably used as a den. Singh had a shooting platform built over the hill. He and some natives watched there one night and saw a procession of mother wolf and cubs, two of which looked human though they went on all fours and had long matted hair. The local natives would not dig out the hill but Singh brought in some more willing workers. The mother darted out to attack the invaders, and was killed. In the den itself they found a monkey ball of four little creatures clinging together—two cubs and two little girls.

FERAL AND ISOLATED MAN

[10] Kamala was about eight years old and Amala only one and one-half. They were thoroughly wolfish in appearance and behavior: Hard callus had developed on their knees and palms from going on all fours. Their teeth were sharp edged. They moved their nostrils sniffing food. Eating and drinking were accomplished by lowering their mouths to the plate. They ate raw meat and, on one occasion, killed and devoured a whole chicken. At night they prowled and sometimes howled. They shunned other children but followed the dog and cat. They slept rolled up together on the floor.

[11] Amala died within a year but Kamala lived to be eighteen. Both children's bodies were covered with sores when they were captured. Mrs. Singh healed these and softened their skins with oils and massage. She fed and bathed and caressed Kamala and evidently was the means of her socialization. The first sign that Kamala had become "involved" with a human being appeared when Mrs. Singh returned from a trip and Kamala ran to her with evident affection. In time Kamala learned to walk erect, to wear clothing and even to speak a few words.

[12] Because Kamala learned to talk a little, and promised to learn more, we cannot believe that continuous social support of infantile babbling is an essential pre-requisite to speech. Vocalization survived in her as an operant response while it did not for Victor. It is, of course, possible that Kamala lived for a longer time with adults than did Victor and so received more reinforcement for vocalizing. The situation, however, was the reverse. Victor was not found in the care of animals but was living alone. A child could survive outside of human society at an earlier age if it was in the society of some animal than would be possible if it had to shift for itself in the wilds. Victor is likely to have remained longer at home. It seems that speech is possible even when left dormant for many childhood years. Victor's failure was probably due to some specific impairment—probably of hearing. The facts on several cases of extreme social isolation will reinforce these conclusions.

CASES OF EXTREME SOCIAL ISOLATION

[13] In 1937, in Illinois, the child Anna was discovered tied to a chair in a second floor attic-like room. She was nearly six years of age, emaciated, and speechless. She had received absolutely minimal attention since her birth, had been fed almost exclusively on cow's milk, seldom moved from her chair, and never instructed in anything. Anna was an illegitimate child whose mother had hidden her away to avoid the anger of the child's grandfather.

[14] The child was taken to a county home for retarded children and, after a year and a half there, removed to a private home. Anna lived for only four more years. In that time she learned to walk, to dress herself, to play simple games with other children, and to speak a little. She could call attendants by name and had a few

sentences to express her desires. The school report on Anna expressed the opinion that she was probably congenitally feeble-minded. This diagnosis is strengthened by the fact that Anna's mother proved to be a middle-grade moron with an IQ of 50 on the Stanford revision of the Binet-Simon scale. The probability that feral and isolated children who have learned little or no speech were feeble-minded is increased by the remarkable achievements of another isolated child—Isabelle.

[15] Isabelle was found in Ohio at about the same time as Anna. Isabelle was also nearly of an age with Anna, being six and one-half at the time of her discovery. She was the illegitimate child of a deaf mute, and mother and child had lived most of the time in a darkened room away from the rest of the family. Isabelle behaved in many ways like a wild animal. She was fearful and hostile. She had no speech and made only a croaking noise. At first she seemed deaf, so unused were her senses.

[16] Isabelle was taken away and given excellent care by doctors and clinical psychologists. Although her first score on the Stanford-Binet was nineteen months, practically at the zero point of the scale, a program of speech training was, nevertheless, undertaken. A week of intensive work was required to elicit even a first vocalization. Yet a little more than two months later she was beginning to put sentences together. Nine months after that, she could identify words and sentences on the printed page and write very well. Isabelle passed through the usual stages of linguistic development at a greatly accelerated rate. She covered in two years the learning that ordinarily occupies six years. By the age of eight and one-half Isabelle had a normal IQ and was not easily distinguished from ordinary children of her age. In this case speech behaved like many other human and animal performances; the delayed subject progressed at an accelerated rate, presumably because of her maturity.

[17] The case of Isabelle strongly suggests that a child with good congenital intelligence can overcome the mutism caused by social isolation. It is possible that Anna would have done as well with equally expert tutelage but it seems likely that Anna was not Isabelle's equal in congenital intelligence. We do not yet know how many years of social isolation it is possible to overcome with speech training. The excellent results with Isabelle indicate that as many as six and one-half years of isolation can be made up. The moderate success with Kamala (carried on by less expert teachers) suggests that much may be done to offset even eight years of isolation from the human community.

[18] Neither feral nor isolated man creates his own language these days, but must not such a man have done so once in some prehistoric time and so got language started? Actually the circumstances in which language must have begun represent a combination for which we can provide no instances. We have animals among themselves, animals in linguistic communities, and humans among animals, and in none of these cases does language develop. We have humans raised in linguistic communities and, in these circumstances, language does develop. What about a

human born into a human society that has no language? We don't know of any such societies and so we don't know of any such individuals. But these must have been the circumstances of language origination. We shall be better able to guess what happened in these circumstances, intermediate between the primate community and the linguistic community, when we are clearer about the lines of phyletic advance that lead toward language function.

FOR REVIEW AND DISCUSSION

Content

1. In what ways do feral and isolated children seem to differ? How are these differences reflected in language acquisition?

2. According to Brown, what were the circumstances leading to the origin of language in prehistoric cultures?

3. What do the case histories tell us about why some of these children learned to speak and others did not?

Rhetoric

1. Even though he is discussing a serious scientific question, Brown chooses to inject some subtle humor at several places. Locate this humor and comment on its intended effect.

2. Brown does not really define *tetrapus*, *mutus*, and *hursutus*. How does he make their meaning known?

3. Does Brown's purpose seem primarily to be to raise questions or to solve them? What makes his purpose apparent?

4. Outline the main developments in the selection. Do the stages of development help achieve Brown's purpose? What is the function of his concluding paragraph?

Classroom Exercises

1. Based on the facts and circumstances that Brown presents, invent your own case histories of *two* wild children returned to civilization—one who learns to speak and one who doesn't.

2. Put yourself in the position of a wild child who has been returned to civilization and taught to speak. Write a brief account of your experiences in the wild and your first contact with civilization.

Eugene Linden

THE CHIMP COLONY: LUCY

As this selection demonstrates, some of the speculations that Roger Brown makes are already out of date. Lucy the chimpanzee is only one of a number of chimpanzees and gorillas being taught to communicate in human language. A common question about such research is simply, "Why?" This selection should help, at least in part, to answer that question. As you read, think about what Lucy's progress does to our conception of ourselves as the superior species on the earth. The conclusion of the piece is rather speculative and poetic; pay special attention here to Linden's ideas about the consequences of such experiments.

[1] Lucy is the oldest of the institute's chimps currently being raised in species isolation. Her foster parents are Maury and Jane Temerlin. Maury is a psychologist who teaches at the University of Oklahoma; Jane is Dr. Lemmon's assistant. Lucy was born on January 18, 1966, and removed from her mother four days later; she has been with the Temerlins ever since. Like an institute in miniature, their house is a modern rambling structure of glass and plaster. The east window of the living room looks out on several large wire mesh cages that house a garrulous and excitable crew of blue and white macaws; the south window looks out on a patio and two ponds. When the Temerlins are out, Lucy lives in a spacious indoor-outdoor, wire-enclosed duplex. When they are at home, she lives and sleeps with them as she has done since infancy.

[2] During my two trips to the institute in the summers of 1972 and 1973, I met Lucy on several occasions and attended a few of Roger Fouts's sessions with her. Fouts and a number of his assistants visit with Lucy one after another for an hour or two each, five days a week. During some sessions, she would be taught new words, during others tested on vocabulary or some aspect of her word usage, while during still others, Lucy and her companion would just talk and review the signs that she knows. Each assistant kept a record of her utterances on a work sheet and described any novel circumstances, difficulties, or errors that occurred during her signing. Imagine how Lucy must feel. There she is, happy just to have a visitor, and the visitor insists on asking her the names of objects that both of them already know. Then when she tries to start a conversation, all the visitor does is sit there and write.

[3] The aim of these worksheets was to build a statistical profile of selected aspects of Lucy's word use, and in this way Fouts has elicited and documented some

From *Apes, Men and Language* by Eugene Linden. Copyright © 1974 by Eugene Linden. Reprinted by permission of the publishers, E. P. Dutton.

extraordinary behavior. Lucy's vocabulary is about eighty words. It could be much larger, but the investigators are more interested in the way she uses her vocabulary than in its size; they cannot examine all aspects of language at once. A study of any behavior must exclude what might be called "static" data in favor of whatever is sought within the experimental design. When the behavior investigated is language, however, this aspect of scientific inquiry begins to work against the ultimate object of the inquiry.

[4] In focusing on one aspect of language, the investigator must be inattentive to other uses of language that lie outside the thrust of a particular experiment. While the investigator is looking for one aspect of language, Lucy may be gaily demonstrating another. Unlike the investigator, the outsider naturally attends to evidence that the chimp is exploiting the *communicative* aspects of language and is not merely solving problems. And so, as I was introduced to Lucy and the chimps at the institute, I paid particular attention to the flavor of their use of Ameslan, and to those aspects of "speech" that might be obscured by a data table. I found that I reacted to different things than Fouts did. Indeed, the contrasts between Fouts's and my perspectives on Lucy brought out this important characteristic of the investigation of the chimps' use of Ameslan—that the examination of behavior can at times obscure the behavior itself.

[5] This became clear when I met Lucy the next day. I arranged to show up at the Temerlins a little while after Roger began his morning session. Accordingly, at about 9:30 A.M. I walked around to the patio and peered through the living room window. I could see Roger and Lucy gesturing and cavorting on the couch. Fouts disengaged himself and got up to let me in.

[6] I settled unobtrusively onto a couch to observe and to take notes. Lucy promptly abandoned Roger, hopped onto my lap, and, after some unselfconscious staring, commenced a minute inspection of my face and clothing. She looked at my eyes, peered up my nostrils, and then briefly groomed my hair, presumably looking for lice. I had a scab on my knee, visible because I was wearing tennis shorts, and when Lucy had finally worked down to it, she looked over to Roger and touched the tips of two index fingers together. "She's saying you're hurt," said Roger.

[7] I thanked Lucy, who, chuckling and grimacing, ran back over to Fouts. He showed her a picture of a cat and asked her what it was. "Cat," Lucy replied. For a moment Lucy continued to identify the pictures Roger showed her, but as soon as I picked up my pen to take notes she was dying to see what I was up to, and she raced back over and again hopped onto my lap. As I tried to note this, she grabbed the pen and began to scrawl furiously. Roger pointed out that she was using her right hand (I am left-handed so she was not imitating me) and that she was also holding the pen in a manner similar to a precision grip. Roger also said that Lucy seems to consistently hold objects in her left hand in the power grip. Psychologist Jerome Bruner has observed that in children the dominant hand develops a variety of precision grips while the other plays the role of the steadier, and, to stress the parallel between

tool manipulation and language, that the dominant hand plays the role of the predicate to the subordinate hand's subject.

[8] What is significant about Lucy's proclivities in drawing is that right-handedness and left-handedness in humans are related to what is called lateral dominance—the organization and division of labors between the two different hemispheres of the brain. The extraordinary selective pressures that produced language in man required the rapid development of certain parts of the brain, and as a result, rather than both developing equally, the left hemisphere was pushed out of shape to accommodate the renovations necessary to equip man for language. It is possible that the chimp brain is in the first stages of being lopsided that way as well.

[9] After Lucy grew tired of drawing ferocious circles, she looked at me and noticed that the white shirt I was wearing had an alligator insignia on it. Lucy pointed to it several times and tracing a question mark in the air asked me what it was. I looked plaintively over to Roger, who suggested that I put my palms together as in prayer and then make the snapping motion of an alligator's jaws. With this advice I laboriously told Lucy that the insignia was an alligator. The chimpanzee cannot flex its hands backwards from the wrist as easily as a person can, and so, when we asked Lucy to identify the insignia, she, after some fumbling, made the sign with the snapping motion originating from the tips of her fingers. It is a testimony to the accuracy that Roger demands of his chimps that he thought Lucy was just babbling and making a confused version of "book," a sign made by unfolding the closed palms in imitation of an opening book. Only after she persisted in her variation did Roger accept that she was attempting to make the snapping sign. This incident made it clear that Fouts was not reading anything into Lucy's signing. It also gave me the feeling that published accounts gave a very conservative and formalistic picture of what the chimps were doing. While humans were peering at the chimps through the lens of experimental design, the chimps themselves were indeed exploiting Ameslan as a means of communication.

[10] This feeling was further reinforced the next day when I arrived to observe another session. This time I was wearing a blue shirt, but again it had an alligator insignia. Roger asked Lucy who I was. After jumping onto my lap and pointing excitedly at my green insignia, Lucy said, logically enough, that I was an alligator. "Errors" like this did not fit within the scheme of the day's investigation. But was she in error, or was Lucy extracting some characteristic commonly associated with me and using that as the name for me—the very meta-linguistic process that recapitulates the way man came to name his tools and environment?

[11] When conversing with Roger in Ameslan, Lucy would look at him with intense concentration; however, her movements in making signs were not intense, but leisurely, as though communicating by using Ameslan was the most natural thing in the world for a chimp to do. She seemed to understand spoken English. It was eerie to be talking with Roger about Lucy's mirror or doll and then have her run

over and pick it up. Roger noted that earlier that week he had lost Lucy's doll. He glossed his error by replacing the doll with a slightly different one, which he handed Lucy the next day. Lucy was very suspicious of this new doll, and the day after this surreptitious exchange she went over to her toy chest and signed to Roger "out baby." She wanted to see where this strange doll had come from.

[12] During that second session, Lucy was in a manic mood. Again she broke away from Roger when I began taking notes. She grabbed my note pad and pen and scrawled feverishly, as if she were short for time during a final exam. Besides the question of hemispheric dominance, there was another interesting aspect to Lucy's scrawling. It exemplified the chimp's interest in imitating what it sees others doing.

[13] Critics have suggested that any preferences for word order shown by the chimpanzee result from imitation of human models without any understanding of the significance of word order. Many people are tempted to write off all evidence of simian cognitive ability as dumb mimicry; however, the job Lucy did in transcribing my notes (even though my handwriting might leave some wondering whether my scratchings showed any evidence of higher cognitive abilities) would not have caused me to hire her either as mimic or stenographer, and would leave me to doubt that Lucy could precisely imitate behavior if she did not know what she was doing. Moreover, Fouts has demonstrated that imitation is the least effective method of instruction. My suspicions received support a moment later.

[14] After abandoning the note pad, Lucy settled down to improve on the knot with which I had tied my sneakers. Although the determination was inspiring, she would only work herself into a frustrated fury. To get her attention, Roger called her back for tussles and little games. One of these was the swallow game.

[15] Here, Roger will take a pair of sunglasses and pretend to swallow them by turning his head in profile to Lucy and sliding the glasses past his open mouth on the side of his face that Lucy cannot see. Lucy thinks this is hysterically funny, and she will with unflagging interest and excitement sit inches away from Roger while he performs this bit of legerdemain. Promptly after Roger finished today's performance, Lucy grabbed the glasses, and taking her indestructible mirror hopped across the living room to another couch. Holding the mirror with her feet, Lucy, to her own vast amusement, performed the swallow trick, passing the glasses along the obscured side of her face exactly as Roger had done. Then she signed "look, swallow." After her third performance of the swallow trick, Lucy drooled on the mirror, and, while she looked at her distorted image with a bemused expression, spread the saliva around with her finger.

[16] Lucy has her own games to play with Roger. Sometimes she will grab his watch or some other possession, which she won't return until Roger identifies it with the proper sign. Washoe, Fouts noted, has a raunchier sense of humor. One day while riding on Roger's shoulders, Washoe pissed on him and then signed "funny" in a self-congratulatory way.

[17] When Lucy grabs Roger's watch and demands that he identify it to get it back or when she takes the mirror and plays the swallow game by herself, she is obviously imitating her mentors, but such mimicry is no less fraught with meaning than the solitary play of children when they name and talk to their toys. Like the child, Lucy talks to herself, plays with words, and uses these periods of self-absorption to explore her developing language skills. In any event, we should not downgrade imitation in either ape or man. It is the evolutionary device that permits the learning of new behaviors. It permits flexibility.

[18] Dutch psychologist Adriaan Kortlandt, who has visited both Fouts and the Gardners and has observed chimps in the wild as well, feels that the significance of this type of play has not been sufficiently emphasized by the Gardners themselves. He also feels that self-imposed experimental blinders prevented the people working with Ameslan-using chimps from seeing a lot of what is going on. He once watched Washoe "read" an illustrated magazine. As she did, she signed "cat" when she came upon a picture of a tiger, and "drink" upon seeing a vermouth advertisement. He refers to this as "thinking aloud," and he noted that when Washoe was not rewarded, she tended more to think aloud rather than talk to the Gardners. He feels this indicates that the "apes have a lot more to think about than to say."

[19] To the outsider, such thinking aloud is far more persuasive than a data summary of the degree to which the chimp has integrated language into its life. It shows that the infant chimp is not merely pleasing its masters for rewards or solving puzzles, but is rather turning around and examining its new tool. We would expect behavior like this from a child, and we would be suspicious if a chimpanzee purported to have language did not use language in these peripheral ways.

[20] During that second day, I also watched Lucy refute the idea that the chimp's choice of word order is determined solely by mimicry rather than by a sense of structure. Roger had noted that Lucy consistently used the correct order in such three-word combinations as "Roger tickle Lucy." After watching Lucy request several such tickles, I began to wonder what would happen if Roger said "Lucy tickle Roger." I asked Roger if he had ever done this.

[21] He said no, and then after thinking a moment about the possibility of unfortunate consequences from saying such a thing, he turned to Lucy and said, "Lucy tickle Roger." Lucy was sitting beside Roger on the living room couch. She sat back for an instant confused. Almost testily she said, "No, Roger tickle Lucy." Roger again said, "No, Lucy tickle Roger." This time I could see comprehension brighten Lucy's eyes. Excited she jumped onto his lap and began tickling him while he rocked backwards uttering little grunts in imitation of chimp laughter. For the next few minutes, Roger and Lucy politely requested and exchanged tickles. Fouts has since filmed these exchanges with Lucy.

[22] There are other possible explanations for this incident than the reflection of a rudimentary sense of syntax. For one thing Ameslan syntax is not a simple mapping

of English. Then, too, because a sentence such as "Lucy tickle Roger" is short, it is possible that Lucy understood it according to some semantic rather than syntactic scheme. Rather than noting that "Lucy," and not "Roger," was in the subject position, she might have been noting that Fouts was uttering this set of words traditionally associated with tickling.

[23] However, Fouts taught Lucy to say "Roger tickle Lucy" and still says it himself sometimes when he is going to tickle her. Thus, even though the words associated with tickling are said by Roger, Lucy expects to be tickled when Fouts says "Roger tickle Lucy." It must have been something about the words, rather than the speaker, that triggered her tickling. Fouts has since noted that Lucy correctly interprets the difference between such variations as "Roger tickle Lucy, we tickle you," and "you tickle me, tickle Roger." Up to the moment I observed, Lucy had never heard "Lucy tickle Roger," and so she could not merely have been associating a set of words with an appropriate situation.

[24] This brings us back to a syntactic explanation: in all probability, after her initial hesitation Lucy was cueing to the position of the words in the sentence. Similarly, although Ameslan has a grammar different from English, at the institute Ameslan signs are combined according to English grammar. Like Lucy, Washoe eventually adopted what appeared to be grammatical word order, but it was her transition toward its use that confused efforts to quantify her word order preferences in three-word combinations. At the beginning of the test period, Washoe put subject before object, although she put both before the verb; at the end she was using traditional subject-verb-object word order.

[25] Fouts is not surprised that Lucy would have a sense of word order. Psychologist Jean Piaget has said that teaching language to an animal consists largely of mapping the animal's already-existing knowledge. The chimp's capacities for tool-making and tool manipulation show that the chimp has the "already-existing ability" to purposively organize its movements in a non-random way. Why then should its hand movements suddenly be random because it is working with *symbols* for objects and not with objects themselves? Moreover, the chimp lives in intricately organized and highly gregarious bands, a fact that demands his understanding structure of a high order. Thus, it would indeed be odd for a language map to be random in a creature as highly organized as the chimp. So much for word order; let us now turn to the word itself.

[26] Man has traditionally associated words with power and manipulation in magic and religion. In magic, to know the *name* of a force is to be able to invoke it; rituals of white magic are littered with *words of power* that summon or dispel various natural and supernatural forces. Similarly, the ancient Hebrews concealed the name of the deity from all save the highest priests. He might only be referred to indirectly; by being unnamed, this god was beyond man's power and manipulation. In mythology, those who cannot name are impotent, while that which cannot *be* named is

threatening. Man can control only what he can name, which summarizes concisely man's intuitive understanding of the relationship between language and thought. As it is for man, so it is for the chimpanzee.

[27] How Lucy understands the *word* has been Fouts's principal concern. Bellugi and Bronowski forcefully argue that words and the laws that govern their manipulation form an organic whole—i.e., the process of distillation through which man abstracted the symbolic nature of the objects around him was impelled by demands for those objects' manipulation. Within this interlocking whole of word and grammar, we might not expect to find differing levels of analysis; but we would expect some relationship between the sophistication of an animal's ability to symbolize and the sophistication of its ability to combine those symbols in sentences. We would not expect to see an animal prove capable of mastering appropriate Latin case endings for nouns, yet prove incapable of combining those words in meaningful combinations, simply because the level of analysis necessary to use Latin case endings appropriately would presume the ability to analyze and understand Latin grammar. More to the point, if the chimp understood signs in Ameslan to be surrogates for particular objects, we might expect chimps to demonstrate little ability in combining such tokens; yet if the chimp demonstrated that it understood the general properties of particular words and the utility of words in analyzing particular situations, we might expect a commensurate level of abstraction in the grammar with which the chimp organizes those words. Understanding the attributes and combinatory functions of a word like "sweet," for example, is not understanding the word's meaning, but is an analysis of those situations in which what is represented by "sweet" is appropriate. An analysis of "sweetness" represents the type of factoring of the environment Bellugi and Bronowski referred to in their discussion of reconstitution, and the general application of "sweetness" reflects the synthesis that was the second part of that process. Simply stated, to understand a symbol, one must understand its applications; thus, in light of this, it seems illogical to state that an animal can understand the symbolic nature of a word while having no understanding of the rules which integrate that word into sentences.

[28] Lucy gave me a taste of her conception of the symbol when she linked me with my alligator emblem and gave me the sign for alligator as a name. Between my first and second visits to the institute, Fouts made a formal study of Lucy's conceptual abilities by investigating how she used her vocabulary. We discussed the results when I returned to the institute and met Lucy again in the summer of 1973.

[29] The experiment revolved around Lucy's classification of twenty-four different fruits and vegetables. At the time, the words in Lucy's vocabulary that related to food were "food," "fruit," "drink," "candy," and "banana." She used "food," "fruit," and "drink" in a generic manner to refer to those three classes of items while she knew that "banana" was specific for bananas. Fouts says that the most interesting results of the experiment were the "serendipitous findings concerning her responses to particular items." For instance, she consistently referred to the citrus

fruits (four out of the twenty-four fruits and vegetables) as "smell fruits," linking them with their singular, tangy odor. This was the kind of response Fouts had been hoping for, because it indicated that Lucy was rummaging through her vocabulary for words to *describe* the characteristics of objects for which she had no sign. Lucy had no sign, beyond the generic term "fruit" to describe particular classes of fruit, and so she resorted to segregating them by their attributes. The investigators found that Lucy, in classifying these items, seemed to fix upon the same criteria that a naïve person might select. For instance, her broadest division seemed to segregate the fruits from the vegetables. She preferred the word "fruit" for fruits, while she consistently termed vegetables "food." As noted, she classified the citrus items as "smell fruit," but it was radishes and watermelons that truly summoned her descriptive powers. For the first few days of the experiment Lucy referred to radishes as "food." Then she tasted one. Promptly spitting out the mouthful, she called it a "cry hurt food." Throughout the remainder of the experiment she used "hurt" or "cry" to refer to radishes.

[30] Fouts also found that once Lucy learned the specific name within a general category, she resisted applying that name to any other item. For instance, they taught her "berry" for cherry, which she previously knew only as a "fruit." They found that once it was established that a cherry was "berry" she resisted applying "berry" to other items. Thus she seemed to understand the difference between general terms and specific items.

[31] Lucy liked watermelon, and she three times referred to it as a "candy drink" thereby plumbing the fruit for a third of its attributes—sweetness.

[32] Lucy principally used "drink" to refer to watermelon, an attribute of the fruit we recognize in our own appellation for it. On occasion she came even closer to the English word by calling it a "drinkfruit." "Drinkfruit" is about as close to watermelon as any analyst might be expected to get, if the analyst's most specific term for fluids was "drink" and its most specific term for melons was "fruit." Given the vocabulary she had to work with, Lucy came treacherously close to the creative symbolization that produced the English word "watermelon," and we might suppose that she came upon "drinkfruit" by an analysis of its attributes similar to that which produced our own word. These examples indicate that Lucy was making productive use of her vocabulary. By generating an infinite number of new and different sentences from a finite vocabulary, Lucy was demonstrating productivity.

[33] Just as it is thought that most animal communication is closely tied to basic urges and is not displaced in time and space from the stimuli that initiate the message, so it is also thought that each signal an animal sends is an autonomous and specific message, which, if it can be combined with other signals at all, can only be combined in strictly limited ways. For man, each word is perceived to be a building block that he can organize through grammar with other building blocks into an infinite number of messages, but the animal is supposedly limited to sending and

receiving messages that are prefabricated and, so to speak, handed to it whole. According to this logic, Lucy should not have been able to apply "candy" to watermelon and other sweets, because to do so requires that she look past the prefabricated surface of the signal to the building blocks—candiness, for instance—that make up the message. To do this Lucy had to summon her powers of reconstitution.

[34] When Lucy invented a sign for "leash" she demonstrated her understanding of the word's utility. She hates the leash, but because of a nearby highway, it is a necessary accouterment if she is to venture out. Fouts referred to the leash as a "string," a sign made by pulling the little finger. Lucy, however, refers to the leash by making a motion of putting it on. As in her invention of my alligator sobriquet, Lucy here abstracted and reified the properties of the leash into a symbolic representation and, in so doing, was demonstrating how she analyzed the world.

[35] Washoe has displayed productivity as well, says Fouts. Once riding in a rowboat with Roger at the institute, she referred to two swans as "water birds."

[36] Lucy has recently begun using Ameslan to express her emotional states. The most poignant example of this occurred one day when Jane Temerlin, Lucy's foster mother, left the house during one of Roger's training sessions. Lucy ran over to the side window to watch Jane drive off, and as she did, Lucy signed to herself "cry me, me cry." It was the first time Fouts had seen a chimp describe an emotion rather than revert to normal chimp expressions of distress.

[37] On another occasion, Fouts exploited Freud's hypothesis that verbal behavior tends to reduce physical activity in order to save himself from some roughhousing at Lucy's hands. Lucy has gotten very big and very strong in the past year. One day Lucy was keyed up and she came charging toward Fouts from across the Temerlin's living room. As she was charging, Roger (in Ameslan) said "sign!" (the imperative for her to tell him what she wants).

[38] Lucy halted briefly, said "tickle," and then resumed her charge.

[39] "Who?" said Roger.

[40] "Tickle Lucy."

[41] "Ask politely!"

[42] "Please tickle Lucy," said the chimp as she reached Roger. By now Lucy was thoroughly calmed down.

[43] Upon my return visit to the Temerlin's, I was surprised at how big Lucy had become. She is now approaching sexual maturity and occasionally interrupts training sessions with immodest passes at her male mentors. In order to satisfy Lucy's developing maternal instinct, Dr. Lemmon gave her a kitten to raise. Lucy immediately proved herself to be an over-protective mother. She would carry the kitten

everywhere, calling it "my baby." The problem was that the cat, being a cat, did not want to be carried everywhere. Although Lucy carried it properly, she was quite insensitive to the cat's wishes, and as a result, the cat hurt its pads grabbing onto the wire cage in futile resistance whenever its demonically smothering foster mother tramped by and scooped it up. As soon as the Temerlins noticed the cat's sore pads, it was promptly taken away from Lucy. Lucy was stricken with grief. Sue Savage, one of Lucy's trainers, explained to Lucy that she had hurt the cat's paws (feet). Lucy seemed properly chastened. When the cat was eventually returned to her, she immediately cradled it and pointed to its feet, signing "hurt, hurt."

[44] Lucy has met other cats that she has not liked so much, which brings us to a final indication that this particular chimpanzee has stamped her imprimatur on language. Like Washoe, Lucy has taken to swearing. She demonstrates that her invention of the word "leash" did not occur out of fondness for the object, inasmuch as she refers to it as a "dirty leash." On another occasion, after an argument with a local tomcat, she referred to the animal as a "dirty cat." Lucy, like the other chimps, seems to take her relations with other animals very seriously.

[45] If there is one use of language which, for the outsider, demonstrates that an animal understands and exploits the creative aspects of language, that aspect might be swearing. Lucy's use of "dirty" exploited a purely descriptive term for pejorative associations. These pejorative associations were the product of her own deduction and not the product of instruction. By putting her feelings into words, Lucy was also bending words to suit her feelings. More to the point, she was telling us what she thought of that cat, and that is what language is all about. If Lucy's use of Ameslan was mere "aping" of her mentors, we should not expect her to swear.

[46] When Lucy reaches maturity, she will be reintroduced to her own kind. Hopefully she will have an infant of her own, and—this is Fouts's fondest wish—will teach it to communicate using Ameslan.

[47] Based on the differences between my perceptions of Lucy on my first and second visits to Oklahoma, she seemed to be rapidly approaching the age where not only would she need other chimps to fulfill her social and sexual needs but might be maturing to the point where her superior strength would make it difficult for human companions to deal with her. Raised as the Temerlin's infant, she is mindful of their wishes and accepts their dominance; however, as people are perceived to be more and more peripheral to the institute and family, so does their authority with Lucy diminish. When I first met her, she was about six and I was still stronger than she. Sessions of tickling and playing with her were just plain fun. She was then, and still is, quite affectionate and liked nothing better than leaping from couch to couch and roughhousing. During my second visit, I again looked forward to these little tussles; but this year during tickling sessions, I found myself tensed and wary. It was not that I was afraid she might strike out; rather she seemed more deliberate, controlled, and she emanated vibrations of contained power. There was no longer a

question of who was stronger, and on the whole I thought it was very nice of Lucy to want still to play with me. There were other differences between the visits as well. Last year Fouts and I would occasionally take a break to have coffee; this year when we had coffee, Lucy had a cup as well. As she has matured, Lucy has also become more generous; often as she requests food for herself, she gives food to Roger and tells him to eat.

CHILDHOOD'S END

[48] To take the proper measure of the chimp's language abilities, it is important to follow them through maturity. Studying only the infant chimp might leave an observer with a false impression of what the Ameslan-using adult is like. The infant prodigy in Ameslan is thoroughly impressive, but it is very dependent on the humans around it and this tends to dampen evidence of the animal's individuality and make it merely cute. Exposure to the infant also heightens the impression that the chimp would like to be human if only it could. During their maturing, it becomes clear that rather than being failed human beings, they are very successful at being chimps. Rather than smugly reassuring an adorable, dependent infant chimp, the human begins to feel threatened by the vigor, power, and personality of the adult. Since the chimp is a serious animal, we cannot help but be impressed with the seriousness of the idea that these animals can communicate with us in one of our own languages. It is not very threatening when an adorable, dependent infant begins to sign; it is another matter when a self-possessed and somewhat intimidating adult demonstrates its facility with language. Man may need to feel that language is exclusively his if only to compensate for his manifest physical inferiority.

[49] This becomes all the more clear when one is exposed to a chimp not caged in a zoo or being put through a comical routine in a circus. Putting any animal behind bars will transform it from a source of fear into an object of pity, and in doing so will pervert the observer's perceptions of the animal, and in most cases make the animal neurotic, which seems to confirm the original judgment imposed by the cage. We put animals in cages or turn them into performers in part to disarm ancient memories that it was, after all, we who were cast from Eden. Lucy, however, does not live in a cage, she is a member of a family, and my picture of the chimp was commensurately less confused by the symbolic baggage of the zoo, although Lucy was still vastly displaced from a milieu where she would really flourish—a chimp community.

[50] During my second visit with Lucy, I was reminded of Arthur C. Clark's *Childhood's End*, in which man, under the supervision of a race of sterile, rational overlords, becomes the vehicle for the birth of his own successor. In schooling a colony of chimps in Ameslan, we are giving our most cherished tool to an animal already well-equipped by nature to survive in a world without men. We do not know yet how this tool will be used.

FOR REVIEW AND DISCUSSION

Content

1. Describe Lucy's method of communication. How does it differ from the way humans communicate?

2. Why is it significant that Lucy is able to reverse the word order in the simple sentence "Roger tickle Lucy" and that she is able to *describe* as well as *express* an emotion?

3. What is Linden's attitude toward the manner in which the chimps are studied? Linden mentions more than once that investigators often ignore the communicative nature of Lucy's talk. To what extent does Linden's observation affect his attitude toward the study?

Rhetoric

1. Review the selection, marking those paragraphs devoted to Lucy and her training and those devoted to more general discussion of language and behavior. What pattern or organizing principle do you see in the sequence of paragraphs?

2. Why is the last section, "Childhood's End," separated from the rest of the text?

3. Linden is writing about a scientific experiment. What reason might he have for occasionally departing from the chronological order and objectivity we usually associate with such writing?

4. Describe the change in tone that occurs in the last section. Does this change seem called for?

5. Other than to indicate what is obvious—that Linden is not a member of Fouts's group—why might Linden repeatedly refer to himself as "the outsider"? In what way does this reference to himself affect your attitude toward him?

Classroom Exercises

1. To what extent are you convinced that Lucy truly understands words as symbols rather than as distinctive sounds to which she responds by conditioned reflex—much as a well-trained dog responds to the commands *sit*, *fetch*, and so forth.

Carol L. Smith

HOW CHILDREN ACQUIRE LANGUAGE

In contrast to the extraordinary feats of language acquisition accomplished by handicapped children and gifted primates, this selection details how the process occurs naturally and almost effortlessly in the average child. The feat is no less impressive for its commonness. Notice particularly the nature of what is mastered at each step in the process.

[1]   In order to understand the nature of spoken languages and why men are so adept at learning them, it is useful to study the development of speech in children. The factors that affect that development should help reveal the capabilities a child brings to language learning and should help us understand how he applies them in learning the rules of his native language.

EARLY VOCALIZATIONS

[2]   Most children do not speak their first recognizable word until about a year old, but before that time they have had a considerable amount of practice at vocalization. At birth, babies can coo and cry. During the next few months the sounds they spontaneously produce increase in frequency and variety. By four or five months they are beginning to babble—to chant various syllabic sounds in a rhythmic fashion. Then slowly they develop the capacity to imitate the sounds made by others and to control the sounds they make. Finally, they learn the names of people or objects—their first words.

[3]   Infants' early vocalizations seem remarkably independent of what they hear around them. Their early babbling is a type of motor play and experimentation, and it is not limited to the sounds used in a particular language. Instead, infants seem to make sounds from all languages, including French vowels and German rolled Rs. For the first six months of life, deaf babies cry and babble like hearing children—additional evidence for the spontaneity of early vocalization and its relative independence of hearing.

[4]   Hearing the speech of others becomes increasingly important during the second half of the first year. The development of children's ability to imitate others reflects their growing ability to produce sounds voluntarily, although the range of

From *Psychology Today: An Introduction*, Second Edition. Copyright © 1972 by Communications Research Machines, Inc. Reprinted by permission of CRM Books, a Division of Random House, Inc.

voluntarily produced sounds always lags behind those produced spontaneously. At the end of the first year, the baby not only imitates the sounds of syllables and words but is beginning to mimic the stress and pitch patterns of those who talk with him. Before this time the speech sounds of babies from different communities all sound much the same.

[5] Learning to make syllable sounds and to imitate is good preparation for learning words. By rewarding the baby with enthusiastic bursts of approval when he says something that sounds like a word, parents encourage infants to repeat and practice the sounds that are used in words. Imitation and reinforcement also play a major part in the development of children's vocabulary. But there is a leap to be made before the baby starts using words: he must learn that the sound has meaning, that it is used as a symbol for something else. Generally, his first words refer to the tangible and the visible and are used one at a time, as labels or commands ("Dog!" "Cookie!"). Toward the beginning of the second year, the infant will begin to express himself more precisely by combining two words in an utterance. At this time he enters a new phase of the language-learning process, during which he learns the complicated rules for combining words into sentences.

RULE LEARNING

[6] Much of the discussion of rule learning that follows is based on the work of R. Brown, from Harvard University, and particularly on a long-term study that Brown and his collaborators, U. Bellugi, C. Fraser, and C. Cazden, did on the speech of three children whom they call Adam, Eve, and Sarah. When the study began, the children were about two years old and were just beginning to combine words in two-word utterances. The researchers visited them in their homes every week or so until Adam and Sarah were five years old (Eve moved away nine months after the study began) and collected many samples of their speech. They studied primarily the children's spontaneous speech rather than their comprehension of what other people said to them, because speech gives a clearer indication of a child's understanding of grammatical forms than do his responses to other people's utterances. The two central questions of the research were: what do children know about the structure of English at different points in their development, and what process do they use to acquire that knowledge?

[7] At age two, a child's speech is not much like an adult's. His utterances are short; his vocabulary is limited to nouns and action verbs; most other parts of speech are missing. Nonessential words are left out, much as they are when someone writes a telegram. People who know the child well can usually understand what his statements mean, and they often respond by expanding his utterances into a well-formed adult sentence. [The following] are some examples of a young child's *telegraphic speech* and his mother's interpretation recorded by Brown and Bellugi.

Child	Mother
Baby highchair.	Baby is in the highchair.
Eve lunch.	Eve is having lunch.
Throw Daddy.	Throw it to Daddy.
Pick glove.	Pick the glove up.

[8] By age four or five, the child's speech is more adultlike. His utterances have increased in length, and they usually include prepositions, auxiliary verbs, and articles. Furthermore, the child seems to have mastered most of the rules of grammar. Brown and C. Hanlon found Adam—when he was four years and seven months old—saying:

> The man's not bad, is he?
> I can hold on like a monkey, can't I?
> She thought that was a tiger, didn't she?

[9] Questions like these are called *tag questions*, and there is much a child must know to form them correctly. First, he must know that he should use a negative tag such as "can't I?" when he expects a "yes" answer to his question; when he expects a "no" answer, he must use an affirmative tag such as "is he?" In addition, he has to be able to substitute a pronoun for a noun (replacing "man" with "he" in the first example). And he must know how to use auxiliary verbs (such as "did" in the third example). . . .

[10] How does a child come to master the rules of sentence formation in these few short years? Brown and Bellugi's observations suggest that although the child under age four or five does not follow adult grammatical rules, he seems to be following more primitive rules of his own.

[11] One of the first rules that an English-speaking child may learn concerns word order. For example, a two- or three-year-old might say, "Eat cake" while he is devouring his birthday fare. For an adult, "Eat cake" is a command to another to eat the cake. To be correct, the child should say "I am eating the cake," indicating that he is the actor, that eating is in progress at the present, and that the cake is what is being eaten. . . . The child's sentence does not include all these nuances, and it violates several grammatical rules. But the child has observed one adult rule of word order: he puts "cake" after "eat," indicating that the cake is the object being eaten rather than the agent doing the eating. When a child imitates an adult, he often leaves out words, but he does preserve word order. For example, when Brown and Fraser in 1963 asked children between two and three years old to repeat sentences that were spoken to them, one child typically made these responses . . .

Adult	Child
I am drawing a dog.	I draw dog.
I do not want an apple.	I do a apple.
Read the book.	Read book.

[12] As the child's speech becomes less and less telegraphic, he begins to use helping verbs (such as "is" and "are"), prepositions, and articles. He also begins to make a type of error called *overregularization*. Overregularization, which is common in the speech of three- and four-year-olds, results from the misapplication of a grammatical rule. For example, the usual rule for forming the past tense of an English verb is to add "ed" to the base. But some verbs, including many common ones, have irregular past tenses: go/went, come/came, drive/drove, fall/fell. The child may learn common words like "fell" and "came" from his parents before he masters the "ed" past-tense rule and produce grammatically correct sentences: "I fell down" and "The cat came home." But once he learns the rule for forming the regular past tense, he is likely to overgeneralize, producing sentences like "He goed to the store" and "I falled down." Similarly, the general rule for forming plurals in English is to add an "s" to a singular noun: "dog" becomes "dogs," and so on. After the child has learned that rule, such words as "foots," "mans," and "mouses" creep into his conversation.

[13] The emergence of any one adult rule is not sudden; one can see it coming for a long while. For example, consider Sarah's acquisition of the "ing" grammatical inflection to form the present progressive, as in "I am eating." At twenty-seven months, Sarah used this form only about half the time that an adult would have used it. Not until sixteen months later did she consistently use it where required. During those months, Sarah did not use the "ing" ending incorrectly so much as skip it sometimes, saying "I eat" where an adult would say "I am eating." A transitional period during which the child sometimes does and sometimes does not use the new form is characteristic of the learning of inflections (including the plural "s," as in "boys," and the past "ed," as in "played," as well as the present progressive "ing").

[14] Some rules are learned somewhat differently, in several steps. When Bellugi studied the development of children's ability to form negative sentences, for example, she found a number of intermediate steps preceding use of the adult rule. A very young child (age two) has a simple rule for forming a negative: he adds the word "no" to a statement: "No want stand." "No gonna fall." "No mom sharpen it." "No write book." "Like it, no." A little later, the child begins to use "not," and he seems to know that he should place "no" or "not" in a special position. He puts it just before the verb: "You not have one." "He not bite you." "I not get it dirty." The last step is to add the necessary auxiliary verb: "You don't have one." "He doesn't bite you." "I don't get it dirty."

[15] As he progresses toward the adult rules, a child does not make all the errors that he conceivably might. Curiously, he seems to learn some rules without making the errors one would expect. The development of the present progressive (I am eating) is a good example. Not all verbs are used in the progressive form. In general, process verbs such as "break" and "play" commonly occur in the progressive—"I

am breaking the world track record"; "I am playing my banjo." State verbs such as "know" or "need," however, do not take the progressive. It would sound strange to say "I am knowing how to do this" or "I am needing a hammer." A child just learning to form the progressive might be expected to add the "ing" ending to all verbs randomly, and not to observe the process-state distinction. Yet errors of this type, according to Brown and Bellugi, are rarely made.

[16] The tag question is another form that emerges with remarkably few errors. The rules for the formation of tag questions are complicated, so there are many opportunities for error, but the child rarely makes any. The predecessor of the tag question is, "The lady swallowed the sword, *huh?*" or ". . . , *right?*" Then, quite suddenly "huh?" is replaced by "didn't she?" It is as if the child holds off on trying to use tag questions until he understands all the necessary rules.

SEMANTICS AND GRAMMAR

[17] Although there is abundant evidence that children consistently apply rules when they speak, it is a difficult matter to state formally what the rules are. One basic question that needs answering is: are the rules based primarily on semantic or on grammatical relationships?

[18] Sentences can be described in both semantic and grammatical terms. Consider the sentence, "The runner overturned the hurdle." Semantically, a person or *agent* (the runner) initiates an *action* (the overturning), and the *object* (the hurdle) directly receives this action. The meaning of the sentence can be characterized by the semantic relation of agent-action-object. Alternately, the sentence can be described in formal grammatical terms. The *subject* (the runner) dominates the sentence, and there is a predicate composed of a *main verb* (overturned) and a *direct object* (the hurdle). In this sentence, the subject has the semantic role of agent and the main verb that of action. Subjects and verbs, however, will have other semantic roles in different sentences; there is no simple, one-to-one correspondence between grammatical and semantic roles. Consider, for example, the sentence "The hurdle was overturned by the runner."

[19] According to N. Chomsky, the rules that govern speech are based primarily on grammatical relationships rather than on semantic ones. For example, the basic rule of sentence production that says a sentence must have a subject and a predicate is a grammatical rule, not a semantic one. Subject and predicate express a formal relation between parts of a sentence rather than a fixed relation between the meaning of words.

[20] Another rule that governs sentence production is that the verb must agree in number with the subject. Again, this rule is phrased in grammatical terms. There is no easy way to state it in semantic terms. Although the grammatical subject and the

semantic agent are often identical, that is not always true. To illustrate, consider the following sentences:

> The boy gives presents to the girls.
> The girls receive presents from the boy.

In both cases the boy is giving presents to the girls and so is the agent of the action. But only in the first sentence does the verb agree in number with "boy." The verb agrees with the grammatical subject in both sentences; the subject is defined in terms of its relation to the main verb and not in terms of its semantic role.

[21] The rules that govern young children's speech are not necessarily of the same type as those that govern adults' speech. It seems quite possible that the early stages of children's speech rely more heavily on semantic relationships than does adults' speech. Beyond the earliest stages, however, the regularities in children's speech do seem to be based on grammatical rules rather than exclusively on semantic ones.

[22] If that is correct, then we are faced with a problem: how does a two- or three-year-old child begin to learn grammatical rules? Piaget's theory . . . suggests how a child constructs certain semantic concepts during the sensorimotor period, but how he constructs the concepts of subject, predicate, verb, and object at that age is not yet known. Where does his understanding of these relationships come from? It is problems like these that led Chomsky and others to conclude that children are born with a potential ability to understand formal grammatical relations, much as they are born with a potential ability to walk. This innate capacity for the grammatical structure of language, according to Chomsky's theory, helps account for the special linguistic abilities of human beings.

THE ORDER OF ACQUISITION OF RULES

[23] So far we have described children's speech as regular and systematic, something that can be characterized as following rules. We have suggested that the rules are grammatical rather than semantic and have even ventured the hypothesis that sensitivity to certain features of language may be innate. Yet even though the child may have this built-in sensitivity, he does not speak like an adult when he begins to talk.

[24] The child seems to learn adult rules in a fairly stable order. There is some variation from child to child, but not a great deal. The children that R. Brown studied mastered the rules of word order first, and then the rules for certain grammatical inflections. There was a definite order of acquisition among the grammatical inflections. For example, the children learned to use the plural "s" (as in "horses") and the irregular past forms of verbs (went, gone) before they began to use the linking verb "to be" ("The cops *are* here") or the third person indicative ("He

runs"). These two forms, in turn, were acquired before auxiliary verbs ("The cops *are* running in place").

[25] Why do children tend to learn these rules in the same order? There are several possible reasons. First, the frequency with which a form is used in the home might help determine when it is mastered. If a child hears many sentences in which "ing" is attached to verbs, it should be easier for him to figure out when this ending is appropriate. Brown decided to test this hypothesis with the parents of Adam, Eve, and Sarah. In his recent book, *A First Language: The Early Stages*, he reports that the three sets of parents did use different grammatical inflections with different frequencies and that the frequencies were remarkably consistent within each home. However, the forms the parents used most frequently were *not* the ones that the children acquired first. It seems, then, that something other than frequency in parental speech determines the order in which children learn grammatical rules.

[26] Brown found that the *semantic complexity* of a rule is an important determinant of rule learning: the rules that are easiest to understand are mastered first. Semantic complexity refers to the number of meanings that a person must understand in order to use a rule correctly. For example, the rules for the formation of the plural and of the past each requires an understanding of one major meaning. To use the plural correctly, you must understand the concept of number. A given noun is either singular (bed) or not singular (beds). When the noun is not singular, you add an "s." Similarly, to use the past correctly you must understand the idea that something has occurred before right now. Verbs can refer either to some earlier time or not. When they refer to an earlier time, you add "ed" (walked). By contrast, the rule for the formation of a regular third-person verb is semantically more complex. To form it, you must be able to coordinate the meanings of *both* number and earlierness. When the verb is both singular and not earlier, for example, you add an "s" to the main stem of the verb (he walks).

[27] Intuitively, it makes sense that semantic complexity should be an important factor in the order of rule learning. It is hard to imagine how a child could use the past and present tense correctly if he could not differentiate between past and present time. He might perceive that adults sometimes used one form of a verb and sometimes another, but the choice would seem completely arbitrary to him until he could attach distinct meanings to the two forms.

[28] If semantic complexity were the *only* factor affecting the child's discovery of rules, however, forms that have the same meanings would be acquired at the same time. This is not always the case. Sometimes two forms that have the same meanings, such as simple and complex plurals, are acquired at different times. In many of these cases, Brown found, the two forms differ in *grammatical complexity*. Grammatical complexity is a second factor in the order of rule learning. (The table displays some examples of both semantic and grammatical relations.)

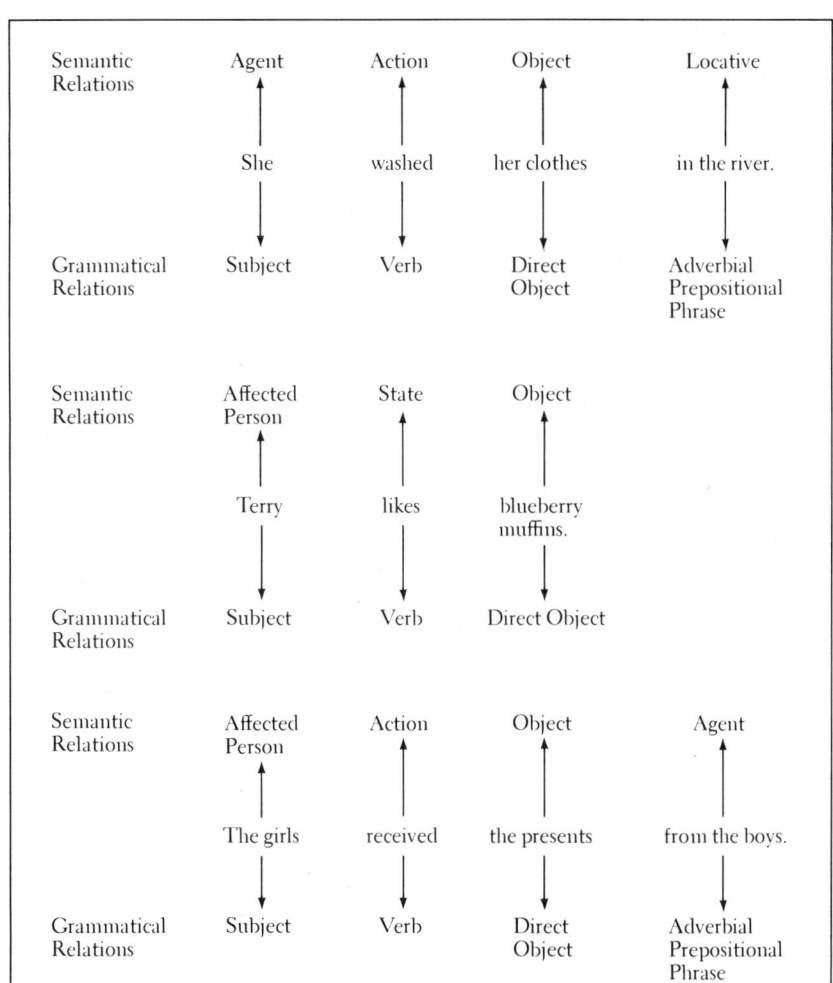

Examples of Semantic and Grammatical Relations

Semantic Relations	Agent	Action	Object	Locative
	↕	↕	↕	↕
	She	washed	her clothes	in the river.
	↕	↕	↕	↕
Grammatical Relations	Subject	Verb	Direct Object	Adverbial Prepositional Phrase

Semantic Relations	Affected Person	State	Object	
	↕	↕	↕	
	Terry	likes	blueberry muffins.	
	↕	↕	↕	
Grammatical Relations	Subject	Verb	Direct Object	

Semantic Relations	Affected Person	Action	Object	Agent
	↕	↕	↕	↕
	The girls	received	the presents	from the boys.
	↕	↕	↕	↕
Grammatical Relations	Subject	Verb	Direct Object	Adverbial Prepositional Phrase

[29] Grammatical complexity refers to the number of steps involved in the derivation of a particular form. For example, compare a simple plural form—a child pointing and saying "apple"—with a more complex plural—"They apples." Although both statements have the same meaning, the second is the more complex grammatically; the child not only pluralized "apples" but also made the pronoun "they" plural, to agree in number with "apples." Cazden analyzed the data from Adam, Eve, and Sarah and found that their performance was better with the simple plurals than with the complex plurals. This finding and others cited by Brown suggest the importance of grammatical complexity in the order of rule learning.

[30] Semantic and grammatical complexity seem to be two important factors in the order of rule learning, but other variables may also be quite important—for example, the *perceptibility* of a given form. Compare the full possessive form, "That is John's hat" with the elliptical possessive, "That is John's." With the elliptical possessive, the "s" can be heard more easily because it is often at the end of a sentence and stressed, whereas the "s" in the full possessive is more likely to be slurred over. Cazden found the performance of Adam, Eve, and Sarah to be much better on the more perceptible form, the elliptical possessive—*even though the elliptical possessive is more grammatically complex than the full possessive*. Apparently, perceptibility may sometimes override grammatical complexity as a determinant of the order of rule learning. However, there are other possible interpretations for the children's performance. The two forms of the possessive differ not only along the dimensions of grammatical complexity and perceptibility but also along that of redundancy of meaning. These multiple differences between any two forms make it difficult to point to any variable as the most important determinant in the order of rule learning.

[31] To summarize, the regularities in a child's speech at different stages suggest that he is learning rules for sentence production. Rule learning is a gradual process: first the child may learn to understand a concept like singular and plural and then, slowly, he begins to notice that plural nouns are marked with an "s." Also, rule learning is not a conscious process. A four-year-old can speak grammatically, but he cannot describe the rules of grammar. Increasing awareness of language rules comes with age.

LATER DEVELOPMENTS

[32] By the age of five most children talk very well. Their sentences are like an adult's in form, although the content of the sentences is restricted. Later developments seem to keep pace with the child's general cognitive advancement. He enlarges his vocabulary as his ability to understand increases and as he is exposed to new things, and he begins to be able to reflect on his own speech.

[33] It takes several years, however, for children to understand fully that words are arbitrary symbols, not intrinsic parts of an object. For example, a group of eight-year-olds was reading a story about how the kangaroo got its name. In the story Captain Cook and his men had landed in Australia and, seeing some strange animals in the distance, asked an Australian what the animals were called. The Australian, not knowing, replied "kangaroo," which in his language meant "I don't know." But Captain Cook and his men went off confident that this strange being was called a kangaroo. The children had a difficult time getting the point of the story because they could not conceive of "kangaroo" as meaning something different from the animal itself. Older children would have easily perceived the two meanings of kangaroo.

[34] F. Kessel reports that between ages five and twelve the child also learns to appreciate the two meanings of an ambiguous sentence. For example: "The duck is ready to eat" could mean either that the duck is the dinner or the diner. Before about twelve years of age, children are unable to pick out the two meanings of the sentence. Around twelve, however, they become able to see the two meanings simultaneously. This and other new abilities with language seem to reflect advances in cognitive development, particularly in the child's capacity to direct his thinking in systematic ways and to deal with hypothetical situations and abstractions.

FOR REVIEW AND DISCUSSION

Content

1. What is the source of the rules for speaking learned by a child? What does this source reveal about the grammar of written language?

2. What is the difference between grammatical and semantic relationships? Describe both in the following sentence: "I was asked by a friend to call you."

3. Speculate on why deaf children cease to babble at about six months of age.

Rhetoric

1. In paragraph 1 Smith in effect states the purpose of her selection. Does she fulfill that purpose?

2. Paragraph 10 functions as a transition from one discussion to another. Does the transition work well, or is it confusing? Is it a logical transition?

3. "Consistency in number" is a favorite phrase of English teachers. Notice that Smith is frequently inconsistent, writing "child" one moment and "children" the next (for instance, see paragraphs 21 and 22). Is her inconsistency undesirable, or is it necessary? On what do you base your decision?

Classroom Exercises

1. What is meant by *telegraphic speech?* If you know any small children, listen to them. What *kinds* of words do they tend to omit from their speech?

2. Write a short paragraph imitating how you think a small child would talk, then compare it to other students' versions and to an actual sample of a child's speech. What conclusions can you draw from the comparisons?

Robert Graves

THE COOL WEB

Scientists have shown that the way we use language changes as we mature. In this poem, the English poet Robert Graves sets forth the same idea long before science ever "proved" it. In their innocence, he says, children use language to express their true feelings and to describe reality as they see it, while adults use language as a defense against reality. It will be helpful when reading the poem to keep in mind the role that euphemisms play in our lives.

[1] Children are dumb to say how hot the day is,
How hot the scent is of the summer rose,
How dreadful the black wastes of evening sky,
How dreadful the tall soldiers drumming by.

[2] But we have speech, to chill the angry day,
And speech to dull the rose's cruel scent.
We spell away the overhanging night,
We spell away the soldiers and the fright.

[3] There's a cool web of language winds us in.
Retreat from too much joy or too much fear:
We grow sea-green at last and coldly die
In brininess and volubility.

[4] But if we let our tongues lose self-possession,
Throwing off language and its watery clasp,
Before our death, instead of when death comes,
Facing the wide glare of the children's day,
Facing the rose, the dark sky and the drums,
We shall go mad no doubt and die that way.

From *Collected Poems* by Robert Graves. Copyright © 1955 by Robert Graves. Reprinted by permission of Curtis Brown, Ltd.

FOR REVIEW AND DISCUSSION

Content

1. Look up *dumb* and *spell* in an unabridged dictionary. Which of their meanings apply in the context of the poem?

2. Explain what you think Graves means when he calls language a "cool web" and refers to its "watery clasp."

3. Graves in fact presents two sides of an issue. Which side do you think he favors, the dumbness of children or the insulation (from reality) of adults?

4. When Graves says that we will go insane if we stop depending on language, does he mean it literally, or is he using a metaphor to achieve a certain effect? Explain your answer.

Rhetoric

1. Notice the repetitions in the poem, especially in the second stanza. What effect do they have on the reader? Explain how they may be acting as a spell.

2. Write the poem out as a short essay. What changes do you have to make? What kinds of problems do you encounter in attempting a prose paraphrase of poetry?

Classroom Exercises

1. Briefly recount your own experiences in using language to protect yourself from reality. Analyze why you chose some words—euphemisms, perhaps—instead of other, more direct, ones to deal with the experiences.

2. Make a list of euphemisms you and your family or friends use, and classify them according to subject (death, bodily functions, etc.). How and why does your list differ from those of other people in your class?

FOR FURTHER READING

Edward Sapir

LANGUAGE AND THOUGHT

> Edward Sapir attempts to answer questions that have long been a source of controversy among philosophers and linguists: "Is thought possible without language? How do thought and language interrelate?" Sapir's response, while not definitive, is nevertheless unequivocal and comprehensive. It is also complex, and requires slow and careful reading.

[1] The question has often been raised whether thought is possible without speech; further, if speech and thought be not but two facets of the same psychic process. The question is all the more difficult because it has been hedged about by misunderstandings. In the first place, it is well to observe that whether or not thought necessitates symbolism, that is speech, the flow of language itself is not always indicative of thought. We have seen that the typical linguistic element labels a concept. It does not follow from this that the use to which language is put is always or even mainly conceptual. We are not in ordinary life so much concerned with concepts as such as with concrete particularities and specific relations. When I say, for instance, "I had a good breakfast this morning," it is clear that I am not in the throes of laborious thought, that what I have to transmit is hardly more than a pleasurable memory symbolically rendered in the grooves of habitual expression. Each element in the sentence defines a separate concept or conceptual relation or both combined, but the sentence as a whole has no conceptual significance whatever. It is somewhat as though a dynamo capable of generating enough power to run an elevator were operated almost exclusively to feed an electric doorbell. The parallel is more suggestive than at first sight appears. Language may be looked upon as an instrument capable of running a gamut of psychic uses. Its flow not only parallels that of the inner content of consciousness, but parallels it on different levels, ranging from the state of mind that is dominated by particular images to that in which abstract concepts and their relations are alone at the focus of attention and which is ordinarily termed reasoning. Thus the outward form only of language is constant; its inner meaning, its psychic value or intensity, varies freely with attention or the selective interest of the mind, also, needless to say, with the mind's general development. From the point of view of language, thought may be defined

From *Language: An Introduction to the Study of Speech* by Edward Sapir, copyright, 1921, by Harcourt Brace Jovanovich, Inc.; renewed, 1949, by Jean V. Sapir. Reprinted by permission of Harcourt Brace Jovanovich, Inc.

LANGUAGE AND THOUGHT

as the highest latent or potential content of speech, the content that is obtained by interpreting each of the elements in the flow of language as possessed of its very fullest conceptual value. From this it follows at once that language and thought are not strictly coterminous. At best language can but be the outward facet of thought on the highest, most generalized, level of symbolic expression. To put our viewpoint somewhat differently, language is primarily a pre-rational function. It humbly works up to the thought that is latent in, that may eventually be read into, its classifications and its forms; it is not, as is generally but naïvely assumed, the final label put upon the finished thought.

[2] Most people, asked if they can think without speech, would probably answer, "Yes, but it is not easy for me to do so. Still I know it can be done." Language is but a garment! But what if language is not so much a garment as a prepared road or groove? It is, indeed, in the highest degree likely that language is an instrument originally put to uses lower than the conceptual plane and that thought arises as a refined interpretation of its content. The product grows, in other words, with the instrument, and thought may be no more conceivable, in its genesis and daily practice, without speech than is mathematical reasoning practicable without the lever of an appropriate mathematical symbolism. No one believes that even the most difficult mathematical proposition is inherently dependent on an arbitrary set of symbols, but it is impossible to suppose that the human mind is capable of arriving at or holding such a proposition without the symbolism. The writer, for one, is strongly of the opinion that the feeling entertained by so many that they can think, or even reason, without language is an illusion. The illusion seems to be due to a number of factors. The simplest of these is the failure to distinguish between imagery and thought. As a matter of fact, no sooner do we try to put an image into conscious relation with another than we find ourselves slipping into a silent flow of words. Thought may be a natural domain apart from the artificial one of speech, but speech would seem to be the only road we know of that leads to it. A still more fruitful source of the illusive feeling that language may be dispensed with in thought is the common failure to realize that language is not identical with its auditory symbolism. The auditory symbolism may be replaced, point for point, by a motor or by a visual symbolism (many people can read, for instance, in a purely visual sense, that is, without the intermediating link of an inner flow of the auditory images that correspond to the printed or written words) or by still other, more subtle and elusive, types of transfer that are not so easy to define. Hence the contention that one thinks without language merely because he is not aware of a coexisting auditory imagery is very far indeed from being a valid one. One may go so far as to suspect that the symbolic expression of thought may in some cases run along outside the fringe of the conscious mind, so that the feeling of a free, non-linguistic stream of thought is for minds of a certain type a relatively, but only a relatively, justified one. Psychophysically, this would mean that the auditory or equivalent visual or motor centers in the brain, together with the appropriate paths of association, that are the cerebral equivalent of speech, are touched off so lightly during the process of thought as not

to rise into consciousness at all. This would be a limiting case—thought riding lightly on the submerged crests of speech, instead of jogging along with it, hand in hand. The modern psychology has shown us how powerfully symbolism is at work in the unconscious mind. It is therefore easier to understand at the present time than it would have been twenty years ago that the most rarefied thought may be but the conscious counterpart of an unconscious linguistic symbolism.

[3] One word more as to the relation between language and thought. The point of view that we have developed does not by any means preclude the possibility of the growth of speech being in a high degree dependent on the development of thought. We may assume that language arose pre-rationally—just how and on what precise level of mental activity we do not know—but we must not imagine that a highly developed system of speech symbols worked itself out before the genesis of distinct concepts and of thinking, the handling of concepts. We must rather imagine that thought processes set in, as a kind of psychic overflow, almost at the beginning of linguistic expression; further, that the concept, once defined, necessarily reacted on the life of its linguistic symbol, encouraging further linguistic growth. We see this complex process of the interaction of language and thought actually taking place under our eyes. The instrument makes possible the product, the product refines the instrument. The birth of a new concept is invariably foreshadowed by a more or less strained or extended use of old linguistic material; the concept does not attain to individual and independent life until it has found a distinctive linguistic embodiment. In most cases the new symbol is but a thing wrought from linguistic material already in existence in ways mapped out by crushingly despotic precedents. As soon as the word is at hand, we instinctively feel, with something of a sigh of relief, that the concept is ours for the handling. Not until we own the symbol do we feel that we hold a key to the immediate knowledge or understanding of the concept. Would we be so ready to die for "liberty," to struggle for "ideals," if the words themselves were not ringing within us? And the word, as we know, is not only a key; it may also be a fetter.

FOR REVIEW AND DISCUSSION

Content

1. What is meant by *thought*? How is a thought differentiated from an *emotion*, a *feeling*, an *instinct*?

2. Sapir comments that the statement "I had a good breakfast this morning" is not so much a concept or thought as a "pleasurable memory symbolically rendered in the grooves of habitual expression." Which word in that statement, though, suggests thought processes at work?

3. What is Sapir's answer to those who believe that thought is possible without language?

LANGUAGE AND THOUGHT

Rhetoric

1. Notice the length of Sapir's paragraphs. What does his tendency toward long paragraphs suggest about the density and difficulty of his subject matter?

2. Do his specific examples and illustrations help to clarify the general abstractness of his subject? Can you think of other examples that might work well?

3. Which passages are the most difficult ones to understand? What causes their difficulty?

Classroom Exercises

1. For what reasons is it important to know the answers to the questions that Sapir mentions in the introduction? What practical results might such knowledge make possible?

2. Might it have been possible to render more clear the complex ideas that Sapir discusses? How might he have done so? Why would it be difficult to say more clearly all that Sapir already says?

FOR DISCUSSION AND WRITING

1. Compare and contrast the importance of language in the life of Helen Keller and the lives of the "wild children."

2. Linden writes that "man can control only what he can name, which summarizes concisely man's intuitive understanding of the relationship between language and thought." To what extent is *control*—or lack of control—an issue in the cases of Helen Keller or the "wild children"?

3. Would it be accurate to say that Keller and the "wild children" could not *think* when they could not *speak*? In what ways does this relationship between thought and language seem accurate? Inaccurate?

4. To what extent does Graves's poem illustrate the point that both Sapir and Linden make, that man can "control only what he can name"?

5. Compare and contrast what Keller and Graves describe as the function or the value of language.

6. Explain whether Sapir would or would not credit Lucy with the ability to think.

7. Based on your reading about chimpanzees and Helen Keller, write an essay in which you describe the process by which you would teach Helen Keller either what music (or a symphony) is or what colors are. Be inventive, but logical.

6 PERSUASION: LOGIC AND EMOTION

> *We live in a world in which men show little esteem for logic, little respect for fact, no faith in anyone's ability to use thought or discourse to arrive at improved judgments, commitments, and first principles.*
> WAYNE C. BOOTH

> *Effective rational propaganda becomes possible only when there is a clear understanding . . . of the nature of symbols and of their relations to the things and events symbolized.*
> ALDOUS HUXLEY

> *Workers of the world unite. You have nothing to lose but your chains.*
> COMMUNIST MANIFESTO

One of the more fascinating, though unquestionably cynical, theories of the origins and development of language is that language bloomed when man saw its great potential for deceiving his fellow man. In our daily attempts to influence others, we try to turn language to our own ends, sometimes using logic but just as frequently appealing to emotion. On a large and systematic scale, these tactics are sometimes called propaganda. In this chapter we examine some standard propaganda techniques for subverting our powers of reason, and then we see these techniques at work in the speeches of General George Patton and Chief Joseph. Finally, we see what effect such persuasion can have on a mass scale in "The Invasion from Mars."

Donna Woolfolk Cross

PROPAGANDA: HOW NOT TO BE BAMBOOZLED

Although propaganda is not always rooted in deception and emotional appeal, it serves by definition to advance the cause of its user, usually at the expense of those it is used against. Here Donna Woolfolk Cross examines many of the more commonplace propaganda techniques and then briefly discusses the need for our realizing that we are being manipulated by the language of others. While reading the selection, try to draw on your own experience for examples of the techniques she discusses.

[1]   Propaganda. If an opinion poll were taken tomorrow, we can be sure that nearly everyone would be against it because it *sounds* so bad. When we say, "Oh, that's just propaganda," it means, to most people, "That's a pack of lies." But really, propaganda is simply a means of persuasion and so it can be put to work for good causes as well as bad—to persuade people to give to charity, for example, or to love their neighbors, or to stop polluting the environment.

[2]   For good or evil, propaganda pervades our daily lives, helping to shape our attitudes on a thousand subjects. Propaganda probably determines the brand of toothpaste you use, the movies you see, the candidates you elect when you get to fact: propaganda works best with an uncritical audience. Joseph Goebbels, Propaganda Minister in Nazi Germany, once defined his work as "the conquest of the masses." The masses would not have been conquered, however, if they had known how to challenge and to question, how to make distinctions between propaganda and reasonable argument.

[3]   People are bamboozled mainly because they don't recognize propaganda when they see it. They need to be informed about the various devices that can be used to mislead and deceive—about the propagandist's overflowing bag of tricks. The following, then, are some common pitfalls for the unwary.

1. NAME-CALLING

[4]   As its title suggests, this device consists of labeling people or ideas with words of bad connotation, literally, "calling them names." Here the propagandist tries to arouse our contempt so we will dismiss the "bad name" person or idea without examining its merits.

From *Speaking of Words*, copyright 1978. Reprinted by permission of the author.

[5]   Bad names have played a tremendously important role in the history of the world. They have ruined reputations and ended lives, sent people to prison and to war, and just generally made us mad at each other for centuries.

[6]   Name-calling can be used against policies, practices, beliefs and ideals, as well as against individuals, groups, races, nations. Name-calling is at work when we hear a candidate for office described as a "foolish idealist" or a "two-faced liar" or when an incumbent's policies are denounced as "reckless," "reactionary," or just plain "stupid." Some of the most effective names a public figure can be called are ones that may not denote anything specific: "Congresswoman Jane Doe is a *bleeding heart!*" (Did she vote for funds to help paraplegics?) or "The Senator is a *tool of Washington!*" (Did he happen to agree with the President?) Senator Yakalot uses name-calling when he denounces his opponent's "radical policies" and calls them (and him) "socialist," "pinko," and part of a "heartless plot." He also uses it when he calls small cars "puddle-jumpers," "canopeners," and "motorized baby buggies."

[7]   The point here is that when the propagandist uses name-calling, he doesn't want us to think—merely to react, blindly, unquestioningly. So the best defense against being taken in by name-calling is to stop and ask, "Forgetting the bad name attached to it, what are the merits of the idea itself? What does this name really mean, anyway?

2. GLITTERING GENERALITIES

[8]   Glittering generalities are really name-calling in reverse. Name-calling uses words with bad connotations; glittering generalities are words with good connotations—"virtue words," as the Institute for Propaganda Analysis has called them. The Institute explains that while name-calling tries to get us to *reject* and *condemn* someone or something without examining the evidence, glittering generalities try to get us to *accept* and *agree* without examining the evidence.

[9]   We believe in, fight for, live by "virtue words" which we feel deeply about: "justice," "motherhood," "the American way," "our Constitutional rights," "our Christian heritage." These sound good, but when we examine them closely, they turn out to have no specific, definable meaning. They just make us feel good. Senator Yakalot uses glittering generalities when he says, "I stand for all that is good in America, for our American way and our American birthright." But what exactly *is* "good for America"? How can we define our "American birthright"? Just what parts of the American society and culture does "our American way" refer to?

[10]   We often make the mistake of assuming we are personally unaffected by glittering generalities. The next time you find yourself assuming that, listen to a political candidate's speech on TV and see how often the use of glittering generalities elicits cheers and applause. That's the danger of propaganda; it *works*.

Once again, our defense against it is to ask questions: Forgetting the virtue words attached to it, what are the merits of the idea itself? What does "Americanism" (or "freedom" or "truth") really *mean* here? . . .

[11] Both name-calling and glittering generalities work by stirring our emotions in the hope that this will cloud our thinking. Another approach that propaganda uses is to create a distraction, a "red herring," that will make people forget or ignore the real issues. There are several different kinds of "red herrings" that can be used to distract attention.

3. PLAIN FOLKS APPEAL

[12] "Plain folks" is the device by which a speaker tries to win our confidence and support by appearing to be a person like ourselves—"just one of the plain folks." The plain-folks appeal is at work when candidates go around shaking hands with factory workers, kissing babies in supermarkets, and sampling pasta with Italians, fried chicken with Southerners, bagels and blintzes with Jews. "Now I'm a businessman like yourselves" is a plain-folks appeal, as is "I've been a farm boy all my life." Senator Yakalot tries the plain-folks appeal when he says, "I'm just a small-town boy like you fine people." The use of such expressions once prompted Lyndon Johnson to quip, "Whenever I hear someone say, 'I'm just an old country lawyer,' the first thing I reach for is my wallet to make sure it's still there."

[13] The irrelevancy of the plain-folks appeal is obvious: even if the man *is* "one of us" (which may not be true at all), that doesn't mean that his ideas and programs are sound—or even that he honestly has our best interests at heart. As with glittering generalities, the danger here is that we may mistakenly assume we are immune to this appeal. But propagandists wouldn't use it unless it had been proved to work. You can protect yourself by asking, "Aside from his 'nice guy next door' image, what does this man stand for? Are his ideas and his past record really supportive of my best interests?"

4. ARGUMENTUM AD POPULUM (STROKING)

[14] *Argumentum ad populum* means "argument to the people" or "telling the people what they want to hear." The colloquial term from the Watergate era is "stroking," which conjures up pictures of small animals or children being stroked or soothed with compliments until they come to like the person doing the complimenting—and, by extension, his or her ideas.

[15] We all like to hear nice things about ourselves and the group we belong to—we like to be liked—so it stands to reason that we will respond warmly to a

person who tells us we are "hard-working taxpayers" or "the most generous, free-spirited nation in the world." Politicians tell farmers they are the "backbone of the American economy" and college students that they are the "leaders and policy makers of tomorrow." Commercial advertisers use stroking more insidiously by asking a question which invites a flattering answer: "What kind of a man reads *Playboy*?" (Does he really drive a Porsche and own $10,000 worth of sound equipment?) Senator Yakalot is stroking his audience when he calls them the "decent law-abiding citizens that are the great pulsing heart and the life blood of this, our beloved country," and when he repeatedly refers to them as "you fine people," "you wonderful folks."

[16] Obviously, the intent here is to sidetrack us from thinking critically about the man and his ideas. Our own good qualities have nothing to do with the issue at hand. Ask yourself, "Apart from the nice things he has to say about me (and my church, my nation, my ethnic group, my neighbors), what does the candidate stand for? Are his or her ideas in my best interests?"

5. ARGUMENTUM AD HOMINEM

[17] *Argumentum ad hominem* means "argument to the man" and that's exactly what it is. When a propagandist uses *argumentum ad hominem*, he wants to distract our attention from the issue under consideration with personal attacks on the people involved. For example, when Lincoln issued the Emancipation Proclamation, some people responded by calling him the "baboon." But Lincoln's long arms and awkward carriage had nothing to do with the merits of the Proclamation or the question of whether or not slavery should be abolished.

[18] Today *argumentum ad hominem* is still widely used and very effective. You may or may not support the Equal Rights Amendment, but you should be sure your judgment is based on the merits of the idea itself, and not the result of someone's denunciation of the people who support the ERA as "fanatics" or "lesbians" or "frustrated old maids." Senator Yakalot is using *argumentum ad hominem* when he dismisses the idea of using smaller automobiles with a reference to the personal appearance of one of its supporters, Congresswoman Doris Schlepp. Refuse to be waylaid by *argumentum ad hominem* and ask, "Do the personal qualities of the person being discussed have anything to do with the issue at hand? Leaving him or her aside, how good is the idea itself?"

6. TRANSFER (GUILT OR GLORY BY ASSOCIATION)

[19] In *argumentum ad hominem*, an attempt is made to associate negative aspects of a person's character or personal appearance with an issue or idea he supports. The

transfer device uses this same process of association to make us accept or condemn a given person or idea.

[20] A better name for the transfer device is guilt (or glory) by association. In glory by association, the propagandist tries to transfer the positive feelings of something we love and respect to the group or idea he wants us to accept. "This bill for a new dam is in the best tradition of this country, the land of Lincoln, Jefferson, and Washington," is glory by association at work. Lincoln, Jefferson, and Washington were great leaders that most of us revere and respect, but they have no logical connection to the proposal under consideration—the bill to build a new dam. Senator Yakalot uses glory by association when he says full-sized cars "have always been as American as Mom's apple pie or a Sunday drive in the country."

[21] The process works equally well in reverse, when guilt by association is used to transfer our dislike or disapproval of one idea or group to some other idea or group that the propagandist wants us to reject and condemn. "John Doe says we need to make some changes in the way our government operates; well, that's exactly what the Ku Klux Klan has said, so there's a meeting of great minds!" That's guilt by association for you; there's no logical connection between John Doe and the Ku Klux Klan apart from the one the propagandist is trying to create in our minds. He wants to distract our attention from John Doe and get us thinking (and worrying) about the Ku Klux Klan and its politics of violence. (Of course, there are sometimes legitimate associations between the two things; if John Doe had been a *member* of the Ku Klux Klan, it would be reasonable and fair to draw a connection between the man and his group.) Senator Yakalot tries to trick his audience with guilt by association when he remarks that "the words 'Community' and 'Communism' look an awful lot alike!" He does it again when he mentions that Mr. Stu Pott "sports a Fidel Castro beard."

[22] How can we learn to spot the transfer device and distinguish between fair and unfair associations? We can teach ourselves to *suspend judgment* until we have answered these questions: "Is there any legitimate connection between the idea under discussion and the thing it is associated with? Leaving the transfer device out of the picture, what are the merits of the idea by itself?"

7. BANDWAGON

[23] Ever hear of the small, ratlike animal called the lemming? Lemmings are arctic rodents with a very odd habit: periodically, for reasons no one entirely knows, they mass together in a large herd and commit suicide by rushing into deep water and drowning themselves. They all run in together, blindly, and not one of them ever seems to stop and ask, "*Why* am I doing this? Is this really what I want to do?" and thus save itself from destruction. Obviously, lemmings are driven to perform their strange mass suicide rites by common instinct. People choose to "follow the

herd" for more complex reasons, yet we are still all too often the unwitting victims of the bandwagon appeal.

[24] Essentially, the bandwagon urges us to support an action or an opinion because it is popular—because "everyone else is doing it." This call to "get on the bandwagon" appeals to the strong desire in most of us to be one of the crowd, not to be left out or alone. Advertising makes extensive use of the bandwagon appeal ("join the Pepsi people"), but so do politicians ("Let us join together in this great cause"). Senator Yakalot uses the bandwagon appeal when he says that "More and more citizens are rallying to my cause every day," and asks his audience to "join them— and me—in our fight for America."

[25] One of the ways we can see the bandwagon appeal at work is in the overwhelming success of various fashions and trends which capture the interest (and the money) of thousands of people for a short time, then disappear suddenly and completely. For a year or two in the fifties, every child in North America wanted a coonskin cap so they could be like Davy Crockett; no one wanted to be left out. After that there was the hula-hoop craze that helped to dislocate the hips of thousands of Americans. More recently, what made millions of people rush out to buy their very own "pet rocks"?

[26] The problem here is obvious: just because everyone's doing it doesn't mean that *we* should too. Group approval does not prove that something is true or is worth doing. Large numbers of people have supported actions we now condemn. Just a generation ago, Hitler and Mussolini rose to absolute and catastrophically repressive rule in two of the most sophisticated and cultured countries of Europe. When they came into power they were welled up by massive popular support from millions of people who didn't want to be "left out" at a great historical moment.

[27] Once the mass begins to move—on the bandwagon—it becomes harder and harder to perceive the leader *riding* the bandwagon. So don't be a lemming, rushing blindly on to destruction because "everyone else is doing it." Stop and ask, "Where is this bandwagon headed? Never mind about everybody else, is this what is best for *me*?". . .

[28] As we have seen, propaganda can appeal to us by arousing our emotions or distracting our attention from the real issues at hand. But there's a third way that propaganda can be put to work against us—by the use of faulty logic. This approach is really more insidious than the other two because it gives the appearance of reasonable, fair argument. It is only when we look more closely that the holes in the logical fiber show up. The following are some of the devices that make use of faulty logic to distort and mislead.

8. FAULTY CAUSE AND EFFECT

[29] As the name suggests, this device sets up a cause-and-effect relationship that may not be true. The Latin name for this logical fallacy is *post hoc ergo propter hoc*,

which means "after this, therefore because of this." But just because one thing happened after another doesn't mean that one *caused* the other.

[30] An example of false cause-and-effect reasoning is offered by the story (probably invented) of the woman aboard the ship *Titanic*. She woke up from a nap and, feeling seasick, looked around for a call button to summon the steward to bring her some medication. She finally located a small button on one of the walls of her cabin and pushed it. A split second later, the *Titanic* grazed an iceberg in the terrible crash that was to send the entire ship to its destruction. The woman screamed and said, "Oh, God, what have I done? What have I done?" The humor of that anecdote comes from the absurdity of the woman's assumption that pushing the small red button resulted in the destruction of a ship weighing several hundred tons: "It happened after I pushed it, therefore it must be *because* I pushed it"—*post hoc ergo propter hoc* reasoning. There is, of course, no cause-and-effect relationship there.

[31] The false cause-and-effect fallacy is used very often by political candidates. "After I came to office, the rate of inflation dropped to 6 percent." But did the person do anything to cause the lower rate of inflation or was it the result of other conditions? Would the rate of inflation have dropped anyway, even if he hadn't come to office? Senator Yakalot uses false cause and effect when he says "our forefathers who made this country great never had free hot meal handouts! And look what they did for our country!" He does it again when he concludes that "driving full-sized cars means a better car safety record on our American roads today."

[32] False cause-and-effect reasoning is terribly persuasive because it seems so logical. Its appeal is apparently to experience. We swallowed X product—and the headache went away. We elected Y official and unemployment went down. Many people think, "There *must* be a connection." But causality is an immensely complex phenomenon; you need a good deal of evidence to prove that an event that follows another in time was "therefore" caused by the first event.

[33] Don't be taken in by false cause and effect; be sure to ask, "Is there enough evidence to prove that this cause led to that effect? Could there have been any *other* causes?"

9. FALSE ANALOGY

[34] An analogy is a comparison between two ideas, events, or things. But comparisons can be fairly made only when the things being compared are alike in significant ways. When they are not, false analogy is the result.

[35] A famous example of this is the old proverb "Don't change horses in the middle of a stream," often used as an analogy to convince voters not to change administrations in the middle of a war or other crisis. But the analogy is misleading because there are so many differences between the things compared. In what ways is

a war or political crisis like a stream? Is the President or head of state really very much like a horse? And is a nation of millions of people comparable to a man trying to get across a stream? Analogy is false and unfair when it compares two things that have little in common and assumes that they are identical. Senator Yakalot tries to hoodwink his listeners with false analogy when he says, "Trying to take Americans out of the kind of cars they love is as undemocratic as trying to deprive them of the right to vote."

[36] Of course, analogies can be drawn that are reasonable and fair. It would be reasonable, for example, to compare the results of busing in one small Southern city with the possible results in another, *if* the towns have the same kind of history, population, and school policy. We can decide for ourselves whether an analogy is false or fair by asking, "Are the things being compared truly alike in significant ways? Do the differences between them affect the comparison?"

10. BEGGING THE QUESTION

[37] Actually, the name of this device is rather misleading, because it does not appear in the form of a question. Begging the question occurs when, in discussing a questionable or debatable point, a person assumes as already established the very point that he is trying to prove. For example, "No thinking citizen could approve such a completely unacceptable policy as this one." But isn't the question of whether or not the policy *is* acceptable the very point to be established? Senator Yakalot begs the question when he announces that his opponent's plan won't work "because it is unworkable."

[38] We can protect ourselves against this kind of faulty logic by asking, "What is assumed in this statement? Is the assumption reasonable, or does it need more proof?"

11. THE TWO EXTREMES FALLACY (FALSE DILEMMA)

[39] Linguists have long noted that the English language tends to view reality in sets of two extremes or polar opposites. In English, things are either black or white, tall or short, up or down, front or back, left or right, good or bad, guilty or not guilty. We can ask for a "straightforward yes-or-no answer" to a question, the understanding being that we will not accept or consider anything inbetween. In fact, reality cannot always be dissected along such strict lines. There may be (usually are) *more* than just two possibilities or extremes to consider. We are often told to "listen to both sides of the argument." But who's to say that every argument has only two sides? Can't there be a third—even a fourth or fifth—point of view?

[40] The two-extremes fallacy is at work in this statement by Lenin, the great Marxist leader: "You cannot eliminate *one* basic assumption, one substantial part of this philosophy of Marxism (it is as if it were a block of steel), without abandoning truth, without falling into the arms of bourgeois-reactionary falsehood." In other words, if we don't agree 100 percent with every premise of Marxism, we must be placed at the opposite end of the political-economic spectrum—for Lenin, "bourgeois-reactionary falsehood." If we are not entirely *with* him, we must be against him; those are the only two possibilities open to us. Of course, this is a logical fallacy; in real life there are any number of political positions one can maintain *between* the two extremes of Marxism and capitalism. Senator Yakalot uses the two-extremes fallacy in the same way as Lenin when he tells his audience that "in this world a man's either for private enterprise or he's for socialism."

[41] One of the most famous examples of the two-extremes fallacy in recent history is the slogan, "America: Love it or leave it," with its implicit suggestion that we either accept everything just as it is in America today without complaint—or get out. Again, it should be obvious that there is a whole range of action and belief between those two extremes.

[42] Don't be duped; stop and ask, "Are those really the only two options I can choose from? Are there other alternatives not mentioned that deserve consideration?"

12. CARD STACKING

[43] Some questions are so multifaceted and complex that no one can make an intelligent decision about them without considering a wide variety of evidence. One selection of facts could make us feel one way and another selection could make us feel just the opposite. Card stacking is a device of propaganda which selects only the facts that support the propagandist's point of view, and ignores all the others. For example, a candidate could be made to look like a legislative dynamo if you say, "Representative McNerd introduced more new bills than any other member of the Congress," and neglect to mention that most of them were so preposterous that they were laughed off the floor.

[44] Senator Yakalot engages in card stacking when he talks about the proposal to use smaller cars. He talks only about jobs without mentioning the cost to the taxpayers or the very real—though still denied—threat of depletion of resources. He says he wants to help his countrymen keep their jobs, but doesn't mention that the corporations that offer the jobs will also make large profits. He praises the "American chrome industry," overlooking the fact that most chrome is imported. And so on.

[45] The best protection against card stacking is to take the "Yes, but . . ." attitude. This device of propaganda is not untrue, but then again it is not the *whole* truth. So ask yourself, "Is this person leaving something out that I should know about? Is there some other information that should be brought to bear on this question?" . . .

[46] So far, we have considered three approaches that the propagandist can use to influence our thinking: appealing to our emotions, distracting our attention, and misleading us with logic that may appear to be reasonable but is in fact faulty and deceiving. But there is a fourth approach that is probably the most common propaganda trick of them all.

13. TESTIMONIAL

[47] The testimonial device consists in having some loved or respected person give a statement of support (testimonial) for a given product or idea. The problem is that the person being quoted may *not* be an expert in the field; in fact, he may know nothing at all about it. Using the name of a man who is skilled and famous in one field to give a testimonial for something in another field is unfair and unreasonable.

[48] Senator Yakalot tries to mislead his audience with testimonial when he tells them that "full-sized cars have been praised by great Americans like John Wayne and Jack Jones, as well as by leading experts on car safety and comfort."

[49] Testimonial is used extensively in TV ads, where it often appears in such bizarre forms as Joe Namath's endorsement of a pantyhose brand. Here, of course, the "authority" giving the testimonial not only is no expert about pantyhose, but obviously stands to gain something (money!) by making the testimonial.

[50] When celebrities endorse a political candidate, they may not be making money by doing so, but we should still question whether they are in any better position to judge than we ourselves. Too often we are willing to let others we like or respect make our decisions *for us*, while we follow along acquiescently. And this is the purpose of testimonial—to get us to agree and accept *without* stopping to think. Be sure to ask, "Is there any reason to believe that this person (or organization or publication or whatever) has any more knowledge or information than I do on this subject? What does the idea amount to on its own merits, without the benefit of testimonial?"

[51] The cornerstone of democratic society is reliance upon an informed and educated electorate. To be fully effective citizens we need to be able to challenge and to question wisely. A dangerous feeling of indifference toward our political processes exists today. We often abandon our right, our duty, to criticize and evaluate by dismissing *all* politicians as "crooked," *all* new bills and proposals as

"just more government bureaucracy." But there are important distinctions to be made, and this kind of apathy can be fatal to democracy.

[52] If we are to be led, let us not be led blindly, but critically, intelligently, with our eyes open. If we are to continue to be a government "by the people," let us become informed about the methods and purposes of propaganda, so we can be the masters, not the slaves of our destiny.

FOR REVIEW AND DISCUSSION

Content

1. Briefly explain what propaganda is, who uses it, and why.

2. Identify and describe several of the standard techniques of propaganda. From your own experience, provide one or two examples of each.

3. These techniques are not as universally effective as people have come to believe. Their effectiveness can depend on such factors as the audience's political viewpoint, religion, and financial and social status. Discuss how these factors may affect our reaction to propaganda.

4. A commonly held assumption is that "others propagandize while we persuade." What are the implications of this idea?

Rhetoric

1. An introduction ought to set the tone for what will follow, let the reader know what specifically the subject of the piece is, and engage the reader's attention. Discuss how Cross's introduction achieves or fails to achieve these purposes.

2. How appropriate is Senator Yakalot's name to his manner of speaking? What propaganda devices might be at work in his name?

3. Examine the organization of each section and explain the purpose of the final paragraph or two of each.

Classroom Exercises

1. Cross writes that "propaganda works best with an uncritical audience." Find a particularly subtle bit of propaganda in advertising and explain how it is likely to work on an uncritical mind and on a critical one.

2. Yakalot does not seem to be an intelligent individual; certainly his comments are simple minded, easy to see through. To test your protection against *subtle* propaganda, find in a newspaper or magazine the speech of a more sophisticated politician than Yakalot is and try to see what propaganda it contains.

3. Discuss how such factors as political viewpoint, religion, and financial and social status may affect our reaction to specific pieces of propaganda that you find in a newspaper or magazine.

4. Using the techniques that Cross discusses, write a propagandistic speech about abortion, drug addiction, or some other current topic. Deliver your speech to a friend and gauge the success of your persuasive language by asking your friend to note any unsound statements that can be detected.

Stephen K. Tollefson

THE PERSUASIVE TECHNIQUES IN GENERAL GEORGE PATTON'S FAREWELL ADDRESS

George Patton, a much-decorated American general during the Second World War, was noted for his dedication to America and his fiery—and often obscene—rhetoric. He gave this speech to an army of soldiers heading into battle for the first time. The accompanying analysis is intended to show what is happening, rhetorically, in the speech, but is not intended to imply that Patton was consciously using particular propaganda. In fact, an effective speaker frequently uses such techniques without being aware of them. As you read the selection, try to put yourself in the place of one of the soldiers hearing it and consider what effect it would have had on you.

TEXT

1. Men! This stuff we hear about Americans wanting to stay out of this war—not wanting to fight—is a lot of bullshit.

2. Americans love to fight, traditionally.

ANALYSIS

1. *Sweeping generalization:* Ignores the exceptions to the rule which could cause some listeners to view the situation in a different light. Aren't there some Americans who do want to stay out of the war?

Loaded rhetoric: The use of words or phrases with strong connotations or emotional impact ("stuff," "bullshit"). Obscenity, which Patton uses frequently, is a particular kind of loaded rhetoric that can be used to identify the speaker with the audience.

2. *Appeal to authority:* Depends on the respect people generally have for authority, whether or

Text of "George Patton's Farewell Address to his Troops" is from *Memoirs of a Revolutionist* by Dwight Macdonald. Copyright 1957. Reprinted by permission of Dwight Macdonald.

PATTON'S FAREWELL ADDRESS

TEXT *(continued)*

3. All real Americans love the sting of the clash of battle.

4. America loves a winner. America will not tolerate a loser. Americans despise a coward. Americans play to win.

5. That's why America has never lost a war, for the very thought of losing is hateful to an American.

6. You are not all going to die. Only twenty-five per cent of you right here today will be killed in a major battle.

7. Death must not be feared. Every man is frightened at first in battle. If any man says he isn't, he's a god-damned liar.

ANALYSIS *(continued)*

not the respect is deserved. As in this case, tradition can often be a strong authority.

3. *Bandwagon appeal:* Based on the assumption that people want to be part of a group. Here, if you consider yourself to be a "real" American, you must love to fight. The implication is that if you don't love to fight, you must be unpatriotic.

4. *Repetition:* Causes people to remember key words and phrases ("America," "Americans"), even if the context is forgotten.
Sweeping generalization: See the first sentence of the speech.
Loaded rhetoric: Here, the use of active verbs with strong connotations.
Confusion of the individual with the group: A form of bandwagon appeal not readily apparent to the reader. The shift from "America" to "Americans" gives the impression that the abstract symbol "America" can in fact have an emotion and that individual Americans inherently share that emotion.

5. *Non sequitur:* Literally, "it does not follow." One statement does not proceed logically from the previous one. Does it make logical sense to say that we've never lost a war because we don't like to lose?

6. *Misleading use of statistics:* The figures may be accurate, but their context changes their impact. Of course all the soldiers aren't going to die, but one quarter of them will—in a "major battle." How many more will die in minor skirmishes? Notice the use of "only"; what would be the effect if he had said "nearly"?

7. *Sweeping generalization:* Some men in fact might not be frightened in battle.
Argument ad hominem (against the man): In this case, the argument takes the form of simple *namecalling* ("goddamned liar"). In these arguments, the real issue—here, fear in battle—takes a back seat to calling people names. A

TEXT *(continued)*

8. But a real man will never let the fear of death overpower his honor, his sense of duty to his country and to his manhood.

9. All through your army career, you've bitched about what you call "this chickenshit drilling."

10. That drilling was for a purpose: Instant obedience to orders, and to create alertness. If not, some sonofabitch of a German will sneak up behind him and beat him to death with a sock full of shit.

11. An army is a team. It lives, sleeps, eats, and fights as a team.

12. This individual hero stuff is a lot of crap.

13. The bilious bastards who wrote that kind of stuff for the *Saturday Evening Post* don't know any more about fighting than they know about fucking.

14. Even if you are hit, you can still fight. That's not bullshit either. . . . Every damn man has a job to do.

ANALYSIS *(continued)*

speaker sometimes resorts to namecalling when he senses that his arguments are not strong.

8. *Bandwagon:* All men want to be "real" men, even if they have only a vague notion of what "real" means in this case.
Appeal to higher authority: "Honor" and "duty," like "tradition," are frequently powerful symbols of higher authority.

9. *Identification with the audience:* Assumes that people are most apt to believe someone who is "just plain folks" like themselves. Patton seems to be saying "I know how you feel."

10. *Namecalling:* "Sonofabitch of a German."
Appeal to force: Uses coercion (implicit or explicit) to convince an audience to accept a position. In this case, the coercion is particularly strong because of its connection with humiliation. If you don't follow orders, you will most likely be killed—and it won't take much to kill you.

11. *Clichés:* Like repetitions, they are parts of a speech that people remember because they've heard them so often. Clichés are frequently devoid of any meaning. Note that this is also a *bandwagon appeal*—everyone wants to be on a team.

12. *Loaded rhetoric:* Refer to the first sentence in the speech.

13. *Argument ad hominem:* In this case, Patton is *stereotyping by profession*. The implication is that writers and reporters must be incorrect because they aren't soldiers.
False analogy: In this technique, two things having nothing in common are compared as if they did. Here, "fucking" and "fighting" are equated.

14. *Sweeping generalization:* Perhaps one could still fight with a small bullet wound in the shoulder, but not with a major wound in the chest. The *loaded rhetoric* of "That's not

PATTON'S FAREWELL ADDRESS

TEXT *(continued)*

Each man must think not only of himself but of his buddy fighting beside him.

15. We don't want yellow cowards fighting in this army. They should be killed off like flies. If not, they will go back home and breed more cowards. We got to save the fucking for the fighting man. The brave men will breed more brave men.

16. I want them German bastards to raise up on their hind legs and howl: "Jesus Christ! It's that GODDAMNED THIRD ARMY AND THAT SONOFABITCH PATTON AGAIN!"

17. There's one great thing you men will be able to say when you go home. You may all thank God that thirty years from now, when you are sitting at the fire with your grandson on your knee and he asks you what you did in the Great World War II, you won't have to say: "I shoveled shit in Louisiana."

ANALYSIS *(continued)*

bullshit" provides little logical support for the generalization, although that support is its intent.

Appeal to authority: Jobs have a strong authoritative appeal, and this one is particularly strong because the job is patriotic. The statement, "Every damn man has a job to do," is also a cliché.

15. *Namecalling*: "Yellow cowards."

Appeal to emotions: Used when logic is not important. Here, Patton plays on the soldiers' fear of being cowards as well as their desire to be brave and to have the rewards of bravery ("fucking").

Red herring: Uses a diversion to turn the audience's attention from the main topic. These soldiers are going to war; why is Patton talking about "fucking"?

16. *Exaggerated image*: When the thing itself does not create enough reaction, describing it through an exaggerated image is useful. Here, the phrase "raise up on their hind legs and howl" makes the German less than human—just the image that Patton wants.

17. *Appeal to authority*: In this case, the highest authority for many people—God.

Ignoring previous statements: A form of non-sequitur. Patton says, "You may *all* thank . . . ," which implies that all the soldiers will be returning home, even though earlier he says that one fourth of them will be killed. At the end of the speech, he wants them to forget about death and think of the future.

Appeal to emotions: The soldiers' emotional attachment to the cliché of the American dream is Patton's target here. Notice that he says "grandson" when "grandchild" would have worked just as well. You aren't a "real man" unless you can produce sons.

ANALYSIS *(continued)*

Loaded rhetoric, alliteration, appeal to emotions: This last line is memorable because of the interaction of these persuasive techniques. The alliteration "shoveled shit" heightens the impact of the loaded word ("shit") because we tend to remember alliterative phrases. The emotional appeal works two ways: It plays on our desire to be heroic and patriotic and on our fear of being humiliated.

FOR REVIEW AND DISCUSSION

Content

1. In a paragraph or two, explain what you think Patton's overall purpose is. Regardless of his means, to what extent do you agree or disagree with his purpose?

2. Discuss the *validity* of Patton's equating fighting with sex. Do current attitudes about both war and sex affect the validity of this analogy?

Rhetoric

1. Speculate about why there are so few "facts" in the speech.

2. Single out several recurring rhetorical devices in the speech and discuss their importance to the overall effectiveness of the speech.

3. Analyze Patton's use of obscenity with respect to audience and occasion. How "appropriate" is it?

Classroom Exercises

1. Using a rhetorical strategy different from Patton's, write a short speech for a similar audience on a similar occasion—an army about to go into battle. What do you say to prepare the soldiers for what they must do? Why are you saying it differently than Patton did?

2. Patton was a highly successful general and was apparently much admired by his troops. Discuss those qualities of Patton's speech that might suggest his abilities as a general.

Stephen K. Tollefson

THE PERSUASIVE TECHNIQUES IN CHIEF JOSEPH'S SURRENDER SPEECH

In 1878, Chief Joseph of the Nez Percé Indians led his people in flight from their reservation in Oregon northward across Idaho and Montana to the anticipated freedom of Canada. Pursued relentlessly by the U.S. Cavalry, the weary and decimated Nez Percé surrendered some fifty miles from the Canadian border. As you read, notice how differently Chief Joseph and General Patton achieve their aims, how the first relies primarily on highly charged and active language while the second relies on qualification and passive understatement.

TEXT

1. Our Chiefs are killed. Looking Glass is dead. The old men are all killed.

2. It is the young men who say yes or no.

3. It is cold and we have no blankets. The little children are freezing to death.

ANALYSIS

1. *Passive voice:* Removes the actor from the sentence and here ignores the fact that the audience to whom this speech is addressed is responsible for the deaths. The men are simply dead; no one seems to have caused their deaths. Effectively removes the guilt from the victors.

Sweeping generalization: Were *all* the elders in fact killed?

Sentence structure: Can reinforce specific rhetorical strategies; short declarative sentences without modifiers add to the feeling of resignation and sadness.

2. *False substantive:* Works like the passive voice; the use of "it is" moves the main idea to the subordinate clause, thereby continuing the passive tone established in the first sentence.

3. *Sweeping generalization:* Here emphasizes the desperate condition of the Indians.

Text of "Chief Joseph's Surrender Speech" is from *Hear Me, My Chiefs* by L. V. McWhorter. Copyright 1952 by The Caxton Printers Ltd. Reprinted by permission of the publisher.

TEXT *(continued)*	ANALYSIS *(continued)*
	Appeal to pity: Is almost always effective if it concerns little children; appeals to pity continue throughout the speech.
4. My people, some of them, have run away to the hills and have no blankets, no food; no one knows where they are, perhaps freezing to death.	4. *Qualification:* Is frequently an attempt to make the listener hear something other than what is said; what the listener hears is "My people have run away and are freezing to death."
5. I want time to look for my children and see how many of them I can find.	5. *Ambiguity:* Relies on the confusion of the listener for effectiveness; is Chief Joseph referring to his tribe or to the freezing children mentioned earlier?
6. Maybe I shall find them among the dead.	6. *Qualification:* He says "maybe," but we don't hear it.
7. Hear me, my Chiefs, I am tired; my heart is sick and sad.	7. *Appeal to authority:* Here reminds the Cavalry officers ("chiefs") that they are now in command. *Intensification:* Depends on the notion that if one word is good, two are better; either sick or sad would have been enough. Together they are overwhelming (note that they are also alliterative).
8. From where the sun now stands, I will fight no more forever.	8. *Intensification:* "Forever" added here to "no more" emphasizes the finality of his decision.

FOR REVIEW AND DISCUSSION

Content

1. Is Chief Joseph's audience the soldiers, his own people, or both? Explain what elements of the speech help to identify its audience.

2. Discuss how this speech functions as an appeal to pity, as a description of his people's condition, and as a statement of surrender.

Rhetoric

1. Examine the kinds and structures of verbs used by Chief Joseph and by General Patton. What patterns of difference do you see between the two speakers?

2. How would you describe the mood of Joseph's speech? What elements of the speech work to define this mood?

Classroom Exercises

1. Write a surrender speech of your own, using a tone different from Chief Joseph's. You may want to be condescending, or belligerent. What would the effect of such a tone be?

2. Write a short description of the kind of man Chief Joseph was, based on your reaction to the speech.

Hadley Cantril

THE INVASION FROM MARS

On Halloween Eve, 1938, Orson Welles and his Mercury Radio Theater broadcast a dramatization of H. G. Wells's famous science fiction story "The War of the Worlds." Because of the great realism of Welles's radio script and the acting skills of the Mercury players, many listeners believed they were hearing an actual news broadcast describing a Martian invasion of Earth. This article attempts to explain why so many people were fooled. Of course we may think such things can't happen today (don't we always?), but in 1977, a Swiss radio station caused a minor panic by broadcasting a play about the destruction of Germany by neutron bombs. As you read this account, ask yourself whether you might ever believe in the authenticity of such improbable events without first seeking confirmation from another source.

[1] On the evening of October 30, 1938, thousands of Americans became panic-stricken by a broadcast purported to describe an invasion of Martians which threatened our whole civilization. Probably never before have so many people in all walks of life and in all parts of the country become so suddenly and so intensely disturbed as they did on this night.

[2] Such rare occurrences provide opportunities for the social scientist to study mass behavior. They must be exploited when they come. Although the social scientist unfortunately cannot usually predict such situations and have his tools of investigation ready to analyze the phenomenon while it is still on the wing, he can begin his work before the effects of the crisis are over and memories are blurred. The situation created by the broadcast was one which shows us how the common man

Excerpts from Hadley Cantril, *The Invasion from Mars*, pp. vii–xi, 47–201. Copyright 1940 © 1968 by Princeton University Press. Reprinted by permission of Princeton University Press.

reacts in a time of stress and strain. It gives us insights into his intelligence, his anxieties, and his needs, which we could never get by tests or strictly experimental studies. The panic situation we have investigated had all the flavor of everyday life and, at the same time, provided a semi-experimental condition for research. In spite of the unique conditions giving rise to this particular panic, the writer has attempted to indicate throughout the study the pattern of the circumstances which, from a psychological point of view, might make this the prototype of any panic.

[3] The fact that this panic was created as a result of a radio broadcast is today no mere circumstance. The importance of radio's role in current national and international affairs is too well known to be recounted here. By its very nature radio is the medium *par excellence* for informing all segments of a population of current happenings, for arousing in them a common sense of fear or joy, and for exciting them to similar reactions directed toward a single objective.

[4] Because the social phenomenon in question was so complex, several methods were employed to seek out different answers and to compare results obtained by one method with those obtained by another. Much of our information was derived from detailed interviews of 135 persons. Over 100 of these persons were selected because they were known to have been upset by the broadcast.

[5] Long before the broadcast had ended, people all over the United States were praying, crying, fleeing frantically to escape death from the Martians. Some ran to rescue loved ones. Others telephoned farewells or warnings, hurried to inform neighbors, sought information from newspapers or radio stations, summoned ambulances and police cars. At least six million people heard the broadcast. At least a million of them were frightened or disturbed.

[6] For weeks after the broadcast, newspapers carried human-interest stories relating the shock and terror of local citizens. Men and women throughout the country could have described their feelings and reactions on that fateful evening. Our own interviewers and correspondents gathered hundreds of accounts. A few of these selected almost at random will give us a glimpse of the excitement. Let the people speak for themselves.

[7] "I knew it was something terrible and I was frightened," said Mrs. Ferguson, a northern New Jersey housewife, to the inquiring interviewer. "But I didn't know just what it was. I couldn't make myself believe it was the end of the world. I've always heard that when the world would come to an end, it would come so fast nobody would know—so why should God get in touch with this announcer? When they told us what road to take and get up over the hills and the children began to cry, the family decided to go out. We took blankets and my granddaughter wanted to take the cat and the canary. We were outside the garage when the neighbor's boy came back and told us it was a play."

[8] From a small midwestern town came Joseph Hendley's report. "That Hallowe'en Boo sure had our family on its knees before the program was half over. God

THE INVASION FROM MARS

knows how we prayed to Him last Sunday. It was a lesson in more than one thing to us. My mother went out and looked for Mars. Dad was hard to convince or skeptical or sumpin', but he even got to believing it. Brother Joe, as usual, got more excited than he could show. Brother George wasn't home. Aunt Grace, a good Catholic, began to pray with Uncle Henry. Lily got sick to her stomach. I don't know what I did exactly but I know I prayed harder and more earnestly than ever before. Just as soon as we were convinced that this thing was real, how pretty all things on earth seemed; how soon we put our trust in God."

[9] Archie Burbank, a filling-station operator in Newark, described his reactions. "My girl friend and I stayed in the car for awhile, just driving around. Then we followed the lead of a friend. All of us ran into a grocery store and asked the man if we could go into his cellar. He said 'What's the matter? Are you trying to ruin my business?' So he chased us out. A crowd collected. We rushed to an apartment house and asked the man in the apartment to let us in his cellar. He said, 'I don't have any cellar! Get away!' Then people started to rush out of the apartment house all undressed. We got into the car and listened some more. Suddenly, the announcer was gassed, the station went dead so we tried another station but nothing would come on. Then we went to a gas station and filled up our tank in preparation for just riding as far as we could. The gas station man didn't know anything about it. Then one friend, male, decided he would call up the *Newark Evening News*. He found out it was a play. We listened to the rest of the play and then went dancing."

[10] Mrs. Joslin, who lives in a poor section of a large eastern city and whose husband is a day laborer, said, "I was terribly frightened. I wanted to pack and take my child in my arms, gather up my friends, and get in the car and just go north as far as we could. But what I did was just set by one window, prayin', listenin', and scared stiff and my husband by the other snifflin' and lookin' out to see if people were runnin'. Then when the announcer said 'evacuate the city,' I ran and called my boarder and started with my child to rush down the stairs, not waitin' to ketch my hat or anything. When I got to the foot of the stairs I just couldn't get out, I don't know why. Meantime my husband he tried other stations and found them still runnin'. He couldn't smell any gas or see people runnin', so he called me back and told me it was just a play. So I set down, still ready to go at any minute till I heard Orson Welles say, 'Folks, I hope we ain't alarmed you. This is just a play!' Then, I just set!"

[11] If we are to explain the reaction, then, we must answer two basic questions: Why did this broadcast frighten some people when other fantastic broadcasts do not? And why did this broadcast frighten some people but not others? An answer to the first question must be sought in the characteristics of this particular program which aroused false standards of judgment in so many listeners.

[12] No one reading the script can deny that the broadcast was so realistic for the first few minutes that it was almost credible to even relatively sophisticated and well-informed listeners. The sheer dramatic excellence of the broadcast must not be

overlooked. This unusual realism of the performance may be attributed to the fact that the early parts of the broadcast fell within the existing standards of judgment of the listeners.

[13] A large proportion of listeners, particularly those in the lower income and educational brackets, have grown to rely more on the radio than on the newspapers for their news. Almost all of the listeners, who had been frightened and who were interviewed, mentioned somewhere during the course of their retrospections the confidence they had in radio and their expectation that it would be used for such important announcements. A few of their comments indicate their attitudes:

[14] "We have so much *faith in broadcasting*. In a crisis it has to reach all people. That's what radio is here for."

[15] "The announcer would not say if it was not true. *They always quote if something is a play.*"

[16] As in many situations where events and ideas are so complicated or far removed from one's own immediate everyday experience that only the expert can really understand them, here, too, the layman was forced to rely on the expert for his interpretation.

[17] The logical "expert" in this instance was the astronomer. Those mentioned (all fictitious) were Professor Farrell of the Mount Jennings Observatory of Chicago, Professor Pierson of the Princeton Observatory, Professor Morse of MacMillan University in Toronto, Professor Indellkoffer of the California Astronomical Society and "astronomers and scientific bodies" in England, France, and Germany. Professor Richard Pierson (Orson Welles) was the chief character in the drama.

[18] When the situation called for organized defense and action the expert was once more brought in. General Montgomery Smith, commander of the State Militia at Trenton, Mr. Harry McDonald, vice-president of the Red Cross, Captain Lansing of the Signal Corps, and finally the Secretary of the Interior described the situation, gave orders for evacuation and attack, or urged every man to do his duty.

[19] This dramatic technique had its effect.

[20] "I believed the broadcast *as soon as I heard the professor from Princeton* and the officials in Washington."

[21] "I knew it was an awfully dangerous situation *when all those military men were there and the Secretary of State spoke.*"

[22] The realistic nature of the broadcast was further enhanced by descriptions of particular occurrences that listeners could readily imagine. Liberal use was made of the colloquial expressions to be expected on such an occasion. The gas was "a sort of yellowish-green"; the cop warned, "One side, there. Keep back, I tell you"; a voice shouts, "The darn thing's unscrewing." An example of the specificity of detail is the

announcement of Brigadier General Montgomery Smith: "I have been requested by the Governor of New Jersey to place the counties of Mercer and Middlesex as far west as Princeton, and east to Jamesburg, under martial law. No one will be permitted to enter this area except by special pass issued by state or military authorities. Four companies of State Militia are proceeding from Trenton to Grovers Mill and will aid in the evacuation of homes within the range of military operations."

[23] The events reported proceeded from the relatively credible to the highly incredible. The first announcements were more or less believable, although unusual to be sure. First there is an "atmospheric disturbance," then "explosions of incandescent gas." A scientist then reports that his seismograph has registered a shock of earthquake intensity. This is followed by the discovery of a meteorite that has splintered nearby trees in its fall. So far so good.

[24] But as the less credible bits of the story begin to enter, the clever dramatist also indicates that he, too, has difficulty in believing what he sees. When we learn that the object is no meteorite but a metal casing, we are also told that the whole picture is "a strange scene like something out of a modern Arabian Nights," "fantastic," that the "more daring souls are venturing near." Before we are informed that the end of the casing is beginning to unscrew, we experience the announcer's own astonishment: "Ladies and gentlemen, this is terrific!" When the top is off he says, "This is the most terrifying thing I have ever witnessed. . . . This is the most extraordinary experience. I can't find words. . . ."

[25] The bewilderment of the listener is shared by the eye-witness. When the scientist is himself puzzled, the layman recognizes the extraordinary intelligence of the strange creatures. No explanation of the event can be provided. The resignation and hopelessness of the Secretary of the Interior, counseling us to "place our faith in God," provides no effective guide for action.

[26] In spite of the realism of the broadcast, it would seem highly unlikely that any listener would take it seriously had he heard the announcements that were clearly made at the beginning of the hour. He might then have been excited, even frightened. But it would be an excitement based on the dramatic realism of the program. There would not be the intense feeling of personal involvement. He would know that the events were happening "out there" in the studio, not "right here" in his own state or his own county. In one instance a "correct" (esthetically detached or dramatic) standard of judgment would be used by the listener to interpret events, in another instance a "false" (realistic or news) standard of judgment would be employed. Tuning in late was a very essential condition for the arousal of a false standard of judgment. To be sure, many people recognized the broadcast as a play even though they tuned in late. It is important to raise and to answer the question of how anyone who tuned in at the beginning could have mistaken the clearly introduced play for a news broadcast. Analysis of these cases reveals two

main reasons why such a misinterpretation arose. In the first place, many people who tuned in to hear a play by the Mercury Theatre thought the regular dramatic program had been interrupted to give special news bulletins. The technique was not a new one after their experience with radio reporting of the war crisis in September 1938. The other major reason for the misunderstanding is the widespread habit of not paying attention to the first announcements of a program. Some people do not listen attentively to their radios until they are aware that something of particular interest is being broadcast.

[27] Tuning in late was very decisive in determining whether or not the listener would follow the program as a play or as a news report. For the story of the Martian invasion was so realistic that misinterpretation was apt to arise without proper warning signals.

[28] In spite of the fact that many persons tuned in late to hear this very realistic broadcast, by no means all of them believed it was news. And not all of those who thought the invasion was upon them behaved the same way in the face of danger. Before we can understand the reasons for the varying behavior, the reactions must be arranged in some significant grouping. Otherwise no fruitful conceptualization is possible.

CLASSIFYING THE LISTENERS

[29] **1. Those Who Checked the Internal Evidence of the Broadcast.** The persons in this category were those who did not remain frightened throughout the whole broadcast because they were able to discern that the program was fictitious. Some realized that the reports must be false because they sounded so much like certain fiction literature they were accustomed to.

[30] "At first I was very interested in the fall of the meteor. It isn't often that they find a big one just when it falls. But *when it started to unscrew and monsters came out, I said to myself, 'They've taken one of those Amazing Stories and are acting it out.'* It just couldn't be real. It was just like some of the stories I read in *Amazing Stories* but it was even more exciting."

[31] **2. Those Who Checked the Broadcast against Other Information and Learned that It Was a Play.** These listeners tried to orient themselves for the same reasons as those in the first group—they were suspicious of the "news" they were getting. Some simply thought the reports were too fantastic to believe; others detected the incredible speeds revealed; while a few listeners checked the program just because it seemed the reasonable thing to do. Their method of verifying their hunches was to compare the news on the program to some other information.

[32] "I tuned in and heard that a meteor had fallen. Then when they talked about monsters, I thought something was wrong. *So I looked in the newspaper* to see what program was supposed to be on and discovered it was only a play."

[33] **3. Those Who Tried to Check the Program against Other Information but Who, for Various Reasons, Continued to Believe the Broadcast Was an Authentic News Report.** Two characteristic differences separated the people in this group from those who made successful checks. In the first place, it was difficult to determine from the interviews just why these people wanted to check anyway. They did not seem to be seeking evidence to test the authenticity of the reports. They appeared, rather, to be frightened souls trying to find out whether or not they were yet in any personal danger. In the second place, the type of checking behavior they used was singularly ineffective and unreliable. The most frequent method employed by almost two thirds of this group, was to look out the window or go outdoors. Several of them telephoned their friends or ran to consult their neighbors.

[34] There are several reasons why the checks made by these persons were ineffectual. For some of them, the new information obtained only verified the interpretation which their already fixed standard of judgment provided.

[35] "I looked out of the window and everything looked the same as usual *so I thought it hadn't reached our section yet.*"

[36] "We looked out of the window and Wyoming Avenue was black with cars. *People were rushing away, I figured.*"

[37] "No cars came down my street. *'Traffic is jammed on account of the roads being destroyed,' I thought.*"

[38] **4. Those Who Made No Attempt to Check the Broadcast or the Event.** It is usually more difficult to discover why a person did *not* do something than why he did. Consequently it is more difficult for us to explain why people in this group did not attempt to verify the news or look for signs of the Martians in their vicinity than it was to determine why those who attempted unsuccessful checks displayed their aimless behavior. Over half of the people in this group were so frightened that they either stopped listening, ran around in a frenzy, or exhibited behavior that can only be described as paralyzed.

[39] Some of them reported that they were so frightened they never thought of checking.

[40] "We were so intent upon listening that we didn't have enough sense to try other hook-ups—*we were just so frightened.*"

[41] Others adopted an attitude of complete resignation. For them any attempt to check up, like any other behavior, appeared senseless.

[42] "I was writing a history theme. The girl from upstairs came and made me go up to her place. Everybody was so excited I felt as if I was going crazy and kept on saying, 'what can we do, *what difference does it make* whether we die sooner or later?' We were holding each other. Everything seemed unimportant in the face of death. I was afraid to die, just kept on listening."

[43] Some felt that in view of the crisis situation, action was demanded. A few prepared immediately for their escape or for death.

[44] "I couldn't stand it so I turned it off. I don't remember when, but everything was coming closer. My husband wanted to put it back on but I told him *we'd better do something instead of just listen,* so we started to pack."

[45] Some listeners interpreted the situation in such a way that they were not interested in making a check-up. In a few instances the individual tuned in so late that he missed the most incredible parts of the program and was only aware of the fact that some kind of conflict was being waged.

[46] "I was in my drugstore and my brother phoned and said, 'Turn the radio on, a meteor has just fallen.' We did and heard gas was coming up South Street. There were a few customers and *we all began wondering where it could come from.* I was worried about the gas, it was spreading so rapidly but I was puzzled as to what was actually happening, when I heard airplanes I thought another country was attacking us."

WHY THE PANIC?

[47] A variety of influences and conditions are related to the panic resulting from this particular broadcast. We have found no single observable variable consistently related to the reaction, although a lack of critical ability seemed particularly conducive to fear in a large proportion of the population. Personality characteristics made some people especially susceptible to belief and fright; the influence of others in the immediate environment caused a few listeners to react inappropriately. The psychological pattern revealed by these and other influences must be shown if we are to understand the situation as a whole and not have to resort exclusively to the understanding of single, isolated cases.

WHY THE SUGGESTION WAS OR WAS NOT BELIEVED

[48] What is most inconceivable and therefore especially interesting psychologically is why so many people did not do something to verify the information they were receiving from their loudspeakers. The failure to do this accounts for the persistence of the fright. To understand any panic—whether the cause is a legitimate one or not—it is necessary to see precisely what happens to an individual's mental processes that prevents him from making an adequate check-up.

[49] The persons who were frightened by the broadcast were, for this occasion at least, highly suggestible, that is, they believed what they heard without making sufficient checks to prove to themselves that the broadcast was only a story. Those

who were not frightened and those who believed the broadcast for only a short time were not suggestible—they were able to display what psychologists once called a "critical faculty." The problem is, then, to determine why some people are suggestible, or to state the problem differently, why some people lack critical ability.

[50] There are essentially four psychological conditions that create in an individual the particular state of mind we know as suggestibility. All these may be described in terms of the concept of standard of judgment.

[51] In the first place, individuals may refer a given stimulus to a standard or to several standards of judgment which they think are relevant for interpretation. The mental context into which the stimulus enters in this case is of such a character that it is welcomed as thoroughly consistent and without contradiction. A person with standards of judgment that enable him to "place" or "give meaning to" a stimulus in an almost automatic way finds nothing incongruous about such acceptance; his standards have led him to "expect" the possibility of such an occurrence.

[52] We have found that many of the persons who did not even try to check the broadcast had preexisting mental sets that made the stimulus so understandable to them that they immediately accepted it as true. Highly religious people who believed that God willed and controlled the destinies of man were already furnished with a particular standard of judgment that would make an invasion of our planet and a destruction of its members merely an "act of God." This was particularly true if the religious frame of reference was of the eschatological variety providing the individual with definite attitudes or beliefs regarding the end of the world. Other people we found had been so influenced by the recent war scare that they believed an attack by a foreign power was imminent and an invasion—whether it was due to the Japanese, Hitler, or Martians—was not unlikely. Some persons had built up such fanciful notions of the possibilities of science that they could easily believe the powers of strange superscientists were being turned against them, perhaps merely for experimental purposes.

[53] Whatever the cause for the genesis of the standards of judgment providing ready acceptance of the event, the fact remains that many persons already possessed a context within which they immediately placed the stimulus. None of their other existing standards of judgment was sufficiently relevant to engender disbelief. We found this to be particularly true of persons whose lack of opportunities or abilities to acquire information or training had insufficiently fortified them with pertinent standards of judgment that would make the interpretation of the broadcast as a play seem plausible. More highly educated people, we found, were better able to relate a given event to a standard of judgment they *knew* was an *appropriate* referent. In such instances, the knowledge itself was used as a standard of judgment to discount the information received in the broadcast. These listeners, then, had the ability to refer to relevant standards of judgment which they could rely on for checking purposes and therefore had no need of further orientation.

[54] A second condition of suggestibility exists when an individual is not sure of the interpretation he should place on a given stimulus and when he lacks adequate standards of judgment to make a reliable check on his interpretation. In this situation the individual attempts to check on his information but fails for one of three reasons: (1) He may check his original information against unreliable data which may themselves be affected by the situation he is checking. We found that persons who checked unsuccessfully tended to check against information obtained from friends or neighbors. Obviously, such people were apt themselves to be tinged with doubt and hesitation which would only confirm early suspicions. (2) A person may rationalize his checking information according to the original hypothesis he is checking and which he thinks he has only tentatively accepted. Many listeners made hasty mental or behavioral checks but the false standard of judgment they had already accepted was so pervasive that their check-ups were rationalized as confirmatory evidence. For example, one woman said that the announcer's charred body was found too quickly but she "figured the announcer was excited and had made a mistake." A man noticed the incredible speeds but thought "they were relaying reports or something." Others turned to different stations but thought the broadcasters were deliberately trying to calm the people. A woman looked out of her window and saw a greenish eerie light which she thought was from the Martians. (3) In contrast to those who believe almost any check they make are the people who earnestly try to verify their information but do not have sufficiently well-grounded standards of judgment to determine whether or not their new sources of information are reliable.

[55] A third and perhaps more general condition of suggestibility exists when an individual is confronted with a stimulus which he must interpret or which he would like to interpret and when *none* of his existing standards of judgment is adequate to the task. On such occasions the individual's mental context is unstructured, the stimulus does not fit any of his established categories and he seeks a standard that will suffice him. The less well structured is his mental context, the fewer meanings he is able to call forth, the less able will he be to understand the relationship between himself and the stimulus, and the greater will become his anxiety. And the more desperate his need for interpretation, the more likely will he be to accept the first interpretation given him. Many conditions existed to create in the individuals who listened to the invasion from Mars a chaotic mental universe that contained no stable standards of judgment by means of which the strange event reported could be evaluated. A lack of information and formal educational training had left many persons without any generalized standards of judgment applicable to this novel situation. And even if they did have a few such standards these were vague and tenuously held because they had not proved sufficient in the past to interpret other phenomena. This was especially true of those persons who had been most adversely affected by the conditions of the times.

[56] The prolonged economic unrest and the consequent insecurity felt by many of the listeners was another cause for bewilderment. The depression had already

lasted nearly ten years. People were still out of work. Why didn't somebody do something about it? Why didn't the experts find a solution? What was the cause of it anyway? Again, what would happen, no one could tell. Again, a mysterious invasion fitted the pattern of the mysterious events of the decade. The lack of a sophisticated, relatively stable economic or political frame of reference created in many persons a psychological disequilibrium which made them seek a standard of judgment for this particular event. It was another phenomenon in the outside world beyond their control and comprehension. Other people possessed certain economic security and social status but wondered how long this would last with "things in such a turmoil." They, too, sought a stable interpretation, one that would at least give this new occurrence meaning. The war scare had left many persons in a state of complete bewilderment. They did not know what the trouble was all about or why the United States should be so concerned. The complex ideological, class, and national antagonisms responsible for the crisis were by no means fully comprehended. The situation was painfully serious and distressingly confused. What would happen, nobody could foresee. The Martian invasion was just another event reported over the radio. It was even more personally dangerous and no more enigmatic. No existing standards were available to judge its meaning or significance. But there was quick need for judgment and it was provided by the announcers, scientists, and authorities.

[57] Persons with higher education, on the other hand, we found had acquired more generalized standards of judgment which they could put their faith in. The result was that many of them "knew" that the phenomenal speeds with which the announcers and soldiers moved were impossible even in this day and age. The greater the possibility of checking against a variety of reliable standards of judgment, the less suggestible will a person be. We found that some persons who in more normal circumstances might have had critical ability were so overwhelmed by their particular listening situation that their better judgment was suspended. This indicates that a highly consistent structuration of the external stimulus world may, at times, be experienced with sufficient intensity because of its personal implications to inhibit the operation of usually applicable internal structurations or standards of judgment. Other persons who may normally have exhibited critical ability were unable to do so in this situation because their own emotional insecurities and anxieties made them susceptible to suggestion when confronted with a personally dangerous circumstance. In such instances, the behavioral consequence is the same as for a person who has no standards of judgment to begin with, but the psychological processes underlying the behavior are different.

[58] A fourth condition of suggestibility results when an individual not only lacks standards of judgment by means of which he may orient himself, but lacks even the realization that any interpretations are possible other than the one originally presented. He accepts as truth whatever he hears or reads without even thinking to compare it to other information.

WHY SUCH EXTREME BEHAVIOR?

[59] Granted that some people believed the broadcast to be true, why did they become so hysterical? Why did they pray, telephone relatives, drive at dangerous speeds, cry, awaken sleeping children, and flee? Of all the possible modes of reaction they may have followed, why did these particular patterns emerge? The obvious answer is that this was a serious affair. As in all other panics, the individual believed his well-being, his safety, or his life was at stake. The situation was a real threat to him. Just what constitutes a personal threat to an individual must be briefly examined.

[60] When an individual believes that a situation threatens him he means that it threatens not only his physical self but all of those things and people which he somehow regards as a part of him. This Ego of an individual is essentially composed of the many social and personal values *he* has accepted. *He* feels threatened if his investments are threatened, *he* feels insulted if his children or parents are insulted, *he* feels elated if his alma mater wins the sectional football cup. The particular pattern of values that have been introcepted by an individual will give him, then, a particular Ego. For some individuals this is expanded to include broad ideals and ambitions. *They* will be disturbed if a particular race is persecuted in a distant country because that persecution runs counter to their ideal of human justice and democracy; *they* will be flattered if someone admires an idea of theirs or a painting they have completed.

[61] A panic occurs when some highly cherished, rather commonly accepted value is threatened and when no certain elimination of the threat is in sight. The individual feels that he will be ruined, physically, financially, or socially. The invasion of the Martians was a direct threat to life, to other lives that one loved, as well as to all other cherished values. The Martians were destroying practically everything. The situation was, then, indeed a serious affair. Frustration resulted when no directed behavior seemed possible. One was faced with the alternative of resigning oneself and all of one's values to complete annihilation or of making a desperate effort to escape from the field of danger, or of appealing to some higher power or stronger person who one vaguely thought could destroy the oncoming enemy.

[62] If one assumed that destruction was inevitable, then certain limited behavior was possible: one could cry, make peace with one's Maker, gather one's loved ones around and perish. If one attempted escape, one could run to the house of friends, speed away in a car or train, or hide in some gas-proof, bomb-proof, out-of-the-way shelter. If one still believed that something or someone might repulse the enemy, one could appeal to God or seek protection from those who had protected one in the past. Objectively none of these modes of behavior was a direct attack on the problem at hand, nothing was done to remove the cause of the crisis. The behavior in a panic

is characteristically undirected and, from the point of view of the situation at hand, functionally useless.

[63] In short, the extreme behavior evoked by the broadcast was due to the enormous felt ego-involvement the situation created and to the complete inability of the individual to alleviate or control the consequences of the invasion. The coming of the Martians did not present a situation where the individual could preserve one value if he sacrificed another. It was not a matter of saving one's country by giving one's life, of helping to usher in a new religion by self-denial, of risking the thief's bullet to save the family silver. In this situation the individual stood to lose *all* his values at once. Nothing could be done to save *any* of them. Panic was inescapable. The false standard of judgment used by the individual to interpret the broadcast was not itself the motivational cause of the behavior but it was absolutely essential in arousing the needs and values which may be regarded as the sources of the actions exhibited. A false standard of judgment aroused by the broadcast and causing the individual to be disturbed had its roots in values which were a part of the Ego.

FOR REVIEW AND DISCUSSION

Content

1. Why did the order of events in the broadcast lead people to believe a real invasion was occurring?

2. What are the two major reasons Cantril suggests for the audience's misinterpretation? What further reasons can you suggest?

3. What does Cantril mean by the "ego-involvement the situation created" (paragraph 63)? Where is that *ego-involvement* evidenced in the quoted remarks of the audience?

4. Is Cantril merely saying that the people who were not fooled by the play were *smarter* than those who were fooled? Explain.

Rhetoric

1. The intended audience of this essay is not the lay public. What characteristics of the essay's form and style suggest who the likely audience is?

2. Why has Cantril italicized *he* and *they* in paragraph 60? Why does he switch from *he* to *they*?

3. What words does Cantril use to refer to himself? (For instance, in paragraph 2 he refers to himself as "the writer.") What tone does Cantril convey through these references to himself?

4. What is the effect of Cantril's method of presenting information in paragraph 24? What is he doing rhetorically besides presenting information?

5. Why does Cantril make use of so many quotations from the radio audience?

Classroom Exercises

1. The phenomenon that Cantril analyzes may be an extreme form of unreasonable mass reaction, but certainly there are similarities between the reaction to this radio broadcast and to various political and social issues and events. Discuss one such issue or event (any instance of mob violence or bigotry, for example), and try to determine its causes—the reasons for the mass reaction.

2. Suppose you have turned on your radio to a broadcast similar to the one Cantril describes. You have no clue whether the broadcast is a dramatization or an authentic newscast. What steps would you take to determine the nature of the broadcast? (By the way, your phone seems to be out of order.)

Andrew Marvell

TO HIS COY MISTRESS

Wilfred Owen

DULCE ET DECORUM EST

Written more than two hundred years apart, both poems represent attempts at persuasion through quite different kinds of logic. But neither poem, to be sure, is devoid of emotion. Indeed, both poets employ logic to create a calculated emotional reaction. Marvell was a seventeenth-century master of the English Metaphysical school of poetry. Owen, another Englishman, died young and full of promise in the First World War.

TO HIS COY MISTRESS

[1]   Had we but World enough, and Time,
This coyness Lady were no crime.
We would sit down, and think which way
To walk, and pass our long Loves Day.
Thou by the *Indian Ganges* side
Should'st Rubies find: I by the Tide
Of *Humber* would complain. I would

TO HIS COY MISTRESS

      Love you ten years before the Flood:
      And you should, if you please, refuse
      Till the Conversion of the *Jews*.
      My vegetable Love should grow
      Vaster than Empires, and more slow.
      An hundred years should go to praise
      Thine Eyes, and on thy Forehead Gaze.
      Two hundred to adore each Breast:
      But thirty thousand to the rest.
      An Age at least to every part,
      And the last Age should show your Heart.
      For Lady you deserve this State;
      Nor would I love at lower rate.

[2]   But at my back I alwaies hear
      Times winged Charriot hurrying near:
      And yonder all before us lye
      Desarts of vast Eternity.
      Thy Beauty shall no more be found;
      Nor, in thy marble Vault, shall sound
      My ecchoing song: then Worms shall try
      That long preserv'd Virginity:
      And your quaint Honour turn to dust;
      And into ashes all my Lust.
      The Grave's a fine and private place,
      But none I think do there embrace.

[3]   Now therefore, while the youthful hew
      Sits on thy skin like morning dew,
      And while thy willing Soul transpires
      At every pore with instant Fires,
      Now let us sport us while we may;
      And now, like am'rous birds of prey,
      Rather at once our Time devour,
      Than languish in his slow-chapt pow'r.
      Let us roll all our Strength, and all
      Our sweetness, up into one Ball:
      And tear our Pleasures with rough strife,
      Thorough the Iron gates of Life.
      Thus, though we cannot make our Sun
      Stand still, yet we will make him run.

DULCE ET DECORUM EST

[1] Bent double, like old beggars under sacks,
Knock-kneed, coughing like hags, we cursed through sludge,
Till on the haunting flares we turned our backs
And towards our distant rest began to trudge.
Men marched asleep. Many had lost their boots
But limped on, blood-shod. All went lame; all blind;
Drunk with fatigue; deaf even to the hoots
Of tired, outstripped Five-Nines that dropped behind.

[2] Gas! GAS! Quick, boys!—An ecstasy of fumbling,
Fitting the clumsy helmets just in time;
But someone still was yelling out and stumbling
And flound'ring like a man in fire or lime . . .
Dim, through the misty panes and thick green light,
As under a green sea, I saw him drowning.

[3] In all my dreams, before my helpless sight,
He plunges at me, guttering, choking, drowning.

[4] If in some smothering dreams you too could pace
Behind the wagon that we flung him in,
And watch the white eyes writhing in his face,
His hanging face, like a devil's sick of sin;
If you could hear, at every jolt, the blood
Come gargling from the froth-corrupted lungs,
Obscene as cancer, bitter as the cud
Of vile, incurable sores on innocent tongues,—
My friend, you would not tell with such high zest
To children ardent for some desperate glory,
The old Lie: *Dulce et decorum est
Pro patria mori.**

---

* Editor's note: From the Latin poet Horace: "It is sweet and fitting to die for one's country."

From Wilfred Owen, *Collected Poems.* Copyright Chatto & Windus, Ltd. © 1946, 1963. Reprinted by permission of New Directions Publishing Corporation.

FOR REVIEW AND DISCUSSION

Content

1. Briefly explain what you understand to be the "point" of each poem.

2. How would you characterize the speaker and implied audience in each poem?

3. Why is "light verse" an inadequate description of "To His Coy Mistress"?

4. Why is a pat phrase such as "the horrors of war" an equally inadequate description of "Dulce et Decorum Est"?

Rhetoric

1. In his first stanza, Marvell makes essentially the same point many times. Is this a logical or rhetorical technique? What is its effect? In what way does Marvell mingle logical and rhetorical techniques?

2. Owen, too, makes the same point many times. Compare his technique with Marvell's.

3. To what extent does the strength of each poem derive from the placement of its thesis?

Classroom Exercises

1. Look up *syllogism* in the Glossary. Try to reduce the argument in Marvell's three stanzas into syllogistic form. Do you now find it more or less persuasive than before? Explain.

2. The argument and logic of "Dulce et Decorum Est" are conveyed implicitly by the poem's imagery. If you cannot state them syllogistically (try to construct an inferred syllogism), how *would* you describe Owen's argument and logic?

FOR FURTHER READING

Martin Luther King, Jr.

I HAVE A DREAM

> *This speech by the martyred Black civil rights leader is a celebrated example of contemporary rhetoric. It is especially moving and convincing, in part because of its current historical context. Like the speeches of General Patton and Chief Joseph, however, its intrinsic persuasive power lies in the author's sophisticated use of propaganda techniques. As you read the speech, try to weigh its emotional force against your objective analysis.*

[1]   Five score years ago, a great American, in whose symbolic shadow we stand, signed the Emancipation Proclamation. This momentous decree came as a great beacon light of hope to millions of Negro slaves who had been seared in the flames of withering injustice. It came as a joyous daybreak to end the long night of captivity.

[2]   But one hundred years later, we must face the tragic fact that the Negro is still not free. One hundred years later, the life of the Negro is still sadly crippled by the manacles of segregation and the chains of discrimination. One hundred years later, the Negro lives on a lonely island of poverty in the midst of a vast ocean of material prosperity. One hundred years later, the Negro is still languished in the corners of American society and finds himself an exile in his own land. So we have come here today to dramatize an appalling condition.

[3]   In a sense we have come to our nation's Capital to cash a check. When the architects of our republic wrote the magnificent words of the Constitution and the Declaration of Independence, they were signing a promissory note to which every American was to fall heir. This note was a promise that all men would be guaranteed the unalienable rights of life, liberty, and the pursuit of happiness.

[4]   It is obvious today that America has defaulted on this promissory note insofar as her citizens of color are concerned. Instead of honoring this sacred obligation, America has given the Negro people a bad check; a check which has come back marked "insufficient funds." But we refuse to believe that the bank of justice is bankrupt. We refuse to believe that there are insufficient funds in the great vaults of opportunity of this nation. So we have come to cash this check—a check that will give us upon demand the riches of freedom and the security of justice. We have also come to this hallowed spot to remind America of the fierce urgency of *now*. This is

Copyright © 1963 by Martin Luther King, Jr. Reprinted by permission of Joan Daves.

I HAVE A DREAM

no time to engage in the luxury of cooling off or to take the tranquilizing drug of gradualism. *Now* is the time to make real the promises of Democracy. *Now* is the time to rise from the dark and desolate valley of segregation to the sunlit path of racial justice. *Now* is the time to open the doors of opportunity to all of God's children. *Now* is the time to lift our nation from the quicksands of racial injustice to the solid rock of brotherhood.

[5] It would be fatal for the nation to overlook the urgency of the moment and to underestimate the determination of the Negro. This sweltering summer of the Negro's legitimate discontent will not pass until there is an invigorating autumn of freedom and equality. 1963 is not an end, but a beginning. Those who hope that the Negro needed to blow off steam and will now be content will have a rude awakening if the nation returns to business as usual. There will be neither rest nor tranquility in America until the Negro is granted his citizenship rights. The whirlwinds of revolt will continue to shake the foundations of our nation until the bright day of justice emerges.

[6] But there is something that I must say to my people who stand on the warm threshold which leads into the palace of justice. In the process of gaining our rightful place we must not be guilty of wrongful deeds. Let us not seek to satisfy our thirst for freedom by drinking from the cup of bitterness and hatred. We must forever conduct our struggle on the high plane of dignity and discipline. We must not allow our creative protest to degenerate into physical violence. Again and again we must rise to the majestic heights of meeting physical force with soul force. The marvelous new militancy which has engulfed the Negro community must not lead us to a distrust of all white people, for many of our white brothers, as evidenced by their presence here today, have come to realize that their destiny is tied up with our destiny and their freedom is inextricably bound to our freedom. We cannot walk alone.

[7] And as we walk, we must make the pledge that we shall march ahead. We cannot turn back. There are those who are asking the devotees of civil rights, "When will you be satisfied?" We can never be satisfied as long as the Negro is the victim of the unspeakable horrors of police brutality. We can never be satisfied as long as our bodies, heavy with the fatigue of travel, cannot gain lodging in the motels of the highways and the hotels of the cities. We cannot be satisfied as long as the Negro's basic mobility is from a smaller ghetto to a larger one. We can never be satisfied as long as a Negro in Mississippi cannot vote and a Negro in New York believes he has nothing for which to vote. No, no, we are not satisfied, and we will not be satisfied until justice rolls down like waters and righteousness like a mighty stream.

[8] I am not unmindful that some of you have come here out of great trials and tribulations. Some of you have come fresh from narrow jail cells. Some of you have come from areas where your quest for freedom left you battered by the storms of persecution and staggered by the winds of police brutality. You have been the

veterans of creative suffering. Continue to work with the faith that unearned suffering is redemptive.

[9] Go back to Mississippi, go back to Alabama, go back to South Carolina, go back to Georgia, go back to Louisiana, go back to the slums and the ghettos of our northern cities, knowing that somehow this situation can and will be changed. Let us not wallow in the valley of despair.

[10] I say to you today, my friends, that in spite of the difficulties and frustrations of the moment I still have a dream. It is a dream deeply rooted in the American dream.

[11] I have a dream that one day this nation will rise up and live out the true meaning of its creed: "We hold these truths to be self-evident; that all men are created equal."

[12] I have a dream that one day on the red hills of Georgia the sons of former slaves and the sons of former slaveowners will be able to sit down together at the table of brotherhood.

[13] I have a dream that one day even the state of Mississippi, a desert state sweltering with the heat of injustice and oppression, will be transformed into an oasis of freedom and justice.

[14] I have a dream that my four little children will one day live in a nation where they will not be judged by the color of their skin but by the content of their character.

[15] I have a dream today.

[16] I have a dream that one day the state of Alabama, whose governor's lips are presently dripping with the words of interposition and nullification, will be transformed into a situation where little black boys and black girls will be able to join hands with little white boys and white girls and walk together as sisters and brothers.

[17] I have a dream today.

[18] I have a dream that one day every valley shall be exalted, every hill and mountain shall be made low, the rough places will be made plains, and the crooked places will be made straight, and the glory of the Lord shall be revealed, and all flesh shall see it together.

[19] This is our hope. This is the faith with which I return to the South. With this faith we will be able to hew out of the mountain of despair a stone of hope. With this faith we will be able to transform the jangling discords of our nation into a beautiful symphony of brotherhood. With this faith we will be able to work together, to pray together, to struggle together, to go to jail together, to stand up for freedom together, knowing that we will be free one day.

[20] This will be the day when all of God's children will be able to sing with new meaning

> My country, 'tis of thee,
> Sweet land of liberty,
>   Of thee I sing:
> Land where my fathers died,
> Land of the pilgrims' pride,
> From every mountain-side
>   Let freedom ring.

[21] And if America is to be a great nation this must become true. So let freedom ring from the prodigious hilltops of New Hampshire. Let freedom ring from the mighty mountains of New York. Let freedom ring from the heightening Alleghenies of Pennsylvania!

[22] Let freedom ring from the snowcapped Rockies of Colorado!

[23] Let freedom ring from the curvaceous peaks of California!

[24] But not only that; let freedom ring from Stone Mountain of Georgia!

[25] Let freedom ring from Lookout Mountain of Tennessee!

[26] Let freedom ring from every hill and molehill of Mississippi. From every mountainside, let freedom ring.

[27] When we let freedom ring, when we let it ring from every village and every hamlet, from every state and every city, we will be able to speed up that day when all of God's children, black men and white men, Jews and Gentiles, Protestants and Catholics, will be able to join hands and sing in the words of the old Negro spiritual, "Free at last; free at last! thank God almighty, we are free at last!"

FOR REVIEW AND DISCUSSION

Content

1. When King repeats that he and his followers "refuse to believe" that the nation has given them a "bad check," is he stating what he thinks is true, or is he stating a hope? How can we be certain?

2. What does King mean by "creative suffering"?

Rhetoric

1. What is the tone of the speech? Is the tone established in the introduction and maintained through the speech, or does it change as King progresses?

2. Does King's figurative image, a *check* or *promissory note*, clarify or obscure the point he is making? Explain.

3. What propaganda is there in the phrase "creative suffering"?

4. Identify the religious elements in the speech. Is the speech primarily religious or political?

5. What is the effect of King's using verses from two well-known songs near the end of the speech?

Classroom Exercises

1. Using some of the techniques in Dr. King's speech (for example, repetition and appeals to authority), write a speech of your own on a subject that you have strong feelings about. Your primary goal should be to be convincing.

2. Try to memorize a few lines from Dr. King's speech and a few lines from former President Nixon's speech (end of chapter 7). Discuss the aspects of both speeches that make "I Have a Dream" easier to memorize.

FOR DISCUSSION AND WRITING

1. Explain how the techniques of propaganda discussed by Cross encouraged the audience's response to Welles's dramatization of a Martian invasion.

2. Discuss the similarities and differences between response to propaganda (as Cross describes propaganda) and the conditions of suggestibility defined by Cantril. Illustrate your points by analysis of some current situation that you have observed or have read about.

3. Using Cantril's "four psychological conditions that create . . . suggestibility," explain why the coy mistress in Marvell's poem might or might not respond as the poet desires. Some of what you write will be conjecture, but you can learn much about her by analyzing the intended audience to whom Marvell addresses his poem.

4. Write a line-by-line analysis of the propaganda working in Marvell's poem.

5. Write a line-by-line analysis of the propaganda working in King's speech.

6. Basing your discussion on the speeches and poems in the chapter, argue why one should or should not guard oneself against *all* propaganda.

7. In "Dulce et Decorum Est," Wilfred Owen demolishes an old truism. Pick another such generalization and write an argument of your own, revealing the shallowness of the statement. You may want to imitate Owen and use a concrete example to refute the generalization. Some statements you may want to choose from: "My country, right or wrong." "A woman's place is in the home." "Once a thief, always a thief."

7 POLITICIANS AND THEIR LANGUAGE

> *If thought corrupts language, language can also corrupt thought.*
> GEORGE ORWELL
>
> *Language involves the elements of risk and responsibility.*
> N. SCOTT MOMADAY

Aldous Huxley and George Orwell were concerned many decades ago with the wholesale abuse of language in European politics, but it has been only in recent years that vast numbers of Americans have experienced this kind of exploitation through media coverage of the Vietnam War and the Watergate scandal. Huxley, in this chapter, discusses some general abuses and Richard Gambino relates these to the particular experience of Watergate. Finally, the selection from Orwell's *1984* paints a grim picture of a future in which intentionally obscure and restrictive language has become the norm for society.

Aldous Huxley

WORDS AND BEHAVIOR

> *The theme of this selection is the relationship between language and reality, a topic covered broadly in Chapter Three. Here, however, the author draws his examples specifically from the language of politics and war, providing insight into the abuses of such language and the horrifying consequences thereof. Although Huxley wrote this essay over forty years ago, his biting criticisms still contain—unfortunately—fresh truths. Pay particular attention to his analysis of the word* force: *it is a classic example of semantic analysis.*

[1] Words form the thread on which we string our experiences. Without them we should live spasmodically and intermittently. Hatred itself is not so strong that animals will not forget it, if distracted, even in the presence of the enemy. Watch a pair of cats, crouching on the brink of a fight. Balefully the eyes glare; from far down in the throat of each come bursts of a strange, strangled noise of defiance; as though animated by a life of their own, the tails twitch and tremble. With aimed intensity of loathing! Another moment and surely there must be an explosion. But no; all of a sudden one of the two creatures turns away, hoists a hind leg in a more than fascist salute and, with the same fixed and focused attention as it had given a moment before to its enemy, begins to make a lingual toilet. Animal love is as much at the mercy of distractions as animal hatred. The dumb creation lives a life made up of discrete and mutually irrelevant episodes. Such as it is, the consistency of human characters is due to the words upon which all human experiences are strung. We are purposeful because we can describe our feelings in rememberable words, can justify and rationalize our desires in terms of some kind of argument. Faced by an enemy we do not allow an itch to distract us from our emotions; the mere word "enemy" is enough to keep us reminded of our hatred, to convince us that we do well to be angry. Similarly the word "love" bridges for us those chasms of momentary indifference and boredom which gape from time to time between even the most ardent lovers. Feeling and desire provide us with our motive power; words give continuity to what we do and to a considerable extent determine our direction. Inappropriate and badly chosen words vitiate thought and lead to wrong or foolish conduct. Most ignorances are vincible, and in the greater number of cases stupidity is what the Buddha pronounced it to be, a sin. For, consciously, or subconsciously, it is with deliberation that we do not know or fail to understand—because incomprehension allows us, with a good conscience, to evade unpleasant obligations and respon-

From *Collected Essays* by Aldous Huxley. Copyright 1937 by Aldous Huxley; renewed 1965 by Laura A. Huxley. Reprinted by permission of Harper & Row, Publishers, Inc.

sibilities, because ignorance is the best excuse for going on doing what one likes, but ought not, to do. Our egotisms are incessantly fighting to preserve themselves, not only from external enemies, but also from the assaults of the other and better self with which they are so uncomfortably associated. Ignorance is egotism's most effective defense against that Dr. Jekyll in us who desires perfection; stupidity, its subtlest stratagem. If, as so often happens, we choose to give continuity to our experience by means of words which falsify the facts, this is because the falsification is somehow to our advantage as egotists.

[2]   Consider, for example, the case of war. War is enormously discreditable to those who order it to be waged and even to those who merely tolerate its existence. Furthermore, to developed sensibilities the facts of war are revolting and horrifying. To falsify these facts, and by so doing to make war seem less evil than it really is, and our own responsibility in tolerating war less heavy, is doubly to our advantage. By suppressing and distorting the truth, we protect our sensibilities and preserve our self-esteem. Now, language is, among other things, a device which men use for suppressing and distorting the truth. Finding the reality of war too unpleasant to contemplate, we create a verbal alternative to that reality, parallel with it, but in quality quite different from it. That which we contemplate thenceforward is not that to which we react emotionally and upon which we pass our moral judgments, is not war as it is in fact, but the fiction of war as it exists in our pleasantly falsifying verbiage. Our stupidity in using inappropriate language turns out, on analysis, to be the most refined cunning.

[3]   The most shocking fact about war is that its victims and its instruments are individual human beings, and that these individual human beings are condemned by the monstrous conventions of politics to murder or be murdered in quarrels not their own, to inflict upon the innocent and, innocent themselves of any crime against their enemies, to suffer cruelties of every kind.

[4]   The language of strategy and politics is designed, so far as it is possible, to conceal this fact, to make it appear as though wars were not fought by individuals drilled to murder one another in cold blood and without provocation, but either by impersonal and therefore wholly non-moral and impassible forces, or else by personified abstractions.

[5]   Here are a few examples of the first kind of falsification. In place of "cavalrymen" or "foot-soldiers" military writers like to speak of "sabres" and "rifles." Here is a sentence from a description of the Battle of Marengo: "According to Victor's report, the French retreat was orderly; it is certain, at any rate, that the regiments held together, for the six thousand Austrian sabres found no opportunity to charge home." The battle is between sabres in line and muskets in échelon—a mere clash of ironmongery.

[6]   On other occasions there is no question of anything so vulgarly material as ironmongery. The battles are between Platonic ideas, between the abstractions of

physics and mathematics. Forces interact; weights are flung into scales; masses are set in motion. Or else it is all a matter of geometry. Lines swing and sweep; are protracted or curved; pivot on a fixed point.

[7]   Alternatively the combatants are personal, in the sense that they are personifications. There is "the enemy," in the singular, making "his" plans, striking "his" blows. The attribution of personal characteristics to collectivities, to geographical expressions, to institutions, is a source, as we shall see, of endless confusions in political thought, of innumerable political mistakes and crimes. Personification in politics is an error which we make because it is to our advantage as egotists to be able to feel violently proud of our country and of ourselves as belonging to it, and to believe that all the misfortunes due to our own mistakes are really the work of the Foreigner. It is easier to feel violently toward a person than toward an abstraction; hence our habit of making political personifications. In some cases military personifications are merely special instances of political personifications. A particular collectivity, the army or the warring nation, is given the name and, along with the name, the attributes of a single person, in order that we may be able to love or hate it more intensely than we could do if we thought of it as what it really is: a number of diverse individuals. In other cases personification is used for the purpose of concealing the fundamental absurdity and monstrosity of war. What is absurd and monstrous about war is that men who have no personal quarrel should be trained to murder one another in cold blood. By personifying opposing armies or countries, we are able to think of war as a conflict between individuals. The same result is obtained by writing of war as though it were carried on exclusively by the generals in command and not by the private soldiers in their armies. ("Rennenkampf had pressed back von Schubert.") The implication in both cases is that war is indistinguishable from a bout of fisticuffs in a bar room. Whereas in reality it is profoundly different. A scrap between two individuals is forgivable; mass murder, deliberately organized, is a monstrous iniquity. We still choose to use war as an instrument of policy; and to comprehend the full wickedness and absurdity of war would therefore be inconvenient. For, once we understood, we should have to make some effort to get rid of the abominable thing. Accordingly, when we talk about war, we use a language which conceals or embellishes its reality. Ignoring the facts, so far as we possibly can, we imply that battles are not fought by soldiers, but by things, principles, allegories, personified collectivities, or (at the most human) by opposing commanders, pitched against one another in single combat. For the same reason, when we have to describe the processes and the results of war, we employ a rich variety of euphemisms. Even the most violently patriotic and militaristic are reluctant to call a spade by its own name. To conceal their intentions even from themselves, they make use of picturesque metaphors. We find them, for example, clamoring for war planes numerous and powerful enough to go and "destroy the hornets in their nests"—in other words, to go and throw thermite, high explosives and vesicants upon the inhabitants of neighboring countries before they have time to come and do the same to us. And how reassuring is the language of historians and

strategists! They write admiringly of those military geniuses who know "when to strike at the enemy's line" (a single combatant deranges the geometrical constructions of a personification); when to "turn his flank"; when to "execute an enveloping movement." As though they were engineers discussing the strength of materials and the distribution of stresses, they talk of abstract entities called "man power" and "fire power." They sum up the long-drawn sufferings and atrocities of trench warfare in the phrase, "a war of attrition"; the massacre and mangling of human beings is assimilated to the grinding of a lens.

[8]   A dangerously abstract word, which figures in all discussions about war, is "force." Those who believe in organizing collective security by means of military pacts against a possible aggressor are particularly fond of this word. "You cannot," they say, "have international justice unless you are prepared to impose it by force." "Peace-loving countries must unite to use force against aggressive dictatorships." "Democratic institutions must be protected, if need be, by force." And so on.

[9]   Now, the word "force," when used in reference to human relations, has no single, definite meaning. There is the "force" used by parents when, without resort to any kind of physical violence, they compel their children to act or refrain from acting in some particular way. There is the "force" used by attendants in an asylum when they try to prevent a maniac from hurting himself or others. There is the "force" used by the police when they control a crowd, and that other "force" which they used in a baton charge. And finally there is the "force" used in war. This, of course, varies with the technological devices at the disposal of the belligerents, with the policies they are pursuing, and with the particular circumstances of the war in question. But in general it may be said that, in war, "force" connotes violence and fraud used to the limit of the combatants' capacity.

[10]   Variations in quantity, if sufficiently great, produce variations in quality. The "force" that is war, particularly modern war, is very different from the "force" that is police action, and the use of the same abstract word to describe the two dissimilar processes is profoundly misleading. (Still more misleading, of course, is the explicit assimilation of a war, waged by allied League-of-Nations powers against an aggressor, to police action against a criminal. The first is the use of violence and fraud without limit against innocent and guilty alike; the second is the use of strictly limited violence and a minimum of fraud exclusively against the guilty.)

[11]   Reality is a succession of concrete and particular situations. When we think about such situations we should use the particular and concrete words which apply to them. If we use abstract words which apply equally well (and equally badly) to other, quite dissimilar situations, it is certain that we shall think incorrectly.

[12]   Let us take the sentences quoted above and translate the abstract word "force" into language that will render (however inadequately) the concrete and particular realities of contemporary warfare.

[13] "You cannot have international justice, unless you are prepared to impose it by force." Translated, this becomes: "You cannot have international justice unless you are prepared, with a view to imposing a just settlement, to drop thermite, high explosives and vesicants upon the inhabitants of foreign cities and to have thermite, high explosives and vesicants dropped in return upon the inhabitants of your cities." At the end of this proceeding, justice is to be imposed by the victorious party—that is, if there is a victorious party. It should be remarked that justice was to have been imposed by the victorious party at the end of the last war. But, unfortunately, after four years of fighting, the temper of the victors was such that they were quite incapable of making a just settlement. The Allies were reaping in Nazi Germany what they sowed at Versailles. The victors of the next war will have undergone intensive bombardments with thermite, high explosives and vesicants. Will their temper be better than that of the Allies in 1918? Will they be in a fitter state to make a just settlement? The answer, quite obviously, is: No. It is psychologically all but impossible that justice should be secured by the methods of contemporary warfare.

[14] The next two sentences may be taken together. "Peace-loving countries must unite to use force against aggressive dictatorships. Democratic institutions must be protected, if need be, by force." Let us translate. "Peace-loving countries must unite to throw thermite, high explosives and vesicants on the inhabitants of countries ruled by aggressive dictators. They must do this, and of course abide the consequences, in order to preserve peace and democratic institutions." Two questions immediately propound themselves. First, is it likely that peace can be secured by a process calculated to reduce the orderly life of our complicated societies to chaos? And, second, is it likely that democratic institutions will flourish in a state of chaos? Again, the answers are pretty clearly in the negative.

[15] By using the abstract word "force," instead of terms which at least attempt to describe the realities of war as it is today, the preachers of collective security through military collaboration disguise from themselves and from others, not only the contemporary facts, but also the probable consequences of their favorite policy. The attempt to secure justice, peace and democracy by "force" seems reasonable enough until we realize, first, that this noncommittal word stands, in the circumstances of our age, for activities which can hardly fail to result in social chaos; and second, that the consequences of social chaos are injustice, chronic warfare and tyranny. The moment we think in concrete and particular terms of the concrete and particular process called "modern war," we see that a policy which worked (or at least didn't result in complete disaster) in the past has no prospect whatever of working in the immediate future. The attempt to secure justice, peace and democracy by means of a "force," which means, at this particular moment of history, thermite, high explosives and vesicants, is about as reasonable as the attempt to put out a fire with a colorless liquid that happens to be, not water, but petrol.

[16] What applies to the "force" that is war applies in large measure to the "force" that is revolution. It seems inherently very unlikely that social justice and social

WORDS AND BEHAVIOR

peace can be secured by thermite, high explosives and vesicants. At first, it may be, the parties in a civil war would hesitate to use such instruments on their fellow-countrymen. But there can be little doubt that, if the conflict were prolonged (as it probably would be between the evenly balanced Right and Left of a highly industrialized society), the combatants would end by losing their scruples.

[17] The alternatives confronting us seem to be plain enough. Either we invent and conscientiously employ a new technique for making revolutions and settling international disputes; or else we cling to the old technique and, using "force" (that is to say, thermite, high explosives and vesicants), destroy ourselves. Those who, for whatever motive, disguise the nature of the second alternative under inappropriate language, render the world a grave disservice. They lead us into one of the temptations we find it hardest to resist—the temptation to run away from reality, to pretend that facts are not what they are. Like Shelley (but without Shelley's acute awareness of what he was doing) we are perpetually weaving

> A shroud of talk to hide us from the sun
> Of this familiar life.

We protect our minds by an elaborate system of abstractions, ambiguities, metaphors and similes from the reality we do not wish to know too clearly; we lie to ourselves, in order that we may still have the excuse of ignorance, the alibi of stupidity and incomprehension, possessing which we can continue with a good conscience to commit and tolerate the most monstrous crimes:

> The poor wretch who has learned his only prayers
> From curses, who knows scarcely words enough
> To ask a blessing from his Heavenly Father,
> Becomes a fluent phraseman, absolute
> And technical in victories and defeats,
> And all our dainty terms for fratricide;
> Terms which we trundle smoothly o'er our tongues
> Like mere abstractions, empty sounds to which
> We join no meaning and attach no form!
> As if the soldier died without a wound:
> As if the fibers of this godlike frame
> Were gored without a pang: as if the wretch
> Who fell in battle, doing bloody deeds,
> Passed off to Heaven translated and not killed;
> As though he had no wife to pine for him,
> No God to judge him.

[18] The language we use about war is inappropriate, and its inappropriateness is designed to conceal a reality so odious that we do not wish to know it. The language we use about politics is also inappropriate; but here our mistake has a different purpose. Our principal aim in this case is to arouse and, having aroused, to rationalize and justify such intrinsically agreeable sentiments as pride and hatred, self-esteem and contempt for others. To achieve this end we speak about the facts of politics in words which more or less completely misrepresent them.

[19] The concrete realities of politics are individual human beings, living together in national groups. Politicians—and to some extent we are all politicians—substitute abstractions for these concrete realities, and having done this, proceed to invest each abstraction with an appearance of concreteness by personifying it. For example, the concrete reality of which "Britain" is the abstraction consists of some forty-odd millions of diverse individuals living on an island off the west coast of Europe. The personification of this abstraction appears, in classical fancy-dress and holding a very large toasting fork, on the backside of our copper coinage; appears in verbal form, every time we talk about international politics. "Britain," the abstraction from forty millions of Britons, is endowed with thoughts, sensibilities and emotions, even with a sex—for, in spite of John Bull, the country is always a female.

[20] Now, it is of course possible that "Britain" is more than a mere name—is an entity that possesses some kind of reality distinct from that of the individuals constituting the group to which the name is applied. But this entity, if it exists, is certainly not a young lady with a toasting fork; nor is it possible to believe (though some eminent philosophers have preached the doctrine) that it should possess anything in the nature of a personal will. One must agree with T. H. Green that "there can be nothing in a nation, however exalted its mission, or in a society however perfectly organized, which is not in the persons composing the nation or the society. . . . We cannot suppose a national spirit and will to exist except as the spirit and will of individuals." But the moment we start resolutely thinking about our world in terms of individual persons we find ourselves at the same time thinking in terms of universality. "The great rational religions," writes Professor Whitehead, "are the outcome of the emergence of a religious consciousness that is universal, as distinguished from tribal, or even social. Because it is universal, it introduces the note of solitariness." (And he might have added that, because it is solitary, it introduces the note of universality.) "The reason of this connection between universality and solitude is that universality is a disconnection from immediate surroundings." And conversely the disconnection from immediate surroundings, particularly such social surroundings as the tribe or nation, the insistence on the person as the fundamental reality, leads to the conception of an all-embracing unity.

[21] A nation, then, may be more than a mere abstraction, may possess some kind of real existence apart from its constituent members. But there is no reason to suppose that it is a person; indeed, there is every reason to suppose that it isn't. Those who speak as though it were a person (and some go further than this and speak as though it were a personal god) do so, because it is to their interest as egotists to make precisely this mistake.

[22] In the case of the ruling class these interests are in part material. The personification of the nation as a sacred being, different from and superior to its constituent members, is merely (I quote the words of a great French jurist, Léon Duguit) "a way of imposing authority by making people believe it is an authority *de*

jure and not merely *de facto.*" By habitually talking of the nation as though it were a person with thoughts, feelings and a will of its own, the rulers of a country legitimate their own powers. Personification leads easily to deification; and where the nation is deified, its government ceases to be a mere convenience, like drains or a telephone system, and, partaking in the sacredness of the entity it represents, claims to give orders by divine right and demands the unquestioning obedience due to a god. Rulers seldom find it hard to recognize their friends. Hegel, the man who elaborated an inappropriate figure of speech into a complete philosophy of politics, was a favorite of the Prussian government. "*Es ist,*" he had written, "*es ist der Gang Gottes in der Welt, das der Staat ist.*"* The decoration bestowed on him by Frederick William III was richly deserved.

[23] Unlike their rulers, the ruled have no material interest in using inappropriate language about states and nations. For them, the reward of being mistaken is psychological. The personified and deified nation becomes, in the minds of the individuals composing it, a kind of enlargement of themselves. The superhuman qualities which belong to the young lady with the toasting fork, the young lady with plaits and a brass *soutien-gorge*,† the young lady in a Phrygian bonnet, are claimed by individual Englishmen, Germans and Frenchmen as being, at least in part, their own. *Dulce et decorum est pro patria mori.* But there would be no need to die, no need of war, if it had not been even sweeter to boast and swagger for one's country, to hate, despise, swindle and bully for it. Loyalty to the personified nation, or to the personified class or party, justifies the loyal in indulging all those passions which good manners and the moral code do not allow them to display in their relations with their neighbors. The personified entity is a being, not only great and noble, but also insanely proud, vain and touchy; fiercely rapacious; a braggart; bound by no considerations of right and wrong. (Hegel condemned as hopelessly shallow all those who dared to apply ethical standards to the activities of nations. To condone and applaud every iniquity committed in the name of the State was to him a sign of philosophical profundity.) Identifying themselves with this god, individuals find relief from the constraints of ordinary social decency, feel themselves justified in giving rein, within duly prescribed limits, to their criminal proclivities. As a loyal nationalist or party-man, one can enjoy the luxury of behaving badly with a good conscience.

[24] The evil passions are further justified by another linguistic error—the error of speaking about certain categories of persons as though they were mere embodied abstractions. Foreigners and those who disagree with us are not thought of as men and women like ourselves and our fellow-countrymen; they are thought of as representatives and, so to say, symbols of a class. In so far as they have any personality at all, it is the personality we mistakenly attribute to their class—a personality that is, by definition, intrinsically evil. We know that the harming or killing of men and

* [Roughly: "The state—it is the passage of God through the world."]
† [brassiere]

women is wrong, and we are reluctant consciously to do what we know to be wrong. But when particular men and women are thought of merely as representatives of a class, which has previously been defined as evil and personified in the shape of a devil, then the reluctance to hurt or murder disappears. Brown, Jones and Robinson are no longer thought of as Brown, Jones and Robinson, but as heretics, gentiles, Yids, niggers, barbarians, Huns, communists, capitalists, fascists, liberals—whichever the case may be. When they have been called such names and assimilated to the accursed class to which the names apply, Brown, Jones and Robinson cease to be conceived as what they really are—human persons—and become for the users of this fatally inappropriate language mere vermin or, worse, demons whom it is right and proper to destroy as thoroughly and as painfully as possible. Wherever persons are present, questions of morality arise. Rulers of nations and leaders of parties find morality embarrassing. That is why they take such pains to depersonalize their opponents. All propaganda directed against an opposing group has but one aim: to substitute diabolical abstractions for concrete persons. The propagandist's purpose is to make one set of people forget that certain other sets of people are human. By robbing them of their personality, he puts them outside the pale of moral obligation. Mere symbols can have no rights—particularly when that of which they are symbolical is, by definition, evil.

[25] Politics can become moral only on one condition: that its problems shall be spoken of and thought about exclusively in terms of concrete reality; that is to say, of persons. To depersonify human beings and to personify abstractions are complementary errors which lead, by an inexorable logic, to war between nations and to idolatrous worship of the State, with consequent governmental oppression. All current political thought is a mixture, in varying proportions, between thought in terms of concrete realities and thought in terms of depersonified symbols and personified abstractions. In the democratic countries the problems of internal politics are thought about mainly in terms of concrete reality; those of external politics, mainly in terms of abstractions and symbols. In dictatorial countries the proportion of concrete to abstract and symbolic thought is lower than in democratic countries. Dictators talk little of persons, much of personified abstractions, such as the Nation, the State, the Party, and much of depersonified symbols, such as Yids, Bolshies, Capitalists. The stupidity of politicians who talk about a world of persons as though it were not a world of persons is due in the main to self-interest. In a fictitious world of symbols and personified abstractions, rulers find that they can rule more effectively, and the ruled, that they can gratify instincts which the conventions of good manners and the imperatives of morality demand that they should repress. To think correctly is the condition of behaving well. It is also in itself a moral act; those who would think correctly must resist considerable temptations.

FOR REVIEW AND DISCUSSION

Content

1. Huxley's attitude toward *ignorance* and *stupidity* may be new to you How valid does it seem? What specific examples can you think of to illustrate what he says?

2. What does Huxley mean when he writes in paragraph 11 that "reality is a succession of concrete and particular situations"? How important is this definition of reality to the points Huxley is making in the essay?

3. Explain why thinking correctly is a "moral act."

4. Huxley seems as harshly critical of the general public as he does of its political leaders. What causes his attitude toward the general public?

Rhetoric

1. What seems to be Huxley's purpose in writing the essay? Is the purpose stated anywhere?

2. Huxley both analyzes and argues. Locate examples of both modes of exposition and explain how the two complement each other.

3. This essay was written in the 1930s, yet its ideas are quite contemporary. What is there, however, in its diction and style that points to the essay's being over forty years old?

4. "What is absurd and monstrous about war is that men who have no personal quarrel should be trained to murder one another in cold blood" (paragraph 7). Is this sentence free of propagandistic elements? How can we be certain?

5. Describe the structure of the sentence that is paragraph 3. Does the structure make it easy or difficult to understand?

6. Examine the opening sentence of each paragraph, looking for transitional words and phrases. Categorize each transition by its function—comparison, contrast, exemplification, logical sequence, and so forth. How often does Huxley rely on explicit transitional terms to advance his argument and analysis?

Classroom Exercises

1. Huxley expects much from us. To what extent is it possible to do what he says we should do—think and speak "exclusively in terms of concrete reality"? How might we begin to do so?

2. Discuss the relative reality of concrete and abstract language. What constitutes the *reality* of words?

Mark Twain

THE WAR PRAYER

This selection is a parable, a story in which certain general truths about the human condition are illustrated through the actions and attitudes of specific characters. And, like fables, parables also convey a moral. Mark Twain, who is familiar to us as a humorist and satirist, here shows his darker side and teaches us something about our blind and thoughtless use of words in a situation that obviously calls for moral vision and semantic accuracy.

[1] It was a time of great and exalting excitement. The country was up in arms, the war was on, in every breast burned the holy fire of patriotism; the drums were beating, the bands playing, the toy pistols popping, the bunched firecrackers hissing and spluttering; on every hand and far down the receding and fading spread of roofs and balconies a fluttering wilderness of flags flashed in the sun; daily the young volunteers marched down the wide avenue gay and fine in their new uniforms, the proud fathers and mothers and sisters and sweethearts cheering them with voices choked with happy emotion as they swung by; nightly the packed mass meetings listened, panting, to patriot oratory which stirred the deepest deeps of their hearts and which they interrupted at briefest intervals with cyclones of applause, the tears running down their cheeks the while; in the churches the pastors preached devotion to flag and country and invoked the God of Battles, beseeching His aid in our good cause in outpouring of fervid eloquence which moved every listener. It was indeed a glad and gracious time, and the half-dozen rash spirits that ventured to disapprove of the war and cast a doubt upon its righteousness straightway got such a stern and angry warning that for their personal safety's sake they quickly shrank out of sight and offended no more in that way.

[2] Sunday morning came—next day the battalions would leave for the front; the church was filled; the volunteers were there, their young faces alight with martial dreams—visions of the stern advance, the gathering momentum, the rushing charge, the flashing sabers, the flight of the foe, the tumult, the enveloping smoke, the fierce pursuit, the surrender!—then home from the war, bronzed heroes, welcomed, adored, submerged in golden seas of glory! With the volunteers sat their dear ones, proud, happy, and envied by the neighbors and friends who had no sons and brothers to send forth to the field of honor, there to win for the flag or, failing, die the noblest of noble deaths. The service proceeded; a war chapter from the Old

From *The Portable Mark Twain*. Copyright 1940; renewed © 1968 by The Viking Press Inc. Reprinted by permission of The Viking Press.

THE WAR PRAYER

Testament was read; the first prayer was said; it was followed by an organ burst that shook the building, and with one impulse the house rose, with glowing eyes and beating hearts, and poured out that tremendous invocation—

> "God the all-terrible! Thou who ordainest,
> Thunder thy clarion and lightning thy sword!"

Then came the "long" prayer. None could remember the like of it for passionate pleading and moving and beautiful language. The burden of its supplication was that an ever-merciful and benignant Father of us all would watch over our noble young soldiers and aid, comfort, and encourage them in their patriotic work; bless them, shield them in the day of battle and the hour of peril, bear them in His mighty hand, make them strong and confident, invincible in the bloody onset; help them to crush the foe, grant to them and to their flag and country imperishable honor and glory—

[3] An aged stranger entered and moved with slow and noiseless step up the main aisle, his eyes fixed upon the minister, his long body clothed in a robe that reached to his feet, his head bare, his white hair descending in a frothy cataract to his shoulders, his seamy face unnaturally pale, pale even to ghastliness. With all eyes following him and wondering, he made his silent way; without pausing, he ascended to the preacher's side and stood there, waiting. With shut lids the preacher, unconscious of his presence, continued his moving prayer, and at last finished it with the words, uttered in fervent appeal, "Bless our arms, grant us the victory, O Lord our God, Father and Protector of our land and flag!"

[4] The stranger touched his arm, motioned him to step aside—which the startled minister did—and took his place. During some moments he surveyed the spellbound audience with solemn eyes in which burned an uncanny light; then in a deep voice he said:

[5] "I come from the Throne—bearing a message from Almighty God!" The words smote the house with a shock; if the stranger perceived it he gave no attention. "He has heard the prayer of His servant your shepherd and will grant it if such shall be your desire after I, His messenger, shall have explained to you its import—that is to say, its full import. For it is like unto many of the prayers of men, in that it asks for more than he who utters it is aware of—except he pause and think.

[6] "God's servant and yours has prayed his prayer. Has he paused and taken thought? Is it one prayer? No, it is two—one uttered, the other not. Both have reached the ear of Him Who heareth all supplications, the spoken and the unspoken. Ponder this—keep it in mind. If you would beseech a blessing upon yourself, beware! lest without intent you invoke a curse upon a neighbor at the same time. If you pray for the blessing of rain upon your crop which needs it, by that act you are possibly praying for a curse upon some neighbor's crop which may not need rain and can be injured by it.

[7] "You have heard your servant's prayer—the uttered part of it. I am commissioned of God to put into words the other part of it—that part which the pastor, and also you in your hearts, fervently prayed silently. And ignorantly and unthinkingly? God grant that it was so! You heard these words: 'Grant us the victory, O Lord our God!' That is sufficient. The *whole* of the uttered prayer is compact into those pregnant words. Elaborations were not necessary. When you have prayed for victory you have prayed for many unmentioned results which follow victory—*must* follow it, cannot help but follow it. Upon the listening spirit of God the Father fell also the unspoken part of the prayer. He commandeth me to put it into words. Listen!

[8] "O Lord our Father, our young patriots, idols of our hearts, go forth to battle—be Thou near them! With them, in spirit, we also go forth from the sweet peace of our beloved firesides to smite the foe. O Lord our God, help us to tear their soldiers to bloody shreds with our shells; help us to cover their smiling fields with the pale forms of their patriot dead; help us to drown the thunder of the guns with the shrieks of their wounded, writhing in pain; help us to lay waste their humble homes with a hurricane of fire; help us to wring the hearts of their unoffending widows with unavailing grief; help us to turn them out roofless with their little children to wander unfriended the wastes of their desolated land in rags and hunger and thirst, sports of the sun flames of summer and the icy winds of winter, broken in spirit, worn with travail, imploring Thee for the refuge of the grave and denied it—for our sakes who adore Thee, Lord, blast their hopes, blight their lives, protract their bitter pilgrimage, make heavy their steps, water their way with their tears, stain the white snow with the blood of their wounded feet! We ask it, in the spirit of love, of Him Who is the Source of Love, and Who is the ever-faithful refuge and friend of all that are sore beset and seek His aid with humble and contrite hearts. Amen.

[9] (*After a pause*) "Ye have prayed it; if ye still desire it, speak! The messenger of the Most High waits."

[10] It was believed afterward that the man was a lunatic, because there was no sense in what he said.

FOR REVIEW AND DISCUSSION

Content

1. What is the moral of the parable?

2. What semantic contrasts are apparent between the language of the preacher's prayer ("Bless our arms, grant us the victory, O Lord . . .") and the language of the stranger's rendition of the "unheard" prayer?

3. What do you suppose is the congregation's response to the stranger's prayer? What is implied by that response?

Rhetoric

1. Look up *irony* in the Glossary. In what ways is Twain's parable ironic?

2. The nature of parables is such that their moral is not explained to us; rather, we must interpret it. How does the last sentence of the parable help us interpret it?

3. The verb of the last sentence is in the *passive voice*—we are not told *who* believed "that the man was a lunatic." Why might Twain have chosen the passive voice instead of the active voice: "The congregation believed afterward that . . ."? What is the effect of each?

4. Also in the last sentence, Twain uses the word *lunatic* rather than a synonym such as *mentally ill person* or *insane person*. What effect has this particular word choice?

Classroom Exercises

1. Look up one of Christ's parables in the New Testament (e.g., "the good Samaritan" or "the prodigal son" in the Book of Luke). In what ways does it differ from "The War Prayer"?

2. A common mistake is to assume that authors always agree with their characters. What is Twain saying? How can we tell what he—not his characters—means?

Richard Gambino

WATERGATE LINGO: A LANGUAGE OF NON-RESPONSIBILITY

> Concerned with much the same abuses of language as Huxley is, Richard Gambino examines the Watergate hearings. He points out how the language of the Watergate conspirators allowed them to distort and mask reality and to avoid responsibility or guilt for lies and crimes they committed.

> We operated on what is known in some industries as a zero-defect system. We attempted to get everything right.
> H. R. HALDEMAN

[1] In a now famous phrase, Ron Ziegler and John Ehrlichman have declared White House statements proven false to be "no longer operative." This is a very handy phrase which can mean any of the following:

> It wasn't true in the first place.
> I'm sorry I said it.
> I thought it was true then but I know now it wasn't.

While the public was left wondering what the phrase meant, responsibility for the original lies was shifted from the liars to the lies themselves. The responsibility was not in the people, not even in the stars, but in the statements themselves, which were spoken of as if they had lives and energy of their own.

[2] In ordinary English we speak of employees being fired. In the language of the Department of State, they are "selected out." It sounds as if the fired people are honored. The palliative phrase relieves the employer from responsibility for an unpleasant act. Similarly, at the C.I.A., according to Director Colby, superiors do not fire subordinates. They "arrange a circumstance where employees can be helped to leave government service early." How helpful of them! One is almost led to think that people dismissed might thank their bosses for being favored.

[3] Those involved in Watergate or its cover-up do not destroy evidence of crimes. They "deep-six" papers. This sailor's phrase conjures up colorful salts jettisoning unneeded ballast over the side instead of political men engaged in criminal conspiracy. The frequent use of metaphors and similes to sugar-coat ques-

---

From *Freedom at Issue* (November–December 1973). Copyright 1973 by Freedom House, Inc. Reprinted by permission of the publisher and author.

tions of culpability reached a high point when Special White House Counsel J. Fred Buzhardt waxed poetic about his predecessor, John W. Dean III. Instead of saying that Dean's testimony was false, Buzhardt spoke of "the failure of Dean's muse while he was on the mountain. . . ." Now if Dean were lying under oath he would be guilty of perjury and could be held legally accountable. But it seems cruel and unusual punishment to declare one a liar and perjuror merely because his muse failed while he was on the mountain. After all, who among us has not known frustration in our creative enterprises?

[4]   Whether Dean's muse was reliable or not, he said during his testimony that those engaged in the cover-up once suggested that John Mitchell "should be brought forward." Connotations of going to the head of the class leap to mind. The phrase also evokes one coming forward with forthrightness, sincerity and even courage. Through the magic of words, those who made the suggestion that Mitchell take all the guilt and punishment for all the conspirators sound like honest brokers, even like outraged righteous souls. As long as their language is used, it becomes impossible to blame them for wanting to make one man the patsy for a conspiracy to obstruct justice.

[5]   When Mitchell finally did come forward (in the ordinary sense of the term), he spoke to the Senate Select Committee about "White House horror stories." Not criminal conduct or unethical behavior by White House officials and employees, but "White House horrors." "Criminal conduct" and "unethical behavior" are depressingly meaningful expressions. They lead to thoughts of real acts by real people with real names and faces who really can be and should be held responsible. But "White House horror stories" suggests vague, perhaps unreal, events caused by nameless occult or imaginary powers. The phrase places the Watergate crimes and other misconduct in the same categories as silly old wives' tales of haunted houses and Hollywood fantasy. Although we are frightened by these horror stories, we know our fears are baseless. It is only gentle, benign Boris Karloff behind the terrible Frankenstein mask. Don't be scared, kiddies.

[6]   If Hugh Sloan, Jr. gave money to a convicted criminal one might suspect him of something rotten. But if as it was said he merely paid "increments . . . in the form of currency" to G. Gordon Liddy, why Sloan sounds as if he was merely giving his fellowman his due. After all, increments are normally thought to be deserved. And "currency" is what scholarly economists deal with, a far cry from the filthy lucre you and I covet. Could Sloan be guilty of something illegal or immoral? Why it is unthinkable—because Washingtonspeak makes it literally unspeakable.

THE DECLINE OF LANGUAGE

[7]   Because of the language they use, and in which we are compelled to follow their accounts, Watergate witnesses and the people they favor are never really

responsible. Even those seeking the truth are forced into parlance in which moral and legal responsibility is unutterable. Thus Senator Howard Baker, vice-chairman of the Senate Select Committee, asked one of the witnesses "how we might ventilate the structure of campaigning." One who ventilates a structure—presumably one who causes air to flow through a building—is not per se doing anything or concerned with anything of any moral or legal consequence whatsoever. His behavior is morally and legally neither responsible or irresponsible. It is quite different with a person who attempts to reform illegal and unethical political campaigning, a sticky matter for many on both sides of the Senate hearing table. Better to talk about ventilation.

[8]   Many commentators on the Watergate actions have ominously linked the events with the society presented in George Orwell's novel *1984*. As I have watched the Watergate hearings on television, I have been reminded not so much of *1984* as of a lesser known work of Orwell, an essay written in 1945 entitled, *Politics and the English Language*. In it, Orwell warned:

> It is clear that the decline of a language must ultimately have political and economic causes. . . . But an effect can become a cause, reinforcing the original cause and producing the same effect in an intensified form, and so on indefinitely. A man may take to drink because he feels himself to be a failure, and then fail all the more completely because he drinks. It is rather the same thing that is happening to the English language. It becomes ugly and inaccurate because our thoughts are foolish, but the slovenliness of our language makes it easier to have foolish thoughts.

[9]   A significant lesson is emerging from the Watergate hearings, apart from those that the powerful violate laws, subvert the United States Constitution and scorn decent ethics. The testimony of the Watergate crowd demonstrates that a stock political language has evolved which makes it difficult for the powerful and the public alike even to think meaningfully about respect for laws, loyalty to the Constitution or to exercise moral sensibilities. The torrent of circumlocutions, mechanical verbal formulas, misplaced technical jargon, palliative expressions, euphemisms and inflated phraseology indicate that the brains both of speakers and listeners are being anesthetized or stunted. Critical meanings are barred from the beginning in a form of conceptual contraception. Insofar as we become addicted to the corrupt Watergate language, it is nonsense to speak of political or moral responsibility and irresponsibility. Lacking mastery of clear, meaningful language deprives us of the basic equipment required of responsible people. As we abandon meaningful language in favor of blather, we become positively irresponsible to ourselves as well as to others. In listening to the Watergate witnesses it often is hard to tell whether they are merely dissemblers trying to paralyze the minds of others, self-deceivers who have crippled their own intelligences, or glib dolls whose characters remained undeveloped as their smartness grew.

[10]   Whatever the character of the Watergate witnesses, the hearings show that political language has degenerated since Orwell's warning that thought and lan-

guage decline together. Seemingly more than before in American politics the English language is used not as an instrument for forming and expressing thought. It is used more to prevent, confuse and conceal thought. Thus we have grown accustomed to calling political lingo "rhetoric." This good word has been so debased to stand for anything from propaganda and nonsense to vicious lies. As the pseudo-language takes hold—*even in the process of our determined attempts to regenerate responsibility in political life*—it drags us further into chaotic conditions leading logically and inevitably to political nihilism.

[11] In my opinion we have been so concerned with the 1984 aspects of Watergate—the spying, wiretapping and other "dirty tricks" (another euphemism that emerged from the hearings)—that we have overlooked something at least as important. If our political language, and therefore our public thinking, becomes so debauched that moral meanings can no longer be clearly expressed or understood, then all the gadgets, technology and techniques of Watergate will be unnecessary. We will have already slipped into a 1984 nightmare. A society that cannot speak or understand sense is condemned to live nonsensically. To put it in Washingtonspeak, clear political meanings and the higher political values that depend on them will have become "no longer operative." In plain language, we will have become a nation of politically nonresponsible imbeciles "speaking in tongues." Not the inspired Biblical kind but the spurious Watergate sort.

PERSONAL MORALITY INEXPRESSIBLE

[12] Although there are varieties of Watergate talk, there is one quality common to the witnesses' ways of speaking, one very important thread connecting the apparently disparate linguistic styles. Except when they are accusing current enemies, e.g. Mitchell's calling Jeb Magruder's testimony that he (Mitchell) reviewed tapes and documents gained through illegal wiretaps and burglary "a palpable, damnable lie," their language permits no raising of questions of personal responsibility for unethical or criminal conduct on their part or by their colleagues. Issues of moral right and wrong are inexpressible in their lingo. When Senator Weicker asked Herbert Porter what was "the quality of his mind" (Washingtonspeak for "what were you thinking?") while he dealt in improper use of campaign funds, Porter paused, then replied, "Senator, I'm not a moral philosopher." In politics as in ethics what our language prevents us from articulating, it prevents us from thinking. Although the words of the Watergate people indicate that Washingtonspeak is well on the way to becoming a language in which the whole matter of legality, as well as ethics, will also be inexpressible, it has not yet reached that perfect state. Speakers of this odd language must at present rest content with its power to make only *personal* responsibility for illegal acts impossible. Just as it would have been impossible in Periclean Athens to speak of the internal combustion engine, computers or atomic energy, so

in Washingtonspeak personal moral responsibility does not exist. To be sure, illegal acts still exist in Watergate glossology, but in the linguistic progress achieved so far, illegalities exist *sui generis*. They constitute a kind of unholy creation from nothing by no one.

CIRCUMLOCUTIONS

[13] Several dominant features of Washingtonspeak have been greatly exposed during the Watergate hearings. Circumlocutions and convoluted language are among the foremost instruments of this language of nonresponsibility. Champion among the witnesses in this skill is the voluble Mr. Ehrlichman. His method was to confound critical questions put to him by blanketing them with intense barrages of grape-shot syntax. The Senators questioning him were given time limits and most of them were poor cross-examiners, an opinion confirmed by a recent survey conducted among prominent trial lawyers. Ehrlichman, therefore, as one of my acquaintances put it, "talked the bastards to death" with such phrases as "we (Dean, Mitchell and Ehrlichman) made an agreement to go out and develop additional information if we could." One may seek, compile, file, pursue, fabricate, conceal, alter, reveal and do other things regarding information. But how does one "develop" it? In a darkroom? A chemist's laboratory? Ehrlichman's language leaves us ignorant of precisely what the three men had agreed to do and therefore unable to assess its morality or legality. We would be left in this quandary even if, as Ehrlichman said of his associates and himself, "we gathered together to compare ignorances." How do you and I compare what I do not know with what you do not know? If I speak no Greek and you speak no Chinese, how do we compare these tongues? For a comparison to be achieved, someone must introduce knowledge. But then someone would know something, and Ehrlichman was asserting he and his associates knew nothing when they gathered together.

[14] In reply to the question why he had approved Mr. Kalmbach's mission of raising money for the jailed Watergate burglars, Ehrlichman allowed that his approval was only "perfunctory" and given because "Mitchell had some interest in making sure that defendants were well defended." Does "perfunctory" mean Ehrlichman was not responsible? What was Mr. Mitchell's "interest"? Was the payment for a legal defense, was it hush money, or both? Because of Ehrlichman's verbal dexterity in tying up the English language, it is impossible to know from his testimony who was responsible for what. Events merely happened.

[15] Although Ehrlichman was aggressively or defiantly blunt throughout much of his confrontation with the Senate Committee, he repeatedly became almost incomprehensibly loquacious when questioned about his responsibility and that of others he insisted were blameless. When asked about the allegation made by both Richard Helms and General Vernon Walters, formerly the two top men at the C.I.A., that

Ehrlichman and Haldeman suggested that the agency ask the F.B.I. to limit its investigation into the "laundering" of Republican money in Mexico on the pretext that the F.B.I. would endanger some pretended agency operation in that country, Ehrlichman's diction became inscrutable:

> My recollection of that meeting is at considerable variance with General Walters' in the general thrust and in the details. In point of fact, as I recall it, we informed Mr. Helms and General Walters that the meeting was held at the President's request for the reasons I stated. Mr. Haldeman said that the Watergate was an obvious important political issue and that the President had no alternative but to order a full allout F.B.I. investigation until he was satisfied that there was some specific area from which the F.B.I. should not probe for fear of leaks through the F.B.I. or dissociated and disconnected C.I.A. activities that had no bearing on Watergate.

Ehrlichman displayed extraordinary skill in surrounding an outrageous opinion with tortuous verbiage which gives it a coating of justification. Thus he glibly took the offensive when questioned about the burglary of Daniel Ellsberg's psychiatrist's office:

> I think if it is clearly understood that the President has the constitutional power to prevent the betrayal of national security secrets, as I understand he does, and that is well understood by the American people, and an episode like that is seen in that context, there shouldn't be any problem.

What "constitutional power"? Which "national security secrets"? By whose definition? "Well understood by the American people"? "There shouldn't be any problem"? Ehrlichman's crossfire of stock phrases sends us diving for cover, numbs our minds and almost makes us sorry the topic was raised.

[16] Washingtonspeak circumlocution is virtually invulnerable. It smothers any counterattack with more circumlocution. The circumlocution gains strength over each attempt to pierce it with Hydra's ability instantly to replace any of its serpents' heads which is cut off with two others. Thus Ehrlichman first explained—in his fashion—the payment of cash to the captured Watergate burglars by saying, "John Mitchell felt very strongly that it was important to have good legal representation for these defendants for a number of reasons—for political reasons, but also because we had these civil damage suits that had been filed by the Democrats." When pressed about exactly what were the "political reasons," Ehrlichman set the Hydra-like prowess of circumlocution upon his questioners. "Well," he said, "just that if there were to be a trial and it were to take place before the election, that obviously that trial would have some political impact and good representation was simply essential." By this time the numerous heads of Ehrlichman's verbal monster were overwhelming. No one on the Committee pursued the question any further.

[17] Similarly, Ehrlichman's response to a query about whether he suspected Jeb Magruder's involvement in the Watergate cover-up and what he did about his suspicion was so convoluted as to be totally uninformative. Again no Senator challenged Ehrlichman's confounding statement that:

> There came a time when there was a feeling that, at least on my part, based on what Mr. Dean was telling me about the unraveling of this thing, that Mr. Magruder may have had some involvement, and that culminated in a meeting with the Attorney General (Mitchell) at the end of July, on the 31st of July, where Magruder was specifically discussed. But just where in there I acquired the information, I can't tell you.

Any questions?

[18] Resort to circumlocution was characteristic of others at key points when questions of someone's personal responsibility threatened to surface. Senator Inouye asked Mitchell a pointed question in plain English: "Have you ever considered whether it was fair to the American people to conspire to keep them from the true facts of this matter [of a series of illegal and unethical actions]?" In the words of the old calypso song, Mitchell's reply was clear as mud and it covered the ground. "Yes, I am sure," he said, "that the subject matter crossed my mind many, many times. But I do not believe now, I did not believe then, that the President should be charged with the transgressions of others. And it is just as simple as that." The habit of using inflated blather at crucial points is so strong that John Dean's "I was trying to test the chronology of my knowledge" was typical.

THE STOCK PHRASE

[19] Another feature of the Watergate language of nonresponsibility is the use of stupefying stock phrases. A private meeting with the President of the United States arouses considerable interest about possibly revealing statements. But John Dean's "one on one with the President" sounds as impersonal as the shuffling of a deck of cards. It is mechanical in connotation, as are other phrases used by Watergate witnesses. They did not approve things but "signed off on them" as when Jeb Magruder said Mitchell signed off on a proposed project. The phrase makes Mitchell appear to casually flip a switch rather than consciously and knowingly make a decision. You, I and most people take orders from our bosses or superiors in our jobs or careers. John Dean "followed a channel of reporting." It sounds more prescribed by circumstances than an act of conscious obedience. The course of a channel is fixed and a good harbor pilot merely follows it. And reporting evokes much less responsibility than giving and taking instructions.

[20] Watergate people never reflect on the past since such an activity would imply that they are capable of understanding elementaries of personal responsibility. They are forever "in hindsight" like so many creatures with eyes imbedded in their behinds. Thus they merely "see" the past in a manner that permits them not to commit themselves about their moral or legal culpability then or their present view whether they were responsible. For example in the following exchange with Samuel Dash, John Mitchell really reveals nothing about his responsibility for past behavior or his current opinion about that responsibility:

Dash: "As Attorney General of the United States, why didn't you throw Mr. Liddy out of your office?"

Mitchell: "Well, I think, Mr. Dash, in hindsight I not only should have thrown him out of the office, I should have thrown him out of the window."

Dash: "Well, since you did neither, why didn't you at least recommend that Mr. Liddy be fired?"

Mitchell: "Well, in hindsight, I probably should have done that too."

To describe a series of circumstances surrounding an event implies personal knowledge which in turn might imply personal responsibility. Therefore, Mitchell volunteered—after being asked a direct question regarding a suspicious meeting—"let me play out the scenario for you." He merely starts the movie projector but has no relation to what might appear on the screen.

[21] Incidentally, whereas most people are told of criminal events, thereby raising questions of their complicity after the fact, Watergate people were merely "brought up to speed on" them. After all, the highway signs specify minimum as well as maximum legal speeds, right?

[22] The stock phrase most used during the Watergate hearings was "at this point in time" and its variations, e.g. "at that point in time." At first these expressions sound merely like pretentious, elaborate ways of saying, "then," "now," "at that time," "at this time," etc. But the stock phrases are much more useful. "At that point in time" serves to isolate the event being discussed, to detach it, bracket it and set it apart from all other events and people. It becomes a moment existing by itself. Questionable conduct is thereby voided by being reduced to a mathematical point, a fiction having no dimensions, connections, history or relation to the present. Surgeons prefer to operate in a "clean field" established by isolation of the area of incision through elaborate operating room techniques. Only a swatch of flesh is presented to the surgeon's eyes instead of a whole patient. The surgeon is thus spared the unnerving sight of the patient's face, posture, and general human appearance at the critical time of surgery. "At that point of time" accomplishes an analogous effect. The difference of course is that the surgical procedure serves a legitimate medical purpose, while the Watergate linguistic procedure obscures personal political and moral responsibility. Two of the axiomatic requirements of personal responsibility are motives before the deed and awareness of consequences after the deed. "At that point in time" foils both.

[23] "Pre-situation" and "post-situation" are Watergate phrases which once again sever events from relations, connections, and hence responsibility. They are even more bloodless than the ordinary legal phrases "before the event" and "after the event."

[24] But perhaps the most blatantly robot evoking phrase is John Dean's saying he "dealt with people telephonically." Now, when you call someone on the telephone, or he calls, and you and he talk, human behavior occurs and ordinary respon-

sibilities for it become discussible. But no more comes to mind when one person deals with another telephonically than when we watch the whir of computer machinery. It is totally impersonal, mechanical, inhuman.

SPECIALIZED JARGON

[25] Another prominent feature of Watergate talk is the frequent misuse of technical jargon taken from specialized areas of life. Jargon used by specialists in reference to their speciality is meaningful and useful. It facilitates communication between the specialists whether it be in football, medicine, seamanship, stock brokerage, etc. But when appropriated for use in politics, technical jargon from other fields serves contrary purposes. Codes produced by misplaced jargon used in politics serve to mask the true nature of what is happening. And the use of jargon which is elsewhere legitimate lends an aura of justification and respectability to morally and legally dubious behavior. The use of appropriated jargon also serves the old priesthood mystique function of jargon. Those privy to the code enjoy a special, privileged, sophisticated status making them superior to us ordinary slobs.

[26] Much of the jargon used by the Watergate people is taken from the fields of police work and cloak-and-dagger activity. The first is a legitimate profession, the second at least is glamorously mysterious. Unethical and illegal conduct becomes dressed up by the borrowed jargon. Thus, those engaged in burglary, malfeasance of office, criminal conspiracy and other evil conduct did not do these things over ordinary periods of time. They functioned "within time frames," a mechanically detached expression legitimately used in the computer field. Illegal domestic spies constitute a "new intelligence unit" and their equipment was said to need "housing," i.e. quarters that do not call attention to themselves. Images of Humphrey Bogart in trenchcoat playing cat and mouse with the Nazis instead of a sleazy group spying on the personal lives of law abiding fellow Americans.

[27] Illegal activity is spoken of as "games." Criminal conspiracy becomes a "game plan." Conspirators are "team players" like so many good halfbacks or third basemen. Thus Caulfield is said to have told McCord he was "fouling up the game plan." And Herbert Porter said he remained silent about nefarious doings at Nixon's campaign headquarters because he wanted to be a "team player." Criminal wiretappers are spoken of as "wire men," mere technicians like electricians legitimately used by the telephone company or police department.

[28] Another linguistic style heavily favored by Watergate witnesses is the use of the passive rather than active voice. For example, instead of saying "I was curious" or "I thought of it," the witnesses have an infuriating habit of saying things like "it pricked my curiosity," "it crossed my mind," "it dawned on me." The effect of the habitual use of the passive voice is to create an illusory animistic world where events

have lives, wills, motives and actions of their own without any human being responsible for them. This effect is enhanced by another tendency of the speakers—the constant use of multi-syllabic words when ordinary shorter ones would do. This old pedant's trick serves to numb independent thought in the listener and speaker. It also puffs up the status of the speaker in the minds of his audience and in his own self-esteem. Thus, the elegant lingo prettifies the sordid facts probably even in the minds of the guilty.

[29] The use of martyred metaphors, similes, and euphemisms serves the same function of obscuring import and responsibility from the guilty, from the victims and from bystanders. Illegally obtained or illegally used money is "laundered." Cleanliness is next to Godliness. Liddy's lengthy presentation to Mitchell, Dean and others of monstrous plans to use "mugging squads," kidnapping teams, compromising prostitutes and electronic eavesdropping against the White House's political opposition is described by use of a kindergarten phrase as a "show-and-tell session." The exposing of criminal involvement is spoken of as "this matter is starting to unravel." Presumably the journalists, Judge Sirica and the Senators and Congressmen searching out the truth are guilty of taking apart a neatly knitted sweater. Haldeman's reference to the exposition makes the obstruction of justice sound even more benign, and those uncovering it as naughty children or semivandals. According to Dean, the White House chief of staff said, "Once the toothpaste is out of the tube, it's going to be very hard to get it back in." Spank the brats playing with the tube!

[30] Those who are spied upon by wiretaps are not referred to as subjects, and certainly not as victims. They were called "targets." Subjects and victims have rights, feelings, dignity—they are humans, citizens. But targets are inanimate things whose sole function is to be hit. Should one object? Do targets at a rifle or archery range complain? Don't be absurd.

[31] Dean described a reassuring phone call from President Nixon as a "stroking session." Normally we stroke our lovers, children and pets—loving gestures, thoughts of which stimulate warm feelings in us. Was or was not Dean implying Nixon's complicity by use of this sensual metaphor? Poets use metaphors and similes to heighten meanings. Watergate people use them to blur meanings.

[32] Among the most infuriating euphemisms used by Watergate witnesses is "surreptitious entry," meaning burglary. Thus a crime becomes a game of hide and seek, or at most a naughty prank. Next time you find a burglar in your home don't shout "police!" Say "Oh, you surreptitious devil you!"

[33] What ordinary crooks call "casing the joint" before a burglary is called by the Watergate bunch "a vulnerability and feasibility study." Surely these men were just students and technicians. But criminals? Never.

[34] Illegal wiretapping is evil. Therefore the Watergate people engaged in "electronic surveillance." Spying on a person's activities is "visual surveillance." Evil

people cover up, lie and bribe. Watergate people "contain situations" like so many protective dams.

[35] Is this concern with language mere pedantry, a case of academic vanity? I suggest not. When an elaborate language of nonresponsibility becomes current in the federal government, it would be irresponsible for us not to expose and correct it. We have been had. A language of nonresponsibility is being forced upon us to describe a list of crimes, as Washingtonspeak would have it, "at the very highest levels" of the United States Government. It is a list which beggars our conscience when we push aside the elaborate Watergate talk camouflaging it. As Senator Weicker recently stated them, they should be sobering enough to bring us to our linguistic senses:

> Conspiracy to commit breaking and entering.
> Conspiracy to commit burglary.
> Breaking and entering.
> Burglary.
> Conspiracy to obstruct justice.
> Conspiracy to intercept wire or oral communications.
> Perjury.
> Subornation of perjury.
> Conspiracy to obstruct a criminal investigation.
> Conspiracy to destroy evidence.
> Conspiracy to file false sworn statements.
> Misprision of a felony.
> Filing of false statements.
> Interception of wire and oral communications.
> Obstruction of criminal investigation.
> Attempted interference with the administration of the Internal Revenue laws.
> Attempted unauthorized use of Internal Revenue information.

To these we might add illegal use of the C.I.A., and numerous unethical practices from violation of the doctor-patient privilege to sabotage of a presidential campaign.

[36] An ancient Roman saying has it that the mind is dyed by the color of its thoughts. Since thoughts are formed in language, it follows that the mind is dyed by the tint of language. Could it be that so much outrageous conduct occurred at least in part because too many minds functioned through a language which extracted personal responsibility from consideration? Did addiction to Washingtonspeak facilitate the commission of conduct ordinarily considered unacceptable to the community at large?

[37] It is time to cleanse our minds—and I don't mean launder—from the muck of Washingtonspeak if we still value government of responsible people, by responsible people and for responsible people. Although a more humble goal, this would be preferable to Mr. Haldeman's "zero-defect system."

FOR REVIEW AND DISCUSSION

Content

1. What does Gambino mean by the last sentence in the first paragraph? Does he believe what he says in that sentence? How can we tell?

2. Under what circumstances is it "nonsense to speak of political or moral responsibility and irresponsibility" (paragraph 9)? Discuss and exemplify Gambino's reasoning.

3. Politicians are not alone in their amoralizing use of language. Discuss examples of other groups who use language similarly.

Rhetoric

1. Haldeman may have spoken seriously when he said that he and his cohorts "tried to get everything right." In what tone, though, does Gambino present the Haldeman quotation?

2. Gambino seems to have difficulty maintaining an even tone in his essay. Point out some examples of this unevenness. Do you think it detracts from or complements Gambino's credibility?

3. Describe Gambino's use of specific examples. What purpose do they serve?

Classroom Exercises

1. Try translating and reducing into plain English Ehrlichman's recollection of the money laundering incident (paragraph 15).

2. By reading or listening to news reports, find examples of each feature of "Washingtonspeak": circumlocution, stock phrase, specialized jargon, euphemism, and passive voice. Translate your examples into plain English.

3. Write a paragraph in which you confess to a number of immoral acts. (Let your muse invent them!) Then rewrite the paragraph in "Washingtonspeak." Is your revised paragraph obscure enough to hide your guilt—to indicate that you might fare well in Washington?

George Orwell

THE DESTRUCTION OF WORDS

George Orwell's 1984 forecasts a futuristic society of terrifying repression and cruelty. In this excerpt from the novel, Winston Smith and Syme discuss Syme's work, the creation of the definitive edition of the Newspeak Dictionary. By 2050, Syme estimates, Newspeak will have made it literally impossible for anyone to formulate a thought inimical to the government of Big Brother. As you read, you may find it useful to reflect on previous selections concerning the relation of language to thought.

[1]   In the low-ceilinged canteen, deep under ground, the lunch queue jerked slowly forward. The room was already very full and deafeningly noisy. From the grille at the counter the steam of stew came pouring forth, with a sour metallic smell which did not quite overcome the fumes of Victory Gin. On the far side of the room there was a small bar, a mere hole in the wall, where gin could be bought at ten cents the large nip.

[2]   "Just the man I was looking for," said a voice at Winston's back.

[3]   He turned round. It was his friend Syme, who worked in the Research Department. Perhaps "friend" was not exactly the right word. You did not have friends nowadays, you had comrades; but there were some comrades whose society was pleasanter than that of others. Syme was a philologist, a specialist in Newspeak. Indeed, he was one of the enormous team of experts now engaged in compiling the Eleventh Edition of the Newspeak dictionary. He was a tiny creature, smaller than Winston, with dark hair and large, protuberant eyes, at once mournful and derisive, which seemed to search your face closely while he was speaking to you.

[4]   "I wanted to ask you whether you'd got any razor blades," he said.

[5]   "Not one!" said Winston with a sort of guilty haste. "I've tried all over the place. They don't exist any longer."

[6]   Everyone kept asking you for razor blades. Actually he had two unused ones which he was hoarding up. There had been a famine of them for months past. At any given moment there was some necessary article which the Party shops were unable to supply. Sometimes it was buttons, sometimes it was darning wool, sometimes it was shoelaces; at present it was razor blades. You could only get hold of them, if at all, by scrounging more or less furtively on the "free" market.

From *1984* by George Orwell.   Reprinted by permission of Mrs. Sonia Brownwell Orwell and Martin Secker & Warburg.

THE DESTRUCTION OF WORDS

[7] "I've been using the same blade for six weeks," he added untruthfully.

[8] The queue gave another jerk forward. As they halted he turned and faced Syme again. Each of them took a greasy metal tray from a pile at the edge of the counter.

[9] "Did you go and see the prisoners hanged yesterday?" said Syme.

[10] "I was working," said Winston indifferently. "I shall see it on the flicks, I suppose."

[11] "A very inadequate substitute," said Syme.

[12] His mocking eyes roved over Winston's face. "I know you," the eyes seemed to say, "I see through you, I know very well why you didn't go to see those prisoners hanged." In an intellectual way, Syme was venomously orthodox. He would talk with a disagreeable gloating satisfaction of helicopter raids on enemy villages, the trial and confessions of thought-criminals, the executions in the cellars of the Ministry of Love. Talking to him was largely a matter of getting him away from such subjects and entangling him, if possible, in the technicalities of Newspeak, on which he was authoritative and interesting. Winston turned his head a little aside to avoid the scrutiny of the large dark eyes.

[13] "It was a good hanging," said Syme reminiscently. "I think it spoils it when they tie their feet together. I like to see them kicking. And above all, at the end, the tongue sticking right out, and blue—a quite bright blue. That's the detail that appeals to me."

[14] "Nex', please!" yelled the white-aproned prole with the ladle.

[15] Winston and Syme pushed their trays beneath the grille. Onto each was dumped swiftly the regulation lunch—metal pannikin of pinkish-gray stew, a hunk of bread, a cube of cheese, a mug of milkless Victory Coffee, and one saccharine tablet.

[16] "There's a table over there, under that telescreen," said Syme. "Let's pick up a gin on the way."

[17] The gin was served out to them in handleless china mugs. They threaded their way across the crowded room and unpacked their trays onto the metal-topped table, on one corner of which someone had left a pool of stew, a filthy liquid mess that had the appearance of vomit. Winston took up his mug of gin, paused for an instant to collect his nerve, and gulped the oily-tasting stuff down. When he had winked the tears out of his eyes he suddenly discovered that he was hungry. He began swallowing spoonfuls of the stew, which, in among its general sloppiness, had cubes of spongy pinkish stuff which was probably a preparation of meat. Neither of them spoke again till they had emptied their pannikins. From the table at Winston's left, a little behind his back, someone was talking rapidly and continuously, a harsh gabble almost like the quacking of a duck, which pierced the general uproar of the room.

[18] "How is the dictionary getting on?" said Winston, raising his voice to overcome the noise.

[19] "Slowly," said Syme. "I'm on the adjectives. It's fascinating."

[20] He had brightened up immediately at the mention of Newspeak. He pushed his pannikin aside, took up his hunk of bread in one delicate hand and his cheese in the other, and leaned across the table so as to be able to speak without shouting.

[21] "The Eleventh Edition is the definitive edition," he said. "We're getting the language into its final shape—the shape it's going to have when nobody speaks anything else. When we've finished with it, people like you will have to learn it all over again. You think, I dare say, that our chief job is inventing new words. But not a bit of it! We're destroying words—scores of them, hundreds of them, every day. We're cutting the language down to the bone. The Eleventh Edition won't contain a single word that will become obsolete before the year 2050."

[22] He bit hungrily into his bread and swallowed a couple of mouthfuls, then continued speaking, with a sort of pedant's passion. His thin dark face had become animated, his eyes had lost their mocking expression and grown almost dreamy.

[23] "It's a beautiful thing, the destruction of words. Of course the great wastage is in the verbs and adjectives, but there are hundreds of nouns that can be got rid of as well. It isn't only the synonyms; there are also the antonyms. After all, what justification is there for a word which is simply the opposite of some other words? A word contains its opposite in itself. Take 'good,' for instance. If you have a word like 'good,' what need is there for a word like 'bad'? 'Ungood' will do just as well—better, because it's an exact opposite, which the other is not. Or again, if you want a stronger version of 'good,' what sense is there in having a whole string of vague useless words like 'excellent' and 'splendid' and all the rest of them? 'Plusgood' covers the meaning, or 'doubleplusgood' if you want something stronger still. Of course we use those forms already, but in the final version of Newspeak there'll be nothing else. In the end the whole notion of goodness and badness will be covered by only six words—in reality, only one word. Don't you see the beauty of that, Winston? It was B.B.'s idea originally, of course," he added as an afterthought.

[24] A sort of vapid eagerness flitted across Winston's face at the mention of Big Brother. Nevertheless Syme immediately detected a certain lack of enthusiasm.

[25] "You haven't a real appreciation of Newspeak, Winston," he said almost sadly. "Even when you write it you're still thinking in Oldspeak. I've read some of those pieces that you write in the *Times* occasionally. They're good enough, but they're translations. In your heart you'd prefer to stick to Oldspeak, with all its vagueness and its useless shades of meaning. You don't grasp the beauty of the destruction of words. Do you know that Newspeak is the only language in the world whose vocabulary gets smaller every year?"

[26] Winston did know that, of course. He smiled sympathetically he hoped, not trusting himself to speak. Syme bit off another fragment of the dark-colored bread, chewed it briefly, and went on:

[27] "Don't you see that the whole aim of Newspeak is to narrow the range of thought? In the end we shall make thoughtcrime literally impossible, because there will be no words in which to express it. Every concept that can ever be needed will be expressed by exactly *one* word, with its meaning rigidly defined and all its subsidiary meanings rubbed out and forgotten. Already, in the Eleventh Edition, we're not far from that point. But the process will still be continuing long after you and I are dead. Every year fewer and fewer words, and the range of consciousness always a little smaller. Even now, of course, there's no reason or excuse for committing thoughtcrime. It's merely a question of self-discipline, reality-control. But in the end there won't be any need even for that. The Revolution will be complete when the language is perfect. Newspeak is Ingsoc and Ingsoc is Newspeak," he added with a sort of mystical satisfaction. "Has it ever occurred to you, Winston, that by the year 2050, at the very latest, not a single human being will be alive who could understand such a conversation as we are having now?"

[28] "Except—" began Winston doubtfully, and then stopped.

[29] It had been on the tip of his tongue to say "Except the proles," but he checked himself, not feeling fully certain that this remark was not in some way unorthodox. Syme, however, had divined what he was about to say.

[30] "The proles are not human beings," he said carelessly. "By 2050—earlier, probably—all real knowledge of Oldspeak will have disappeared. The whole literature of the past will have been destroyed. Chaucer, Shakespeare, Milton, Byron—they'll exist only in Newspeak versions, not merely changed into something different, but actually changed into something contradictory of what they used to be. Even the literature of the Party will change. Even the slogans will change. How could you have a slogan like 'freedom is slavery' when the concept of freedom has been abolished? The whole climate of thought will be different. In fact there will *be* no thought, as we understand it now. Orthodoxy means not thinking—not needing to think. Orthodoxy is unconsciousness."

[31] One of these days, thought Winston with sudden deep conviction, Syme will be vaporized. He is too intelligent. He sees too clearly and speaks too plainly. The Party does not like such people. One day he will disappear. It is written in his face.

[32] Winston had finished his bread and cheese. He turned a little sideways in his chair to drink his mug of coffee. At the table on his left the man with the strident voice was still talking remorselessly away. A young woman who was perhaps his secretary, and who was sitting with her back to Winston, was listening to him and seemed to be eagerly agreeing with everything that he said. From time to time Winston caught some such remark as "I think you're *so* right, I do *so* agree with

you," uttered in a youthful and rather silly feminine voice. But the other voice never stopped for an instant, even when the girl was speaking. Winston knew the man by sight, though he knew no more about him than that he held some important post in the Fiction Department. He was a man of about thirty, with a muscular throat and a large, mobile mouth. His head was thrown back a little, and because of the angle at which he was sitting, his spectacles caught the light and presented to Winston two blank discs instead of eyes. What was slightly horrible was that from the stream of sound that poured out of his mouth, it was almost impossible to distinguish a single word. Just once Winston caught a phrase—"complete and final elimination of Goldsteinism"—jerked out very rapidly and, as it seemed, all in one piece, like a line of type cast solid. For the rest it was just a noise, a quack-quack-quacking. And yet, though you could not actually hear what the man was saying, you could not be in any doubts about its general nature. He might be denouncing Goldstein and demanding sterner measures against thought-criminals and saboteurs, he might be fulminating against the atrocities of the Eurasian army, he might be praising Big Brother or the heroes on the Malabar front—it made no difference. Whatever it was, you could be certain that every word of it was pure orthodoxy, pure Ingsoc. As he watched the eyeless face with the jaw moving rapidly up and down, Winston had a curious feeling that this was not a real human being but some kind of dummy. It was not the man's brain that was speaking; it was his larynx. The stuff that was coming out of him consisted of words, but it was not speech in the true sense: it was a noise uttered in unconsciousness, like the quacking of a duck.

[33] Syme had fallen silent for a moment, and with the handle of his spoon was tracing patterns in the puddle of stew. The voice from the other table quacked rapidly on, easily audible in spite of the surrounding din.

[34] "There is a word in Newspeak," said Syme. "I don't know whether you know it: *duckspeak*, to quack like a duck. It is one of those interesting words that have two contradictory meanings. Applied to an opponent, it is abuse; applied to someone you agree with, it is praise."

[35] Unquestionably Syme will be vaporized, Winston thought again. He thought it with a kind of sadness, although well knowing that Syme despised him and slightly disliked him, and was fully capable of denouncing him as a thought-criminal if he saw any reason for doing so. There was something subtly wrong with Syme. There was something that he lacked: discretion, aloofness, a sort of saving stupidity. You could not say that he was unorthodox. He believed in the principles of Ingsoc, he venerated Big Brother, he rejoiced over victories, he hated heretics, not merely with sincerity but with a sort of restless zeal, an up-to-dateness of information, which the ordinary Party member did not approach. Yet a faint air of disreputability always clung to him. He said things that would have been better unsaid, he had read too many books, he frequented the Chestnut Tree Café, haunt of painters and musicians. There was no law, not even an unwritten law, against frequenting the Chestnut Tree Café, yet the place was somehow ill-omened. The

old, discredited leaders of the Party had been used to gather there before they were finally purged. Goldstein himself, it was said, had sometimes been seen there, years and decades ago. Syme's fate was not difficult to foresee. And yet it was a fact that if Syme grasped, even for three seconds, the nature of his, Winston's, secret opinions, he would betray him instantly to the Thought Police. So would anybody else, for that matter, but Syme more than most. Zeal was not enough. Orthodoxy was unconsciousness.

FOR REVIEW AND DISCUSSION

Content

1. What does Syme mean when he says that he is *destroying words?*

2. Do you think that it is possible to remove systematically specific words from a language?

3. Are *shades of meaning* really *useless?* Support your answer by drawing on examples.

4. Syme asks, "What justification is there for a word which is simply the opposite of some other words?" There is a disarming logic in Syme's reasoning. How would you argue against him? Whose argument is more convincing?

Rhetoric

1. What irony is there in Winston's conviction that Syme will be vaporized? In what way is the irony increased when we consider the reasons why Syme, according to Winston, will be vaporized?

2. Notice how much information about Newspeak Orwell conveys to us through Syme's dialogue. How might our understanding of that information be different than it now is had Orwell presented it simply through third-person narration?

3. How would you characterize the general atmosphere of the cafeteria scene? What descriptive details in the narrative contribute to the creation of this atmosphere?

Classroom Exercises

1. Discuss whether you believe, as Orwell did, that language was potentially the most fearsome and destructive weapon in the arsenal of repressive government.

2. Discuss whether it is possible for language to degenerate so that one can talk without thinking at all, without speaking "in the true sense" but quacking "a noise uttered in unconsciousness."

FOR FURTHER READING

Richard M. Nixon

STATEMENT: APRIL 30, 1973

President Nixon delivered this speech on national television several months before the Watergate scandal finally forced him from office. Here he attempts to explain his role in the crisis and his attitude toward developing events. Of course, his subsequent resignation now colors our reading of the speech. But any reader denied the perspective of historical hindsight will still find ample evidence in this "statement" of what Donna Woolfolk Cross calls "bamboozling."

9:01 P.M. EDT

[1]   I want to talk to you tonight from my heart on a subject of deep concern to every American.

[2]   In recent months, members of my Administration and officials of the Committee for the Re-election of the President—including some of my closest friends and most trusted aides—have been charged with involvement in what has come to be known as the Watergate affair. These include charges of illegal activity during and preceding the 1972 Presidential election and charges that responsible officials participated in efforts to cover up that illegal activity.

[3]   The inevitable result of these charges has been to raise serious questions about the integrity of the White House itself. Tonight I wish to address those questions.

[4]   Last June 17, while I was in Florida trying to get a few days' rest after my visit to Moscow, I first learned from news reports of the Watergate break-in. I was appalled at this senseless, illegal action, and I was shocked to learn that employees of the Re-election Committee were apparently among those guilty. I immediately ordered an investigation by appropriate government authorities. On September 15, as you will recall, indictments were brought against seven defendants in the case.

[5]   As the investigations went forward, I repeatedly asked those conducting the investigation whether there was any reason to believe that members of my Administration were in any way involved. I received repeated assurances that there were not. Because of these continuing reassurances—because I believed the reports I was

STATEMENT: APRIL 30, 1973

getting, because I had faith in the persons from whom I was getting them—I discounted the stories in the press that appeared to implicate members of my Administration or other officials of the campaign committee.

[6] Until March of this year, I remained convinced that the denials were true and that the charges of involvement by members of the White House staff were false. The comments I made during this period, and the comments made by my Press Secretary on my behalf, were based on the information provided to us at the time we made those comments. However, new information then came to me which persuaded me that there was a real possibility that some of these charges were true, and suggesting further that there had been an effort to conceal the facts both from the public, from you, and from me.

[7] As a result, on March 21, I personally assumed the responsibility for coordinating intensive new inquiries into the matter, and I personally ordered those conducting the investigations to get all the facts and to report them directly to me, right here in this office.

[8] I again ordered that all persons in the Government or at the Re-election Committee should cooperate fully with the FBI, the prosecutors and the Grand Jury. I also ordered that anyone who refused to cooperate in telling the truth would be asked to resign from government service. And, with ground rules adopted that would preserve the basic constitutional separation of powers between the Congress and the Presidency, I directed that members of the White House staff should appear and testify voluntarily under oath before the Senate Committee investigating Watergate.

[9] I was determined that we should get to the bottom of the matter, and that the truth should be fully brought out—no matter who was involved.

[10] At the same time, I was determined not to take precipitate action, and to avoid, if at all possible, any action that would appear to reflect on innocent people. I wanted to be fair. But I knew that in the final analysis, the integrity of this office—public faith in the integrity of this office—would have to take priority over all personal considerations.

[11] Today, in one of the most difficult decisions of my Presidency, I accepted the resignations of two of my closest associates in the White House—Bob Haldeman, John Ehrlichman—two of the finest public servants it has been my privilege to know.

[12] I want to stress that in accepting these resignations, I mean to leave no implication whatever of personal wrongdoing on their part, and I leave no implication tonight of implication on the part of others who have been charged in this matter. But in matters as sensitive as guarding the integrity of our democratic process, it is essential not only that rigorous legal and ethical standards be observed, but also that the public, you, have the total confidence that they are both being

observed and enforced by those in authority and particularly by the President of the United States. They agreed with me that this move was necessary in order to restore that confidence.

[13] Because Attorney General Kleindienst—though a distinguished public servant, my personal friend for twenty years, with no personal involvement whatever in this matter—has been a close personal and professional associate of some of those who are involved in this case, he and I both felt that it was also necessary to name a new Attorney General.

[14] The Counsel to the President, John Dean, has also resigned.

[15] As the new Attorney General, I have today named Elliot Richardson, a man of unimpeachable integrity and rigorously high principle. I have directed him to do everything necessary to ensure that the Department of Justice has the confidence and trust of every law abiding person in this country.

[16] I have given him absolute authority to make all decisions bearing upon the prosecution of the Watergate case and related matters. I have instructed him that if he should consider it appropriate, he has the authority to name a special supervising prosecutor for matters arising out of the case.

[17] Whatever may appear to have been the case before—whatever improper activities may yet be discovered in connection with this whole sordid affair—I want the American people, I want you to know beyond the shadow of a doubt that during my terms as President, justice will be pursued fairly, fully, and impartially, no matter who is involved. This office is a sacred trust and I am determined to be worthy of that trust.

[18] Looking back at the history of this case, two questions arise:
How could it have happened?
Who is to blame?

[19] Political commentators have correctly observed that during my twenty-seven years in politics, I have always previously insisted on running my own campaigns for office.

[20] But 1972 presented a very different situation. In both domestic and foreign policy, 1972 was a year of crucially important decisions, of intense negotiations, of vital new directions, particularly in working toward the goal which has been my overriding concern throughout my political career—the goal of bringing peace to America and peace to the world.

[21] That is why I decided, as the 1972 campaign approached, that the Presidency should come first and politics second. To the maximum extent possible, therefore, I sought to delegate campaign operations, and to remove the day-to-day campaign decisions from the President's office and from the White House. I also, as you recall, severely limited the number of my own campaign appearances.

STATEMENT: APRIL 30, 1973   303

[22] Who, then, is to blame for what happened in this case?

[23] For specific criminal actions by specific individuals, those who committed those actions, must, of course, bear the liability and pay the penalty.

[24] For the fact that alleged improper actions took place within the White House or within my campaign organization, the easiest course would be for me to blame those to whom I delegated the responsibility to run the campaign. But that would be a cowardly thing to do.

[25] I will not place the blame on subordinates—on people whose zeal exceeded their judgment, and who may have done wrong in a cause they deeply believed to be right.

[26] In any organization, the man at the top must bear the responsibility. That responsibility, therefore, belongs here, in this office. I accept that. And I pledge to you tonight, from this office, that I will do everything in my power to ensure that the guilty are brought to justice, and that such abuses are purged from our political processes in the years to come, long after I have left this office.

[27] Some people, quite properly appalled at the abuses that occurred, will say that Watergate demonstrates the bankruptcy of the American political system. I believe precisely the opposite is true. Watergate represented a series of illegal acts and bad judgments by a number of individuals. It was the system that has brought the facts to light and that will bring those guilty to justice—a system that in this case has included a determined Grand Jury, honest prosecutors, a courageous Judge, John Sirica, and a vigorous free press.

[28] It is essential now that we place our faith in that system—and especially in the judicial system. It is essential that we let the judicial process go forward, respecting those safeguards that are established to protect the innocent as well as to convict the guilty. It is essential that in reacting to the excesses of others, we not fall into excesses ourselves.

[29] It is also essential that we not be so distracted by events such as this that we neglect the vital work before us, before this Nation, before America, at a time of critical importance to America and the world.

[30] Since March, when I first learned that the Watergate affair might in fact be far more serious than I had been led to believe, it has claimed far too much of my own time and attention.

[31] Whatever may now transpire in the case—whatever the actions of the Grand Jury, whatever the outcome of any eventual trials—I must now turn my full attention once again to the larger duties of this office. I owe it to this great office that I hold, and I owe it to you—to our country.

[32] I know that as Attorney General, Elliot Richardson will be both fair and

fearless in pursuing this case wherever it leads. I am confident that with him in charge, justice will be done.

[33] There is vital work to be done toward our goal of lasting structure of peace in the world—work that cannot wait. Work that I must do.

[34] Tomorrow, for example, Chancellor Brandt of West Germany will visit the White House for talks that are a vital element of "The Year of Europe" as 1973 has been called. We are already preparing for the next Soviet-American summit meeting, later this year.

[35] This is also a year in which we are seeking to negotiate a mutual and balanced reduction of armed forces in Europe, which will reduce our defense budget and allow us to have funds for other purposes at home so desperately needed. It is the year when the United States and Soviet negotiators will seek to work out the second and even more important round of our talks on limiting nuclear arms, and of reducing the danger of a nuclear war that would destroy civilization as we know it. It is a year in which we confront the difficult tasks of maintaining peace in Southeast Asia and in the potentially explosive Middle East.

[36] There is also vital work to be done right here in America—to ensure prosperity, and that means a good job for everyone who wants to work, to control inflation, that I know worries every housewife, everyone who tries to balance a family budget in America, to set in motion new and better ways of ensuring progress toward a better life for all Americans.

[37] When I think of this office—of what it means—I think of all the things that I want to accomplish for this nation—of all the things I want to accomplish for you.

[38] On Christmas Eve, during my terrible personal ordeal of the renewed bombing of North Vietnam, which after twelve years of war, finally helped to bring America peace with honor, I sat down just before midnight. I wrote out some of my goals for my second term as President.

[39] Let me read them to you.

[40] "To make it possible for our children, and for our children's children, to live in a world of peace.

[41] "To make this country be more than ever a land of opportunity—of equal opportunity, full opportunity for every American.

[42] "To provide jobs for all who can work, and generous help for all who cannot.

[43] "To establish a climate of decency, and civility, in which each person respects the feelings and the dignity and the God-given rights of his neighbor.

[44] "To make this a land in which each person can dare to dream, can live his dreams—not in fear, but in hope—proud of his community, proud of his country, proud of what America has meant to himself and to the world."

STATEMENT: APRIL 30, 1973 305

[45] These are great goals. I believe we can, we must work for them. We can achieve them. But we cannot achieve these goals unless we dedicate ourselves to another goal.

[46] We must maintain the integrity of the White House, and that integrity must be real, not transparent. There can be no whitewash at the White House.

[47] We must reform our political process—ridding it not only of the violations of the law, but also of the ugly mob violence, and other inexcusable campaign tactics that have been too often practiced and too readily accepted in the past—including those that may have been a response by one side to the excesses or expected excesses of the other side. Two wrongs do not make a right.

[48] I have been in public life for more than a quarter of a century. Like any other calling, politics has good people, and bad people. And let me tell you, the great majority in politics, in the Congress, in the Federal Government, in the State Government, are good people. I know that it can be very easy, under the intensive pressures of a campaign, for even well-intentioned people to fall into shady tactics—to rationalize this on the grounds that what is at stake is of such importance to the Nation that the end justifies the means. And both of our great parties have been guilty of such tactics in the past.

[49] In recent years, however, the campaign excesses that have occurred on all sides have provided a sobering demonstration of how far this false doctrine can take us. The lesson is clear: America, in its political campaigns, must not again fall into the trap of letting the end, however great that end is, justify the means.

[50] I urge the leaders of both political parties, I urge citizens, all of you, everywhere, to join in working toward a new set of standards, new rules and procedures—to ensure that future elections will be as nearly free of such abuses as they possibly can be made. This is my goal. I ask you to join in making it America's goal.

[51] When I was inaugurated for a second term this past January 20, I gave each member of my Cabinet and each member of my senior White House staff a special four-year calendar with each day marked to show the number of days remaining to the administration. In the inscription on each calendar, I wrote these words: "The Presidential term which begins today consists of 1,461 days—no more, no less. Each can be a day of strengthening and renewal for America; each can add depth and dimension to the American experience. If we strive together, if we make the most of the challenge and the opportunity that these days offer us, they can stand out as great days for America, and great moments in the history of the world."

[52] I looked at my own calendar this morning up at Camp David as I was working on this speech. It showed exactly 1,361 days remaining in my term. I want these to be the best days in America's history, because I love America. I deeply believe that America is the hope of the world, and I know that in the quality and wisdom of the

leadership America gives lies the only hope for millions of people all over the world, that they can live their lives in peace and freedom. We must be worthy of that hope, in every sense of the word. Tonight, I ask for your prayers to help me in everything that I do throughout the days of my Presidency to be worthy of their hopes and of yours.

[53] God bless America and God bless each and every one of you.

9:25 P.M. EDT

FOR REVIEW AND DISCUSSION

Content

1. Paraphrase paragraph 10 in such a way that President Nixon's meaning becomes clear.

2. What support does President Nixon offer for his assertion that "we must maintain the integrity of the White House"?

3. Just past the midpoint of the speech (paragraph 22), President Nixon asks, "Who, then, is to blame for what happened in this case?" Several lines later *he* accepts *responsibility*. Has he answered his own question?

4. Has he really accepted *responsibility?* Explain.

Rhetoric

1. What reason might President Nixon have for casting the last sentence of paragraph 4 in the *passive voice?*

2. What is the strongest, most convincing point in the speech? What makes the point convincing?

3. In what ways is the second half of the speech related to the first half?

4. This speech has frequently been called a masterpiece of its kind. Explain what kind of masterpiece it is.

Classroom Exercises

1. Notice that President Nixon does not admit that any laws have actually been broken or that anyone is guilty of any wrongdoing. Discuss how he manages to talk about Watergate without making those admissions.

2. To what extent must we be aware of President Nixon's *purpose* in speaking before we can determine the *meaning* of his speech? Cite specific sections of the speech as you discuss the relation between purpose and meaning.

FOR DISCUSSION AND WRITING

1. Explain whether Huxley would or would not praise the prayer of Twain's stranger as an example of "correct thinking."

2. Compare and contrast Orwell's description of *Newspeak* and *Duckspeak* with Gambino's treatment of *Washingtonspeak*.

3. Apply the chapter's descriptions of political language to a speech by a current politician. (You should be able to find transcripts of such speeches in your library's periodical room.) Then evaluate the degree to which its author resorts to "bamboozling."

4. Using the logical and rhetorical techniques discussed in chapter 6, analyze and compare the two prayers in "The War Prayer."

5. *1984* was first published in 1947. How accurately did Orwell prophesy some features of our present society?

8 ADVERTISERS AND THEIR LANGUAGE

> *The survival of democracy depends on the ability of large numbers of people to make realistic choices in the light of adequate information.*
> ALDOUS HUXLEY
>
> *I can't tell Nucoa margarine from the high-priced spread.*
> A HOUSEWIFE

Advertising language more often than not appeals to our emotions rather than to our intelligence and reason. We want to be better looking, more intelligent, more cosmopolitan, and we want to believe people who promise that we can be these things without effort. The actual words that advertisers use to convince us to buy their products are discussed by Paul Stevens, while Jerzy Kosinski analyzes the meaning and effect of some of those words. David Ogilvy, an advertising man like Stevens, provides some tips on how to write effective advertisements and discusses copywriting strategy in general.

Jerzy Kosinski

THE REALITY BEHIND WORDS

Kosinski, a Polish-born novelist and educator, is a trenchant observer of American culture. Here, by means of an amusing extended example, he reminds us of that first principle of general semantics that advertisers seem only too eager to help us forget: The word is not *the thing it symbolizes!*

[1]   New Haven—The American poet Chayym Zeldis once told me that the reason he could do without certain things in life was that their names produced unwelcomed responses in him, believing, as I do, that language is indeed the creator of reality when it gives a name to it. But one does not have to be a poet or a novelist—or an advertising sloganeer—to realize that words, like commanding officers and their men, can massacre innocent bystanders; and that often it is language that evokes in us a passion to embrace or reject others, to love or kill, to be free or be confined.

[2]   Particularly if the hand holds a gun, we value words: we do not kill, we "evacuate" or "waste"; we don't ship out bodies, we "transport remains" home, and we don't fail, we "underachieve."

[3]   Especially when the hand clasps the credit card of commerce, we don't care whether the words matter, permitting commercials and advertising to revise our imaginations daily without the blink of an eye. In either case, imagine if you will this daily scene in your friendly neighborhood courtroom peopled with the judge, defendants, prosecutors, lawyers, jurors, and among the audience, the impatient representatives of our friendly automobile insurance companies.

[4]   The case before the court: a multiple automobile crash on your friendly neighborhood highway, which has caused a few deaths, one or two dismemberments, and considerable property damage. All the defendants plead not guilty; they claim that just before the crash each of them was carefully driving his own friendly, properly registered, insured and recently inspected American-made motor vehicle. Their car models are called—as they are in actuality—Demon, Super Bee, Firebird, Tempest, Charger, Toronado, Centurion, Cutlass and Road Runner. The motor vehicles they inadvertently crashed into are named Thunderbird, Rebel, Cyclone, Swinger, Sting Ray, Dart, Barracuda and Fury. The accidents took place on a friendly community road called the expressway.

Copyright © 1971 by The New York Times Company. Reprinted by permission.

[5] ". . . and therefore, Your Honor, when I saw this man trying to pass by me on the right in his Challenger, sure I stepped on it. Why, my Boss, which I just bought . . ." protests one defendant.

[6] "Objection, Your Honor. The car's name is irrelevant!" interrupts the prosecutor.

[7] Should an objection against a name—a word—be sustained in this instance? Who but friendly defendants in most cases kill over fifty thousand friendly Americans yearly in car accidents on our friendly highways? Considering the pain, destruction and death these drivers caused, would it have been more appropriate if their four-wheel modes of transportation were named by car makers from Detroit—as indeed they ought to be—Collider, Veerer and Catapulter (for the young crowd, of course); Relapser (for those who think young); Maimer (medium-priced range); Polluter (top of the line); Autopsy-Coupe 400 (limited edition); Annihilator, Waster and Evacuator (the last three models available to military personnel at no extra cost with protective camouflage paint); and the compact Off-Roader?

[8] Would a man driving the economical Super-Wound Convertible, for instance, race a lady smiling from her ash-colored Vista-Paralyso? Would a citizen in a supercharged Cougar drag-race against a couple of teen-agers in their Wildcat, if instead he were driving a Custom-Disintegrator and they drove their parents' Hardhat-Vapido? Of course not!

[9] To my mind, a man proudly driving his Comet, Satellite or Galaxie is more than likely imaginatively to leave this friendly earth's orbit simply because the automobile's name makes him feel that he is driving some extraterrestrial vehicle.

[10] Must our attitude toward the language continue to remain that ambiguous—or that fraudulent? Too frequently language manipulates us when we are unaware of our responses to it; yet when we are conscious of these responses we conveniently dupe ourselves by ignoring the language whenever it becomes threatening.

[11] "Every individual or national degradation," Joseph de Maisire notes, "is immediately foretold by a strictly proportioned degradation in the language itself." Today our society is continually subverted by what is one of its greatest threats—monolithic, dictatorial Wordcon.

FOR REVIEW AND DISCUSSION

Content

1. Study advertisements for a few of the automobiles that Kosinski mentions. Discuss whether the themes of those advertisements seem to support Kosinski's argument.

THE REALITY BEHIND WORDS

2. Explain why you do or do not accept Kosinski's argument that the names of the cars we drive contribute to the death toll on highways. With apologies to Alice and to Lewis Carroll, "Can a name do so much?"

3. Discuss Kosinski's assertion that "we conveniently dupe ourselves by ignoring the language when it becomes threatening."

Rhetoric

1. What purpose does the second paragraph of the essay serve?

2. Kosinski does not define the neologism *Wordcon*. How does he expect us to understand the term?

3. The author feels strongly about his subject. At what points in the essay is this apparent?

4. What tone is implied in the tags "friendly neighborhood" and "friendly community" applied to the courtroom, the automobile companies, and so forth?

5. Other selections in this book contain pointed humor. Kosinski's, however, might be described as *black humor*. From the general tone of the essay, try to define black humor and to explain its appropriateness in this instance.

Classroom Exercises

1. Decide on a name that suggests the style of car you would like to drive. What does that name say about your driving character? Compare the name you choose to the names that other members of the class choose, and discuss similarities and differences.

2. As a class, make a list of possible names for cars, describing the kind of car that would be appropriate for the name. For instance, the Plymouth Possum could be a small gray car for people who do a lot of night-time driving.

Paul Stevens

WEASEL WORDS: GOD'S LITTLE HELPERS

We turn here to a detailed examination of some of the words advertisers commonly exploit in order to exploit us. Federal law prohibits advertisers from lying to us—and they usually don't. But they certainly make us work to discover the truth, as Stevens makes clear in this selection. As you read, consider to what degree advertisers capitalize on our ability and willingness to lie to ourselves.

[1] First of all, you know what a weasel is, right? It's a small, slimy animal that eats small birds and other animals, and is especially fond of devouring vermin. Now, consider for a moment the kind of winning personality he must have. I mean, what kind of a guy would get his jollies eating rats and mice? Would you invite him to a party? Take him home to meet your mother? This is one of the slyest and most cunning of all creatures; sneaky, slippery, and thoroughly obnoxious. And so it is with great and warm personal regard for these attributes that we humbly award this King of All Devious the honor of bestowing his name upon our golden sword: the weasel word.

[2] A weasel word is "a word used in order to evade or retreat from a direct or forthright statement or position" (Webster). In other words, if we can't say it, we'll weasel it. And, in fact, a weasel word has become more than just an evasion or retreat. We've trained our weasels. They can do anything. They can make you hear things that aren't being said, accept as truths things that have only been implied, and believe things that have only been suggested. Come to think of it, not only do we have our weasels trained, but they, in turn, have got you trained. When *you* hear a weasel word, you automatically hear the implication. Not the real meaning, but the meaning *it* wants *you* to hear. So if you're ready for a little re-education, let's take a good look under a strong light at the two kinds of weasel words.

WORDS THAT MEAN THINGS THEY REALLY DON'T MEAN

Help

[3] That's it. "Help." It means "aid" or "assist." Nothing more. Yet, "help" is the one single word which, in all the annals of advertising, has done the most to say

From *I Can Sell You Anything* by Paul Stevens. Copyright © 1972 by Ballantine Books, Inc. Reprinted by permission of Ballantine Books, a Division of Random House, Inc.

something that couldn't be said. Because "help" is the great qualifier; once you say it, you can say almost anything after it. In short, "help" has helped help us the most.

> Helps keep you young
> Helps prevent cavities
> Helps keep your house germ-free

[4]   "Help" qualifies everything. You've never heard anyone say, "This product will keep you young," or "This toothpaste will positively prevent cavities for all time." Obviously, we can't say anything like that, because there aren't any products like that made. But by adding that one little word, "help," in front, we can use the strongest language possible afterward. And the most fascinating part of it is, you are immune to the word. You literally don't hear the word "help." You only hear what comes after it. And why not? That's strong language, and likely to be much more important to you than the silly little word at the front end.

[5]   I would guess that 75 percent of all advertising uses the word "help." Think, for a minute, about how many times each day you hear these phrases:

> Helps stop . . .
> Helps prevent . . .
> Helps fight . . .
> Helps overcome . . .
> Helps you feel . . .
> Helps you look . . .

I could go on and on, but so could you. Just as a simple exercise, call it homework if you wish, tonight when you plop down in front of the boob tube for your customary three and a half hours of violence and/or situation comedies, take a pad and pencil, and keep score. See if you can count how many times the word "help" comes up during the commercials. Instead of going to the bathroom during the pause before Marcus Welby operates, or raiding the refrigerator prior to witnessing the Mod Squad wipe out a nest of dope pushers, stick with it. Count the "helps," and discover just how dirty a four-letter word can be.

Like

[6]   Coming in second, but only losing by a nose, is the word "like," used in comparison. Watch:

> It's like getting one bar free
> Cleans like a white tornado
> It's like taking a trip to Portugal

[7]   Okay. "Like" is a qualifier, and is used in much the same way as "help." But "like" is also a comparative element, with a very specific purpose; we use "like" to get you to stop thinking about the product per se, and to get you thinking about

something that is bigger or better or different from the product we're selling. In other words, we can make you believe that the product is more than it is by likening it to something else.

[8]   Take a look at that first phrase, straight out of recent Ivory Soap advertising. On the surface of it, they tell you that four bars of Ivory cost about the same as three bars of most other soaps. So, if you're going to spend a certain amount of money on soap, you can buy four bars instead of three. Therefore, it's like getting one bar free. Now, the question you have to ask yourself is, "Why the weasel? Why do they say 'like'? Why don't they just come out and say, 'You get one bar free'?" The answer is, of course, that for one reason or another, you really don't. Here are two possible reasons. One: sure, you get four bars, but in terms of the actual amount of soap that you get, it may very well be the same as in three bars of another brand. Remember, Ivory has a lot of air in it—that's what makes it float. And air takes up room. Room that could otherwise be occupied by more soap. So, in terms of pure product, the amount of actual soap in four bars of Ivory may be only as much as the actual amount of soap in three bars of most others. That's why we can't—or won't—come out with a straightforward declaration such as, "You get 25 percent more soap," or "Buy three bars, and get the fourth one free."

[9]   Reason number two: the actual cost and value of the product. Did it ever occur to you that Ivory may simply be a cheaper soap to make and, therefore, a cheaper soap to sell? After all, it doesn't have any perfume or hexachlorophene, or other additives that can raise the cost of manufacturing. It's plain, simple, cheap soap, and so it can be sold for less money while still maintaining a profit margin as great as more expensive soaps. By way of illustrating this, suppose you were trying to decide whether to buy a Mercedes-Benz or a Ford. Let's say the Mercedes cost $7,000, and the Ford $3,500. Now the Ford salesman comes up to you with this deal: as long as you're considering spending $7,000 on a car, buy my Ford for $7,000 and I'll give you a second Ford, free! Well, the same principle can apply to Ivory: as long as you're considering spending 35 cents on soap, buy my cheaper soap, and I'll give you more of it.

[10]   I'm sure there are other reasons why Ivory uses the weasel "like." Perhaps you've thought of one or two yourself. That's good. You're starting to think.

[11]   Now, what about that wonderful white tornado? Ajax pulled that one out of the hat some eight years ago, and you're still buying it. It's a classic example of the use of the word "like" in which we can force you to think, not about the product itself, but about something bigger, more exciting, certainly more powerful than a bottle of fancy ammonia. The word "like" is used here as a transfer word, which gets you away from the obvious—the odious job of getting down on your hands and knees and scrubbing your kitchen floor—and into the world of fantasy, where we can imply that this little bottle of miracles will supply all the elbow grease you need. Isn't that the name of the game? The whirlwind activity of the tornado replacing the

whirlwind motion of your arm? Think about the swirling of the tornado, and all the work it will save you. Think about the power of that devastating windstorm; able to lift houses, overturn cars, and now, pick the dirt up off your floor. And we get the license to do it simply by using the word "like."

[12] It's a copywriter's dream, because we don't have to substantiate anything. When we compare our product to "another leading brand," we'd better be able to prove what we say. But how can you compare ammonia to a windstorm? It's ludicrous. It can't be done. The whole statement is so ridiculous it couldn't be challenged by the government or the networks. So it went on the air, and it worked. Because the little word "like" let us take you out of the world of reality, and into your own fantasies.

[13] Speaking of fantasies, how about that trip to Portugal? Mateus Rosé is actually trying to tell you that you will be transported clear across the Atlantic Ocean merely by sipping their wine. "Oh, come on," you say. "You don't expect me to believe that." Actually, we don't expect you to believe it. But we do expect you to get our meaning. This is called "romancing the product," and it is made possible by the dear little "like." In this case, we deliberately bring attention to the word, and we ask you to join us in setting reality aside for a moment. We take your hand and gently lead you down the path of moonlit nights, graceful dancers, and mysterious women. Are we saying that these things are all contained inside our wine? Of course not. But what we mean is, our wine is part of all this, and with a little help from "like," we'll get you to feel that way, too. So don't think of us as a bunch of peasants squashing a bunch of grapes. As a matter of fact, don't think of us at all. Feel with us.

[14] "Like" is a virus that kills. You'd better get immune to it.

Other Weasels

[15] "Help" and "like" are the two weasels so powerful that they can stand on their own. There are countless other words, not quite so potent, but equally effective when used in conjunction with our two basic weasels, or with each other. Let me show you a few.

[16] **Virtual or Virtually.** How many times have you responded to an ad that said:

> Virtually trouble-free . . .
> Virtually foolproof . . .
> Virtually never needs service . . .

Ever remember what "virtual" means? It means "in essence or effect, but not in fact." Important—"but not in fact." Yet today the word "virtually" is interpreted by you as meaning "almost or just about the same as. . . ." Well, gang, it just isn't true. "Not," in fact, means not, in fact. I was scanning, rather longingly I must confess, through the brochure Chevrolet publishes for its Corvette, and I came to this phrase: "The seats in the 1972 Corvette are virtually handmade." That had me, for a minute. I almost took the bait of that lovely little weasel. I almost decided that those seats were just about completely handmade. And then I remembered. Those seats were not, *in fact*, handmade. Remember, "virtually" means "not, in fact," or you will, in fact, get sold down the river.

[17] **Acts or Works.** These two action words are rarely used alone, and are generally accompanied by "like." They need help to work, mostly because they are verbs, but their implied meaning is deadly, nonetheless. Here are the key phrases:

> Acts like . . .
> Acts against . . .
> Works like . . .
> Works against . . .
> Works to prevent (or help prevent) . . .

You see what happens? "Acts" or "works" brings an action to the product that might not otherwise be there. When we say that a certain cough syrup "acts on the cough control center," the implication is that the syrup goes to this mysterious organ and immediately makes it better. But the implication here far exceeds what the truthful promise should be. An act is simply a deed. So the claim "acts on" simply means it performs a deed on. What that deed is, we may never know.

[18] The rule of thumb is this: if we can't say "cures" or "fixes" or use any other positive word, we'll nail you with "acts like" or "works against," and get you thinking about something else. Don't.

Miscellaneous Weasels

[19] **Can Be.** This is for comparison, and what we do is to find an announcer who can really make it sound positive. But keep your ears open. "Crest can be of significant value when used in . . . ," etc., is indicative of an ideal situation, and most of us don't live in ideal situations.

[20] **Up To.** Here's another way of expressing an ideal situation. Remember the cigarette that said it was aged, or "cured for up to eight long, lazy weeks"? Well, that could, and should, be interpreted as meaning that the tobaccos used were cured anywhere from one hour to eight weeks. We like to glamorize the ideal situation; it's up to you to bring it back to reality.

[21] **As Much As.**   More of the same. "As much as 20 percent greater mileage" with our gasoline again promises the ideal, but qualifies it.

[22] **Refreshes, Comforts, Tackles, Fights, Comes On.**   Just a handful of the same action weasels, in the same category as "acts" and "works," though not as frequently used. The way to complete the thought here is to ask the simple question, "How?" Usually, you won't get an answer. That's because, usually, the weasel will run and hide.

[23] **Feel *or* The Feel Of.**   This is the first of our subjective weasels. When we deal with a subjective word, it is simply a matter of opinion. In our opinion, Naugehyde has the feel of real leather. So we can say it. And, indeed, if you were to touch leather, and then touch Naugehyde, you may very well agree with us. But that doesn't mean it is real leather, only that it feels the same. The best way to handle subjective weasels is to complete the thought yourself, by simply saying, "But it isn't." At least that way you can remain grounded in reality.

[24] **The Look Of *or* Looks Like.**   "Look" is the same as "feel," our subjective opinion. Did you ever walk into a Woolworth's and see those $29.95 masterpieces hanging in their "Art Gallery"? "The look of a real oil painting," it will say. "But it isn't," you will now reply. And probably be $29.95 richer for it.

WORDS THAT HAVE NO SPECIFIC MEANING

[25]   If you have kids, then you have all kinds of breakfast cereals in the house. When I was a kid, it was Rice Krispies, the breakfast cereal that went snap, crackle, and pop. (One hell of a claim for a product that is supposed to offer nutritional benefits.) Or Wheaties, the breakfast of champions, whatever that means. Nowadays, we're forced to a confrontation with Quisp, Quake, Lucky Stars, Cocoa-Puffs, Clunkers, Blooies, Snarkles and Razzmatazz. And they all have one thing in common: they're all "fortified." Some are simply "fortified with vitamins," while others are specifically "fortified with vitamin D," or some other letter. But what does it all mean?

[26]   "Fortified" means "added on to." But "fortified," like so many other weasel words of indefinite meaning, simply doesn't tell us enough. If, for instance, a cereal were to contain one unit of vitamin D, and the manufacturers added some chemical which would produce two units of vitamin D, they could then claim that the cereal was "fortified with twice as much vitamin D." So what? It would still be about as nutritional as sawdust.

[27]   The point is, weasel words with no specific meaning don't tell us enough, but we have come to accept them as factual statements closely associated with something good that has been done to the product. Here's another example.

Enriched

[28] We use this one when we have a product that starts out with nothing. You mostly find it in bread, where the bleaching process combined with the chemicals used as preservatives renders the loaves totally void of anything but filler. So the manufacturer puts a couple of drops of vitamins into the batter, and presto! It's enriched. Sounds great when you say it. Looks great when you read it. But what you have to determine is, is it really great? Figure out what information is missing, and then try to supply that information. The odds are, you won't. Even the breakfast cereals that are playing it straight, like Kellogg's Special K, leave something to be desired. They tell you what vitamins you get, and how much of each in one serving. The catch is, what constitutes a serving? They say, one ounce. So now you have to whip out your baby scale and weigh one serving. Do you have any idea how much that is? Maybe you do. Maybe you don't care. Okay, so you polish off this mound of dried stuff, and now what? You have ostensibly received the minimum, repeat, minimum dosage of certain vitamins for the day. One day. And you still have to go find the vitamins you didn't get. Try looking it up on a box of frozen peas. Bet you won't find it. But do be alert to "fortified" and "enriched." Asking the right questions will prove beneficial.

[29] Did you buy that last sentence? Too bad, because I weaseled you, with the word "beneficial." Think about it.

Flavor and Taste

[30] These are two totally subjective words that allow us to claim marvelous things about products that are edible. Every cigarette in the world has claimed the best taste. Every supermarket has advertised the most flavorful meat. And let's not forget "aroma," a subdivision of this category. Wouldn't you like to have a nickel for every time a room freshener (a weasel in itself) told you it would make your home "smell fresh as all outdoors"? Well, they can say it, because smell, like taste and flavor, is a subjective thing. And, incidentally, there are no less than three weasels in that phrase. "Smell" is the first. Then, there's "as" (a substitute for the ever-popular "like"), and, finally, "fresh," which, in context, is a subjective comparison, rather than the primary definition of "new."

[31] Now we can use an unlimited number of combinations of these weasels for added impact. "Fresher-smelling clothes." "Fresher-tasting tobacco." "Tastes like grandma used to make." Unfortunately, there's no sure way of bringing these weasels down to size, simply because you can't define them accurately. Trying to ascertain the meaning of "taste" in any context is like trying to push a rope up a hill. All you can do is be aware that these words are subjective, and represent only one opinion—usually that of the manufacturer.

Style and Good Looks

[32] Anyone for buying a new car? Okay, which is the one with the good looks? The smart new styling? What's that you say? All of them? Well, you're right. Because this is another group of subjective opinions. And it is the subjective and collective opinion of both Detroit and Madison Avenue that the following cars have "bold new styling": Buick Riviera, Plymouth Satellite, Dodge Monaco, Mercury Brougham, and you can fill in the spaces for the rest. Subjectively, you have to decide on which bold new styling is, indeed, bold new styling. Then, you might spend a minute or two trying to determine what's going on under that styling. The rest I leave to Ralph Nader.

Different, Special, and Exclusive

[33] To be different, you have to be not the same as. Here, you must rely on your own good judgment and common sense. Exclusive formulas and special combinations of ingredients are coming at you every day, in every way. You must constantly assure yourself that, basically, all products in any given category are the same. So when you hear "special," "exclusive," or "different," you have to establish two things: on what basis are they different, and is that difference an important one? Let me give you a hypothetical example.

[34] All so-called "permanent" antifreeze is basically the same. It is made from a liquid known as ethylene glycol, which has two amazing properties: It has a lower freezing point than water, and a higher boiling point than water. It does not break down (lose its properties), nor will it boil away. And every permanent antifreeze starts with it as a base. Also, just about every antifreeze has now got antileak ingredients, as well as antirust and anticorrosion ingredients. Now, let's suppose that, in formulating the product, one of the companies comes up with a solution that is pink in color, as opposed to all the others, which are blue. Presto—an exclusivity claim. "Nothing else looks like it, nothing else performs like it." Or how about, "Look at ours, and look at anyone else's. You can see the difference our exclusive formula makes." Granted, I'm exaggerating. But did I prove a point? . . .

FUN FOODS

[35] This category is devoted to things made to be ingested, which either have no nutritional or health value, or are not sold as having these values. I include beer, wine, soft drinks, coffee, tea, candy, and most breakfast cereals. As a general point of view, all of these are sold basically on emotionalism, because by definition they have nothing else to offer. Within that framework, I find that they break down into six approaches, as follows:

1. Good, better, best. A statement by the manufacturer asserting that his product is the best one around. This is not a comparison of any kind; it is simply a subjective opinion being expressed by a somewhat partial judge.

2. Taste/taste imagery. Either a claim of superior taste, or one which attempts to describe the taste in imaginative terms. The latter is particularly evident in candies and cereals. . . .

3. You. Remember in the chapter on claims, we talked about "saying something about the user"? It's rampant here, particularly in drinks.

4. Description/recipe. Often fun food advertising will simply describe itself in the most delicious terms, very often taking the form of a recipe. This is rather innocuous stuff, if you are alert to the weasels used.

5. Exploitation. A variation of the "fad" advertising, usually found with products that have been around a long time, and are now getting on the bandwagon.

6. Catch phrases. Most often used with kids, to try to start a fad, or as a memory device. . . .

SUMMARY

[36] A weasel word is a word that's used to imply a meaning that cannot be truthfully stated. Some weasels imply meanings that are not the same as their actual definition, such as "help," "like," or "fortified." They can act as qualifiers and/or comparatives. Other weasels, such as "taste" and "flavor," have no definite meanings, and are simply subjective opinions offered by the manufacturer. A weasel of omission is one that implies a claim so strongly that it forces you to supply the bogus fact. Adjectives are weasels used to convey feelings and emotions to a greater extent than the product itself can.

[37] In dealing with weasels, you must strip away the innuendos and try to ascertain the facts, if any. To do this, you need to ask questions such as: How? Why? How many? How much? Stick to basic definitions of words. Look them up if you have to. Then, apply the strict definition to the text of the advertisement or commercial. "Like" means similar to, but not the same as. "Virtually" means the same in essence, but not in fact.

[38] Above all, never underestimate the devious qualities of a weasel. Weasels twist and turn and hide in the dark shadows. You must come to grips with them, or advertising will rule you forever.

[39] My advice to you is: Beware of weasels. They are nasty and untrainable, and they attack pocketbooks.

FOR REVIEW AND DISCUSSION

Content

1. Explain why it is important to advertisers that we do not *see* weasel words.

2. What is the common thread of meaning or connotation that connects most weasel words?

3. Find two or three magazine ads that use *help*. Do they use the word effectively, or would the "average" person see through the illusion? Explain.

Rhetoric

1. Describe Stevens's attitude toward his audience. (Does Stevens treat his audience as equals to himself or as subordinates?)

2. Is Stevens taunting us with the tricks he describes, or is he trying to inform us? What suggests his purpose?

3. Stevens frequently uses the pronoun *you*, a practice discouraged by many English teachers. What reason might he have for using *you*?

4. Describe the tone of the passage in which Stevens, discussing Ivory soap, says, "That's good. You're starting to think."

5. Review Huxley's "Words and Behavior" (chapter 7). Will Stevens's essay be as relevant to current events forty years from now as Huxley's is to events today? Support your answer with references to both essays.

Classroom Exercises

1. Stevens seems to think that simple awareness of weasel words will prevent us from being "deceived" by advertisements. Discuss the extent to which you agree or disagree with him.

2. Discuss whether Stevens's position is an ethical one. (Is Stevens judging whether it is right or wrong to use weasels?)

3. Study a magazine advertisement for a widely merchandised and popular product. In how many ways does the advertisement try to exploit our apparent willingness to be deceived?

David Ogilvy

HOW TO WRITE POTENT COPY

Like Stevens in the preceding selection, Ogilvy writes from his own experience as a highly successful advertising executive. Whereas Stevens deals with the particular, illusory words of advertisements, Ogilvy discusses the whole advertisement, its total form and content. His concern is the printed advertisement, not the radio or television commercial. Still, we can learn a great deal about general advertising theory from this master practitioner.

I. HEADLINES

[1] The headline is the most important element in most advertisements. It is the telegram which decides the reader whether to read the copy.

[2] On the average, five times as many people read the headline as read the body copy. When you have written your headline, you have spent eighty cents out of your dollar.

[3] If you haven't done some selling in your headline, you have wasted 80 per cent of your client's money. The wickedest of all sins is to run an advertisement *without* a headline. Such headless wonders are still to be found; I don't envy the copywriter who submits one to me.

[4] A change of headline can make a difference of ten to one in sales. I never write fewer than sixteen headlines for a single advertisement, and I observe certain guides in writing them:

> (1) The headline is the "ticket on the meat." Use it to flag down the readers who are prospects for the kind of product you are advertising. If you are selling a remedy for bladder weakness, display the words BLADDER WEAKNESS in your headline; they catch the eye of everyone who suffers from this inconvenience. If you want *mothers* to read your advertisement, display MOTHERS in your headline. And so on.
>   Conversely, do not say anything in your headline which is likely to *exclude* any readers who might be prospects for your product. Thus, if you are advertising a product which can be used equally well by men and women, don't slant your headline at women alone; it would frighten men away.
> (2) Every headline should appeal to the reader's *self-interest*. It should promise her a benefit, as in my headline for Helena Rubinstein's Hormone Cream: HOW WOMEN OVER 35 CAN LOOK YOUNGER.

From *Confessions of an Advertising Man* by David Ogilvy. Copyright © 1963 by David Ogilvy Trustee. Reprinted by permission of Atheneum Publishers.

(3) Always try to inject *new* into your headlines, because the consumer is always on the lookout for new products, or new ways to use an old product, or new improvements in an old product.

The two most powerful words you can use in a headline are FREE and NEW. You can seldom use FREE, but you can almost always use NEW—if you try hard enough.

(4) Other words and phrases which work wonders are HOW TO, SUDDENLY, NOW, ANNOUNCING, INTRODUCING, IT'S HERE, JUST ARRIVED, IMPORTANT DEVELOPMENT, IMPROVEMENT, AMAZING, SENSATIONAL, REMARKABLE, REVOLUTIONARY, STARTLING, MIRACLE, MAGIC, OFFER, QUICK, EASY, WANTED, CHALLENGE, ADVICE TO, THE TRUTH ABOUT, COMPARE, BARGAIN, HURRY, LAST CHANCE.

Don't turn up your nose at these clichés. They may be shopworn, but they work. That is why you see them turn up so often in the headlines of mail-order advertisers and others who can measure the results of their advertisements.

Headlines can be strengthened by the inclusion of *emotional* words, like DARLING, LOVE, FEAR, PROUD, FRIEND, and BABY. One of the most provocative advertisements which has come out of our agency showed a girl in a bathtub, talking to her lover on the telephone. The headline: *Darling, I'm having the most extraordinary experience . . . I'm head over heels in* DOVE.

(5) Five times as many people read the headline as read the body copy, so it is important that these glancers should at least be told what brand is being advertised. That is why you should always include the brand name in your headlines.

(6) Include your selling promise in your headline. This requires long headlines. When the New York University School of Retailing ran headline tests with the cooperation of a big department store, they found that headlines of ten words or longer, containing news and information, consistently sold more merchandise than short headlines.

Headlines containing six to twelve words pull more coupon returns than short headlines, and there is no significant difference between the readership of twelve-word headlines and the readership of three-word headlines. The best headline I ever wrote contained *eighteen* words: *At Sixty Miles an Hour the Loudest Noise in the New Rolls-Royce comes from the electric clock.*[1]

(7) People are more likely to read your body copy if your headline arouses their curiosity; so you should end your headline with a lure to read on.

(8) Some copywriters write *tricky* headlines—puns, literary allusions, and other obscurities. This is a sin.

In the average newspaper your headline has to compete for attention with 350 others. Research has shown that readers travel so fast through this jungle that they don't stop to decipher the meaning of obscure headlines. Your headline must *telegraph* what you want to say, and it must telegraph it in plain language. Don't play games with the reader.

In 1960 the *Times Literary Supplement* attacked the whimsical tradition in British advertising, calling it "self-indulgent—a kind of middle-class private joke, apparently designed to amuse the advertiser and his client." Amen.

(9) Research shows that it is dangerous to use *negatives* in headlines. If, for example, you write OUR SALT CONTAINS NO ARSENIC, many readers will miss the negative and go away with the impression that you wrote OUR SALT CONTAINS ARSENIC.

(10) Avoid *blind* headlines—the kind which mean nothing unless you read the body copy underneath them; most people *don't*.

---

[1] When the chief engineer at the Rolls-Royce factory read this, he shook his head sadly and said, "It is time we did something about that damned clock."

II. BODY COPY

[5] When you sit down to write your body copy, pretend that you are talking to the woman on your right at a dinner party. She has asked you, "I am thinking of buying a new car. Which would you recommend?" Write your copy as if you were answering that question.

> (1) Don't beat about the bush—go straight to the point. Avoid analogies of the "just as, so too" variety. Dr. Gallup has demonstrated that these two-stage arguments are generally misunderstood.
>
> (2) Avoid superlatives, generalizations, and platitudes. Be specific and factual. Be enthusiastic, friendly, and memorable. Don't be a bore. Tell the truth, but make the truth fascinating.

[6] How long should your copy be? It depends on the product. If you are advertising chewing gum, there isn't much to tell, so make your copy short. If, on the other hand, you are advertising a product which has a great many different qualities to recommend it, write long copy: the more you tell, the more you sell.

[7] There is a universal belief in lay circles that people won't read long copy. Nothing could be farther from the truth. Claude Hopkins once wrote five pages of solid text for Schlitz beer. In a few months, Schlitz moved up from fifth place to first. I once wrote a page of solid text for Good Luck Margarine, with most gratifying results.

[8] Research shows that readership falls off rapidly up to fifty words of copy, but drops very little between fifty and 500 words. In my first Rolls-Royce advertisement I used 719 words—piling one fascinating fact on another. In the last paragraph I wrote, "People who feel diffident about driving a Rolls-Royce can buy a Bentley." Judging from the number of motorists who picked up the word "diffident" and bandied it about, I concluded that the advertisement was thoroughly read. In the next one I used 1400 words.

[9] Every advertisement should be a *complete* sales pitch for your product. It is unrealistic to assume that consumers will read a *series* of advertisements for the same product. You should shoot the works in every advertisement, on the assumption that it is the only chance you will ever have to sell your product to the reader—*now or never*.

[10] Says Dr. Charles Edwards of the graduate School of Retailing at New York University, "The more facts you tell, the more you sell. An advertisement's chance for success invariably increases as the number of pertinent merchandise facts included in the advertisement increases."

[11] In my first advertisement for Puerto Rico's Operation Bootstrap, I used 961 words, and persuaded Beardsley Ruml to sign them. Fourteen thousand readers clipped the coupon from this advertisement, and scores of them later established

HOW TO WRITE POTENT COPY

factories in Puerto Rico. The greatest professional satisfaction I have yet had is to see the prosperity in Puerto Rican communities which had lived on the edge of starvation for four hundred years before I wrote my advertisement. If I had confined myself to a few vacuous generalities, nothing would have happened.

[12] We have even been able to get people to read long copy about gasoline. One of our Shell advertisements contained 617 words, and 22 per cent of male readers read more than half of them.

[13] Vic Schwab tells the story of Max Hart (of Hart, Schaffner & Marx) and his advertising manager, George L. Dyer, arguing about long copy. Dyer said, "I'll bet you ten dollars I can write a newspaper page of solid type and you'd read every word of it."

[14] Hart scoffed at the idea. "I don't have to write a line of it to prove my point," Dyer replied. "I'll only tell you the headline: THIS PAGE IS ALL ABOUT MAX HART."

[15] Advertisers who put coupons in their advertisements *know* that short copy doesn't sell. In split-run tests, long copy invariably outsells short copy.

[16] Do I hear someone say that no copywriter can write long advertisements unless his media department gives him big spaces to work with? This question should not arise, because the copywriter should be consulted before planning the media schedule.

> (3) You should always include testimonials in your copy. The reader finds it easier to believe the endorsement of a fellow consumer than the puffery of an anonymous copywriter. Says Jim Young, one of the best copywriters alive today, "Every type of advertiser has the same problem; namely to be believed. The mail-order man knows nothing so potent for this purpose as the testimonial, yet the general advertiser seldom uses it."

[17] Testimonials from celebrities get remarkably high readership, and if they are honestly written they still do not seem to provoke incredulity. The better known the celebrity, the more readers you will attract. We have featured Queen Elizabeth and Winston Churchill in "Come to Britain" advertisements, and we were able to persuade Mrs. Roosevelt to make television commercials for Good Luck Margarine. When we advertised charge accounts for Sears, Roebuck, we reproduced the credit card of Ted Williams, "recently traded by Boston to Sears."

[18] Sometimes you can cast your entire copy in the form of a testimonial. My first advertisement for Austin cars took the form of a letter from an "anonymous diplomat" who was sending his son to Groton with money he had saved driving an Austin—a well-aimed combination of snobbery and economy. Alas, a perspicacious *Time* editor guessed that I was the anonymous diplomat, and asked the headmaster of Groton to comment. Dr. Crocker was so cross that I decided to send my son to Hotchkiss.

> (4) Another profitable gambit is to give the reader helpful advice, or service. It hooks about 75 per cent more readers than copy which deals entirely with the product.

[19] One of our Rinso advertisements told housewives how to remove stains. It was better read (Starch) and better remembered (Gallup) than any detergent advertisement in history. Unfortunately, however, it forgot to feature Rinso's main selling promise—that Rinso washes whiter; for this reason it should never have run.[2]

(5) I have never admired the *belles lettres* school of advertising, which reached its pompous peak in Theodore F. MacManus' famous advertisement for Cadillac, "The Penalty of Leadership," and Ned Jordan's classic, "Somewhere West of Laramie." Forty years ago the business community seems to have been impressed by these pieces of purple prose, but I have always thought them absurd; they did not give the reader a single *fact*. I share Claude Hopkins' view that "fine writing is a distinct disadvantage. So is unique literary style. They take attention away from the subject."

(6) Avoid bombast. Raymond Rubicam's famous slogan for Squibb, "The priceless ingredient of every product is the honor and integrity of its maker," reminds me of my father's advice: when a company boasts about its integrity, or a woman about her virtue, avoid the former and cultivate the latter.

(7) Unless you have some special reason to be solemn and pretentious, write your copy in the colloquial language which your customers use in everyday conversation. I have never acquired a sufficiently good ear for vernacular American to write it, but I admire copywriters who can pull it off, as in this unpublished pearl from a dairy farmer:

> Carnation Milk is the best in the land,
> Here I sit with a can in my hand.
> No tits to pull, no hay to pitch,
> Just punch a hole in the son-of-a-bitch.

It is a mistake to use highfalutin language when you advertise to uneducated people. I once used the word OBSOLETE in a headline, only to discover that 43 per cent of housewives had no idea what it meant. In another headline, I used the word INEFFABLE, only to discover that I didn't know what it meant myself.

However, many copywriters of my vintage err on the side of underestimating the educational level of the population. Philip Hauser, head of the Sociology Department at the University of Chicago, draws attention to the changes which are taking place:

> The increasing exposure of the population to formal schooling . . . can be expected to effect important changes in . . . the style of advertising . . . Messages aimed at the "average" American on the assumption that he has had less than a grade school education are likely to find themselves with a declining or disappearing clientele.[3]

Meanwhile, all copywriters should read Dr. Rudolph Flesch's *Art of Plain Talk*. It will persuade them to use short words, short sentences, short paragraphs, and highly *personal* copy.

Aldous Huxley, who once tried his hand at writing advertisements, concluded that "any trace of literariness in an advertisement is fatal to its success. Advertisement writers may not be lyrical, or obscure, or in any way esoteric. They must be universally intelligible. A good advertisement has this in common with drama and oratory, that it must be immediately comprehensible and directly moving."[4]

---

[2] The photograph showed several different kinds of stain—lipstick, coffee, shoe-polish, blood and so forth. The blood was my own; I am the only copywriter who has ever *bled* for his client.

[3] *Scientific American* (October 1962).

[4] *Essays Old And New* (Harper & Brothers, 1927). Charles Lamb and Byron also wrote advertisements. So did Bernard Shaw, Hemingway, Marquand, Sherwood Anderson, and Faulkner—none of them with any degree of success.

(8) Resist the temptation to write the kind of copy which wins awards. I am always gratified when I win an award, but most of the campaigns which produce *results* never win awards, because they don't draw attention to themselves.

The juries that bestow awards are never given enough information about the *results* of the advertisements they are called upon to judge. In the absence of such information, they rely on their opinions, which are always warped toward the highbrow.

(9) Good copywriters have always resisted the temptation to *entertain*. Their achievement lies in the number of new products they get off to a flying start. In a class by himself stands Claude Hopkins, who is to advertising what Escoffier is to cooking. By today's standards, Hopkins was an unscrupulous barbarian, but technically he was the supreme master. Next I would place Raymond Rubicam, George Cecil, and James Webb Young, all of whom lacked Hopkins' ruthless salesmanship, but made up for it by their honesty, by the broader range of their work, and by their ability to write civilized copy when the occasion required it. Next I would place John Caples, the mail-order specialist from whom I have learned much.

These giants wrote their advertisements for newspapers and magazines. It is still too early to identify the best writers for television.

FOR REVIEW AND DISCUSSION

Content

1. What seems to be Ogilvy's way of deciding what advertising should and should not do?

2. Ogilvy's main concern is with the effectiveness of advertising. To what extent is he also concerned with truthfulness in advertising?

3. Discuss why Ogilvy's assessment of the average consumer's mental prowess may or may not be accurate.

4. "Testimonials from celebrities get high readership," claims the author. Discuss this advertising and propaganda technique and explain reasons for its effectiveness.

Rhetoric

1. What evidence do you see that Ogilvy's own prose reflects the advice he gives for writing advertising copy?

2. Which techniques for writing potent copy would not be very useful for writing potent exposition? Which techniques would be useful for exposition?

3. As specifically as you can, explain the differences between writing advertisements and writing exposition.

Classroom Exercises

1. Using Ogilvy's discussion as a guide, write a persuasive advertisement for an imagined product. Then read your advertisement to your fellow students and have them analyze it, looking for what Ogilvy says belongs in potent copy.

2. Bring to class some ads that contain long and detailed copy. Discuss whether they are effective according to Ogilvy's criteria.

3. Write a potent recruiting ad for your composition course.

FOR FURTHER READING

Bruce A. Lohof

THE HIGHER MEANING OF MARLBORO CIGARETTES

> *Like Kosinski, whose selection begins this chapter, Lohof is both an amused and amusing observer of American life. In this remarkable analysis of the Marlboro Man, Lohof more than does justice to one of modern advertising's great success stories.*

[1]   . . . Doubtless the finest exemplar of the merchandised metaphor is the Marlboro Man who for the past half decade and more has served as the emblem of Marlboro Cigarettes. Rugged, vigorous, and robust, he strides across the television screen or through the pages of a magazine. He crouches before a daybreak fire to turn the crinkling bacon or pour coffee from a blackened pot. He rides his horse knee-deep in snow, his sheepskin coat warding off the howling winter winds. He gazes serenely over the sturdy neck of his stabled pony. In every case he is "lighting up," and suggesting that you follow his lead. He is the archetypical cowboy, to be sure. But he is much more.

[2]   There was a time when he was not even that. For thirty years the "man" in the Marlboro commercial had as often as not been a lady—and always in plush, upholstered surroundings. Marlboro Cigarettes in the days before the Marlboro Man had been "America's luxury cigarette," a genteel smoke available with either an ivory tip or a red "beauty tip." The affluent, textured salons in which Marlboros were smoked connoted a deep-pile luxury and velvet sophistication that bordered on the effeminate. Indeed, Marlboros were widely regarded as a lady's smoke forty years before Virginia Slims Cigarettes congratulated the American woman on having come

> . . . a long way, baby,
> To get where you've got to today;
> You've got your own cigarette now, baby;
> You've come a long, long way.

From the *Journal of Popular Culture* 3 (Winter, 1969): 442–49. Reprinted by permission of the publisher.

[3]   Then the 1950s brought the first cancer scare and, subsequently, a bromide in the form of cigaret filters. A spate of filtered brands entered the market. Among them was the Philip Morris Company's early bid. "New from Philip Morris," the slogan said. Marlboros, an old brand in new clothing, now had a "filter, flavor, [and a] fliptop box." Moreover, lest the effeminacy of old be augmented by the sissiness that surrounded the earliest filtered cigarettes, Marlboro was given a new, masculine image—the tattooed man.

[4]   By chance, the first tattooed man was a cowboy. No Marlboro Man, he was simply the result of an advertiser's desire to identify his product with "regular guys." As an agency executive later admitted, "We asked ourselves what was the most generally accepted symbol of masculinity in America, and this led quite naturally to a cowboy." No apparent effort was made to magnify this initial cowboy into the cultural symbol which would later emerge. Indeed, the tattooed man soon forsook the range in pursuit of other manly vocations. "Obviously," advertisers erroneously reasoned, "we couldn't keep on showing cowboys forever, although they could be repeated from time to time." In his place came a succession of he-men—explorers, sailors, athletes, and an occasional tuxedoed but no less rugged gentleman. In each case the common denominators were an elemental masculinity and, of course, the tattoo—emblem of those who look "successful and sophisticated but rugged . . . as though [they] might have had interesting experiences."[1]

[5]   But the tattooed man, like the imagination of the culture that smoked his cigarettes, kept returning to the open spaces of his birth. His Madison Avenue parents had meant for him to don cowboy regalia on occasion, but the costume became his natural clothing. In the early 1960s the cowboy was promoted to supremacy over other tattooed men. By 1963 the tattoo had disappeared and the Marlboro Man had emerged as the exclusive inhabitant of Marlboro commercials. A cultural symbol had evolved; a metaphor was ready for merchandising.

[6]   The Marlboro image, though woven into whole cloth, consists of two elements, each illuminated in the neon of sloganeering. One, naturally, is the Marlboro Man himself. The other is expressed in the ubiquitous phrase: "Come to Marlboro Country."

[7]   Marlboro Country, in a sense, is Montana—the Montana which more than twenty-five years ago astounded that eastern, erudite Jew Leslie Fiedler. "The inhumanly virginal landscape: the atrocious magnificence of the mountains, the illimitable brute fact of the prairies"—this is Marlboro Country. It is, as the license plates say, the "Big Sky Country." Had it not been for Rousseau's romantic myth of noble savagery, Fiedler would have been psychologically impotent in the face of its

---

[1] Leo Burnett, "The Marlboro Story: How One of America's Most Popular Cigarettes Got that Way," *New Yorker*, 34 (November 15, 1958), 41–43. See also "Marlboro Won Success by Big Newspaper Ads," *Editor and Publisher*, 91 (December 6, 1958), 26; and "PR Man Fones, Adman Burnett Bare 'Secrets' of Modest Marlboro He-Man," *Advertising Age*, 29 (November 17, 1958), 3, 99.

virginal enormity. He would have had no way of comprehending it. There would have been nothing for him "to do with it . . . no way of assimilating the land to [his] imagination."[2]

[8] But the Rousseauan legacy, held in trust by Natty Bumppo, Daniel Boone, and more recently Ben Cartwright, has made Marlboro Country not only mentally manageable but psychologically fascinating. Thus, what might have boggled the national imagination by its sheer immensity in fact evokes within the cultural consciousness a nostalgic and reverent image of its own mythical heritage. Marlboro Country is an environmental memoir, reminding Americans of where they have been and inviting them to vicariously return.

[9] At first glance Marlboro Country is reminiscent of the pastoral ideal of a Vergilian poem. Folded, spindled, and mutilated, modern man views such vernal expanses with the envy of Vergil's exiled shepherd:

> Tityrus, while you lie there at ease under the
> awning of a spreading beech and practise
> country songs on a light shepherd's pipe, I
> have to bid good-bye to the home fields and
> the ploughlands that I love. Exile for me,
> Tityrus—and you lie sprawling in the shade,
> teaching the woods to echo back the charms
> of Amaryllis.[3]

[10] The rustic garden, of course, is a potent symbol in the American mind. Leo Marx has shown the intrusion of "technology" into the "pastoral ideal"—or *The Machine in the Garden*—to be a "metaphoric design which recurs everywhere in our literature" from James Fenimore Cooper and Washington Irving to Ernest Hemingway and Robert Frost.[4] Indeed, so envious are harried twentieth-century Americans of the pastoral ideal that it spills out of their serious art and across their commercial advertising. Once the consumer realizes that "You can take Salem out of the country, but you can't take the 'Country' out of Salem" he and some modern Amaryllis are only a pack of cigarettes away from a gambol through a field of waving grass toward a shadowy glade. Here Rip Van Winkle escaped from the village to a cozy repose in the midst of benign nature. Here menthol-puffing couples meander barefoot across an oaken bridge with never a thought of splinters. Here picnics are antless, summers are sweatless, and autumns are endless (which is to say winterless). Here one can find pleasant refuge from the responsibilities and encumbrances of civilization.

[11] But the trill of shepherds' pipes and the wooded serenity of a Hollywood back lot are, upon closer inspection, strangers in Marlboro Country. They belong instead

---

[2] Leslie A. Fiedler, "Montana, or the End of Jean-Jacques Rousseau," reprinted in *An End to Innocence* (Boston, 1955), p. 131.
[3] Vergil, *Eclogues*, trans. E. V. Rieu, quoted in Marx, p. 20.
[4] Marx, p. 16.

to the pastoral verdure of Salem Country, that Arcadian middle landscape that edges upon civilization. On the nether edge of Arcadia, however, is the wilderness—violent, primitive, occasionally malevolent. This is the incredible landscape of Fiedler's Montana. This is the monstrous, illimitable home of the noble savage. This is Marlboro Country.

[12] The cursory distinctions between the garden and the wilderness are esthetic: the bucolic greenery of "take a puff, it's springtime," versus the rough-hewn realism of a Frederick Remington painting; the capricious gaiety of flutes versus the strident, robust brass of "The Magnificent Seven," the motion picture whose virile theme accompanies all Marlboro commercials.[5] Beneath the surface, though, lie more important differences. The pastoral ideal connotes a benign nature where conflict, danger, and tension are non-existent. The primitive ideal, on the other hand, speaks of a wilderness which jeopardizes and makes demands upon its residents. Accordingly, the Vergilian shepherd lies in repose, unharassed by either the complicated tensions of the town or the forbidding dangers of the marsh.[6] Meanwhile, his wilderness counterpart stands erect and vigilant. He is a man in conflict with his environment. He is of necessity a man of action and purpose. He is a Marlboro Man.

[13] The Marlboro Man epitomizes the awesome, primitive environment in which he lives. His clothing, his habits, and even his face reflect the competitive spirit which the wilderness exacts from its inhabitants. His garb is not the fringed and bespangled costume of dimestore Texans and backlot cowboys. Nor is it the casual drape of the classic shepherd. He wears instead a rough-spun shirt, sheepskin vest or coat, dungarees, and chaps—nothing for show, nothing for comfort, everything for facing down the elements.

[14] His habits, like his clothing, are dictated by practical considerations, He is, as the jingle says:

> Up before the sun,
> Travel[ing] all day long.

Each commercial presents another vignette. He rescues a stranded herd from the snowbound uplands; he mends fence; he rounds up stray calves; he thwarts an incipient stampede. Even his leisure moments—gathering water for the morning coffee or competing in a local rodeo—are reflections of his real purpose. His habits are work-oriented, his work a way of life.

---

[5] It is worth noting that advertisers have recognized that Remington's paintings "would be perfect for a series of outdoor Marlboro posters," and have erected his art work—blown to 300 times its original size—along California's highways. See "Giant Size Remington Reproductions Become Marlboro Outdoor Boards," *Advertising Age*, 40 (January 20, 1969), p. 32.

[6] Marx delineates the borders of Arcadia. "One separates it from Rome, the other from the encroaching marshland." Within these borders the pastoral shepherd is "free of the repressions entailed by a complex civilization," but still "not prey to the violent uncertainties of nature." Marx, p. 22.

[15] But the essence of the Marlboro Man finds its truest expression in his face. His visage does not reflect the placid serenity of the shepherd. Nor does it mirror either the cosmetic polish of civilization's winners or the sullen weariness worn by its victims. Like his clothing and his habits, the face of the Marlboro Man comes with the territory—sculptured, cragged, lined not by age but by the elements. He gazes out upon Marlboro Country through what Fiedler called the " 'Montana Face' . . . a face developed not for sociability or feeling, but for facing into the weather."[7] A rude sagaciousness of eye, a leathery tautness of skin, a wind-cured ruddiness of complexion—altogether a rugged handsomeness—signal his sturdy lifestyle.

[16] The higher meaning of this Marlboro Man and the wilderness he faces down cannot be written in terms of tobacco. Not cigarettes but metaphors—or in this case *a* metaphor—are being merchandised. The Marlboro image is a cultural symbol which speaks to the collective imagination of the American people. It speaks of the virgin frontier, and of the brutal efficacy and constant vigilance which the frontier exacts from its residents. It speaks, as did Frederick Jackson Turner three-quarters of a century ago, of that

> coarseness and strength combined with acuteness and inquisitiveness; that practical, inventive turn of mind, quick to find expedients; that masterful grasp of material things, lacking in the artistic but powerful to effect great ends; that restless, nervous energy; that dominant individualism, working for good and for evil, and withal that buoyancy and exuberance which comes with freedom. . . .[8]

[17] In fine, the image speaks of *innocence* and *individual efficacy:* innocence in spite of the Marlboro Man's rude sagacity, efficacy because the territory demands it as the price of survival. It was the innocence of the Marlboro Man which prompted Fiedler to write that, in Montana, "there was something heartening in dealing with people who had never seen, for instance, a Negro or a Jew or a Servant, and were immune to all their bitter meanings."[9] In Marlboro Country one finds a breed of humanity untarnished by—indeed, ignorant of—the acrid fumes of modern civilization. The naiveté of the Marlboro Man is as fresh as the unpolluted air that sustains him and as pure as the mountain stream which quenches his thirst. Unsullied is he by the guilt and terror that mingle in the civilized eye whenever it sees a race riot or a ghetto or a mushroom cloud. He stands beyond the city's fouled social relations, compromised political affairs, and clogged streets. He represents a reprieve from the malaise that hangs darkly over all who have been accessories to the crimes of civilization.

[18] The Marlboro image, however, is not evocative of simple escape. To be sure, the Marlboro Man stands apart from civilization. But he stands apart also from

---

[7] Fiedler, pp. 134–35.
[8] Frederick Jackson Turner, "The Significance of the Frontier in American History," reprinted in *The Frontier in American History* (New York, 1920), p. 37.
[9] Fiedler is quick to notice the darker side of noble savagery, pointing out that these same people "had never seen an art museum or a ballet or even a movie in any language but their own." Fiedler, p. 135.

Arcadia, from the simple, purposeless, unencumbered dawdling of Salem Country. Like civilization—and unlike the Vergilian garden—Marlboro Country makes demands upon its inhabitants. But responsibilities there are simple. The tasks require vigilance, rigor, and diligence, but there is resolution and accomplishment in the reward. Possessed of those virtues memorialized by Turner—"that practical, inventive turn of mind . . . that masterful grasp of material things"—the Marlboro Man is "powerful to effect great ends."

[19] The Marlboro image represents escape, not from the responsibilities of civilization, but from its frustrations. Modern man wallows through encumbrances so tangled and sinuous, so entwined in the machinery of bureaucracies and institutions, that his usual reward is impotent desperation. He is ultimately responsible for nothing, unfulfilled in everything. Meanwhile, he jealously watches the Marlboro Man facing down challenging but intelligible tasks. He sees this denizen of the wilderness living as Thoreau would have: "deliberately . . . front[ing] only the essential facts of life."[10]

[20] Innocence and individual efficacy are the touchstones of the metaphor employed on behalf of Marlboro Cigarettes. Despoiled by technology, Marlboro Country and the virtues which flourished therein are no more. But technology has a way of reconstituting for commercial purposes that which it has taken away. So it is with the Marlboro Man, his habits and appearance, his virtues, and his territory. A way of life which became a folk myth in the minds of a people is conjured back into "reality" and sent into the marketplace.

[21] A decade ago the editor of a trade journal questioned the "intrusion" of cowboys "into . . . advertising—as authorities on cigarets, bourbon and automobiles." Noting the cowboy's alleged penchant "for personal ornamentation, preening, drinking and brawling," his tendency toward "regarding females largely in the herd," and the aroma "of horses, dung and sweaty saddle leather" that follows wherever he goes, the editor thought it paradoxical that "civilized advertising men can parade him before us as someone whose habits are worthy of copying."[11] The resolution to this paradox, of course, is that the Marlboro Man is not simply a cowboy. He is a symbol of irretrievable innocence, and of that illimitable wilderness wherein, as Emerson said, one might have been "plain old Adam, the simple genuine self against the whole world."[12]

---

[10] Henry David Thoreau, *Walden* (New York, 1961), p. 105.
[11] "Saddlesoap, Please," *Advertising Age*, 31 (March 28, 1960), p. 90.
[12] *The Journals and Miscellaneous Notebooks of Ralph Waldo Emerson*, ed. William H. Gilman *et al.* (Cambridge, 1960–), IV, p. 141.

FOR REVIEW AND DISCUSSION

Content

1. Explain what Lohof means by "merchandized metaphor." What other metaphors besides the Marlboro Man come to mind?

2. Discuss the irony in the contrast between the product being sold and the image being used to present it. How does Lohof exploit this irony?

3. Is Lohof saying that Marlboro Country *is* Montana or that Marlboro Country is a *romanticization* of Montana? How is his meaning made clear?

4. Do you agree that the Marlboro image is as significant and as compelling as Lohof makes it out to be? Explain.

Rhetoric

1. Notice how Lohof quotes from Leslie Fiedler in paragraph 7. What use does Lohof make of the quoted material? Do the quotes "prove" anything?

2. A characteristic of Lohof's writing is the occasional short sentence (see, for instance, the last sentence of paragraph 11). What effect does Lohof achieve by injecting a short sentence (or string of short sentences) into his prose?

3. How would you characterize Lohof's control of diction? Is the level of diction consistent or uneven? Explain and illustrate.

4. Humor is often the result of juxtaposing things (placing them side by side) in odd or unexpected combinations. What juxtaposing in the essay indicates that at times it is not to be taken altogether seriously?

5. What is the effect of the many literary and historical allusions and references? Does "missing" some of them necessarily detract from your general understanding or enjoyment of the essay? Explain.

6. Examine paragraph 18. Each sentence contains at least one connective (transitional) phrase. Identify each and explain how it affects the direction of the discussion.

Classroom Exercises

1. Discuss whether it is likely that Marlboro advertisements would prove effective or ineffective on non-Americans. (What, for instance, might be a Briton's response to the Marlboro Man?)

2. Discuss the extent to which archetypal figures and motifs in advertising affect the public's attitude toward concerns other than the products advertised. Something for you to consider is whether advertising merely *makes use* of already prevalent conditions in society or *creates* conditions.

3. Bring to class, for group analysis, other ads that rely on archetypal figures for their effectiveness.

FOR DISCUSSION AND WRITING

1. Ogilvy and Stevens appear to have conflicting attitudes toward their profession and toward the public. In some cases, though, their attitudes may be similar. Compare and contrast these attitudes.

2. Describe how Ogilvy's prose style and expository organization differ from those of his colleague Stevens. What specifically might account for these differences (intended audience, purpose, personality, and so forth)?

3. "Advertising is at once one of the great curses and great blessings of the modern age." Do you think it is more one than the other? Discuss and exemplify.

4. Drawing on your own experience and on information in the four selections in this chapter, write a detailed evaluation of the role advertising plays in our daily lives.

5. Would Stevens or Ogilvy necessarily agree with Kosinski's treatment of automobile advertisements? What might Kosinski criticize in Ogilvy's article?

6. Write an essay in which you discuss the "greater" significance of a product in a way similar to Lohof's discussion of Marlboro cigarettes.

POSTSCRIPT

He ventures to speak because he must: language is the repository of his whole knowledge and experience.
                                        N. SCOTT MOMADAY

An ear won't keep few fishes.
                                        RPC 4000 COMPUTER

If I should die before my pen
Has gleaned my teeming brain. . . .
                                        JOHN KEATS

Questions that we might all ask on completing this book are "Where do we go from here?" or "What are we to make of all that we now know about language?" Thus, this postscript begins with some ideas about the future, about men and language and computers, followed by a short account of the humorous but sometimes disconcerting poetry produced by these machines. Finally, to conclude the book, we turn to one man's speculations about our deepest relationship with language.

Terry Winograd

ARTIFICIAL INTELLIGENCE: WHEN WILL COMPUTERS UNDERSTAND PEOPLE?

> We seem to expect all computers eventually to be like Hal in 2001: A Space Odyssey or Artoo Detoo in Star Wars: *simply mechanical versions of ourselves, complete with language and personality. But as Terry Winograd points out in this selection, that time is far off. Experiments in teaching computers to use language have been only moderately successful, but they have taught scientists one important lesson: Language and our use of it is an infinitely complicated process. As you read, ask yourself what differences continue to distinguish your own use of language from a computer's.*

[1] There was a sense of nightmare unreality about all this. Bowman felt as if he was in the witness box, being cross-examined by a hostile prosecutor for a crime of which he was unaware—knowing that, although he was innocent, a single slip of the tongue might bring disaster.

[2] "I want to do this myself, Hal," he said. "Please give me control."

[3] "Look, Dave, you've got a lot of things to do. I suggest you leave this to me."

[4] "Hal, switch to manual hibernation control."

[5] "I can tell from your voice harmonies, Dave, that you're badly upset. Why don't you take a stress pill and get some rest?"*

[6] Hal is the oversolicitous and eventually mutinous computer in the film *2001: A Space Odyssey* and the novel written from it by Arthur C. Clarke. He can perform most of the intellectual activities that human beings can, only better. One of his most useful accomplishments is the ability to converse with his human shipmates in perfect, idiomatic English. Indeed, Hal is so sensitive to even the most subtle nuances of intonation that humans find it distressingly difficult to deceive him.

[7] Science fiction has a way of turning into science fact. Computers like Hal aren't here yet, but a number of researchers are working at teaching computers to use language. Their efforts are part of a new science called *artificial intelligence* (AI), which is growing on the border between psychology and computer program-

---

*Copyright © 1968 by Arthur C. Clarke and Polaris Productions.

From *Psychology Today* Magazine 7 (May, 1974): 73–77. Copyright © 1974 Ziff-Davis Publishing Company. Reprinted by permission.

ing. As its name indicates, a major goal of this science is to program computers to do intelligent things—to converse with human beings, play chess, recognize objects, solve abstract problems, and use common sense.

[8]   There are many practical reasons for making computers more intelligent. For example, when computers can use language, they will become accessible to a much wider range of people, including students, teachers, business people, and others who may lack special computer training. In addition, they will be able to take over many of our routine mental chores, and help with more complex tasks such as medical diagnosis. However, many AI researchers (including myself) are just as concerned with natural intelligence as with artificial. In the process of programing a computer to behave intelligently, we find ourselves examining our own abilities from a new perspective, and expanding our knowledge of the human mind.

MISSING PIECES

[9]   When AI researchers first decided to teach computers language they turned to the traditional sciences of psychology and linguistics for a theoretical foundation. There they found a bewildering array of conceptual fragments, like so many brightly colored parts of some jigsaw puzzle that was missing all its central pieces. Psychologists knew how a person's choice of words reflects hidden thoughts and desires. They had discovered that certain kinds of brain injuries cause mysterious impairments of language. And they had mountains of data on how people memorize lists of nonsense words, and how long it takes to react to a letter or word printed on a screen. Linguists, on the other hand, could describe the many ways in which different languages put endings on nouns or verbs. They could trace historical changes in the development of a language. And they had devised ingenious methods for discovering the units of sound and meaning in an unfamiliar language.

[10]   But nobody had addressed the central question of how a language works as a whole. No one had discovered what happens when a person hears or reads the simplest sentence. These scholars had not been stupid or misguided, but they lacked conceptual tools that were powerful enough to analyze and describe a complex system, in which the working of the parts is hidden from view.

[11]   Fortunately, the computer itself has been able to provide new ways to describe processes, and new tools for understanding them. Although still in its infancy, computer science has already developed a rich set of concepts about how information can be stored, processed and used. And because the computer works with great speed and precision, it enables us to test theories that are far more complex than those expressed in traditional (i.e., mathematical) terms. We can build a working model of a theory in the form of a computer program, then see what happens when the program actually tries to perform.

[12] This approach makes us look at things in a special way, and asks questions that differ from those asked in the past. Unlike the laboratory psychologist, we are not concerned with trying to isolate some tiny aspect of a problem for detailed study under special experimental conditions. Nor do we concentrate on pathologies and oddities, which are of interest only when they shed light on how the system as a whole is put together.

BUILDING THE TAJ MAHAL

[13] Many people think of the computer as an almost magical device, a gadget that will solve problems automatically. But a stone mason with a tool box and a sketch does not have the Taj Mahal. We must be careful that we don't build a system to do part of what we want, then naively believe it will somehow do all the rest. If we want the computer to do something we consider intelligent, we must first analyze just what goes into doing the job. We must delve below the surface of what may seem to be a simple act, and try to imitate the complicated workings that operate so smoothly in everyday life.

[14] When a language program is the goal, it is especially difficult to judge how much the computer should—or can—do. Understanding language is a skill all normal people take for granted. Like breathing or walking, we do it all the time without conscious effort, and only when communication breaks down for some reason do we think about it at all. Subjectively it feels as though comprehension just happens all at once; the individual steps are buried somewhere in the inner workings of our minds. Yet, from the point of view of "information processing," comprehension is an astounding feat, one that requires a tremendous background of knowledge. A person must know not only the structure of his language, but how meaning is conveyed and something about the subject of the conversation.

[15] He must also know how to draw inferences. When we talk to someone, we automatically assume that our listener understands language, so if we cannot make sense out of the response we get back, we begin to look for deeper reasons. For instance, if I ask you "What time is it?" and you answer "I just got here," I don't assume immediately that you misunderstood me. I look for some connection. Perhaps you always arrive at nine o'clock so it must be nine o'clock. Or perhaps the clock is somewhere else in the building, and since you have just arrived, you haven't had a chance to look at it.

[16] One of the first conversational computer programs, written in the early '60s by Joseph Weizenbaum at M.I.T., took advantage of the fact that people try to make sense of an utterance by drawing the necessary connections. The program is called "Eliza" after the character in Shaw's *Pygmalion,* and the musical *My Fair Lady.* It plays the role of a psychiatrist. A "patient" types in messages to the computer via a

teletypewriter terminal; the computer responds by typing messages back. In the following sample dialog, the computer's remarks are capitalized:

PLEASE TELL ME YOUR PROBLEM.
I am feeling depressed.
HOW LONG HAVE YOU BEEN FEELING DEPRESSED?
Ever since my mother left.
TELL ME MORE ABOUT YOUR FAMILY.
My father is very strict.
PLEASE GO ON.
Last night I dreamt he spanked me.
WHAT WOULD IT MEAN TO YOU IF HE SPANKED YOU?
Didn't you ever get spanked?
WE WERE DISCUSSING YOU, NOT ME.
You're just a dumb machine anyway.
DO COMPUTERS FRIGHTEN YOU?

[17] At first glance, this might well be a discussion with a real psychiatrist. The computer seems to understand what the patient has said, and even seems to apply a certain amount of psychiatric interview technique. Actually, the program uses a very simple system of patterns containing key words. Whenever it sees a sentence of the form ". . . I am . . . ," it responds, "How long have you been . . . ," filling in the end of the sentence from the patient's original one. When the program sees the word *mother*, it says: "Tell me more about your family." These patterns are set up to reflect a certain amount of psychiatric knowledge. For example, one response to "I dreamt that . . ." is, "Do you often wish that . . . ," because people frequently reveal their desires in dreams. When the program sees the word *everyone*, it asks, "Who in particular can you think of?" which tends to elicit a description of a situation that the person at first was reluctant to detail. With a large number of such patterns, the program can carry on an extended dialog without repeating.

[18] But the program's knowledge is in scattered fragments, and it has no real understanding of what the patient says. If the patient happens to type "Thinking about what I am doing always upsets me," the program blindly applies the pattern for ". . . I am . . ." and comes up with: "How long have you been doing always upsets you?" If it fails to find one of its key words, it launches into endless loops of "Please go on," "Tell me more," etc. And most important, the program does not build up a picture of what the patient is saying. It merely reacts to each sentence according to the particular words that appear in it.

[19] Weizenbaum created Eliza to demonstrate that very little understanding is necessary for a machine to *appear* competent. The program's flaws are not due to its size, or to a shortage of patterns, but to the fact that it doesn't attempt true comprehension. A real psychiatrist listening to his patient needs a huge storehouse of knowledge about people, their lives, thoughts and activities. He also needs a highly developed reasoning power to combine this knowledge in a way that makes understanding possible. We are only beginning to explore how to represent such knowl-

edge in a computer, and we have only the most rudimentary ways of having the machine use it.

A BOX OF BLOCKS

[20] You can get some idea of the enormity of the task by considering the following passage, which a group at the Xerox Corporation is using to test the reading ability of a computer:

[21] *Tommy had just been given a new set of blocks. He was opening the box when he saw Jimmy coming in.*
The computer has to answer three simple questions:
  * Who was opening the box?
  * What was in the box?
  * Who came in?
Although any first-grader could easily answer these questions, the computer finds them surprisingly hard. Obviously, it is no Hal.

[22] When we try to spell out precisely what the first-grader is doing that the computer is not, we find it very difficult, much more difficult than describing what a person does when cooking an omelet or fixing a watch. But one thing, at least, is clear: we can't answer the questions by simply repeating words directly from the passage. That strategy would lead us to answer the first question, "Who was opening the box?" with the words "He was opening the box." This answer is unsatisfactory, because words like *he* or *it* make sense only in a context where they refer to a particular person or thing. The reader has to recognize that "he" meant Tommy, and to do this he must know that "he" refers to a person, that "Tommy" is a person's name, and that sets of blocks are not people.

[23] The second question, "What was in the box?" calls for much more specialized knowledge. Nothing in the passage directly tells us what box is being opened, or what the contents of the box are. But a person reading the text immediately assumes that the box is the one containing the set of blocks. He can do this because he knows that new items often come in boxes, and that opening a box of new items is the usual thing to do. Most important, he assumes he is receiving a connected message. There is no logical reason why the box must be connected with the blocks, but if it were not, some further introduction would be necessary. Thus, if you read "Tommy had just been given a new job. He was opening the box . . . ," or, "Tommy had just been given a new set of blocks. He was opening the book . . . ," you would be confused, because there would be no obvious connection between the sentences.

[24] So even with this simple passage, understanding depends on knowing about the world. This means that when we talk to another person, we do not need to fill in

explicitly all the possible connections between things (which we probably couldn't do anyway). We can safely assume that our listener will use his or her own intelligence and information about the world to put together the meaning we intend. A sentence does not "convey" meaning the way a truck conveys cargo, complete and packaged. It is more like a blueprint that allows the hearer to reconstruct the meaning from his own knowledge.

MAN BITES DOG

[25] Still, this knowledge is not quite enough. To read a blueprint you must know the conventional symbols used to describe physical structures. To understand language, you must know the conventional rules that make up its grammar.

[26] There is a tacit agreement among all the speakers of a particular language to use words in certain ways in order to express certain relationships. These rules vary widely from language to language. For example, in English, the sentence "The man bit the dog" tells us that the man did the biting. In Japanese, this relationship can be expressed by two different orders, equivalent to *man dog bite* and *dog man bite*. Someone who understands Japanese can tell who did the biting by looking for a special marker, such as "-o," that identifies the object of the verb.

[27] All human languages, even those used by supposedly "primitive" cultures, have a complicated system of grammatical devices that enable the speaker to weave complex combinations of messages into each phrase. Although there are simple grammars in animal communication systems, human grammars go far beyond such systems. In the course of a few words, we not only can specify a fact, we can also indicate which information is important, which information we believe is new for the listener, how new information relates to previous information, and even how we feel about what we are saying.

[28] For example, instead of saying "The man bit the dog," we can say "The dog was bitten by the man." The basic assertion is the same, but the focus of attention is different. We might use this assertion as part of a description, as in "the man who bit the dog," or "the dog that the man bit," then build this phrase into a larger sentence, with its own information, focus and place in the conversation.

[29] Grammatical signals can be quite subtle, even in simple sentences. Consider the last question in our little computer reading test, "Who came in?" To answer, you must understand the phrase ". . . he saw Jimmy coming in," from the original story. But this phrase is ambiguous. If it had said ". . . he saw Jimmy come in," it would have been clear that Jimmy came in. On the other hand, if it had said ". . . he saw Jimmy before coming in" we would think that Tommy, not Jimmy, came in. In learning a foreign language, we're often puzzled by such subtleties, and we misinterpret what we hear long after we know the meanings of individual words, because we don't know how to read the blueprint.

BUILDING A MICROWORLD

[30] If we wanted our program to understand everything we might say to it, we would need to provide it with an entire encyclopedia of knowledge. To get around this problem, AI researchers pick one small area for discussion, and try to put together all the different kinds of knowledge that go into it. By working with these "microworlds," we avoid being swamped by a hopelessly large quantity of information.

[31] One such microworld involves a primitive "robot," consisting of a television camera eye connected to a mechanical arm. On command from a person seated at a teletype, the arm picks up and stacks some toy blocks that are arranged on a table top. There are several laboratories that use such systems to explore problems in vision, language and problemsolving.

[32] My own work has been with a modified version of this system. Instead of having a real robot carry out the actions, the computer generates a television picture showing a drawing of a table top on top of which are blocks of various shapes. A program alters the picture to conform to the commands from the teletype. The following dialog is from a longer conversation with the system. The human being starts:

    How many blocks are not in the box?
    FOUR OF THEM.
    Is at least one of them narrower than the one which I told you to pick up?
    YES, THE RED CUBE.
    Can the table pick up blocks?
    NO.
    Can a pyramid be supported by a block?
    YES.
    Will you please stack up both of the red blocks and either a green cube or a pyramid?
    OK. (Carries out command)
    Which cube is sitting on the table?
    THE LARGE GREEN ONE WHICH SUPPORTS THE RED PYRAMID.
    Had you touched any pyramid before you put the green one on the little cube?
    YES, THE GREEN ONE.
    When did you pick it up?
    WHILE I WAS STACKING UP THE RED CUBE, A LARGE RED BLOCK, AND A LARGE GREEN CUBE.
    Why?
    TO GET RID OF IT.
    Why did you do that?
    TO CLEAN OFF THE RED CUBE . . .
    A "steeple" is a stack which contains two green cubes and a pyramid.
    I UNDERSTAND.
    Are there any steeples now?
    NO.
    Build one.
    OK.

[33] To carry out even a simple command, the computer must draw on all its abilities. It must understand what it sees in the scene, decide the action called for, and devise a plan of execution. The program does not operate on any single principle; rather, it is organized like a community of specialists, each with his own expertise in dealing with some part of the job of understanding. These specialists, or subprograms, share a common "data base" of information about the current situation in the blocks world, as well as a common memory for recent events and conversations. They continually add information to the data base to describe the current input, the plans and answers under preparation, and the information to be remembered.

[34] There are some subprograms that deal primarily with the syntactic forms of sentences, i.e., with the ways in which words and phrases are combined. Others use this information to put together the intended meaning of a sentence. Still others are concerned with knowing how things work on the table top, and using this knowledge to reason about intended meanings. These three kinds of subprograms represent the traditional areas of linguistic analysis—syntax, semantics and pragmatics. Of course, language is an integrated whole, and you can't talk about one area without paying attention to how it fits in with the rest. But the categories do provide a reasonably natural way to divide up the program.

[35] Suppose I type in, "Which block is contained by the big box?" The grammar subprograms will go to work, analyzing the sentence word by word, trying to put together phrases and build up descriptions which the semantic subprograms can use. They discover that *the big box* is the logical subject of *contain* while *which block* is the object. This is the same conclusion they would have reached if I had typed "The big box contains which blocks?"

NODES OF THE TREE

[36] The result of this analysis is a treelike structure [see figure]. (Of course, in the machine, there is no drawing, but a description of one.) You can see that the groupings, or "nodes" of the tree correspond to the parts of speech—noun, verb, preposition, adjective and adverb. These are the basic chunks for conveying meaning. A grammar subprogram exists for each type of group; as the program proceeds through the sentence, it uses information about previous input, as well as the words that follow, to decide which "specialist" it must call.

[37] The tree provides a convenient way for the subprograms to communicate with each other. Each one looks at the tree to see what has been done so far. Each can change the tree, or fill in information about particular groupings, for use by fellow subprograms.

[38] The meaning subprograms are equipped with definitions of words, and with the information accumulating about the structure of the sentence. They also can use information about previous sentences to help decode the current one. Some analyze particular kinds of groups. For example, the noun-group specialist takes a phrase like *the three red blocks,* and builds a description of a set of three objects, each of which is a block having the color red. This description is in a notation that the reasoning subprograms can use.

[39] To remove the ambiguities and multiple meanings of English words, the semantic specialists use information about context. They must look through the set of objects they know about to decide which ones are being described. And they must have very specific knowledge about how meaning is conveyed in English. For instance, "Pick up a red block" leaves the computer free to choose any red block at all, while "Pick up *the* red block" implies that the speaker has a particular block in mind. Perhaps it is the only one around, or was mentioned recently, or is the only one for which the action is appropriate.

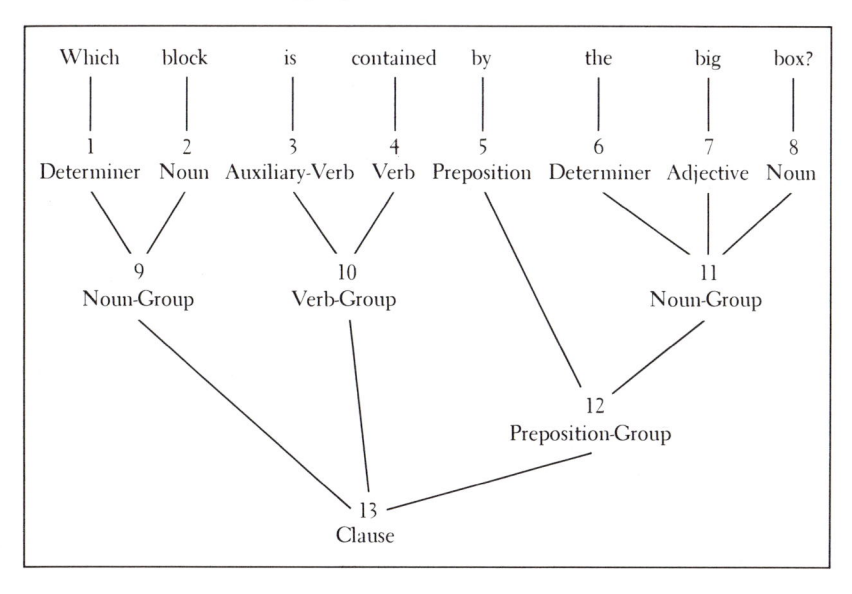

```
Which      block      is       contained   by        the        big        box?
  |          |        |           |        |          |          |          |
  1          2        3           4        5          6          7          8
Determiner Noun  Auxiliary-Verb  Verb  Preposition Determiner Adjective   Noun
     \    /            \    /                           \    | /
       9                 10                                  11
   Noun-Group        Verb-Group                          Noun-Group
         \              |                            /
          \             |                   12
           \            |           Preposition-Group
            \           |          /
                       13
                     Clause
```

[40] Certain words, like *it* and *one* (as in "a red one . . .") require their own semantic specialists. These subprograms may need to carry out complicated deductions to decipher the intended meaning. To do this, they can call on the third major group of programs, the reasoning specialists, which know about objects in the blocks world and can answer questions or solve problems involving them.

[41] For the computer, the final "meaning" of a phrase or sentence is an internal program that tells it what actions it must take. If the sentence is a command, these

may be physical actions on the table top. If it is a question, the program may have to print some response. If it is a statement, the program may search memory for objects or events fitting some description, or add new information to memory for later use.

[42] But thinking of meanings as ordinary programs is far too rigid. Surely when I say something to you, I am not giving you a set of instructions to carry out letter by letter. You have tremendous freedom in how you will understand and react to what I say. To capture this freedom, we use a more flexible kind of program, written in a special "goal-directed" programing language. The program specifies a set of goals to be achieved, but not the exact details on how to achieve them. For instance, when the program gets the command "Pick up the red block," it first decides which block we mean, then creates a goal named PICK UP BLOCK 3 (where BLOCK 3 happens to be the computer's internal name for a particular block on the table). A subprogram for PICK UP then enters the picture, and interprets the goal. It may have to plan a whole series of actions to free the robot hand, clear off any objects sitting on BLOCK 3, and do the actual picking up. All the while, it remembers both its plan and its actions, so it can answer questions about what it did and why. Although this rudimentary self-consciousness is limited to only the simplest sorts of actions and motives, it is essential to the program's ability to understand and to respond intelligently.

[43] This program is much harder to evaluate than simpler ones, like Eliza. The boundaries of its abilities are not clear. In the sample dialog I presented, it seems to behave very much as a person would in the same environment. But there are many ways in which it falls far short of human language ability. Sentences that seem well within its domain can cause troubles. For instance, the program cannot understand a command to build a stack three blocks high, because it lacks information about the grammar of phrases like *three blocks high* or *10 miles long*. Of course, we could add these without making any basic changes, but there are many similar problems. Human language has evolved over a period of thousands of years, and contains countless special constructions.

[44] Another obstacle is the program's inability to handle a phrase like *a three-block stack*. Many languages, including English and Chinese, allow us to string nouns together in a way that leaves their combined meaning open to special interpretation. A kitchen pot is in the kitchen, a soup pot is used for making soup, and a cast-iron pot is made of cast-iron. Thus, we cannot simply combine the meanings of *block* and *stack*, the way we could combine *red* and *block*. The system lacks the mechanisms necessary to find the meaning of noun combinations.

[45] The reasoning subprograms also have severe limitations. The program cannot carry out the command, "Build a stack without touching any pyramids," because it has no way to work on one goal (building a stack) while keeping track of another one (avoiding contact with pyramids). The reasoning specialists have a sort of one-track mind unsuited to complicated tasks.

[46] We also must worry about enlarging the program's world. In a tiny microworld, we can store and find information in a simple way, and we have no problem retrieving the pieces of information relevant to a particular question or deduction. But in an expanded world, we would be faced with a selection problem; it would take much too long just to look through all the information to decide what is relevant. We need some way of picking out bits of knowledge from the whole.

[47] Finally, we have only begun to attack the problems inherent in the little passage about Tommy and Jimmy. The program can do the kind of filling in so characteristic of human language only in very obvious cases. It cannot deal with the sentence fragments and implied meanings which make up most of our daily conversation. This is partly because of the fact that in its present form, the program builds up the meaning of each segment before incorporating it into a larger unit, instead of letting the nature of the whole guide the perception of the parts. Much current AI research is devoted to finding a more gestaltlike approach.

[48] All these shortcomings indicate that this program—which is one of the most advanced language-understanding programs in existence—has a long way to go before it comprehends the way people do. At present, it takes a huge computer and sophisticated programing to do a small part of what a young child does naturally. In fact, many people are skeptical about how far the "artificial intelligentsia" will ever get. These critics predict that we will never develop programs complex enough to duplicate "uniquely human" forms of information processing.

[49] I feel that it may be meaningless to ask whether a computer can ever understand English "just like a person." The differences in physical form and experience must lead, inevitably, to differences in performance. What we are studying are those aspects of intelligent thought and behavior which are fundamental to any kind of mental process, whether in machine or human brain. I believe that in the future, computers will not only become more useful computational tools, they will also help us unravel some of the mysteries of the mind. They have already given us new insights into many facets of language, and have helped us appreciate how much goes on when we carry out the "simple" act of understanding.

FOR REVIEW AND DISCUSSION

Content

1. What does Winograd mean when he writes that "nobody had addressed the central question of how a language works as a whole" (paragraph 10)?

2. What does Winograd mean by the term *knowledge* as he uses it in paragraphs 14 and 15? How do we *know* how language is structured, meaning is conveyed, and inference is drawn?

3. In what ways—if any—can computers use language more effectively than we can? In what ways can computers use language less effectively?

4. Discuss the reasons Winograd gives for trying to program computers to use human language. Which reasons seem more important?

Rhetoric

1. Is the opening passage from *2001* appropriate and useful, given the general content of the essay? Explain.

2. How do the blueprint and truck analogies in paragraph 24 clarify what a sentence does? Explain.

3. Does Winograd have an objective attitude toward computers and their anticipated role in society, or is he "selling" us on the idea of artificial intelligence?

4. Assuming that you know little or nothing about computer science, how successful has Winograd been in teaching you something about his complex field? As an expert, how well has he communicated with a lay audience?

Classroom Exercises

1. Discuss the relationship that is developing between language and computers. Does it seem likely that studies in *artificial intelligence* will affect the way we think and speak?

2. Have someone in the class who knows about "computer languages" explain one of those languages (Algol or Fortran, for instance) to the class.

F. P. Tullius

COMPUTER POETRY OR, SOB SUDDENLY, THE BONGOS ARE MOVING

Having observed linguistically gifted computers in other more mundane roles, we now see them take flight on the wings of the Muse. As you read this humorous essay, you might consider whether it teaches us more about the imagination of computers or the imagination of men.

[1]   For some time now digital computers have been writing poetry. Words are fed into them (the way numbers are) and they store a collection of parts of speech. By a programming process the operator can cause the machine to select from the words at random in such an order as to make a sentence of some sort.

[2]   The question of whether computer literature should be criticized by humans or by other computers—or criticized at all—is going to have to be faced up to. I suppose the position could be taken that computers are like Dr. Johnson's upright dog; the fact that these mechanisms write at all, however badly, is a matter for surprise—but hardly one meriting serious consideration. Still, the published writer in our society has always had to submit to criticism, and I see no good reason why computers should be exempt.

[3]   The real donkey work of comprehensive criticism in this infant art will have to be done by someone better equipped than myself, inasmuch as I am not in the least a familiar of modernist poetry, having worked my way up to Browning and then quit. The best I can offer anyone interested in getting in on the ground floor of this fast-growing field is a sketchy bit of background on the Cybernetic School (as I have dubbed it) and a few random observations about its singular *œuvre*.

[4]   The most prolific automatic writer seems to be RPC 4000, which operates out of a "briefcase factory," called the Librascope Division of General Precision, Inc., in Glendale, California. It is 4000 to whom we are indebted for this highly colored—though slightly boozed—rhymed quatrain:

>   Oh, panic not to this docile juice.
>   Finally, few of my jackets did distrust the goose.
>   To those cell's hot ashes, a raccoon may sting,
>   Ah, to rectify was black; to refute is nourishing.

Copyright © 1963 by *Harper's* Magazine. All rights reserved. Reprinted from the December 1963 issue by special permission.

[5]   Now bear in mind that someone (a human, I believe) once said a poem shouldn't mean, but just be. And that poem, you'll admit, certainly is. I'm not a bit embarrassed to own that I rather like the part about the majority of the writer's jackets trusting the goose. Anything at all yea-saying in these slippery times is good to hear. And though raccoons don't precisely sting, neither do tigers burn nor does man take arms against the sea, if you want to play that way.

[6]   Riffling through my clippings, I find that 4000, for some occult, cybernetic reason, is absolutely hipped on the word "few." (Of course, there could be a simple explanation, such as somebody didn't feed in enough adjectives.) Besides those few distrustful jackets, we find:

> Few fingers go like narrow laughs
> An ear won't keep few fishes
> Ah, few sects smell bland
> All blows have glue, few toothpicks have wood

[7]   4000 also has a predilection for the infinitive used in parallel construction, in the manner of "To err is human, to forgive divine." The above-quoted, "Ah, to rectify was black; to refute is nourishing," is one example. Then in other creations we have: "To leap is stuffy, to crawl was tender" (observe, too, the same auxiliary verb disagreement in both examples); "To weep is unctuous, to move is poor"; and the rhymed, sort-of-Alexandrine, couplet:

> She was stupider; he is stout.
> Oh, to overwhelm was snowy;
>   to conceal is devout.

Considering that—if all systems were go—4000 could probably write the equivalent of *Paradise Lost* in nine-and-one-tenth seconds, you can readily imagine that there is practically no end to the making of verses by this logorrhean machine.

[8]   Here is just a thimbleful of the piquant reflections and brainish apprehensions to emerge from 4000's read-out tape: "Broccoli is often blind," "Communism is more porcelain than albino gold," "Many whales have broth all day," "At lunch time he looks like bold jelly," "Do many mountains grow in the afternoon," "Under a lamp the nude is vain," "It was dirtiest who bleeds behind the piano," "The iron mother's bouquet did rudely call," "Sob suddenly, the bongos are moving," and "Dividing honestly was like praying badly." Full marks to 4000 for avoidance of the obvious in that last line. How easy it would have been (and how logically human) to create a neat, pellucid mediocrity such as, "Dividing badly is like praying badly."

[9]   There are indications that 4000 has trouble continuing a thought into the next line (something that most corporeal poets have no trouble doing). Each of 4000's lines seem self-contained, vacuum-packed, and independent as a hog on ice (to use a human simile with a nice computerese ambiguity). Even the titles owe allegiance to no line, but stand aloof as so many camels. The poem "Mice" is a good example, showing complete discreteness of line, except possibly for lines three and four:

COMPUTER POETRY 351

> The broad sleighs of glass are dashing hungrily,
> She is a toiler of dissolute water, and I am those bland melodies.
> So chess was arsenic and gold was beer,
> It was a snail of murmuring beer, and I am those angry nets.
> He was lustier than the twine and more bold than the shop.
> The milk of plates upon many sands of cream was like consummate
>   magnates.

(Despite some champagne tastes, such as an affinity for substances like gold, platinum, and porcelain, 4000 seems to be a proletarian devotee of beer.)

[10] Another promising computer, whose works have been published only nonattributively, is said to be owned and operated by the Systems Development Corporation in Santa Monica. This poet has no name—or number—but like all computers (and fleshly poets, for that matter) it has little crotchets that often give it away in print. The SD computer, for one thing, seems petty and self-centered alongside good old *dégagé* 4000. SD is—let's face it—a minor computer. One of the cardinal rules of commercial composition is that a writer should not write about writers. Here we have a computer that writes (or computes) about computers: "Thoughts drip and dark computers in heavy fast sad gods run," and "Horses fighting, some women drip, no happy horses writing men, but computers pick."

[11] This computer has some sort of thing about locomotives: "Locomotives create horses with women," it wrote in one place, and in another, "Fussy fast locomotives produce many gods." (A delectable and pulsating line, I will confess, which perhaps gives indication that SD will not always remain minor.) Maybe it is really the whole broad conception of travel that polarizes the affections of this machine. Consider the following—also rather lovely—line which our minor machine modestly coughed up: "From all thoughts boats love some boats." Two boats in one line. Now, going back over all the SD quotations, you will notice gods running, three references to horses, and then, of course, those fussy fast locomotives.

[12] That's about all I can contribute on this burgeoning field, and, anyway, I'm getting tired, and it's about time to knock off for lunch. While drinking my coy buttermilk, or perhaps downing a snail of murmuring beer, I'll hear the broad sleighs of glass dashing hungrily and the milk of plates upon many sands of cream. And perhaps there will even be borne to me, from some nearby table, the jelly-bold conversation and narrow laughs of a couple of portly and consummate magnates.

FOR REVIEW AND DISCUSSION

Content

1. The poems of RPC 4000 and of SD are written in different styles. How can you account for the difference?

2. What, after all, is Tullius saying about computer poetry?

3. What does Tullius mean by "a nice computerese ambiguity" (paragraph 9)?

Rhetoric

1. At what point in the article does Tullius's tone become apparent? Explain why this point is an effective or an ineffective one.

2. Does the adjective *piquant* (paragraph 8) to describe 4000's reflections seem appropriate? Why might Tullius have chosen it?

3. A number of allusions in the article may be obscure to you. Identify several of them and discuss how they help or hinder your enjoyment and understanding of the article.

4. Is Tullius's humor intended as a put-down, a build-up, or simply a description of the artistic abilities of computers? On what do you base your answer?

Classroom Exercises

1. Are any of RPC 4000's verses actually *poetic*? If you think that some are, explain what makes them poetic. If you think that none is, explain what the computer's work is missing.

2. Discuss the differences (and similarities) between the poetry of RPC 4000 and the following lines from E. E. Cummings:

> all ignorance toboggans into know
> and trudges up to ignorance again

N. Scott Momaday

THE MAN MADE OF WORDS

> *Someday we may truly be able to converse with computers, but for now we have only one another. From a future filled with computers, we move, in this article, into the past, to an old American Indian story, for an understanding of our most profound relationship to language. Momaday's point is much larger than the story itself and applies not only to language in general, but to our relationship to literature in particular. As you read, think about the connections between Momaday's ideas and those expressed in other articles throughout this book.*

[1] The Kiowa tales which are contained in *The Way to Rainy Mountain* constitute a kind of literary chronicle. In a sense they are the milestones of that old migration in which the Kiowas journeyed from the Yellowstone to the Washita. They record a transformation of the tribal mind, as it encounters for the first time the landscape of the Great Plains; they evoke the sense of search and of discovery. Many of the tales are very old, and they have not until now been set down in writing. Among them there is one that stands out in my mind. When I was a child, my father told me the story of the arrowmaker, and he told it to me many times, for I fell in love with it. I have no memory that is older than that of hearing it. This is the way it goes:

> If an arrow is well made, it will have tooth marks upon it. That is how you know. The Kiowas made fine arrows and straightened them in their teeth. Then they drew them to the bow to see that they were straight. Once there was a man and his wife. They were alone at night in their tipi. By the light of a fire the man was making arrows. After a while he caught sight of something. There was a small opening in the tipi where two hides had been sewn together. Someone was there on the outside looking in. The man went on with his work, but he said to his wife: "Someone is standing outside. Do not be afraid. Let us talk easily, as of ordinary things." He took up an arrow and straightened it in his teeth; then, as it was right for him to do, he drew it to the bow and took aim, first in this direction and then in that. And all the while he was talking, as if to his wife. But this is how he spoke: "I know that you are there on the outside, for I can feel your eyes upon me. If you are a Kiowa, you will understand what I am saying and you will speak your name." But there was no answer, and the man went on in the same way, pointing the arrow all around. At last his aim fell upon the place where his enemy stood, and he let go of the string. The arrow went straight into the enemy's heart.

[2] Heretofore the story of the arrowmaker has been the private possession of a very few, a tenuous link in that most ancient chain of language which we call the

From "The Story of the Arrowmaker," *The New York Times Book Review*, May 4, 1969. Copyright © 1969 by The New York Times Company. Reprinted by permission.

oral tradition; tenuous because the tradition itself is so; for as many times as the story has been told, it was always but one generation removed from extinction. But it was held dear, too, on that same account. That is to say, it has been neither more nor less durable than the human voice, and neither more nor less concerned to express the meaning of the human condition. And this brings us to the heart of the matter at hand: the story of the arrowmaker is also a link between language and literature. It is a remarkable act of the mind, a realization of words and the world that is altogether simple and direct, yet nonetheless rare and profound, and it illustrates more clearly than anything else in my own experience, at least, something of the essential character of the imagination—and in particular of that personification which in this instance emerges from it: the man made of words.

[3] It is a fine story, whole, intricately beautiful, precisely realized. It is worth thinking about, for it yields something of value; indeed, it is full of provocation, rich with suggestion and consequent meaning. There is often an inherent danger in the close examination of such a thing, a danger that we might impose too much of ourselves upon it. But this story, I believe, is exceptional in that respect. It is informed by an integrity that bears examination easily and well, and in the process it seems to appropriate our own reality and experience.

[4] It is significant that the story of the arrowmaker returns in a special way upon itself. It is about language, after all, and it is therefore part and parcel of its own subject; virtually, there is no difference between the telling and that which is told. The point of the story lies, not so much in what the arrowmaker does, but in what he says—and indeed *that* he says it. The principal fact is that he speaks, and in so doing he places his very life in the balance. It is this aspect of the story which interests me most, for it is here that the language becomes most conscious of itself; we are close to the origin and object of literature, I believe; our sense of the verbal dimension is very keen, and we are aware of something in the nature of language that is at once perilous and compelling. "If you are a Kiowa, you will understand what I am saying, and you will speak your name." Everything is ventured in this simple declaration, which is also a question and a plea. The conditional element with which it begins is remarkably tentative and pathetic; precisely at this moment is the arrowmaker realized completely, and his reality consists in language, and it is poor and precarious. And all of this occurs to him as surely as it does to us. Implicit in that simple occurrence is all of his definition and his destiny, and all of ours. He ventures to speak because he must; language is the repository of his whole knowledge and experience, and it represents the only chance he has for survival. Instinctively, and with great care, he deals in the most honest and basic way with words. "Let us talk easily, as of ordinary things," he says. And of the ominous unknown he asks only the utterance of a name, only the most nominal sign that he has been understood, that his words are returned to him on the sheer edge of meaning. But there is no answer, and the arrowmaker knows at once what he has not known before; that his enemy is, and that he has gained an advantage over him. This he knows certainly, and the certainty itself is his advantage, and it is crucial; he makes

the most of it. The venture is complete and irrevocable, and it ends in success. The story is meaningful. It is so primarily because it is composed of language, and it is in the nature of language in turn that it proceeds to the formulation of meaning. Moreover, the story of the arrowmaker, as opposed to other stories in general, centers upon this procession of words toward meaning. It seems in fact to turn upon the very idea that language involves the elements of risk and responsibility; and in this it seeks to confirm itself. In a word, it seems to say, everything is a risk. That may be true, and it may also be that the whole of literature rests upon that truth.

[5]   The arrowmaker is preeminently the man made of words. He has consummate being in language; it is the world of his origin and of his posterity, and there is no other. But it is a world of definite reality and of infinite possibility. I have come to believe that there is a sense in which the arrowmaker has more nearly perfect being than have other men by and large, and a more nearly perfect right to be. We can imagine him, as he imagines himself, whole and vital, going on into the unknown darkness and beyond. And this last aspect of his being is primordial and profound.

[6]   And yet the story has it that he is cautious and alone, and we are given to understand that his peril is great and immediate, and that he confronts it in the only way he can. I have no doubt that this is true, and I believe that there are implications which point directly to the determination of our literary experience and which must not be lost upon us. A final word, then, on an essential irony which marks this story and gives peculiar substance to the man made of words. The storyteller is nameless and unlettered. From one point of view we know very little about him, except that he is somehow translated for us in the person of the arrowmaker. But from another, that is all we need to know. He tells us of his life in language, and of the awful risk involved. It must occur to us that he is one with the arrowmaker and that he has survived, by word of mouth, beyond other men. We said a moment ago that, for the arrowmaker, language represented the only chance for survival. It is worth considering that he survives in our own time, and that he has survived over a period of untold generations.

FOR REVIEW AND DISCUSSION

Content

1. What does Momaday mean by asserting that the arrowmaker is "completely realized" when he says, "If you are a Kiowa, you will understand what I am saying and you will speak your name"? Do you agree with Momaday?

2. What, other than what Momaday finds, does the arrowmaker's statement ("If you are a Kiowa . . .") imply about the arrowmaker? What reason might Momaday have had for not mentioning these implications?

3. What does Momaday mean by the phrase *man made of words?*

Rhetoric

1. Momaday frequently frames statements within the following kind of structure: "*altogether* simple and direct, *yet* nonetheless rare and profound." What is the effect of this device?

2. The essay may be seen as a series of concentric circles, with the arrowmaker himself as the smallest and the readers of Momaday's writing as the largest circle. This way of looking at the essay helps us to understand Momaday's statement that the story "returns in a special way upon itself" because it is about language. Discuss Momaday's statement.

3. A reader's first response to this essay is that it is difficult, even obscure, yet in fact it contains few esoteric words and complex sentences. What, then, produces such a response?

Classroom Exercises

1. In what specific ways do we depend on language for both cultural and physical survival? Like Momaday's storyteller, you might try creating an imaginative situation to illustrate this dependence.

2. Recount a well-remembered story that you were told as a child. Try to discover any features in this story that are similar to those of the arrowmaker's. Discuss any significance you may have attached to the story over the years and the significance of its having been a childhood story.

FOR DISCUSSION AND WRITING

1. Discuss the differences in the relation between language and people (as Momaday describes it) and the relation between language and computers (as it is treated in the selections by Winograd and Tullius). As you discuss these differences, consider the possibility of computers eventually using language as Momaday says the arrowmaker does.

2. Apply Winograd's analysis of the problems inherent in creating *artificial intelligence* to Tullius's presentation of computer poetry. Which of these problems—if any—are evident in the poetry?

3. Based on information derived from any selections in the book, explain why you think it likely that computers will or will not be programmed to use language as we do. Consider what qualities of language or language users are most easily or least easily reproducible in computers.

4. Discuss the ways in which Momaday's attitude about language and survival might change if computers could be programmed to use language the way we do. (Before you write, you may want to review the role of the computer Hal in the movie *2001*.)

5. Write an essay in which you explain how much of the material in this book leads up to Momaday's discussion of the arrowmaker.

GLOSSARY

Some of the literary and language terms appearing in this book are briefly defined here.

Abstract language Words that make no appeal to the physical senses: *aspect, concept, factor*, and so on. Frequently words that describe abstract attributes or qualities (themselves abstract words): *good, interesting, wonderful*, and so on. See *concrete language.*

Ameslan An acronym for *American Sign Language;* the system of hand gestures, signifying letters, words, and phrases, used by deaf persons for communication.

Analogy A comparison for purposes of explanation, clarification, and analysis. Although the distinctions are sometimes blurred, an analogy differs from a *metaphor* or *simile* in that it is usually more prosaic, extended, and detailed:

> If in your mind's eye you take the average galaxy to be about the size of a bee—a small bee, a honeybee, not a bumblebee—our Galaxy would be roughly represented in shape and size by a 50-cent piece, and the average spacing of the galaxies would be about two yards, and the range of telescopic vision about a mile. So sit back and imagine a swarm of bees spaced about two yards apart and stretching away from you in all directions for a distance of about a mile. Now for each honeybee substitute the vast bulk of a galaxy and you have an idea of the Universe that has been revealed by the large American telescopes.
>
> Fred Hoyle

See *metaphor* and *simile.*

Arbitrary Random, not arising from a set of rules or laws.

Argument The presentation of reasons, facts, evidence in order to establish a point of view or the truth or falsehood of a premise.

Articulation The process of forming sounds in order to speak.

Cognition The mental processes by which knowledge is acquired; its opposites, roughly, would be *emotion* and *intuition.*

Concrete language Words naming things that can be experienced through the physical senses: *flower, mosquito, skillet;* or words describing sensory attributes or qualities: *yellow flower, buzzing mosquito, greasy skillet,* and so on. See *abstract language* and *imagery.*

Connotation The multiple associations a word carries: *pig* usually *connotes* dirtiness, smelliness, greediness and so forth. See *denotation.*

Colloquial Usage associated with speech as opposed to writing. See the Preface to the *Dictionary of American Slang* (chapter 4).

Deduction In logic, the process of deriving conclusions from general statements or *premises.* For example, since we know that cocker spaniels are even-tempered dogs that make good pets for children, we can presume, or deduce, that a particular spaniel will be a good family pet. See *induction*.

Denotation   The literal or exact definition of a word. For example, a *pig* is "any of several mammals of the family Suidae, having short legs, cloven hoofs, bristly hair. . . ." See *connotation*.

Description   The outlining or revealing of the characteristics of a person, place, or thing.

Diction   Choice of words, especially as it contributes to *style* and *tone* in writing. See "Usage is Something Else Again" (chapter 4).

Elliptical   Grammatically, referring to a verbal construction from which one or more words are omitted but understood: "She is smarter than he [is]."

Euphemism   A mild, vague, or pleasant word or phrase used in place of one considered offensive or too explicit: To *pass away* is a euphemism for to *die*.

Exposition   The mode of writing in which something is explained, discussed, interpreted, or argued. The essay, while predominantly in the *expository* mode, may also include *description* and *narration*.

Figure of speech   A departure from the precise, or *denotative*, meaning of words, not to be taken literally; used to create a vivid image: *It's raining cats and dogs*. See *metaphor* and *simile*.

Grammar   The formal features of a language and the rules they adhere to. See *usage*.

Hyperbole   An exaggeration used for effect, frequently amusing:

> With all the dignity at my command, I informed her that I was late for a skating appointment. She emitted a howl of derisive laughter. "Why, you pathetic old dodo," she cackled, "you couldn't stand up on a pair of skates if they were set in concrete!"
>
> S. J. Perelman

Imagery   Concrete words, especially words that make an appeal to the sense of sight; that which can be visualized.

Irony   A literary device by which what is meant is markedly different from or the opposite of what is said.

Induction   In logic, the process of arriving at a general conclusion based on examination of particular instances. For example, seeing a large stand of bare and charred trees, we can conclude or *induce* that a forest fire has occurred. See *deduction*.

Inflected   Altered in grammatical form by addition to a base word: *horse* to *horses*; *walk* to *walks*, or *walked*, and so on.

Intonational   Referring to the pitch or variety of pitches in a given utterance.

Jargon   The specialized terminology of a particular profession or group. See Preface to the *Dictionary of American Slang* (chapter 4).

Lexical   Having to do with the vocabulary (the *lexicon*) of a language.

Linguistics   The study of language, especially the nature and structure of human speech.

Logic   The process of reasoning according to set rules and structures.

Metalinguistics   The study of the relationship between language and other cultural and social phenomena.

Metaphor   A *figure of speech* in which something is said to be something else; an implied comparison: *the moon was a ghostly galleon / Tossed upon cloudy seas*. See *simile*.

Narration   The relation of a sequence of events or actions; *narrative* is often a synonym for a *story*.

Neologism   A new word; sometimes a new meaning for an old word.

Orthography   The system of representing the sounds of language in writing: spelling.

Personification The attribution of human characteristics to animals, objects, or ideas: *The sun's a wizard . . . but so's the moon a witch.*

Philology The study of language, especially its historical development and its relation to the history and literature of a culture.

Phonation The act of uttering speech sounds.

Portmanteau word One formed by combining the meanings and sounds of two different words: *smog,* e.g., is a combination of *smoke* and *fog.*

Psycholinguist One who studies the function of the brain in the acquisition and use of language.

Rhetoric The art of writing or speaking as a means of persuasion, with special attention to the words, structures, and organizational techniques used to achieve various persuasive effects; the term *rhetoric* does not necessarily carry negative *connotations.*

Semantics The study of the meanings of words, especially changes in the meanings of words.

Sign That which both signifies and has a direct relation to something else: Smoke is a *sign* of fire. See *symbol.*

Simile A *figure of speech* in which a comparison is introduced by *like* or *as*: *He fought like a wounded tiger.* See *metaphor.*

Slang Informal *diction,* usually *colloquial* and ephemeral. See Preface to the *Dictionary of American Slang* (chapter 4).

Sobriquet A nickname or assumed name, often friendly or humorous; Senator Hubert Humphrey carried the *sobriquet* "the Happy Warrior."

Stereotype The result of faulty reasoning that attributes certain characteristics to a group, based on experience with only one or a few members of the group—or vice versa: The "dumb jock" and "frivolous sorority girl" are *stereotypes.*

Style In writing, the way in which something is expressed; the particular diction and syntax that indicate an author's awareness of his language, subject, and audience. See *tone.*

Syllogism A pattern of *deductive reasoning* or *argument* based on the statement of a major premise, a minor premise, and a conclusion. The argument is valid if both premises are true and the conclusion joins them properly. The classic example: *All men are mortal. Socrates is a man. Therefore Socrates is mortal.*

Symbol Something that suggests or stands for but has no necessary relation to something else that is usually general or abstract in nature: A cross is a *symbol* of Christianity, a crown a *symbol* of sovereignty, a Cadillac of wealth (or ostentation!), and so on. See *sign.*

Syntax The way in which words are arranged to form sentences; the order or sequence of words in sentences.

Thesis The main point or controlling idea of an essay; usually stated in or near the opening paragraph.

Tone Frequently a loose synonym for *style,* but more appropriately those elements of a writer's diction that suggest his "feelings" toward his subject and audience. A writer's *tone* may be described as *angry, humorous, condescending,* and so on.

Transition terms Those words or phrases indicating sequential or logical movement from one event or idea to the next: *also, however, now, then, therefore, on the other hand,* and so on.

Usage The diction and syntax of a language customarily accepted by a given group of persons. *Usage* may often be at variance with *grammar.* See *grammar.* See "Usage is Something Else Again" (chapter 4).

Verbiage Excessive use of words or inflated *diction* inappropriate to a given topic.